Divine Democracy

Divine Democracy

Political Theology after Carl Schmitt

MIGUEL VATTER

UNIVERSITY PRESS

Oxford University Press is a department of the University of Oxford. It furthers
the University's objective of excellence in research, scholarship, and education
by publishing worldwide. Oxford is a registered trade mark of Oxford University
Press in the UK and certain other countries.

Published in the United States of America by Oxford University Press
198 Madison Avenue, New York, NY 10016, United States of America.

© Oxford University Press 2021

All rights reserved. No part of this publication may be reproduced, stored in
a retrieval system, or transmitted, in any form or by any means, without the
prior permission in writing of Oxford University Press, or as expressly permitted
by law, by license, or under terms agreed with the appropriate reproduction
rights organization. Inquiries concerning reproduction outside the scope of the
above should be sent to the Rights Department, Oxford University Press, at the
address above.

You must not circulate this work in any other form
and you must impose this same condition on any acquirer.

Library of Congress Cataloging-in-Publication Data
Names: Miguel Vatter, author.
Title: Divine democracy : political theology after Carl Schmitt / [Miguel Vatter].
Description: New York, NY : Oxford University Press, [2021] |
Includes bibliographical references and index.
Identifiers: LCCN 2020018270 (print) | LCCN 2020018271 (ebook) |
ISBN 9780190942359 (hardback) | ISBN 9780190942366 (paperback) |
ISBN 9780190942380 (epub) | ISBN 9780190942397 (online)
Subjects: LCSH: Schmitt, Carl, 1888–1985—Influence. | Political theology. |
Democracy—Religious aspects—Christianity. | Christianity and politics.
Classification: LCC BT83.59 .V38 2021 (print) |
LCC BT83.59 (ebook) | DDC 261.7—dc23
LC record available at https://lccn.loc.gov/2020018270
LC ebook record available at https://lccn.loc.gov/2020018271

Contents

Acknowledgements   vii

Introduction: Political Theology and Democratic Legitimacy in the 20th Century   1

1. Carl Schmitt and Sovereignty   21
2. Eric Voegelin and Representation   67
3. Jacques Maritain and Human Rights   97
4. Ernst Kantorowicz and Government   133
5. Jürgen Habermas and Public Reason   189

Conclusion—"Only a god can resist god": Gnosticism and Political Theology   241

References   257
Index   285

Acknowledgements

Many friends have generously discussed political theology with me and commented on my texts on this subject over the years: Hauke Brunkhorst, Gonzalo Bustamante, Julie Cooper, Renato Cristi, Mick Dillon, Jorge Dotti (†), Roberto Esposito, Andreas Greiert, Agnes Heller (†), Nicholas Heron, Lucien Jaume, James Martel, John McCormick, Cary Nederman, Diego Rossello, Quentin Skinner, Helen Tartar (†), José-Luis Villacañas, Samuel Weber, and Jessica Whyte. Not being myself a historian, I was lucky to have encountered early on two medieval historians who opened new horizons for me: in high school, Jack Ullman, who suggested I read Kantorowicz's biography of Frederick II, and in college, Francis Oakley, who gave me my early training in the history of ideas. I am fortunate to count on the friendship and advice of Simona Forti, who read through the whole manuscript. The ideas found in these pages have been presented at several conferences over the years, but one in particular, "Sovereignty, Religion, and Secularism: Interrogating the Foundations of Polity," Carl Friedrich von Siemens Stiftung, Munich, July 2018, stands out for the intense and productive discussions I had with some of the participants, including Bruce Rosenstock, Cécile Laborde, Montserrat Herrero, and Vincent Lloyd. I thank the organizer, Robert Yelle, for his generous invitation. Finally, I am grateful to my editor at Oxford, Angela Chnapko, for believing in the project. My greatest debt of gratitude, as always, is to Vanessa Lemm, who shepherded an amorphous book project to its current form, and to our children Lou, Esteban, Alizé, and Sebastian, who make it all worthwhile.

The germ for this book is found in a series of lectures I delivered in the graduate seminar of Roberto Esposito at the Istituto Scienze Umane, Naples, Italy, in November 2009; in a long paper I presented in September 2010 at the American Political Science Association Annual Meeting in Washington, DC, entitled "Political Theology without Sovereignty: Some 20th Century Examples (Voegelin, Maritain, Badiou)"; and in the Introduction to my edited volume from 2011, *Crediting God: Sovereignty and Religion in the Age of Global Capitalism* (New York: Fordham University Press). I consolidated my interpretation of Maritain in the 2013 article "Politico-Theological

Foundations of Universal Human Rights: The Case of Maritain," *Social Research 80* (1): pp. 233–60. Chapter 3 in this volume is a much revised and expanded version of this article. This book is anchored on the reading of Schmitt's conception of political theology that I proposed in the 2016 chapter "The Political Theology of Carl Schmitt," in *The Oxford Handbook of Carl Schmitt*, edited by Jens Meierhenrich and Oliver Simons, pp. 245–68 (New York: Oxford University Press). Chapter 1 is a considerably revised and updated version of the above text. The interpretation of Kantorowicz offered in Chapter 4 draws upon some material from my 2019 essay "Liberal Governmentality and the Political Theology of Constitutionalism," in *Sovereignty in Action*, edited by Neil Walker and Bas Leijssenaar, pp. 115–43 (New York: Cambridge University Press). Lastly, the Conclusion is based on my 2019 discussion of Blumenberg in "'Only a God can resist a God': Political Theology between Polytheism and Gnosticism," *Political Theology 20* (6): pp. 472–97. I thank all the editors and publishers for permission to use this material.

Introduction

Political Theology and Democratic Legitimacy in the 20th Century

The problem of democratic political theology

Political theology is a discourse developed in the 20th century that looks back on a millennial history in which western societies tightly interwove religion and politics, as political rulers sought support in religion and religions pursued political power. Have we left this past behind because we are now living in a secular age? Political theology takes a critical view on the claim that the modern Atlantic republican revolutions, responsible for the emergence of modern representative democracy, led to a definitive divorce of the political from the theological. But political theology is also a postmodern and post-secular discourse that seeks to reconfigure both religion and politics in a new democratic constellation.[1] Nearly forty years ago, the French theorist of democracy Claude Lefort penned a remarkably influential article on the problem of political theology. He concluded that religion resists and insists in modern secular politics because it is 'an expression of the unavoidable ... difficulty democracy has of reading its story' (Lefort 2006, 187). What makes it difficult for modern democracy to tell its own secular story is the problem of the legitimacy of power.

Carl Schmitt, who first coined the term, argued that political theology was inevitably implied in any legitimation discourse. Legitimacy assumes that the activity of ruling and being ruled, at some basic level, is good and should be sanctified. The idea of legitimacy intertwines political rule and spiritual salvation.[2] For this same reason, Schmitt believed that power is legitimate

---

[1] For one recent and influential narrative bringing these three elements of political theology together see (Taylor 2007).

[2] Schmitt considered Jacob Burckhardt's claim that power is always evil as the highest expression of atheism (Schmitt 1988, 57; 2007, 60). For examples of wide-ranging discussions of the connection between the exercise of legitimate power and salvation in political theology, see (Taubes 1983; Esposito 1988; Assmann 2002; and Kahn 2011).

2   DIVINE DEMOCRACY

only when it assumes the form of sovereignty and obeys the principle that *salus populi suprema lex esto* ('the salvation of the people shall be the supreme law'). The global resurgence of sovranists and sovereignism suggests that this belief is gaining ground within liberal, secular societies. At the same time, if modern democracy is characterized by any single trait, it is surely the insight that 'power belongs to none of us'.[3] Theorists of democracy are sceptical whether there exists any real evidence or full-proof demonstration that justifies why some privileged individual or group ought to rule over any other. The regular deployment of democratic elections is not about choosing the true representatives, but about assuring that we can always get rid of them.[4] This tension between the idea of legitimacy and representative democracy is the terrain on which political theology operates. Schmitt sought to understand and exploit this tension. He claimed that it gave rise to a congenital 'crisis' of legitimation in liberal democratic regimes. His first formulation of political theology was a plea to reinstate absolute sovereignty and maintain the monarchical principle under conditions of modern mass democracy. It led him to support the Nazi dictatorship.

The focus of this book is the development of political theology after Schmitt and in reaction to the emergence of totalitarian regimes.[5] It puts forward two general hypotheses about this development. The first hypothesis is that after Schmitt political theology takes a 'democratic turn'. It seeks to overcome the tension between democracy and legitimacy by displacing the primacy of sovereignty as the locus of solutions to the modern crisis of legitimation. In the western political tradition, the legitimacy of rule connects to democracy in two basic senses. Ruling is legitimate as far as it meets with the approval and support of those subject to it. Legitimacy therefore depends at some basic level on the possibility of unifying a group of individuals into a people. Schmitt believed that this unification required the representative to

---

[3] See (Rancière 2009; and Ober 2010) for arguments with respect to ancient democracy. Lefort formulates the point as follows with regard to modern democracy: 'of all the regimes we know, [democracy] is the only one to have represented power in such a way as to show that power is an *empty place*' (Lefort 2006, 159). On the inbuilt demand for the contestation of power in modern democracies, see also (Pettit 1997; and Rosanvallon 2006). Contemporary political science has shown that there exists a fundamental indeterminacy about who is the 'people' that is supposed to exercise the supreme power in modern democracy. For some aspects of this debate, see (Rosanvallon 1998; Espejo 2011; and Näsström 2015).

[4] See (Pitkin 1967; and Przworski, Stokes, and Manin 1999).

[5] My study of political theology does not have a 'comparative' aspiration, much less does it present an 'encyclopaedic' overview of the ways in which politics and religion were combined either in western or in world history. It seeks to explain the interest and pertinence of political theology as a discursive regularity in contemporary political theory.

be sovereign. After Schmitt, the discourse of political theology orients itself around the task of developing forms of political representation that unify a people without or beyond sovereignty. These forms of unification can be either representative or direct; they can have a rational ground based on the public exercise of discussion and debate, but they can also have a mystical ground based on the exercise of charismatic qualities and ritual practices of acclamation. In this book I suggest that a consideration of this 'political theology without sovereignty' is particularly useful to understand the non-electoral forms of popular participation that are linked up with the phenomenon of populism.

The other root along which legitimacy connects with democracy is broadly constitutional. Rule is legitimate as far as the laws and commands it issues are authorized in accordance with a 'higher' law. Legitimacy here is a function of legality or the 'rule of law', where the legal rights and obligations have the peculiarity of being somehow inherent or natural to the people rather than a product of the institutions that rule over them.[6] Schmitt believed that the rule of law stands or falls on the authority of the sovereign whose commands are taken as law. After Schmitt, the discourse of political theology is more interested in the converse proposition, namely, in the idea that sovereignty depends on normative orders that underlie it and exceed the control of the state. In this book I suggest that this 'political theology without sovereignty' can help us understand the emergence of forms of constitutionalism that seek to establish a pre- or supra-political government over the state itself associated with the phenomenon of neoliberalism.

The second hypothesis is that the displacement of sovereignty in 20th century political theology takes two distinct paths: one follows the hegemonic role of Christianity in the western approach to the legitimacy of power and its relation to democracy. The other path takes its bearings from the traditions of Judaism and Islam as they flow into western philosophical and political culture in late antiquity and in the medieval period. Generalizing to an extreme degree, one can say that Christian political theology after Schmitt displaces sovereignty by pivoting on the idea that legitimacy is a function of the political unity of a people achieved through its political *representation*, as befits its Christological doctrinal structure.[7] In this sense, from my perspective

---

[6] I mean this description to be wide enough to include the idea of 'natural right' in the Greek philosophical tradition and in the Jewish tradition, but I also take it to refer to the Roman and medieval republican idea that peoples are products of their constitutions.
[7] On Christian political theology as a discourse on politics that arises because of theology, see (Scott and Cavanaugh 2008; Cavanaugh, Bailey, and Hovey 2011; and Hovey and Phillips 2015),

what makes a given political theology 'Christian', in the last instance, is the focus on the 'representative' character of democracy. By way of contrast, and once again generalizing, one can say that non-Christian, alternative political theologies displace sovereignty by pivoting on the idea that democracy is a function of a people's fidelity to a *higher law*, as befits a prophetological and messianic doctrinal structure. From this perspective, what makes a given political theology 'Jewish' or 'Islamic', in the end, is the focus on the 'direct' character of democracy.[8]

Argument and structure of book

Does liberal democracy require a politico-theological foundation? This book will not pretend to answer this complicated and controversial question head on.[9] Rather, I propose to approach the problem by considering the following: if contemporary democracy requires legitimacy, and if legitimacy is a politico-theological construction, then the question of the possibility of a democratic political theology acquires substantial importance. For if it turned out that political theology cannot be democratic, as Schmitt initially surmised, then raising the question of the legitimacy of liberal democracy risks the conclusion that liberal democracy is in a permanent crisis or is

---

among others. Their approach to the discourse of political theology does not focus on the problem of legitimacy and government as I do in this book. Influenced by theologians like Karl Barth, Reinhold Niebuhr, Paul Tillich, Jürgen Moltmann, Stanley Hauerwas, etc., this approach to Christian political theology tends to assume that politics and theology are separate spheres with their autonomous logics. My discussion of Christian political theology, instead, takes seriously as a point pioneered by the U.S. historian of religion Erwin Goodenough and the German theologian Erik Peterson, for whom Christian theology was always already traversed by Hellenistic and Roman philosophical, political, and legal categories (Goodenough 1969; and Peterson 1997). Thus, my focus is on Christian political theology as a jurisprudential discourse first, and a theological discourse only secondarily. What interests me are the productive tensions and exchanges between political theology and political theory. By political theory I understand a discourse that offers a genealogy and an archaeology of the legitimacy of legal and political orders.

[8] I discuss the development of Jewish political theology in *Living Law. Jewish Political Theology from Hermann Cohen to Hannah Arendt* (Oxford University Press, 2021). Hereafter referred to as *Living Law*.

[9] For different attempts and strategies to address this question that refer to political theology, see (Asad 2003; Böckenförde 2006; Milbank 2006; Agamben 2007a; Gillespie 2008; Cavanaugh 2009; Kahn 2011; Lupton and Hammill 2012; Havers 2013; Kahn 2014; and Gregory 2015), among others. For a recent critique of postsecular claims about the religious foundations of liberalism and their normative consequences, see (Laborde 2017). Like Seyla Benhabib and Jean Cohen, Laborde also considers Schmitt's political theology to lie at the basis of the postsecular critiques of liberalism. See (Benhabib 2010; Cohen 2013; and Laborde 2014).

caught up in a performative contradiction.[10] So this book is concerned with answering the question: can political theology be democratic?

I argue that in the 20th century, several significant political philosophers answered this question by saying: 'Yes, provided that political theology can discard sovereignty.' Christianity, Judaism, and Islam contain teachings that can be employed to articulate a political theology without sovereignty: Christianity because of the message of universal love and peace expounded by its founder, Judaism and Islam because of their theocratic foundations, according to which the only real sovereign is a radically transcendent and ultimately unknowable God. But this remark is only the start of the problem, not only for the obvious reason that all three monotheistic religions also have been employed to offer a foundation to sovereignty. Rather, the more serious problem is that in order to develop a conception of democratic legitimacy it is not enough to reject sovereignty on 'religious' or 'theological' grounds. One also needs to show, positively, how the transposition of certain theological concepts and teachings into the sphere of law and politics leads to the kind of concrete institutions and practices that make up modern democracy. These are concrete institutions like free elections of representatives, legal systems based on the protection of individual rights, practices of government and administration, and a public sphere in which a public use of reason holds sway. For this reason each chapter discusses a major contributor to the 20th century discourse of Christian political theology (viz., Carl Schmitt, Eric Voegelin, Jacques Maritain, Ernst Kantorowicz, and Jürgen Habermas) by pairing them with a fundamental political concept for modern democracy (viz., sovereignty, representation, universal human rights, government, and public reason). This democratic development of political theology means that the political 'presence' of God in the secular world is no longer figured by hierarchical and sovereign lieutenants like Church, Empire, Nation, but in a series of political institutions, practices, and conceptions of modern democracy that call into question the primacy of sovereignty. Conversely, by reconstructing the different ways in which a series of crucial political concepts are transformed when they become part of a discourse on political theology, I hope to show the overdetermined role that

---

[10] See elaborations of this Schmittian trope of the crisis of liberal democracy in (Mouffe 1999; and Geuss 2001). For Weberian socio-economic arguments as to why political theology no longer has purchase on democratic legitimacy, see (Habermas 2011) and for analogous considerations, (Espejo 2010). But see later in this chapter on the persistence of political theology in Marx and Weber.

Christian religion and theology still play in contemporary democratic political and legal theory.

Chapter 1 discusses the origins of political theology in Schmitt's efforts to refute Hans Kelsen's monistic approach to jurisprudence. Kelsen rejected all dualisms between state and legal system. For him, the idea that the sovereignty of the state stood above and separate from the self-referential system of legal norms produced by a democratic legislative power was an illegitimate transposition of the theological image of God and His Creation into legal science. In order to answer Kelsen's withering critiques of sovereignty, Schmitt makes a juridical recourse to Christology, arguing that it was no coincidence that legal science in the West began with Church law since its scientific character ultimately rested on the transposition of Christian theological concepts into legal and political ones. The chapter proceeds to discuss the contested question whether Schmitt's own political theology is Christian in an orthodox sense, or whether Schmitt simply meant to defend Hobbes's unorthodox idea that the legitimacy of the sovereign rests on its capacity to represent as State the unity of a People much like Christ is the Head of the Church as His mystical body.[11] Erik Peterson rejected Schmitt's attribution of political theology to Christianity because for him the intention behind Trinitarian doctrine was anti-sovranist: it sought to prohibit all identification of the State with the Church. Peterson tried to rescue the democratic credentials of the Christian Church. However, we owe to Giorgio Agamben the insight that a Christian conception of democracy employs the doctrine of the Trinity and a conception of the Christian Church as Christ's mystical and political body not in order to abolish political theology, but so as to displace its discourse from absolute sovereignty to liberal, limited government.[12] The subsequent chapters show in what ways the arc between Peterson's critique of Schmitt and Agamben's identification of the political theology of liberalism was bridged by other theorists of Christian political theology who, in a more concrete fashion, flesh out the connections between Christian theologemes and apparatuses of liberal democratic legitimacy.

Chapter 2 focuses on Eric Voegelin's attempt to think about democratic legitimacy through a politico-theological conception of representation that no longer places the human sovereign at its apex, but instead 'opens' society

---

[11] Against the hypothesis that Schmitt's political theology is Christian, see (Galli 1996; and McCormick 1998). For arguments in favour, see (Meier 2011). For a balanced view, see (Kervégan 2011).

[12] (Agamben 2011).

to the idea of transcendent truth once advocated by Greek philosophy and Christian faith. Following Peterson's critique of Schmitt, Voegelin also believes that the representation of God in and for society exceeds the representative role of the political sovereign. However, for him the veridical Christian representative is no world-denying saint, but rather a freedom fighter against the temptations of Gnosticism encapsulated in secular, revolutionary demands for popular self-rule. This chapter then traces the influence of Voegelin's conception of representation on the contemporary political science debate around the 'return of representation' and the rise of populism, best expressed in the thought of Ernesto Laclau. The chapter shows that contemporary populism manifests the Christian political theological belief in the impossible attainment of popular sovereignty.

Chapter 3 focuses on Jacques Maritain's formulation of Christian democratic political theology that displaces sovereignty in favour of the primacy of human rights. This chapter traces how and why Christian political theology was at the forefront of the turn towards human rights that characterizes politics after World War II.[13] I argue that in the face of the rise of anti-Semitism culminating in the mass extermination of Jews and other minorities, Maritain develops a politico-theological strategy of 'anti-anti-Semitism' that articulates the Pauline focus on individual salvation through faith in terms of a new democratic charter based on the universal respect for individual human rights as the ground for the legitimacy of power. The chapter concludes with a discussion of Saint Paul's Christian 'universalism' as the ultimate basis of radical democratic thought in Alain Badiou. It shows how Badiou remains caught within Maritain's strategy of employing human rights to recognize human difference and plurality within a Christian faith in the universal equality of all with all that simultaneously undermines such recognition.

Chapter 4 locates Ernst Kantorowicz's contribution to the development of Christian democratic political theology in his genealogical explanation for the rise of secular governmentality in modernity.[14] Through a discussion of the intense debates in Anglo-American historiography of medieval political ideas from 1930s through 1960s, my interpretation of Kantorowicz shows that the medieval juridical use of Trinitarian doctrine replaced the idea of monarchic sovereignty inherited through the Roman Empire and

---

[13] On the new historiography of human rights, see (Moyn 2012; 2015).
[14] On the genealogy of governmentality, see (Foucault 2009; and Lemke 2019).

Roman law with a doctrine of liberal government that works in and through constitution-making. In contrast to Agamben's hypothesis that democratic political theology is an 'economic theology' based on the faith in the providential order of free markets, I argue that modern governmentality works by constitutionalizing politics as a condition of possibility for the reduction of politics to economics. The chapter concludes with a discussion of recent sociology of law that defends the hypothesis according to which the rule of law in the West became a real possibility through the clerical revolution that established the legitimacy of the 'constitution' of the Church over against the power of the Christian emperor. My reading of Kantorowicz suggests, to the contrary, that the efforts to constitutionalize Church law were ultimately adopted by secular states in order to develop the forms of democratic governmentality without law that we have come to identify with global normative orders.

Chapter 5 reconstructs the development of Christian political theology put forward by Jürgen Habermas's postsecular account of the communicative ground of democratic legitimacy. The focus of the chapter is Habermas's claim that a democratic understanding of public reason—here taken to be identical with the basic apparatus for generating democratic legitimacy—requires a postsecular 'translation' of monotheistic insights and intuitions into 'reasons' that are also acceptable to a secular or atheist mindset. In giving such a postsecular translation of the religious tradition, Habermas identifies the basis of democratic legitimacy no longer in the 'secularization' of religious beliefs, as Karl Marx and Max Weber had done, but in a 'philosophical' conception of the universality of faith. The chapter concludes with a comparison between Habermas's stance of 'methodological atheism', Ernst Bloch's understanding of the internal relation between Christianity and atheism, Karl Jaspers's idea of a philosophical faith, and Jacques Derrida's hypothesis that messianic faith is necessary for democracy.

In the Conclusion I return to consider Schmitt's claim that the ultimate justification for adopting Christian political theology consists in its being the only viable way to deal with the threat posed by Gnostic mis-archy, or the belief in the evil of power and political rule. Schmitt believed that this Gnostic doctrine motivated all modern revolutionary attempts to radically change society for the better and achieve durable social progress. In this last chapter I reconstruct Hans Blumenberg's strategy in rejecting Schmitt's construal of political theology of sovereignty as a function of 'restraining' the drift of the modern, secular age into increasing anarchy and disorder while at the same time responding to the Gnostic challenge to political power. For Blumenberg this strategy was captured by Goethe's motto *nemo contra deum nisi deus ipse* [against a god, only a god]. Opposing Schmitt's Christological reading of the motto, Blumenberg's interpretation shows a new appreciation for the polytheism and pantheism that characterized pagan civil religions. I situate Blumenberg's interpretation within a republican understanding of worldly power that affirms its value insofar as it is oriented to the ideal of no-rule or non-domination and is institutionalized in the form of constitutional separation of powers. The discussion between Schmitt and Blumenberg on the meaning of Goethe's mysterious motto stands here as symbol of the limits of all Christian political theology in defending democratic forms of legitimacy.

Question of method: Political theology and the debate on secularization

If the theorems of secularization were true, the discourse of political theology would have no reason to exist. But contemporary thinkers like Charles Taylor and Jürgen Habermas argue that modern liberal democracies are 'postsecular' forms of society in which 'religious communities continue to exist in a context of ongoing secularization'.[15] Schmitt constructed political theology having in view this coming postsecular society, and as a reaction to Weber's and Marx's theories of Modernity as a process of secularization that would render religion obsolete. In his classic work, *The Legitimacy of the Modern Age*, Hans Blumenberg established that the fundamental starting point for a treatment of political theology lies in the sociological debate on secularization that Schmitt engaged with Weber.[16] Schmitt conceived of political theology as a contribution to the 'sociology of concepts' that Weber pioneered.[17] He understood political theology as the study of the transfer of theological concepts developed within the Christian Church into the secular law and politics of the early modern states.[18] Schmitt clearly intended

---

[15] (Habermas 2003, 104). For an alternative vision of postsecularism, see (Taylor 2007; 2011).

[16] For a good recapitulation of the debate between Schmitt and Blumenberg, see (Bragagnolo 2011).

[17] The first three chapters of *Political Theology* appeared with the title "Sociology of the Concept of Sovereignty and Political Theology" in a 1922 edited book in honour of the recently deceased Weber, *Erinnerungsgabe für Max Weber*.

[18] Schmitt presents political theology as 'a sociology of juristic concepts' (Schmitt 1988, 37, 42), whereby what is studied are the 'fundamentally systematic and methodical analogies' (ibid., 37) between jurisprudence and theology. This study gives rise to hypotheses such as: 'the exception in jurisprudence is analogous to the miracle in theology' (ibid., 36), or: 'the modern constitutional state

political theology as a discourse that would rework several signature themes of Weber's sociology, including: the problem of legitimacy; the question of power as the monopoly of legitimate use of violence (*Gewalt*); and the process of secularization of Protestantism. But in defining secularization as a function of political theology, Schmitt in fact reversed and rejected the theory of secularization developed during the 19th century by French and German sociology, which receives perhaps its most notable systematization in Weber's sociology of religion.

Weber's sociology of religion contains two distinct, even opposite, motifs that are pertinent in order to capture the conceptual horizon within which political theology developed in the early 20th century. The first motif centres on an account of Modernity and modernization as a process of secularization.[19] Secularization in this sense is allied with the idea of rationalization as a 'disenchantment' of the world through the expansion of means-end practical and scientific rationalities.[20] The second motif centres on the charismatic or messianic characteristics of spiritual and political movements that bring into the world absolute, substantive value orientations or standpoints. The dialectical interaction of these two motifs determines the fundamental problem of Weber's thought, namely, the question of how to conduct one's life or *Lebensführung*.[21] Despite Weber's comparativist approach to the phenomenon of religion, and his willingness to extend 'ascetic' and 'disenchanting' powers to all so-called world or axial religions, the central religion on the basis of which he builds his hypothesis of the secular rationalization of the world remains Protestantism. For Weber, Protestantism represents a paradigmatic case of inner-worldly asceticism that is ultimately responsible for both capitalism and positivism (as well as liberalism) or, in short, for 'Modernity' as we know it. Prophetic Judaism, instead, offers the principal paradigm for his reflections on charismatic authority.

The key concept through which Weber developed his account of secularization is the Pauline conception of 'vocation' (*Beruf*). As Weber famously

---

triumphed together with deism, a theology and a metaphysics that banished the miracle from the world' (ibid.), or: 'all the identities that recur in the political ideas and in the state doctrines of the nineteenth century rest on such conceptions of immanence' (ibid., 49).

[19] On the debate on secularization, see (Monod 2002; Casanova 2013; Gregory 2017; and Hunter 2017).
[20] For a classic discussion, see (Habermas 1984a). On the typologies of rationality, see (Kalberg 1980).
[21] On the question of *Lebensführung* as central in Weber's thought see (Hennis 2000).

illustrates in his book on *The Protestant Ethic and the Spirit of Capitalism*, this New Testament idea becomes 'secularized' by Luther and Calvin whereby it acquires the meaning of a secular or worldly 'profession' (Weber 1958, 207–210). What began as a messianic category in Paul ends up being, in the discourse of secularization, the doctrine that the salvation of the individual is no longer dependent on the Messiah, nor even on God, but is achievable solely by 'following' the path outlined by one's worldly vocation.[22] As Voegelin puts it: Protestantism offers a path to salvation in and through the progress of 'civilization', 'the discipline and economic success which certified salvation to the Puritan saint' (Voegelin 1952, 129). Taylor's recent reconstruction of the Reformation follows Voegelin: 'there were not to be any more ordinary Christians and super-Christians. The renunciative vocations were abolished. All Christians alike were to be totally dedicated' to their salvation (Taylor 2007, 77). In the secular age, individual salvation would come about by an autonomous moral re-ordering of individuals (Taylor 2007, 27) achieved by adopting 'a disciplined personal life', a 'well-ordered society', and a 'correct inner stance' (Taylor 2007, 82).[23] According to Voegelin's and Taylor's narratives, starting with the Reformation the idea of salvation gradually receives a form that lacks all reference to divine transcendence.[24]

Voegelin believed that Marxism was the most historically effective 'secularizing' movement in late modernity. By adopting Ludwig Feuerbach's thesis that religion is merely the self-alienation of the human being, Marx concluded that the more the human being recognizes its social essence, the more it 'becomes conscious that he himself is God'. From this follows the Nietzschean 'consequence [that] man is transfigured into superman' (Voegelin 1952, 125). From here the step is a short one to divide human beings into inferior and superior 'races' or 'types', which then feeds into totalitarian ideologies.[25]

---

[22] See the discussion in (Agamben 2005).
[23] These are the elements of what Taylor calls the 'modern social imaginary' in (Taylor 2004).
[24] Taylor speaks of a 'secular age' characterized by an 'immanent frame' in which 'the eclipse of all goals beyond human flourishing becomes conceivable' (Taylor 2007, 19). Voegelin calls this secular idea of salvation, or 'the fallacious immanentization of the Christian *eschaton*' (Voegelin 1952, 122) by the name of Gnosticism.
[25] According to Voegelin, Gnosticism believes 'in an expansion of the soul to the point where God is drawn into the existence of man. . . . For the men who fall into these experiences divinize themselves by substituting more massive modes of participation in divinity for faith in the Christian sense' (Voegelin 1952, 124). Political religions correspond to these 'more massive modes of participation in divinity' and which culminate in modern totalitarianism. See also (Voegelin 1994). I discuss the idea of 'political religion' and the difference with political theology in the chapters dedicated to Voegelin and Maritain.

The link that Voegelin draws from Marxism to Weberian secularization, and from the latter to totalitarianism, is dubious, even preposterous, if taken as a thesis on intellectual history. Yet it is not entirely lacking in significance if studied considering the question of how the debate on secularization is employed by the discourse of political theology. For Weber's version of secularization, at one level, cannot be so neatly distinguished from the version of secularization given previously by Marx. According to Weber, Protestantism ultimately stands as a symbol of the possibility that all religious values will eventually receive purely worldly or secular realizations. The Weberian thesis can be rephrased as follows: unless religion—the aspiration to transcendence—is 'translated' back into a non-religiously constructed social reality (composed of power and economic relations, the growth of objective knowledge, systems of human law, etc.), then it is religion, and not the world, that shall perish.

This implication of Weber's secularization principle is precisely the point that Marx had already made in *On the Jewish Question*. In this early text, secularization receives two meanings. First, it refers to the *social and political* processes that realize religious values. This idea is captured by Marx's apparently paradoxical claim according to which the values of Christianity are not realized in the Christian confessional states but only in the liberal, 'neutral' state.[26] For in the former, those who do not share the official state religion are at best 'tolerated', whereas only in liberal states that uphold the principle of non-establishment of religion by the state can everyone be treated according to their proper human dignity as befits the doctrine that all human beings were 'made in the image' of God.[27] Marx's point is that to be a true Christian, that is, to live in the truth that all of God's creatures are equal before God, means to respect the liberty and equality of all, and this just means to live in a liberal state that is 'methodologically' atheistic.[28]

---

[26] "The perfected Christian state is rather the *atheist* state, the *democratic* state, the state which relegates religion to the level of the other elements of civil society" (Marx 1975, 222).

[27] Marx's insight is potentially compatible with Nietzsche's thesis that the modern and secular struggle for human equality in the form of 'atheistic' movements like socialism, liberalism, and feminism all seek to realize the Christian ideal: "the *democratic* movement is the heir to the Christian movement" (Nietzsche 1989, 202). What is called today 'postsecularism' is an elaboration of these insights. Postsecularism points out that the modern state constructs 'religion' as a private activity in order to be able to establish itself as a public space of neutrality and equal respect, and, conversely, in establishing itself along these liberal lines, the state becomes the perfect realization of Christian ideals. For an interesting collection of essays on these themes, see (Sullivan et al. 2015).

[28] Marx's insight remains operative in Habermas's construal of public reason as a function of 'methodological atheism'.

More polemically, Marx considers that the true realization of Judaism is not the life of 'Halakhic Man.' Rather, for Marx Judaism is realized in capitalism and bourgeois civil society, that is, in a system in which universal equality is premised on establishing money as the universal form of exchange value. In sum, for Marx, being a Christian in modernity does not mean ascribing to a given faith denomination. It means—speaking ethico-politically—being a liberal democrat.[29] Likewise, being a Jew in modernity does not mean studying and following the Torah. It means—speaking ethico-politically—having to worship the only true God of civil society, namely, capital.[30] For Marx, religion lacks a *politics and an ethics* of its own. The 'sacred' has no social effectivity at all: to have any effect on the world, the sacred has to become 'profane', it has to secularize itself, it has to cease being sacred.[31] That is why capitalism, where 'everything sacred becomes profane', can also be understood as the drive to pure effectivity or will to power.[32] Marx joins up with Nietzsche once again.

The second meaning of secularization that Marx gives in *On the Jewish Question* is 'abolitionist' with respect to religion. If the values of religion acquire reality only in their social-political realization, and if the logic of sociopolitical reality is neither religious nor theological, then it follows that by unfolding its own immanent logic, society will necessarily end up abolishing religion. Borrowing a term from Voegelin, Taylor believes this sense of secularization is inseparable from the belief that the modern world is a 'closed' world of immanence.[33] Viewed from the perspective of Marx's historical materialism, if religion persists in Modernity, this only means that the immanent logic of the social world has not yet unfolded completely. Religion is symbolic of the self-division or alienation of society; it gives expression to the continued existence of a form of society that is not fully human, whose conditions block the awareness or recognition of the truth that human nature is through and through a social essence.[34] That is why, with the social

---

[29] For readings of "On the Jewish Question" that cover this ground, see (Bosteels 2013; and Brown 2014).

[30] For the connection of this point with Walter Benjamin's fragment "Capitalism as Religion," see the discussion in (Hamacher 2002; Löwy 2009; and Weber 2013), among many others.

[31] On this motif from a politico-theological perspective, see (Agamben 2007b).

[32] For an early analysis of this step from Marx to Nietzsche in the context of the debate with Antonio Negri and the Workerist movement in Italy, see (Cacciari 1977). And for Negri's most recent critique of political theology, see (Negri 2015).

[33] See (Taylor 2007, 556; and Voegelin 1952, 158). The distinction between 'open' and 'closed' worlds originally comes from Bergson. On its meanings in Bergson, see (Lefebvre and White 2012).

[34] These not fully human social conditions are experienced as 'alienation', 'reification', and 'pathology'. For these categories, see (Honneth 2007).

realization of the human social essence, which must take the form of a social revolution, religion will be dissolved.

The discourse of political theology in the 20th century radically changes the meaning of secularization developed by Marx and Weber. The category of secularization is not abandoned. Rather, political theology exposes the secret reliance on theological ideas and distinctions in Marx's and Weber's apparently secular articulation of the idea of secularization.[35] It then affirms this theological basis of secularization in order to claim that the process of modernization has both theological conditions of possibility and religious finalities. In sum, for Schmitt, and, more generally, for the 20th-century discourse of political theology, the term 'secularization' refers to the fact that were it not for its *hidden theological meaning,* socio-political reality would be lacking in *historical effectivity.* Political theology therefore rejects the Marxist and Weberian hypothesis that religious values acquire reality only when they are transposed into social-political reality, which in turn evinces a positivist, social-scientific logic of its own. Political theology aims to refute the abolitionist hypothesis found in the modern theorem of secularization.

The discourse of political theology seeks to undermine, from the inside, the premises of positivist social sciences, first sociology, then political science, and, more recently, political economy, by showing that their constitutive socio-economic-political categories are derivative of theological categories, and not vice versa.[36] Thus, Schmitt takes up the crucial feature of all socio-political reality, namely, the persistence of conflict, war, and revolution, and claims to show its inherently theological source.[37] Such a reversal of Marx and Weber is also at work in Schmitt's most famous thesis, namely, his definition of the 'concept of the political' in terms of the authority to define who is friend and who is enemy. For Schmitt, all socio-political realities (all 'political unities') depend on some representative person having the

---

[35] Thus, from this politico-theological viewpoint, Marx's discourse on secularization itself relies on religious distinctions between Christianity and Judaism in order to articulate its abolitionist hypothesis. Indeed, the abolitionist thesis has often been understood as if Marx applied a radical form of messianism to his narrative on communism. Similar considerations apply to Weber's use of theological terms like 'vocation' or 'charisma'. Schmitt considered Weber's conception of charismatic authority to have been his own original contribution to the discourse of political theology.

[36] Claims to the effect that certain theologies already contain a social science, or the related claim that certain theologies offer the theoretical presuppositions of modern social science, are found in the already cited Taylor, Milbank, Gillespie. For political economy, see now (Leshem 2017).

[37] On war and revolution as the decisive social categories of modernity, see (Arendt 1990; and Foucault 1997), who reflect the standpoints of Marx (all society is class struggle) and Weber (all politics is a form of war).

sole authority to make the decision on war, and this decision is theologically structured.[38]

The contemporary discussion on postsecularism has internalized the discourse of political theology in the 20th century and its critique of the Marxist and Weberian secularization theorems. A growing body of work attempts to show that western rule of law, and a fortiori the system of liberal rights, is rooted in the Christian tradition.[39] Others argue that the distinction between 'religious' and 'secular' is itself of Christian origin, and therefore its employment in the public sphere stands in tension with the supposed 'neutrality' of the liberal state.[40] In general, western public intellectuals from Charles Taylor and Talal Asad to Jürgen Habermas and Richard Dworkin have argued that the belief in a purely 'secular' foundation of liberalism is an illusion, and that we should move to a 'postsecular' vision of the role of religion in the public sphere.

For Cécile Laborde, the most damaging postsecular critique of the liberal 'two-way protection' of religious freedom and non-establishment of religion is the Schmittian challenge that liberalism 'is merely another religion'.[41] If this claim were to be true, then liberalism would be both 'judge and party' whenever it seeks to defend the freedom of religion or that of association. Liberalism would turn out to be structurally biased whenever it comes to realizing 'politico-legal values of free exercise and non-establishment' through its public use of reason (Laborde 2017, 39). Laborde's response to the challenge of political theology is to argue that this postsecular critique may have a valid point with respect to certain forms of liberal secularism, like the French idea of *laïcité*, but it does not affect Rawlsian or political 'egalitarian liberalism' because the latter is by definition not itself 'grounded in any comprehensive metaphysical, ontological, or ethical doctrine. It does not seek to enforce a substantively liberal and secular way of life on citizens, but instead affirms political principles of justice.... As a political doctrine it can be endorsed ... from a variety of otherwise conflicting conceptions of the good' (Laborde 2017, 40).

However, this answer seems to preclude the possibility that politico-theological considerations are at work when it comes to discussing and

---

[38] On the concept of the political in Schmitt I refer to my discussion in (Vatter 2008).
[39] For some examples, see (Berman 1983; Tierney 1982; Waldron 2002; and Moyn 2015).
[40] For some examples, (Asad 2003; and Anidjar 2006; 2014).
[41] (Laborde 2017, 38). She mentions Schmitt's political theology in the context of the liberalism-as-religion thesis in (Laborde 2017, 25).

deciding on 'constitutional essentials' using public reason. Or, put another way, Laborde might not consider seriously enough the possibility that all constitutionalism is 'religious' constitutionalism in one sense or another, including liberal constitutionalism.[42] In my opinion, this is because the question of political theology and its relation to democratic legitimacy remains underexplored. My analysis of the discourse on Christian political theology undertakes such a preliminary exploration. It does so by adopting as its *guiding-thread* the problem of democratic legitimacy. For political theology contributes to the discourse on secularization by developing the category of legitimacy. However, there are also good reasons to question whether modern democracy requires the category of legitimacy. Indeed, the upshot of the prolonged debate between Schmitt and Blumenberg on secularization is perhaps just the recognition of the inadequacy and internal tension of the concept of 'democratic legitimacy'. This debate offers the methodological approach I adopt in this book.

Blumenberg's first critique of Schmitt's idea of secularization, in *The Legitimacy of the Modern Age*, imputes to Schmitt the fallacy of having projected onto Modernity his own understanding of the dualism between legality and legitimacy. For Blumenberg, 'legitimacy' requires by definition a reference to some transcendent source of value and order, transmitted through history, whereas 'legality' refers to a synchronic, self-referential system of abstract norms (Blumenberg 1996, 107–8). On this view, 'for the political theorist Carl Schmitt, secularisation is a category of legitimacy' (Blumenberg 1996, 108) because the legitimacy of Modernity would necessarily have to be characterized by the transfer of 'medieval' theological concepts into 'modern' secular concepts.

In his response to Blumenberg's critique, Schmitt demands a shift from approaching secularization based on 'philosophy of history' or 'sociology of concepts' focused on 'Modernity' as a process of rationalization, towards a properly politico-theological approach to secularization, centred on the question of legitimacy in democratic societies.[43] Schmitt reminds

---

[42] As famously suggested in (Stepan 2000).

[43] According to Schmitt, Blumenberg conflated political theology with the entirely different question of the relation between theology and 'philosophy of history', and the various debates as to whether philosophy of history in modernity is a secularized version of a Christian or Jewish 'history of salvation' (*Heilsgeschichte*). In the second edition of *The Legitimacy of the Modern Age* Blumenberg in fact criticizes the different versions of the 'secularization theorem' that seek to explain the possibility of modern philosophy of history found in Karl Löwith, Rudolf Bultmann, Hans Jonas, and Odo Marquard (Blumenberg 1996, 35–72). In the recently published correspondence between Blumenberg and Schmitt, the letter written by Blumenberg on the seventh of August 1975 is particularly telling, insofar as it attempts to establish a bridge with Schmitt on the ground of their mutual

Blumenberg that when he defined 'secularization' as the study of the translation or transposition of concepts from theology to jurisprudence he was not making a claim about 'philosophy of history' nor about the periodization of the shift from the middle ages to the modern age. Blumenberg's thesis that modernity is somehow a 'self-legitimating' process that requires no such transposition of concepts missed Schmitt's point. Rather, for Schmitt there is an *internal* correlation between political theology as transposition of theological into jurisprudential concepts and the project of securing 'legitimacy' for the legal and social order of modern society. Schmitt's point is that what counts is the capital difference between legitimacy and legality. If one accepts this difference, then it does not matter how the project of Modernity finds its 'legitimacy', and whether it does so by breaking with the medieval worldview, because in any case it is caught up in a discourse on political theology. To what extent Schmitt may be right about legitimacy, and what follows from it for democratic political theory, is the leading question that motivates the discussion of Christian political theology in this book.

In their correspondence and in his later writings, Blumenberg responded to Schmitt by proposing a different approach to the question of how secularization relates to legitimacy. Blumenberg suggests dropping entirely the category of secularization if one seeks to explain historical transitions between medieval and modern periods. The category of secularization inevitably assumes a 'wall of separation' between 'religion' and 'politics'. From the Marxist-Weberian viewpoint on secularization, politics will eventually break through the wall and make 'religion' superfluous. From the Schmittian and postsecular viewpoints, there exists an underlying need for religion that subverts any claim on the part of politics to determine its destiny entirely autonomously or immanently.[44]

Blumenberg breaks free from these two viewpoints by pointing out that the distinction between religion and politics as relatively autonomous yet interacting domains is already operative in the Hellenistic age. In this sense, a form of secularism is already found in Hellenism and does not need to wait for Modernity. This same insight is of capital importance to the genealogies

---

interest in Goethe's motto *Nemo contra deus nisi deus ipse*, and their mutual rejection of Löwith's attempt to identify historical consciousness of the moderns with eschatological themes (Blumenberg 2007, 132–33).

[44] This view is now echoed in (Diamantides and Schütz 2018), where the underlying persistence of religion is linked to a supposed human emotional need to assume certain beliefs and rituals on blind trust or faith, which no amount of rationalization can eliminate.

of modern secularism proposed by Kantorowicz and Habermas, both of which show that the remote origins of concepts of secular politics are to be found in the Hellenistic discursive intermixing of philosophy, theology, and politics. Prior to the medieval period, in which philosophy and politics were constituted as 'handmaidens' to revealed monotheistic religions, 'religion' was always already traversed and constituted by political and legal categories. What is called 'Christianity' was, always already, Greco-Roman. It was constituted by the application of categories drawn from Hellenistic philosophy and Roman law to biblical teachings, in much the same sense as the modern 'liberal' state was always already 'Christian' and 'Jewish' because it was no less constituted by the application of Christian and Jewish religious teachings. The one constant in this back and forth between politics and law, on one side, and philosophy and theology, on the other, is precisely the mutual translation of these discourses into one another. These considerations strongly support Agamben's methodological definition of political theology as the discourse that studies the analogies and conceptual transpositions not only from theology to law and politics, but also and primarily from law and politics to theology.[45]

However, Blumenberg considers that the Hellenistic age was free of the modernist conceit that politics will supplant religion or, conversely, that religion underlies all politics. In Hellenistic thought, the mutual dependence of religion and politics is captured by the expression 'Athens *and* Jerusalem' as the underlying pathos for the problem of legitimacy. Far from establishing a 'wall of separation' between religion and politics, Blumenberg suggests that in Hellenistic times each was inviting the participation of the other in view of articulating solutions to the problem of legitimacy. Interestingly, historical scholarship points to the Hellenistic period as being the first in which something like a 'political theology' is discernible.[46] Schmitt is therefore correct to prioritize the problem of legitimacy over the secularization hypothesis, but he is mistaken to believe that a proper understanding of legitimacy necessarily leads to his view of secularization. For Blumenberg, the exemplarity of the Hellenistic context indicates that the priority of legitimacy requires *discarding* all secularization talk along with the belief in a 'wall of separation' that somehow gives credence to such talk.

---

[45] See (Agamben 1998; 2008; 2011).
[46] See (Goodenough 1928; Peterson 2011; and Dvornik 1966).

The exchange between Schmitt and Blumenberg uncovers an additional methodological principle for the study of political theology. For in this exchange Schmitt and Blumenberg agree that the ultimate context from which the problem of legitimacy emerges is the permanent struggle against Gnosticism in western political thought. By Gnosticism, Blumenberg and Schmitt both have in mind the phenomenon of *hatred of power* or *mis-archy*, that is, the tendency to resort to a radically transcendent source of salvation in order to end the disasters wrought by political power on earth. According to Blumenberg, the conflict between the Gnostic rejection of the world and the attempt to give political reality to the 'love of the world' (*amor mundi*) is a constant problem area that keeps being reoccupied in western history.

For Schmitt, the only effective response to the Gnostic challenge is a Christian discourse of legitimate power, that is, a Christian political theology. Blumenberg disagrees. He admits that Schmitt is correct to claim that modernity has met the challenge of Gnosticism by reducing 'legitimacy' to 'legality'. But he rejects Schmitt's representation of modern legality as if it were an expression of modern Gnosticism: an example of human self-divinization that stands in rebellion against God as the ultimate source of the legitimacy of power. On the contrary, Blumenberg suggests that the Hellenistic articulation of 'Athens and Jerusalem' already offered ways to think about legitimacy as a function of legality, but in such a way that it avoids the Gnostic temptation of misarchy. A full consideration of this hypothesis leads beyond the bounds of this investigation and requires engaging the discourse of Jewish political theology.

1
Carl Schmitt and Sovereignty

On the scientific and polemical meanings of political theology

The concept of political theology did not exist before Schmitt baptized it in 1922 with his book *Political Theology*.[1] In the last chapter of *Political Theology* Schmitt gave a decidedly polemical meaning to the concept. Citing Cardinal Newman's dictum that 'no medium exists . . . between catholicity and anarchism', he went on to agree with Donoso Cortés's imperious call to govern through dictatorship as the only realistic counter to Bakunin's project of 'spreading Satan' through anarchism and socialism (Schmitt 1988, 53, 63–4).[2] However, the first three chapters of *Political Theology* are not polemical in the above sense.[3] When, decades later, in *Political Theology II* Schmitt returns to discuss his early book, he emphasizes the 'scientific' meaning of political theology.[4] Political theology is scientific when it studies how concepts

---

[1] Schmitt says that in *Political Theology* he 'introduced the phrase "political theology" to literature' (Schmitt 2008c, 35); see also his claim in a letter to a student that 'the coining of the term "political theology" in fact comes from me' (Mohler 1995, 119, cited in Meier 2011, 202, n. 48).

[2] The polemical concept of 'political theology' takes as its object the 'hatred' of power that develops in the late 19th-century Russian nihilist and anarchist tradition, culminating in many ways with Bakunin, and which finds in Dostoevsky's novels its most influential depiction. On this Russian context of Schmitt's polemical use of political theology, see (Paléologue 2004; McCormick 2010; and Forti 2014). A related literary context that is important for Schmitt's polemical use of political theology is now discussed in (Hoibraaten 2011). The importance of the Russian development of political theology was already pointed out by (Voegelin 1952). The polemical meaning of political theology is highlighted in (Meier 1995; 2011). Mehring argues that the theorem of secularization placed Schmitt before a disjunction in the early 1920s: whether to employ political theology in its scientific form in order to draw attention to the religious roots of the project of modernity, or whether to employ political theology in a polemical way, in order to propose a 'political' deployment of Catholicism in the sense of counter-Enlightenment figures like de Maistre and Donoso Cortés (Mehring 2009, 125–26).

[3] Mehring suggests Schmitt was undecided in the early 1920s as to whether to employ political theology in its 'scientific' form in order to draw attention to the religious roots of the project of modernity, or whether to employ political theology in a polemical way, in order to propose a 'political' deployment of Catholicism in the sense of counter-Enlightenment figures like de Maistre and Donoso Cortés (Mehring 2009, 125–26).

[4] This is the meaning of political theology found in (Böckenförde 1983; Blumenberg 1996; Galli 1996; Kantorowicz 1997; Assmann 2002; Kervégan 2005; Agamben 2008; and Kahn 2011). In his intellectual biography of Schmitt, Mehring follows Assmann and distinguishes between a 'historically descriptive' and a 'politically engaged' sense of political theology (Mehring 2009, 124–29). For an

developed in theology and jurisprudence are 'transposed' from one area to the other, 'among which harmonious exchanges are permitted and meaningful' (Schmitt 2008c, 108). Schmitt's famous version of the secularization theorem, namely, the claim that 'all significant concepts of the modern theory of the state are secularized theological concepts' (Schmitt 1988, 36), is based on this analogy between theology and jurisprudence. The study of these analogies is the subject matter of political theology as a way of doing the 'sociology of concepts'. *Political Theology* applied this sociological methodology to the concept of sovereignty.

Contemporary approaches to Schmitt are divided into two opposed tendencies. On the one hand, there is an effort to separate Schmitt's discourse on political theology from what are assumed to be his main contributions to political science and jurisprudence in works like *Constitutional Theory* and *The Concept of the Political*.[5] On the other hand, there is an effort to deny or downplay the validity of these contributions on the grounds that his entire thought is caught up with political theology in its 'polemical' meaning and is vitiated by his anti-liberalism and his anti-Judaism.[6] Both approaches to Schmitt lose much of their appeal once the discourse of political theology is shown to have a defensible meaning for political science and jurisprudence. This includes Schmitt's hypothesis that 'all political concepts, images, and terms have a polemical meaning' because they are fashioned in light of 'a specific conflict and are bound to a concrete situation'.[7] This hypothesis applies equally to the concept of political theology. It was Erik Peterson, originally a close friend and collaborator of Schmitt's, who pointed out that the 'polemical' context of the discourse of political theology originates in what he calls 'monotheism as a political problem'. This is the Hellenistic context that witnessed the theoretical effort to ground the power of the human sovereign on the analogy with the idea of God as King of the world.[8]

This 'polemical' context of the discourse on political theology produced an inflationary use of the term whereby very different concepts—Jewish

early use of the concept in the field of medieval intellectual history, seemingly without reference to Schmitt, see (Oakley 1968).

[5] For recent examples, see (Kalyvas 2009; Loughlin 2015; and Lindahl 2015a).
[6] For variants of this claim, see (Holmes 1993; Lilla 2001; and Müller 2003).
[7] Cited in (Blumenberg 2007, 30).
[8] See the homonymous work in (Peterson 2011). The 1960s reception in German theology of Schmitt's 'political theology' also falls within this polemical understanding of the term; see (Metz 1970).

'theocracy', Roman 'civil theology', French and North American revolutionary conceptions of 'civil religion', Egyptian, Byzantine, Russian, or even National Socialist forms of 'political religion', the 'theologico-political' solutions given by Spinoza and Hobbes to the wars of religion—are all collapsed under the same concept.[9] It is no accident that in *Political Theology II* Schmitt explicitly acknowledges the manifold equivocations the term 'political theology' gives rise to.[10]

In this chapter I propose one way to traverse and join together the scientific and the polemical meanings of political theology throughout Schmitt's oeuvre without neglecting or minimizing either side of the question. My starting hypothesis is that both the scientific and the polemical approaches to political theology arise from what Schmitt calls the problem of 'political unity and its presence or representation' (Schmitt 2008c, 72). Political unity refers to what Schmitt from early on calls 'political form', and what he would later call 'concrete order'.[11] Schmitt's main claim is that such political unity or order is always and only possible through a Christological conception of 'representation': 'to represent means to make an invisible being visible and present through a publicly present one' (Schmitt 1996c, 243).[12] This conception of political representation is what the jurisprudential wisdom of the Catholic Church, as a concrete legal and political order, teaches. According to Schmitt's interpretation, this teaching was preserved and transmitted to the modern doctrine of sovereignty by Thomas Hobbes. In turn, this theologically informed conception of representation is what the modern American and French revolutions rejected, replacing it instead by a democratic conception of representation where the representatives advocate for their electors rather than standing-for a transcendent principle of political unity.

---

[9] Meier assumes a continuity between the Roman idea of civil theology in Varro and Bakunin's use of 'political theology'. All of this is mixed together in Schmitt's concept 'political theology', which thus designates 'the opposition between authority and anarchy, between faith in revelation and atheism, between obedience to and rebellion against the supreme sovereign' (Meier 2011, 171). For a narrative that places these theologico-political discourses into a continuum, see the Introduction to (Vries 2006). By way of contrast, I brought attention to the discontinuity between theologico-political discourses in the Introduction to (Vatter 2010).

[10] 'There are many political theologies because there are, on the one hand, many different religions, and, on the other hand, many different kinds and methods of doing politics' (Schmitt 2008c, 66).

[11] For a recent discussion of these concepts in Schmitt, see (Meierhenrich and Simons 2017).

[12] Schmitt refers to this kind of representation where something transcendent is made visible in an immanent political order with the term *Räpresentation* and opposes it to the 'modern' idea of a 'representative' who takes our place in a deliberative assembly because he or she collects a majority of our votes. This modern kind of representation Schmitt refers to by the term of *Stellvertretung*.

Schmitt says that the analogies between theology and jurisprudence reflect the fact that these two 'sciences' developed in the west within 'concrete orders' like the Catholic Church in the medieval period and the modern Westphalian system of states in the early modern period (Schmitt 2008c, 108).[13] The politico-theological representation of political unity thus becomes the ground of legal order: it explains the possibility of jurisprudence. But this same conception of representation also accounts for the 'polemical' register of political theology. Schmitt believed that, in virtue of its capacity to 'represent' Christ on earth, the Christian Church offered itself as a bulwark against the power of both liberalism and capitalism, behind which lurks the threat of atomism and anarchism.[14]

At this point it is important to address one possible objection to my choice of representation as the crucial concept through which to capture the main features of Schmitt's discourse on political theology. Political theorists who have employed Schmitt's thought in order to develop a 'radical democratic' political thought, from Antonio Negri and Chantal Mouffe to Andreas Kalyvas and Hans Lindahl, have primarily focused their attention on the concept of constituent power rather than on the concept of representation.[15] Indeed, in *Constitutional Theory* Schmitt remarks that the idea of constituent power is also a concept of political theology since, when Spinoza first articulated this concept through the idea of *natura naturans*, he was basically secularizing the medieval idea of God as *potestas constituens*. For Schmitt, both are 'part of the theory of political theology'.[16] However, the validity of this claim is doubtful and Schmitt never provides any further evidence, apart from the quick reference to Spinoza, that the republican conception of constituent power can be captured by his discourse of political theology. The fact that in *Constitutional Theory* he appropriates Spinoza to his discourse on political theology, while a few years later in *The Leviathan in the State Theory of Thomas Hobbes* he defends Hobbes as the true political theologian and opposes him to Spinoza's 'liberalism', is indicative of the difficulty of inscribing constituent power within political theology.[17]

---

[13] I follow here the hypothesis of (Kervégan 2009, 96–97).
[14] For recent engagements with this motif, see (Ratzinger 2005; Agamben 2012).
[15] See (Negri 1999; Mouffe 1999; Kalyvas 2005; Lindahl 2015b).
[16] See (Schmitt 2008a, 128). On a related distinction between *potestas absoluta* and *potestas ordinaria* see (Oakley 1998b). For its employment by Schmitt, see (Frank 2010; and Ojakangas 2012).
[17] For a convincing argument that Schmitt remains committed to the 'monarchical principle' even in his discussion of constituent power in *Constitutional Theory*, see (Cristi 2011).

This chapter's second thesis argues that Schmitt's focus on representation as the basis of jurisprudence was a reaction against Kelsen's legal positivism and the English school of pluralism who, some years before, offered two visions of jurisprudence without sovereignty. Both 'scientific' approaches to jurisprudence called into question the parallelism between God and State. The English school of pluralism questioned the parallelism in order to defend the legitimacy of churches, universities, and labour unions to resist the commands of the state when these commands called for actions that went against either the conscience or the freedom of association of its members. Kelsen questioned the parallelism because he believed that a democratic state was possible only on condition that its legal commands were seen to issue out of a constitutional, self-referential, and immanent system of norms.

This chapter's third and final thesis is that Schmitt's later work abandons the idea that his scientific discourse on political theology is necessarily linked with the ideas of sovereignty, absolutism, and dictatorship. Instead, Schmitt attempts to place democracy at the heart of political theology by considering the possibility that Greco-Roman political concepts were transferred into Judeo-Christian theological concepts, reversing his earlier theorem of secularization. This 'democratic turn' in his political theology was itself motivated by a polemical engagement with Peterson's critique of his political theology. However, Schmitt's response to Peterson still employs the category of representation in order to offer a political interpretation of the Christian doctrine of the Trinity and its relation to democratic legitimacy.

Schmitt versus Kelsen: Christology, legal personality, and the application of law

Schmitt developed the scientific meaning of political theology in response to Kelsen's rejection of the very idea of legal personality. Schmitt claims that he was the first to draw attention to the 'fundamentally systematic and methodological analogies' between theology and jurisprudence as far back as his first book, *Der Wert des Staates und die Bedeutung des Einzelnen* from 1914. However, he clearly organizes his discussion in *Political Theology* as a refutation of Kelsen, who 'has the merit of having stressed since 1920 the methodical relationship of theology and jurisprudence' (Schmitt 1988, 39). In this context, he refers to Kelsen's book *Der soziologische und der juristische Staatsbegriff. Kritische Untersuchung des Verhältnisses von Staat und Recht*

[The sociological and juridical concept of the state. Critical investigation of the relations between state and law]. Thus, at least as concerns the scientific meaning of political theology, Schmitt is reacting to Kelsen rather than the other way around. In order to make sense of what political theology means for Schmitt, then, it is imperative to begin with Kelsen's account of the same.[18]

In an early article dedicated to juridical fictions, Kelsen discusses the idea of a juridical person, understood as a being existing independently of the system of norms, and endowed with duties and rights (Kelsen 1919, 631). For Kelsen, this juridical person is merely a useful 'personification of a complex of norms' (Kelsen 1919, 631); the legal person is a fiction that has no corresponding reality. Yet, Kelsen points out that it is the most natural of mistakes to 'hypostasize' this fiction and consider it 'as if' it were a real person, just as happens when one hypostasizes mental functions into the idea of a 'soul' or, in the case of physical motion, into the idea of a 'force' (Kelsen 1919, 634–35). In all these cases, a tautology is turned into two entities.[19] Kelsen's fundamental thesis is that a scientific approach to law depends entirely on unmasking the role played by the juridical person within a legal system. A scientific or objective approach to the law is only possible on the basis of 'the sovereignty of the law [*Souveranität des Rechtes*] (or, what is the same, of the State), that is, when one recognises the legal order [*Rechtsordnung*] as a self-standing system of norms *not derived from a higher order* [*Ordnung*]' (Kelsen 1919, 652, emphasis mine). Without the critique of the hypostasis of such legal persons, there is no true science of right.

Three years later, in *Der soziologische und der juristische Staatsbegriff*, Kelsen advances the radical claim that the idea of a 'unique-single [*einig-einzigen*] State' is a hypostatization of the legal order analogous to the hypostatization of the unity of nature in the person of the monotheistic God (Kelsen 1981, 220). In both cases, a person (God or State, both conceived as persons) is posited as transcending the complex of norms,

---

[18] For recent defences of Schmitt's scientific, rather than polemic, approach to political theology, see (Chen 2006; and Espejo 2010), who nevertheless do not discuss the central question of the significance of political theology for jurisprudence. The importance of Kelsen for Schmitt's conception of political theology is highlighted in (Baume 2009), who also correctly emphasizes that the fundamental problem that a political theology is called to solve is that of the unity of the state, or political unity, through a theory of representation.

[19] The second sense of a juridical fiction (*fictio juris*) does not have an inherent relation to a reality that it falsifies. This second kind of juridical fiction is entirely legitimate because it does not claim to refer to any entities outside of the complex of norms, and instead merely refers to ways in which to move within this complex of norms, for instance when the law refers to someone as the 'father' of a child, for the purposes of law, although they are not the biological father of the child (Kelsen 1919, 639–41). All translations from the German are mine.

presenting itself as endowed with an 'absolute will' as the 'creative' source of the norm-complex (Kelsen 1981, 222–23). The idea that state 'sovereignty' stands above the legal order is due to the misunderstanding of the idea of juridical person.[20]

According to Kelsen, the hypostatization of the juridical person is foundational to both Christian theology and to the doctrine of the state [*Staatslehre*]. These two discourses provide a way of reconnecting God with Nature, and state with law, that the hypostatization of legal personhood previously separated. But for Kelsen, the 'solutions' provided by theology and doctrine of the state are entirely 'mystical'. In theology this solution takes the form of the doctrine of the 'two natures' of Christ, who must be entirely divine and entirely human, found in Christology (Kelsen 1981, 230–33). In the doctrine of the state the solution conceives of the state as both 'above and below' the legal order. Expressed more clearly, theology and the doctrine of the state both require worldly 'representatives' of their transcendent persons. Thus, by 1922 Kelsen had already identified the logic that accounts, simultaneously, for the secularization theorem and the concept of structural analogies between theology and jurisprudence, exactly the complex of issues Schmitt takes up in *Political Theology*.

In his celebrated article, 'God and the State,' originally published in *Logos* in 1922, Kelsen explains the analogy and parallelism between theological and political concepts as a function of the need to give 'intuitive expression' for the unity of the world (in the case of God) or the unity of laws (in the case of the state) through 'the anthropomorphic mental aid of personification' (Kelsen 1973, 68).[21] The state is 'the person . . . the personification of law' (Kelsen 1973, 69). The structural analogies between theology and jurisprudence are possible not only thanks to the personification of order but also through the hypostatization of this person, for it is the latter that imputes a substance to the function of unity and thus creates a dualism between God and world, state and legal system. Implicit in the possibility of hypostatization is the idea that law is a command, for then the step to personalize the law and understand it as a command of someone (the state as person) is a natural fallacy.

---

[20] For a discussion of Kelsen's critique of all dualistic conceptions of the state, see (Brunkhorst 2011).
[21] 'The concept of legal order enables us to apprehend as a unity the multitude of legal relations between individuals. But the abstract unity of the legal order is rendered palpable in the idea of a person, whose will signifies the content of this legal order, just as the will of God finds expression in the world-order' (Kelsen 1973, 69).

The correct view, for Kelsen, is to deny any such dualism between state and law: 'the state in every respect can only be the legal order.... The theory of the legal state [*Rechtsstaat*] can concede no part of the state to stand outside the law . . . this state of general state-theory is identical as an order with law, and as a person is merely the personification, the anthropomorphic expression, of the unity of law' (Kelsen 1973, 69–70). Although Kelsen does not employ the concept of 'representation' in this context, it is clear that his theory of the hypostatization of personification entails a concept of representation as the making present or visible again of something that is not presently visible. As a jurisprudential discourse, political theology addresses the question of who or what represents or personifies the state. For Kelsen, political representation acquires this importance only because of the fallacy entailed in understanding the person of the state as a real thing, as transcending the complex of norms.[22] Representation presupposes 'the pseudo-existence of a metalegal, supralegal state': representation is a pseudo-solution to a pseudo-problem (Kelsen 1973, 70).

Kelsen's article 'God and the State' is of interest because it develops a series of aporias or contradictions into which political theology—understood as the doctrine of the hypostatization of the persons of God and of the state—falls due to its doubling up of substances. Illustrated in relation to state and law, the problem is that 'the state is the creator or sustainer of law, and is therefore above the law; but on the other hand is again of the same nature as the law, is subject to the law' (Kelsen 1973, 72). Here Kelsen indicates the quintessential problem of sovereignty and of Bractonian prerogative that would exercise Kantorowicz and many Anglo-American historians of political thought in the 1940s and 1950s. How can the sovereign be simultaneously above and below the law? For Kelsen, this 'logically insoluble problem' receives a pseudo-solution through an account of Christian 'incarnation': 'God transforms Himself into the world, or into its representative, man, in that the divine essentially splits into two persons, God-the-Father and God-the-Son.... This theory of God's incarnation in the world is put forward in theology under the aspect of the self-limitation or self-obligation of God' (Kelsen 1973, 73).

---

[22] As discussed in the next chapter, Voegelin will adopt the defence of representation in his anti-Schmittian development of political theology. Kelsen was keenly aware of the problematic consequences of Voegelin's political theology and dedicated a posthumously published book to refute Voegelin. On this whole episode, see now (Thomassen 2014), who, however, misunderstands the reason why Kelsen would see in Voegelin a political theologian despite Voegelin's well-known critique of 'political religions'.

By identifying the dualism of state and law as the core of 'scientific' political theology, Kelsen claims to show that this discourse merely serves a political purpose and is therefore ideological and not properly scientific. One needs to personify the state only for purposes of ascribing to human acts the character of 'acts of state'. But 'the criterion of ascription to the state can only be a legal one. A human action can be accounted an act of state only when and insofar as it is qualified in a specific manner by a legal norm, is decreed in the system of the legal order' (Kelsen 1973, 76), whereas the doctrine that teaches the dualism of state and law wants to ascribe human acts to the state 'above' the legal order and, nonetheless, still call it a proper 'legal order' or 'public law'. Kelsen believes that this medieval theory of public law simply makes 'a legal act out of a naked act of power', and is essentially the expression of 'an autocratic order directed against a law essentially customary' (Kelsen 1973, 77).[23]

Kelsen's last thesis in 'God and the State', which again anticipates Schmitt, is that the conception of public law in which the sovereign is both above and below the law finds its analogue in the theological idea of a miracle. The sovereign understood as a 'meta- or supralegal state' amounts to the effort of making 'the legally unintelligible intelligible nonetheless—in a legal manner—and to secure belief in a legal miracle' (Kelsen 1973, 78). Although Kelsen does not refer in this text to the idea of a state of exception as being definitive of sovereignty, as Schmitt will do that same year in the opening sentence of *Political Theology*, he already signals Schmitt's identification of the concept of state of exception (in reason of state or public law) and its parallel with the doctrine of miracles in theology.

After having shown the ideological character of political theology, Kelsen arrives at his radically atheistic conclusion: 'God and the state exist only *if and insofar as they are believed in*, and all of their enormous power . . . collapses if the human soul is able to rid itself of this belief' (Kelsen 1973, 80, emphasis mine). The insight that the hypostases of God and state both depend on faith plays a crucial role in the development of Christian democratic political theology. However, what is important at this juncture of the argument is the sense in which Kelsen defines his 'pure theory of law' as a 'purely legal theory of the state, which *gets rid of the idea of a state* distinct from law' and is thus functionally equivalent to a '*stateless* theory of the state' (Kelsen 1973, 81, emphasis mine). Thus, Kelsen's adoption of Bakunin's polemic title *God*

---

[23] Here Kelsen indicates how the modern doctrine of sovereignty and its theory of representation emerges out of the medieval confluence of divine law, imperial Roman law, and common law.

and the State for his own article is an invitation to consider his own legal positivism as an anarchic theory of law. At the end of the text, Kelsen qualifies his anarchism as epistemological because it refutes the claim that the state can be separate from law, while distancing himself from Bakunin's classic anarchist identification of all law with domination.

Schmitt's *Political Theology* is a defence of sovereignty directed against Kelsen's attacks on this concept, and indeed on the very tradition of the European tradition of public law (*jus publicum europaeum*).[24] Schmitt's main argument turns on a discussion of juridical personality, whether it is real or representative, and if so, how it can be represented. In *Roman Catholicism and Political Form*, Schmitt presents his conception of representation [*Räpresentation*], making it into the condition of possibility of political unity. But *Political Theology* has the more arduous task of reconceiving the idea of legal order such that the appeal to representation and thus to the person of the state, the sovereign, is inevitable. This, at least, is the 'scientific' task of the treatise.

Schmitt deploys two arguments to counteract Kelsen's destruction of political theology. The first takes aim at Kelsen's separation of sociology and jurisprudence. Kelsen followed Weber in thinking that sociology studies the relations of power between individuals. Sociology showed that power was 'legitimated' by ideologies that foster belief in divinities and sovereigns and in so doing makes possible the voluntary servitude of the subjects. Jurisprudence, instead, ought to be the science that offers a 'pure' account of law independent from the facticity of power. Schmitt agrees with Kelsen that 'power proves nothing in law' (Schmitt 1988, 17). But, precisely for that reason, law requires an account of the legitimacy of power, that is, an account of 'the connection of actual power with the legally highest power' (Schmitt 1988, 18). Political theology offers an account of the concept of sovereignty that seeks to explain how the abstract complex of norms connects to a concrete complex of power. According to Schmitt, the link to a real person *who must also be a legal person* is a necessary condition for any legal system to acquire a 'political form' and cease being a powerless, apolitical abstraction. As he points out in *Political Theology*, the connection between law

---

[24] The recent defence and reconstruction of 'public law' in (Loughlin 2004; 2010), in this sense, is to be reinterpreted as a broadside against Kelsen's attempted destruction of the tradition of 'public law', and broadly sympathetic to Schmitt's own reconstruction of the same tradition.

and life unavoidably leads back to the problem of legal personality and its 'reality'.[25]

Schmitt's second argument takes up Kelsen's thesis regarding the hypostatization of the person of the state (Schmitt 1988, 18–19), while remaining conscious of its centrality to political theology. On Kelsen's account, 'for juristic consideration there are neither real nor fictitious persons, only points of ascription' and the state is merely 'the point at which ascriptions, which constitute the essence of juristic considerations, "can stop"' (Schmitt 1988, 18–19). According to Schmitt, '[t]he decisive argument [of Kelsen] . . . remains the same: the basis for the validity of a norm can only be a norm: in juristic terms the state is therefore identical with its constitution, with the uniform basic norm' (Schmitt 1988, 19). Schmitt's rebuttal of Kelsen on this front is complex and is made up of several threads.

First, he casts doubt on what Kelsen takes to be the 'unity' of a legal system. For Schmitt this unity is not a theoretical construction, but can only refer to 'the unity of a positive-valid order' (Schmitt 1988, 20). He believes Kelsen fails to show that a complex of norms, a system of laws, emerges out of a constitution without presupposing such a politically concrete order.[26] Kelsen simply avoids the problem of the relation between law and reality by denying the effects of political and sociological realities (concrete orders or groups or associations). Schmitt believes that only the sovereign can hold together the unity of legal order with the unity of 'political reality'.

The second thread of the argument is the thesis that law connects to reality at the point of its application. Schmitt argues that every ascription is based 'on a command' (Schmitt 1988, 20), and thus to deny the difference between state (the person who has authority to issue commands) and law (the point of ascription) is to 'disregard the independent problem of the realization of law' (Schmitt 1988, 21), that is, the problem of legal application.[27] For Schmitt, the state is different from law because the state exists in order to apply law, to give it 'force of law', to decide on its interpretation, to issue a judgment on its basis. Schmitt rejects the idea that the state is merely a law-making power that permits individuals to live 'under the rule of laws (spiritual forces)' as opposed to the 'authority of persons, be they natural or

---

[25] For a discussion of the problem of connecting law to life in Schmitt and Agamben in relation to legal personality, see (Vatter 2016).
[26] For a contemporary explanation and defence of this Schmittian point, see now (Loughlin 2015).
[27] On the problem of application and its significance for Schmitt's jurisprudence, see (Galli 1996; and Vatter 2008) and the literature cited therein.

artificial' (Schmitt 1988, 22). This claim would entail that laws could apply themselves, something that for Schmitt is clearly impossible. Laws need to be applied or enforced or decided by the state; this in turn requires a person who represents the state. The question is what kind of a person is this, a natural or an artificial one?

Schmitt clearly believes that he has found a way beyond the natural/artificial dualism of medieval corporate theory through his politico-theological articulation of the idea of representation. For Schmitt, representation offers the only viable solution to the problem of linking law to life and politics, other than the one offered by Otto von Gierke and his English pluralist followers. In fact, as he admits a few pages later, only Gierke 'answered the basic question on their [law and state] mutual relation by asserting that both are independent factors of human communal life' (Schmitt 1988, 24). Only Gierke does not evade the problem of sovereignty as Kelsen evades it. Both in *Political Theology* and in *The Concept of the Political*, Gierke and the English school of legal pluralism emerge as one of Schmitt's main adversaries. Schmitt argues that Gierke's 'association theory' destroys the idea of a 'centralized authoritarian state' because 'the will of the state or sovereign is not the final source of law but is the organ of the people convoked to express legal consciousness as it emerges from the life of the people'.[28]

Gierke's 'theory of association' appealed to the medieval legal tradition according to which the state was merely a 'community of communities': the state (*civitas*) was itself composed of many associations (*universitates*; sing., *universitas*).[29] On Gierke's broadly associational view, the state ought to 'make' law only as a function of 'ascertaining the legal value of interests as it springs from the people's feeling or sense of right' (Schmitt 1988, 23). The state has no business in dictating the good form of life to society; its role is merely to assure that individuals and groups pursue their interests and values in a rightful way. Schmitt rejects the associational view because he thinks the state 'makes' law in a far more substantial way: 'I will show that the problem of law as a substantial form lies precisely in this act of ascertaining' (Schmitt

---

[28] Gierke, cited in (Schmitt 1988, 24). For a translation of Gierke's main work in legal theory, and a useful historical introduction by the editor Antony Black, see (Gierke 2002).

[29] The English historian J. Neville Figgis, responsible for the Conciliarist revival, was influenced by Gierke and popularized in the Anglophone world the idea according to which medieval political unity was best understood as a 'corporation of corporations'. On Figgis's approach to medieval political theory, see the indispensable (Oakley 1973). The idea of a 'community of communities' or a federal system as the basis of the political unity of a liberal society would resurface in the 1970s with Rawls's *A Theory of Justice*, and it has since received communitarian and libertarian developments in thinkers like Michael Walzer and Chandran Kukathas, respectively.

1988, 23). This is the single most important jurisprudential task of *Political Theology* and the heart of the treatise.

For Schmitt a legal order is a 'substantial form' because only in such a form does law connect with the reality of social life. The task for Schmitt is to show how the life of the sovereign or of the person who represents the state reflects the 'life of the people' without being merely 'artificial'. Motivated by his direct polemic against Gierke, throughout his oeuvre Schmitt turns to Hobbes to fulfil this systematic task. For Gierke, 'the personal will of the ruler is spliced into the state as if into an organic whole', whereas for Schmitt the personal will of the sovereign, qua representative of the state, is not part of the entire state or *civitas*. The sovereign is not part of a greater organic whole on a par with all other civil associations within this state. Where for Gierke, the state merely gives its 'seal of approval' in the form of law to the interests of the people, Schmitt, instead, sees the state as the *only* source of law, which hence requires the *monopoly* of legal authority called sovereignty (Schmitt 1988, 25).

The sovereign state gives 'legal form' to society. This entails much more than merely 'ascertaining' the interests of society that are external to the state, for this would imply that society could 'make' law by itself or was by itself the source of 'legitimacy': 'Every ascertainment and decision contains a constitutive element, an intrinsic value of form. . . . The state thus becomes a form in the sense of a living formation' (Schmitt 1988, 27). In other words, the form of law bequeathed by the state on social interests gives society another kind of 'life'.

In order to explain how a legal form can give life, Schmitt moves on to a discussion of the 'concept of form', and in this way reconnects with the main theme of *Roman Catholicism and Political Form*. The main argument is that 'the legal form is governed by the legal idea and by the necessity of applying a legal thought to a factual situation, which means that it is governed by the self-evolving law in the widest sense. Because the legal idea cannot realize itself, it needs a particular organization and form before it can be translated into reality. That holds true for the formation of a general legal norm into a positive law' (Schmitt 1988, 28). This is the crux of the argument: every law carries a reference to a 'legal idea', that is, to an idea of justice; but every law also has a legal form, that is, an *application* of this idea of justice in the form of an institution or 'particular organization and form'. The seed of Schmitt's subsequent turn away from legal decisionism and adoption of the idea of 'concrete orders' in *Über die drei Arten des rechtswissenschaftlichen Denkens*

[On the three kinds of jurisprudential thinking] is already apparent here.[30] However, for Schmitt it remains always the case that the institution that applies the idea of justice in the form of law needs to be conceived as a legal personality as well, because there is no act of application without a personal act of will or interpretation or decision.[31]

Legal form or legal application of principles of justice (legal ideas) requires a 'conception of personality': 'That *the legal idea cannot translate itself independently is evident from the fact that it says nothing about who should apply it*. In every transformation there is present an *auctoritas interpositio*. A distinctive determination of which individual person or which concrete body can assume such authority cannot be derived from the mere legal quality of a maxim' (Schmitt 1988, 30, emphasis mine). Schmitt's refutation of Kelsen's account of legal ascriptions is here baldly stated, but it is also clear how Schmitt moves from the legal application of a principle of justice (the legal 'idea') to the concept of a legal person who is authorized to make this application or to take this decision. The concept of *auctoritas interpositio* refers to the Roman law conception of a tutor who is 'authorized to act' for a minor who lacks legal autonomy or *sui iuris* status. The reference to this point in Roman law clearly indicates that for Schmitt the proper relation between state and society is that between a tutor and a pupil. In fact, his idea of representation ultimately flows from this Roman legal conception of acting-in-the-place-of-another, which is reworked in the medieval theory of corporate law in relation to the theological idea of the corporate Church (later of the state) as a *corpus mysticum* of Christ.

Schmitt closes his argument against Kelsen by opposing Locke's view, according to whom 'the law gives authority', to Hobbes's view that *auctoritas, non veritas facit legem* [authority, not truth, makes for laws].[32] Only the latter principle is adequate to 'the normative character of the legal decision' because it is aware that 'the legal prescription as the norm of decision only designates how decisions should be made, not who should decide. . . . Accordingly, the question is that of competence, a question that cannot be raised by and much the less answered from the content of the legal quality of a maxim' (Schmitt

---

[30] See (Schmitt 1995). On the idea of concrete orders, see now (Herrero 2015).

[31] Samuel Weber also argues that in Schmitt, 'it is by virtue of the decisive or, rather decisional intervention of a singular subject that "law" can be endowed with "life"' (Weber 2005, 35). However, he does not contextualize Schmitt's solution to the problem of application of law within the medieval juridical understanding of the problem of representation, where the representative is never conceived as merely a 'singular subject'.

[32] (Schmitt 1988, 32) citing Chapter 26 of the Latin edition of *Leviathan*.

1988, 33). For Schmitt, the Hobbesian question, *Quis judicabit?* [who is judge?], will remain the fundamental question for jurisprudence all the way through *Political Theology II*. Who has the *ultimate competence* to determine which of the 'competent authorities' have jurisdiction in each case? This question lies at the heart of the liberal understanding of the limits of state legislation. Yet for Schmitt the attempt to answer it shows the radical untenability of any 'wall of separation' between state and civil society, irrespective of whether this separation is set up to protect religious freedom or economic freedom.

Schmitt versus the English Pluralists: Hobbes and the question of democratic representation

In *Political Theology*, Hobbes's name appears in relation to the centuries-old problem of the proper limits of political and ecclesiastical power. What exercised Schmitt, as it exercised Hobbes, was the question posed in Chapter 42 of the *Leviathan*: should a 'higher' spiritual power, like that claimed by the Christian Church, rule over an 'inferior' material power, like that claimed by the state? European public law—developed by Bodin, Grotius, Pufendorf, Hobbes, and Spinoza—aimed to resolve this question in order to put an end to the endemic 'civil war' between Empire and Church that characterized the medieval *respublica Christiana*.[33] These early modern political and juridical thinkers sought a new concept of political unity that would reconfigure the relation of authority and power between State and Church.[34]

It was generally assumed in medieval political thought that the Pope held the highest spiritual authority (*auctoritas*) and the Holy Roman Emperor wielded supreme earthly power (*potestas*).[35] After the clerical revolution against the Holy Roman Emperor begun by Pope Gregory VII in the 12th century, supporters of a theocratic conception of the Church began to argue

---

[33] See the discussion in (Figgis 1911).

[34] For recent grand narratives on the development of modern sovereignty, see (Loughlin 2010; and Tuck 2016).

[35] As formulated by the "Two Swords" doctrine of Pope Gelasius I: 'Duo sunt . . . quibus principaliter mundus hie regitur: auctoritas sacra pontificum, et regalis potestas' [There are two powers . . . by which this world is chiefly ruled: the sacred authority of the priesthood and the royal power]. See (Schmitt 2003, 61), where he also importantly refers to Neville Figgis as a "real historian." In 1916 Figgis published what is perhaps the first grand narrative of the rise of modern political thought centred on the emergence of the idea of sovereignty, *Studies of Political Thought from Gerson to Grotius 1414–1625* (Figgis 1960).

that the Pope's spiritual power also meant he had 'indirect power' over the Emperor and other kings. In response, emperors and kings began adopting theological figures and arguments to establish 'spiritual' grounds of legitimacy for their secular kingdoms. Hobbes needed to refute the Roman Catholic claim to Papal sovereignty because it placed the absolute character of the sovereign power to determine the public religion of the realm according to the Reformation maxim *cuius regio, eius religio* [whose realm, his religion] into question. At stake was nothing short of Hobbes's attempt to 'fulfill the Reformation'.[36]

In Chapter 42 of the *Leviathan*, Hobbes sets out to refute Cardinal Bellarmine's arguments, in *De Summo Pontefice*, that the Catholic Church has the right to claim supreme civil power wherever Catholic believers are found because the Pope is the head of a 'mystical body' of the Church composed of all believers. Hobbes argued that it makes no sense to say that one (worldly) power is to be subordinate to the other (spiritual) power because 'Subjection, Command, Right and Power are accidents, not of Powers, but of Persons', that is, they are accidents of representatives (Hobbes 2010, 315/347).[37] 'One Power may be subordinate to another, as the art of a Saddler, to the art of a Rider', but from this it does not follow that a saddler is politically subject to a rider. 'Therefore as from the Subordination of an Art, cannot be inferred the Subjection of the Professor; so from the Subordination of a Government, cannot be inferred the Subjection of the Governor' (Hobbes 2010, 315/347).

The whole argument laid out in Chapter 42 depends on Hobbes's understanding of representation, and the crucial claim that power belongs with whoever is the actual representative of the grouping in question. Because of the immense importance of legal personality in Hobbes's argument, Schmitt concludes that Hobbes was well aware of 'the specific reality of legal life inherent in the legal form. The form that he sought lies in the concrete decision, one that emanates from a particular authority.... What matters for the reality

---

[36] I refer here to one of Schmitt's last interpretations of Hobbes, "Die vollendete Reformation. Bemerkungen und Hinweise zu neuen Leviathan-Interpretationen", published in 1965 and now found in (Schmitt 1982). For Schmitt, the problem of the conflict of competences between theology and politics can only come to a real end 'in the same way as the confessional civil wars of the 16th and 17th century: either in a precise answer to the big question *quis judicabit?* Or in an equally precise *itio in partes* [return to the region]—that is, a spatially clear territorial or regional demarcation, in accordance with the principle *cuius regio eius religio*' (Schmitt 2008c, 114). On these concepts to resolve the conflict in early modern German jurisprudence, see (Hunter 2001).

[37] The page numbers refer to the Clarendon edition of 1909, and to the Yale University Press edition respectively.

of legal life is who decides' (Schmitt 1988, 33).[38] It is because they are representatives of a certain sort that sovereigns have the authority to decide cases in the last instance, and because they have this authority, they also have the ultimate power to make law.

In general, the significance of Hobbes for Schmitt's political theology centres on the way Hobbes preserves the idea of legal or political form by building on the Catholic principle of representation as essential for political form, transposing it to the new realm of the modern state.[39] Hobbes retains the Catholic principle of representation despite advocating for the end of the Church's spiritual power as an indirect worldly power.[40] In *Roman Catholicism and Political Form*, Schmitt argues that the political existence of the Catholic Church is significant because it carries forth the principle of representation. The Catholic Church is to be understood as 'a strict realization of the principle of representation' (Schmitt 1996c, 8). In this sense, the Church retains its 'incomprehensible political power' (Schmitt 1996c, 3) irrespective of any 'wall of separation' between spiritual and worldly powers.[41]

Schmitt's thesis is that the Catholic Church is a *complexio oppositorum*, meaning that it can forge a 'unity of the plurality of interests and parties' by virtue of its principle of representation. He expressly opposes this Catholic principle of representation to modern electoral representation because even 'the members of parliament are *representatives of the whole people* and

---

[38] Schmitt appeals to the same conclusion in Chapter 7 of *The Concept of the Political* when he criticizes the liberal idea of rule of law. 'It is clear to a politician that the rule or sovereignty of this type of law [natural law or law of reason/MV] signifies *the rule and sovereignty of men or groups* who can appeal to this higher law and thereby decide its content and how and by whom it should be applied. Hobbes has drawn these simple consequences of political thought without confusion and more clearly than anyone else. He has emphasized time and again that the sovereignty of the law means only the sovereignty of men who draw up and administer this law. The rule of a higher order, according to Hobbes, is an empty phrase if it does not signify politically that certain of this higher order rule over men of a lower order' (Schmitt 2007, 67, emphasis mine).

[39] Here I share the view of (Kervégan 2009).

[40] In similar terms, Schmitt is interested in the 'Catholic philosophers of the counterrevolution' because they apply the lesson drawn from the analogy between juridical and theological concepts. Thus, Donoso Cortés, despite being aware that monarchism was no longer an option in the 19th century, 'was in complete accord with the thought of the Middle Ages, whose construction was juristic. All his perceptions, all his arguments, down to the last atom, were juristic . . . the specific logic of the juristic thinking that culminates in a personal decision' (Schmitt 1988, 52). That is why Donoso Cortés, in the absence of kings, and Hobbes, in the absence of the sovereignty of the Church, both agreed that the principle of political form must lead to 'only one solution: dictatorship. It is the solution that Hobbes also reached by the same kind of decisionist thinking' (ibid.). Donoso Cortés and Hobbes apply the principle of representation that characterized the Church in its political existence.

[41] The outlines of the argument are already found in Tocqueville when he explained the paradox that Christianity was the foundation of American democracy not despite but because of the constitutional principle of non-establishment that kept it separate, and protected, from the vagaries of direct political power. See the discussion of Tocqueville in (Casanova 2011; and Jaume 2011).

thus have an *independent authority* vis-à-vis the voters. Instead of deriving their authority from the individual voter, they continue to derive it from the people' as their 'personification' and 'representative' (Schmitt 1996c, 26, emphasis mine). In other words, Schmitt locates in the political and juridical thought developed within the Catholic Church the origin of a conception of political representation that is neither based on direct elections of the rulers by the ruled, nor dependent on consensual agreements between individuals and their governments. The Catholic principle of representation makes possible a non-democratic way to conjure the presence of the people.[42]

In *Constitutional Theory*, Schmitt postulated that every legitimate state is characterized by 'two opposing formative principles. The first is the principle of identity (specifically the self-identity of the existing people as a political unity, if, by virtue of its own political consciousness and actual will, it has the capacity to distinguish friend and enemy), and the other is the principle of representation, through which the government represents the political unity' (Schmitt 2008a, 247). In the ideal and utopian case where there exists strict identity or homogeneity between the rulers and the ruled, there can be no representation. Representation is only possible when political unity (*complexio*) must be forged out of oppositions (*oppositorum*) that give rise to the need for an authoritative source of binding decisions. The decision can only come from a juridical person who decides, not subjectively or arbitrarily, but as representative of the whole people or community (*civitas*).[43]

The most provocative consequence of Schmitt's political theology is that representation, understood as source of political unity, is neither democratic nor electoral. The idea of a democratic form of representation is ultimately self-contradictory. In one sense, then, for Schmitt political theology—which turns on such an idea of representation—cannot be democratic. However, in another sense, political theology must be democratic because the legitimate representatives must be representatives of a people: 'There is no state without structured elements of the principle of identity' (Schmitt 2008a, 241) because

---

[42] For the debate on whether the roots of modern democracy are to be found in a different interpretation of the principle of organization of the Catholic Church, namely, the feature highlighted in Conciliarism, see (Oakley 1969; 2015). I discuss at length this question in the chapter dedicated to Kantorowicz.

[43] 'The political unity of the people as such can never be present in actual identity and, consequently, must always be represented by men personally' (Schmitt 2008a, 239). 'The presentation of the political unity is an intrinsic part of the form. In every state there must be persons who can say "L´État c'est nous"' (Schmitt 2008a, 241).

'there is no state without people, and that a people, therefore, must always actually be existing as an entity present at hand' (Schmitt 2008a, 239).

The non-democratic conception of popular representation was invented by the Catholic Church when it turned 'the priesthood into an office' (Schmitt 1996c, 14).[44] The idea of a priestly office allowed the Catholic Church to free itself from a dependency on the charismatic gift of religious actors. Thus, 'the priest upholds a position that appears to be completely apart from his concrete personality. Nevertheless he is not the functionary and commissar of republican thinking ... his position is not impersonal, because his office is part of an unbroken chain linked with the personal mandate and concrete person of Christ' (Schmitt 1996c, 14). Here Schmitt assumes that Church authority has a 'descending' structure based on the fact that Peter was the chosen representative of Jesus Christ, who Himself is the Head of the mystical body of all Christian believers, or of the invisible Church.[45] On this reading of the Catholic conception of vicariate representation, the bishop, and in the last instance the Pope as Bishop of Rome, is the representative, the making visible, in the body of the Church, of the invisible Head that is Christ. The bishop, as representative or vicar of Christ as Head of His 'mystical body' as Church, takes on the mask or person of the Lord and repeats the words of the Lord.[46] The bishop 'personifies a role', stands in for Christ, and in this sense makes visible again the invisible head of Christ. Hobbes's and Schmitt's sense of representation relies on this liturgical reservoir of sense. A representative, in other words, is always someone who stands for a divine person.

In *Constitutional Theory*, Schmitt speaks of a 'dialectic' in the concept of representation. The person who is represented by the vicariate representative must be 'a special type of being' who is both visible and invisible (Schmitt 2008a, 243). The representative has the function of standing-for, of making visible again, the person of Christ. More specifically, the person who is represented must be a being that can be 'enhanced' by means of their public re-presentation. The divine person must be a being who gains 'height', 'majesty', and 'dignity' from their being represented to a people.[47] Schmitt is here

---

[44] For a recent discussion of the political theology of office see now (Heron 2018), who takes up the views of Peterson and Agamben. For a critique of Agamben's interpretation of office, see (Hunter 2017).

[45] On the 'descending' structure of Christian ecclesiastical authority, see the essays in (Ullmann 1980).

[46] See (Hofmann 2007, 139, 192–93; Kantorowicz 1997, 59, 102, 159–60).

[47] 'The representative as well as the person represented must maintain a personal dignity.... To represent in an eminent sense can only be done by a person, that is, not simply a "deputy" but an authoritative person or an idea which, if represented, also becomes personified.... Representation

referring to theological problem of the 'kingdom, the power, and the glory' of God.[48] But he has not moved very far from Kelsen's original point, namely, that the theory of legal personality develops in parallel to the Christology of Christian theology, which requires that the transcendent God 'limit' Himself by incarnating Himself as a human being, thereby making possible the very idea of a human 'representative' of Christ.[49]

As Mehring has indicated, in the period from *Political Theology* to *Constitutional Theory* Schmitt relied heavily on the interpretation of the Church advocated by Peterson, according to which the Church 'represents Christ reigning, ruling, and conquering' (Schmitt 1996c, 31).[50] For Peterson, the Christian Event was nothing short of the problem of Christ's crucifixion, resurrection, and elevation to Kingship next to His Father. Schmitt and Peterson agree that the Church is the earthly representative of Jesus understood as the King of a divine Kingdom that belongs to this age. As Christ, Jesus brought to a conclusion the previous age under the rule of Mosaic Law. The political problem of the age after the resurrection of Christ is that for Jesus to be recognized as Christ, His Kingdom must be proclaimed here on earth. Christ must find His obedient subjects here on earth. To elicit this obedience is the goal of the Church, that is, of His earthly representative. In this sense, the priestly office of the representative of Christ exists in order to facilitate the task of elevating Jesus to divine Kingship. Whereas the Puritans argued that such elevation was possible only once the people as a whole became priestly, Hobbes thought that the only way to realize the meaning of 'Jesus is the Christ' was to submit to Leviathan as 'mortall God'.[51]

One of the puzzles about Schmitt's understanding of political theology is how and why he simultaneously advocates the political exemplarity of the Catholic Church and of Hobbes's Leviathan. The Leviathan, after all, was a theoretical construction geared to deny once and for all the 'indirect power' exerted by the Catholic Church (and any other such corporations)

---

invests the representative person with a special dignity because the representative of a noble value cannot be without value' (Schmitt 1996c, 21).

[48] This problem receives opposed developments in Jewish and Christian political theologies. I refer the interested reader to its treatment in *Living Law*.

[49] On the current discussion about representation in Christology, see (Deuser 1999).

[50] The Church 'represents the *civitas humana*. It represents in every moment the historical connection to the incarnation and crucifixion of Christ. It represents the Person of Christ Himself: God become man in historical reality' (Schmitt 1996c, 18). See the discussion in (Mehring 2009).

[51] Hence the importance of the struggle over the Holy Ghost as third person of God in the English Revolution. For the classic treatment of the radical theological ideas of the English Revolution, see (Hill 1972).

on the civil affairs conducted by the state.[52] While this explains the strange *complexio oppositorum* of the Church and the Leviathan in Schmitt's thought, insofar as both employ a vicariate concept of representation undergirding the concept of sovereignty, the possibility that Schmitt wrote his 'Catholic' interpretation of Hobbes in order to contest the English reception of Gierke's associational theory—best exemplified by the proto-communitarianism of Frederic Maitland and J. Neville Figgis, and the socialist theorizing of George Cole and Harold Laski—still requires explanation. All these thinkers shared the desire to demolish what they perceived as Hobbes's deleterious influence on Anglo-American jurisprudence later exemplified by John Austin's legal positivism.[53] In Gierke's theory of law as a function of representative associations based on solidarity, Maitland saw the outlines of a legal theory that could make sense of the English developments in medieval common law limiting the absolute sovereignty of English monarchs. These developments were taken up later by English advocates of Parliamentary supremacy in their struggle against the 'political theology' of James I. In turn, this kind of Parliamentarianism was opposed by Hobbes, who had to develop his own idea of representation in order to counter it.

Seen retrospectively, Hobbes stood at the threshold of a momentous shift in the meaning of political representation. Before his time, the Catholic Church had upheld a politico-theological idea of representation according to which 'the representative is *independent* [from the represented/MV], neither functionary nor agent nor commissioner' (Schmitt 2008a, 245). After him, the American and French Revolutions would introduce the idea that a representative had to be an 'advocate' of the sovereign people to their government.[54] The modern historian of political thought who first indicated the radical difference between the two kinds of representation was none other than Gierke in his work on Althusius. That is why Schmitt accuses Gierke of

---

[52] This is why Patricia Springborg speaks of a basic 'incoherence' in Hobbes's overall strategy when, on the one hand, he attempts to 'secure the king's ecclesiastical supremacy as God's lieutenant, after Moses and Christ' and, at the same time, he 'strengthens the Church's hand by claiming that the Apostles and the bishops are the legitimate representatives of the third person of the Holy Spirit' (Springborg 1996, 362). However, there is no such incoherence if Hobbes is interpreted from the perspective of political theology as Schmitt does.

[53] For this history, see now (Postema 2011).

[54] For anticipations of this idea of representation in English political thought, see (Clarke 1936). On the American Revolution and its new conception of representation, see (Wood 1969). I have discussed the genealogy of this concept of representation and its ambivalent relation with sovereignty in (Vatter 2008). The representative as advocate is defended in (Urbinati 2006).

having confused the real meaning of representation with advocacy (Schmitt 2008a, 247).

In his book *Johannes Althusius und die Entwicklung der Naturrechtlichen Staatstheorien* [Althusius and the development of natural right theories of the state], Gierke sought to reconstruct an alternative system of representation to the one brought to prominence by Grotius and Hobbes via Althusius's federalist political theory. Gierke's provocative claim was that absolutism *could not* be considered a representative political system at all. Gierke linked this alternative concept of representation back to the Conciliarist accounts of representation.[55] In *Constitutional Theory*, Schmitt advocates the exact opposite thesis and does so in Hobbes's name: 'the absolute prince is also *the sole representative* of the political unity of the people. He alone represents the state. As Hobbes puts it, the state has "its unity in the person of the sovereign"; it is "united in the person of the sovereign". Representation first establishes this unity' (Schmitt 2008a, 247). In short, Schmitt employs Hobbes in order to argue that unless a legal system rests on the absoluteness of sovereignty, it will not be 'representative' at all.

For Schmitt, there is no unity of the state or of the people without sovereignty. The sovereign representative exists only as a function of making the unity of the people visible to all of its members. It has absolute authority because it re-presents to all their unity, or state. Properly speaking, no representative can represent all of the members *against* the state. Such a figure is not a representative but merely an advocate of some part of society, but not of the whole. This entire argumentative chain is made possible by Hobbes's axiom on representation according to which 'it is the *Unity* of the Representer [the sovereign], not the *Unity* of the Represented [the individual subjects] that maketh the Person [the People] *One*' (Hobbes 2010, 82/100).

---

[55] (Gierke 1902). Gierke cited as exemplary Nicholas of Cusa's dictum, from book 3, ch. 25 of the *Catholic Concordance*, that 'when they [members of the universal council of the empire] meet in one representative group, the whole empire is assembled [*et dum simul conveniunt in uno compendio repraesentativo totum imperium collectum est*]' (Cusa 1995, 285). Cusa argued that the same principle applied to the elected council or synod of the Church that was to represent the entire Church, of which the Pope was only a part and not a separate 'head' with sovereignty over the Church and its assemblies or councils. On this node of problems, see (Oakley 1981). However, for Schmitt the citation of Cusa proves exactly the contrary of what Gierke maintains, namely, 'the representative is not involved in some form of advocacy but rather in the presentation of the unity of the *whole*' (Schmitt 2008a, 247). Cusa is aptly and ironically chosen as counterexample by Schmitt because of his theory of the 'unity of opposites' or *complexio oppositorum*, which, one may safely presume, Schmitt is trying to take up in his own view of the Catholic Church. The question of whether Schmitt or Gierke is right with respect to Cusa is inordinately complex, not least because, as is well known, Cusa started off as a conciliarist and ended up as an advocate of Papal sovereignty. On representation in Althusius and Cusa, and the debate behind Schmitt's attack on Gierke, see (Hofmann 2007; and Duso 2003).

Hobbes's axiom of representation has recently returned to prominence thanks to the work of Quentin Skinner after some years of relative neglect following Hannah Pitkin's seminal *The Concept of Representation*.[56] Skinner points out how terribly difficult, and possibly misguided, it is to discard Hobbes's conception of representation. For without it, one risks undermining the entire edifice of the modern state as a representative person.[57] And, yet, Schmitt formulates the aporia of parliamentary democracy precisely on this same Hobbesian conception of representation. Either democracy has a direct, and thus not a representative meaning, but then parliamentary democracy becomes a contradiction in terms, or, the political system is representative but then it cannot be democratic (rather, it must be presidential or even dictatorial).[58]

Hobbes's conception of representation is hard to discard because of its internal link to the idea of judicial personation previously discussed. In Chapter 16 of the *Leviathan*, Hobbes defines a person as an actor who acts or utters words either his own, in which case the person is natural, or those of someone else, in which case the person is artificial and 'is said to beare' the other person or 'act in his name'.[59] Hobbes identifies this artificial person with the terms 'Representative, a Lieutenant, a Vicar, an Attorney... and the like' (Hobbes 2010, 81/98). Artificial persons perform actions or speak words that belong to others, as their author; in other words, they act or speak 'by Authority' of the person represented. But for Hobbes it is not necessary to be a real person in order to be represented by an artificial person. Hobbes calls the artificial person or representative 'fictional', when that which is to be represented is an inanimate thing ('a Church, a Hospital, a Bridge') or an individual who cannot give their consent to being impersonated ('Children, Fooles, and Mad-men').

In his discussion of artificial persons, Hobbes relies on the medieval 'fiction' theory of legal personality. According to the 'fiction' theory, a group of people are more than the sum of their parts only when they are 'incorporated'. Furthermore, this 'incorporated body' has no will of its own; it cannot act in any way by itself. For all purposes the 'incorporated body' is the same as an inanimate body or a cognitively impaired body. These bodies require another person to act on their behalf, as their artificial representative, the

---

[56] See (Skinner 2005; 2018; and Pitkin 1967). For the renewal of this debate, see now (Vieira 2017).
[57] I refer to my discussion of this claim in (Vatter 2014b).
[58] See (Schmitt 2001).
[59] For a detailed treatment of Hobbes on representation and its problems, see (Vieira 2009).

same way a tutor represents his or her pupil who is too immature to legally represent themselves. One can see the appeal that a fictional theory of legal personality has for Hobbes's development of a theory of absolute sovereignty, for the fictional theory of the representative detaches it from the social body he is deemed to represent. However the fictional theory, as such, clearly falls short of accounting for the kind of representation that a sovereign king exercises in respect of its kingdom, basically because the kingdom is not composed of inanimate bodies nor is it a collection of minors.[60] On the contrary, as Althusius explains, a kingdom is composed of the 'symbiosis' of smaller associations, organized in a federal way, with the sovereign established by a 'contract of subjection' spelling out the limits of how much the free and federalist society can be governed.

It is at this point, and in order to prepare his prima facie unlikely claim that a free society of individuals would adopt a contract that placed them in absolute subjection to their sovereign, that Hobbes introduces the two central possibilities for artificial representation, one after the other. First, Hobbes proposes the possibility that 'the true God may be personated' (Hobbes 2010, 82/100). Hobbes claims this happened on three occasions: first by Moses, then Jesus Christ, and lastly by the Holy Spirit found in the Apostles and their successors (the Holy Spirit is a Person sent by both God and His Son). Immediately after this theological form of representation, Hobbes introduces his famous consideration about political representation: 'A Multitude of men are made *One* Person, when they are by one man, or one Person, Represented; so that it be done with the consent of every one of that Multitude in particular. For it is the *Unity* of the Representer, not the *Unity* of the Represented, that maketh the Person *One*. And it is the Representer that beareth the Person, and but one Person: And Unity, cannot otherwise be understood in Multitude' (Hobbes 2010, 82/100). Thus, it is Hobbes himself who establishes an analogy between God's representatives and the state's or people's representatives. For that reason it is not implausible for Schmitt to claim that Hobbes is engaging in an exercise of 'political theology', since he is reaffirming the 'unity' of politics and religion, 'the power of the sovereign as

---

[60] It is probably for this very reason that it became necessary to connect the idea of fictional legal personality with the idea of the mystical body of Christ, making the sovereign the stand-in for the head of the mystical body, namely, the lieu-tenant of Christ: this whole process will find its crowning achievement with Hobbes.

the lieutenant of God . . . that brings about the unity of religion and politics' (Schmitt 2008b, 55).[61]

The theoretical construction of the Leviathan subsequently in Chapter 17 does not ultimately help in defining the analogy between God and State that Hobbes established in the previous chapter. For Hobbes famously argues that in order to achieve peace it is necessary that all the individuals 'reduce all their Wills . . . unto one Will: which is as much to say, to appoint one Man, or Assembly of Men, to beare their Person; and every one to owne, and acknowledge himself to be the Author of whatsoever he that beareth their Person, shall Act . . . therein to submit their Wills, every one to his Will, and their Judgment to his Judgment. This is more than Consent, or Concord; it is a reall Unitie of them all, in one and the same Person. . . . This done, the Multitude so united in one Person, is called a Common-wealth, in latine Civitas. This is the generation of that great Leviathan, or rather (to speak more reverently) of that Mortall God, to which we owe, under the Immortall God, our peace and defence. . . . And he that carryeth this Person, is called Soveraigne' (Hobbes 2010, 87–88/104–5). This iconic passage has given rise to a great deal of controversy and confusion in so far as Hobbes here is speaking of two artificial persons, and therefore also of two kinds of representation. On the one hand, there is the Person of the commonwealth, or the united multitude understood as one group personality or as one 'people'. On the other hand, there is the artificial person of the sovereign who bears or impersonates the group personality of the *civitas* or people.

As several commentators have noted, the consent between individuals in appointing one person (the sovereign) to represent them is not enough to establish the representation of the united people by this sovereign. If the first type of representation is analogous to the representation of a corporation by its vicar, the representation that this vicar engages in with respect to the person of the *civitas* is entirely novel because the represented corporation did not exist prior to its representation and only exists insofar as it is represented by the sovereign. As Hasso Hofmann points out, the idea that a king 'represents' the moral person of the state emerges with Grotius and Hobbes. This representative function no longer makes the king analogous to the vicar of a

---

[61] Schmitt did not think Hobbes developed a religiously neutral or liberal idea of sovereignty. In his book on Hobbes (Schmitt 1982) he countenanced this hypothesis, which a few years before had been advanced by Leo Strauss (2008). But, in a typical anti-Semitic gesture, Schmitt brushes the suggestion away by claiming that the 'originators of the revolutionary state-destroying distinction between religion and politics' were Jews, not because they were liberal, but rather because 'the Jews brought about unity from the side of religion' (Schmitt 2008b, 10).

medieval corporation who was still '*majorem singulis, sed minorem universis* [greater than any other individual, but lesser than the community of individuals]'. Instead, the king becomes 'the juridical personification of the state'. This state can only act through the sovereign. In this way, representation has become a way to exert power rather than reflect relationships of solidarity between individual members of a group (Hofmann 2007, 458).

The problem with this idea of sovereign representation based on juridical personification is that the representation of the person of the commonwealth by the person of the sovereign is not based on the consent of the represented individuals. Schmitt was entirely aware of this feature of Hobbes's account: 'the covenant was conceived in an entirely individualistic manner.... If this construct is viewed from its result, from the perspective of the state, what it reveals is that *the state is more than and something different from a covenant concluded by individuals*.... The sovereign-representative person is much more than the sum total of all participating particular wills.... To this extent the new god is *transcendent vis-à-vis all contractual partners*... obviously only in a juristic and not in a metaphysical sense' (Schmitt 2008b, 98, emphasis mine). The Leviathan is a corporation represented by the sovereign as a *personam alicuius gerere*, as a tutor or presidential representative who represents the totality of the people externally, having no relation to the people as a real group personality because the sovereign has been authorized to stand for the people by each singly and not by all as a group. The sovereign is no longer a part (viz., its head) of the body politic, which is designated to represent the whole body, as with the medieval fictional theory of corporations.

In other words, Hobbes makes the artificial person of the sovereign bear the *fictional* person of the People rather than their real personality as an articulated group.[62] Because of the fictional character of his concept of a People, Hobbes is forced to give a 'body' to this fiction or ghost and engages in 'a personification ... of something flesh and blood', namely, of the Leviathan as a body politic. 'The image of the Leviathan is being asked to provide the state with an identity apart from the identity of its representative' (Runciman 2005, 21). Hobbes's dilemma is that the Leviathan cannot be thought on the model of an organic body of the people since then its head (the sovereign) would be singly greater than each member of the body, but smaller than the

---

[62] 'The group of natural persons represented by the sovereign are one person, but only because they are represented by one person, just as a bridge is a person only because it has a person as its representative' (Runciman 2005, 11).

collective body (since he would be only one part of the whole). To avoid this problem, which would nullify his ascription of absolute authority to the sovereign, Hobbes needs to designate the sovereign as the 'soul' of the mechanical body politic, the inanimate machine-state of the Leviathan.[63]

Hobbes relates the metaphor for the sovereign as the 'soul' of the Leviathan to the strange figure from common law called the 'corporation sole', or a corporation composed of only one person, that was Kantorowicz's object of fascination in *The King's Two Bodies*. The King is an office that represents the entire Crown or Realm, but it is an office that is only ever held by one person, the physical king, who lives and dies, while the King remains immortal. In short, the King is a paradoxical 'mortall God' (Runciman 2005, 99). As an officer of the Crown, the physical king is below the law and serves it; as the incarnation of the Crown, the King is above the law.[64] Hobbes 'made the sovereign representative of a corporate entity which could not exist where the sovereign ceased to exist' (Runciman 2005, 100).

On David Runciman's reading, Hobbes adopts the corporativist model for his Leviathan because he needed its 'concession theory' of associations. According to this theory, smaller corporations are brought into existence only by the express concession of the sovereign, who is the only 'real' corporation. But precisely this appeal to the corporate nature of the Leviathan pushes Hobbes into an aporia, which, on Runciman's account, English pluralist theory exploits in its critique of sovereignty. The aporia is the following: if the Leviathan is not a corporation, but merely the personification of the rule of law, then the state is not a group personality and the sovereign represents each individual merely in an individual way. But on this account, no common subjection to one will of all is possible, thus raising the spectre of civil war. Conversely, if the state is granted a group personality to which each individual pays allegiance, as seems to be required by the subjection thesis, then one cannot maintain the concession theory of associations, and

---

[63] On this point, again, Schmitt's insistence on the mechanical nature of the Leviathan seems to have been on the correct path. See the essay, "The State as Mechanism in Hobbes and Descartes" (Schmitt 2008b, 91–103).

[64] Focus on the representational nature of the sovereign sheds light on the long-standing debate in Hobbes scholarship as to whether Hobbes is a thinker of the rule of law, as Michael Oakeshott argued, because he conceives of society as a *societas* of individuals regulated by laws (the Leviathan simply being a personification of this system of rules) (Oakeshott 1996), or whether Hobbes is a thinker of society as a *universitas*, the last inheritor of the corporativist theories bequeathed by the jurisprudence of the Catholic Church, which is Schmitt's and Runciman's hypothesis. For another argument depicting Hobbes as 'a founder of the rule of law tradition' but which does not consider the problem of representation, see (Dyzenhaus 2010).

the group personality of the state will be just one among many group personalities that compete for the allegiance of individuals.

In sketching this aporia of the Leviathan, Runciman unwittingly rehearses exactly the 'two deaths' of the Leviathan that Schmitt pointed out decades earlier in his book on Hobbes. Schmitt argued that the first death of the Leviathan already occurred at the hands of Spinoza's *Theologico-Political Tractatus*, which inverts the priority of public confession over private conscience established by Hobbes. For Spinoza, the highest duty of the state consists in protecting the freedom of thought for each individual. The public confession of the state is only an external cult that must leave the individual free to believe and speak publicly whatever he or she wants (Schmitt 2008b, 56). The second death of the Leviathan takes place when 'the old adversaries, the "indirect" powers of the church and of interest groups, reappeared in that century as modern political parties, trade unions, social organizations, in a word as "forces of society". . . . The Leviathan, in the sense of a myth of the state as the "huge machine", collapsed when a distinction was drawn between the state and individual freedom. That happened when the organizations of individual freedom were used like knives by anti-individualistic forces to cut up the leviathan and divide his flesh among themselves. Thus did the mortal god die for the second time.'[65] It is highly indicative, given the interpretation proposed so far, that Schmitt would end his Hobbes book by defending Hobbes against the critique put forward by Figgis and Laski, basically accusing English pluralism of having given over state power to the mass political party structures that fragment the sovereignty of the state symbolized by the Leviathan.

Of all the English pluralist thinkers, Maitland is the one who most directly attacks the idea of a fictional personality of the group and opposes it to the idea of real group personality. Maitland's famous reconstruction of the juridical figure of the 'corporation sole' was intended as a critique of the Hobbesian construction of sovereignty, since for Maitland such a corporation is but 'a mere ghost of a fiction' (Runciman 2005, 101). Maitland believed

---

[65] (Schmitt 2008b, 73–74). Schmitt's speculation on the 'death' of the Leviathan, the 'mortal god', forms part of the anti-messianic tenor of his political theology. Schmitt's bizarre claim that labour unions function as 'anti-individualistic forces' that 'cut up the leviathan and divide his flesh among themselves' anticipates his discussion in *Land und Meer* of unspecified Jewish 'kabbalists', basing themselves on the messianic writings of Isaak Abravanel, who taught that the Jews stood aside to watch the war between Leviathan and Behemoth, between land and sea monsters, in order to feast on the dead body of the Leviathan in the messianic age (Schmitt 2016, 17). See the discussion by (Gross 2005, 273–78), who rejects entirely the veracity of these speculations. Agamben, instead, takes the political meaning of the messianic banquet seriously (Agamben 2004, 2–3).

that the reason Hobbes's construction failed in England was that the English political system gave rise to the idea of an 'unincorporated body', such as a trust, which has a 'real' personality separate from the individuals composing the trust.[66] Yet this real group personality is not dependent on the concession of the sovereign, which is the case when the personality of the group is only fictional, as held by corporativist theory (Runciman 2005, 67–69).

The idea of a real personality of groups was crucial for the English pluralists for a number of reasons. Endowed with a group personality, the association of individuals is more like a living body politic than a mechanical assemblage of parts. The living body politic requires no 'soul'; it can do without the external, sovereign-appointed 'curator' or 'tutor' as its legal representative. This theory of group personality was the historical, real refutation of Hobbes's theory of representation: for here was a 'Multitude' that, in representing itself to itself, acquired 'Unity'. Pluralist theorists of group personality were on the verge of discovering a third concept of representation, a democratic form of representation that Schmitt had banned from conceptual existence.[67] Hence the enormous threat they posed to his theory.

The pluralist threat was posed at the juridical level, and precisely on the two points that motivated Schmitt's political theology, namely, the relation of law to social life (jurisprudence to sociology) and the problem of political unity through representation. If all law truly emanates from the sovereign, as Hobbes and Schmitt argue, then in order for a group to exist it must follow the law of the sovereign, it must be recognized by the sovereign, and given a concession to exist. Maitland intended to show that in common law it was possible to witness the emanation of law out of these 'unincorporated bodies' composing civil society.

Runciman admirably explains the difference between these two viewpoints with respect to the institution of a marriage as an example of a group personality (and the only corporation that Hobbes allows to be 'natural' and not requiring the concession of the sovereign). A marriage forms an unincorporated body out of two people who share a form of life with common

---

[66] On Maitland's theory of the trust, see (Vatter 2016).

[67] The concept of representation that is most adequate to the idea of group personality is a democratic representation from below. This concept of representation was not invented by English pluralists. Skinner has traced this alternative concept back to English Parliamentarian theorists in the mid 17th century. But its genealogy is still older if one follows the reconstruction of (Hofmann 2007). Hofmann discovers in medieval thought another kind of corporativist representation that is 'democratic' in this sense that it presupposes the identity of governor with governed, which he calls *repraesentatio identitatis*. This type of representation is organic to the group and reflects their solidarity, whereas Hobbes's representative is mechanical and reflects relations of subjection or power.

rules; marriage is not a 'privilege' granted by the state, but the state recognizes the marriage as long as it fulfils certain minimal legal criteria. This raises the following question: does a marriage exist because it fulfils these state-legal criteria, or, vice versa, does a marriage exist because, as a form of life, it generates rules and criteria of its own that the state cannot but recognize through its legal system? Can one be 'married' in a juridically salient sense even though the laws of the state might not recognize this union? Runciman suggests that the answer depends on one's conception of law. If all law is sovereign command, if all valid law stems from the state or its constitution, then the answer is no; but if law originates in forms of life characterized by rule-following, then the answer can be affirmative. 'Where group persons are deemed to be real, the law is nothing more, and nothing less, than an account of the life that surrounds it. The concept of real group personality closes the gap between the world described in law and the world in which men live' (Runciman 2005, 118). By bringing law back down to the life of the association, the Pluralist school managed to connect the sociological and the legal dimensions of political form, as called for by Schmitt's political theology, but in a way contrary to absolute sovereignty.

Laski seems to have been the one who drew out the most radical implications from Gierke's and Maitland's theories of group personality. He states these implications in his first book, *Studies in the Problem of Sovereignty*, which was originally published by Yale University Press in 1917, five years before Schmitt's *Political Theology: Four Chapters on the Concept of Sovereignty*. Even the mere comparison of both titles indicates that Schmitt's book is polemically addressing Laski's attack on sovereignty.

Laski's starting point is Gierke's idea that 'any group of people leading a common life' develops a 'personality that is beyond the personalities of its constituent parts. For us that personality is real. Slowly its personality has compelled the law to abandon the theory of fiction' (Laski 1968, 4). The idea of a group personality requires the rejection of the medieval Roman law tradition of thinking about corporations as having a personality only in a 'fictional' sense.[68] Gierke's point is that, if every association develops a 'real'

---

[68] 'Lawyers, for the most part, have tended to believe that the status of a person is something it is in the power of the state alone to confer, and in this view Austin, doubtless, would have most fully concurred. But surely it is abundantly clear that the personality of associations is primary, that it springs from the fact of their existence, and it is not conceded to them by the state. This concession theory has, it is true, the authority of great men like Savigny behind it. It was urged, in effect by that subtle lawyer Pope Innocent IV when he argued that the corporate person is sheer fiction. That claim, however, is becoming increasingly impossible of acceptance' (Laski 1968, 272).

group personality spontaneously, then it is clear that no 'sovereign' can represent it. Indeed, no 'representation' in the sense of an external political unity is ever needed: no sovereign is needed to bring it into presence since it already exists spontaneously. If there is group personality, then there is no sovereignty. The importance of Laski's *Studies*, published the very same year as Kelsen's article on juridical personality, rests precisely in its ambition to demonstrate the illusion of sovereign authority. This coincidence of aims alone, though on very different jurisprudential grounds, suffices to establish the centrality of Kelsen and Laski in Schmitt's polemics.

Laski's radical thesis is that there is no such thing as 'sovereignty' if by this one understands an attribute of a political entity that elicits 'obedience'. Such an idea of sovereignty is a fiction that has never existed historically, and which gives the lie to the Hobbesian (later Austinian and Schmittian) conceit that law is an authoritative command. Instead, Laski tries to show that all law depends on the 'opinion of the members of the State, and they belong to other groups' (Laski 1968, 12). Laski here is taking up Spinoza's notion that all coercive law depends on the judgment of the person who follows it not on the person who decides its application: 'there is no sanction for law other than the consent of the human mind' (Laski 1968, 14). As a consequence, there is no 'a priori justification which compels their allegiance [to the State] more than the allegiance to Church or to other groups—it [the State] wins the allegiance pragmatically' (Laski 1968, 19).

To illustrate his case, Laski discusses several historical episodes of Church and State relations in 19th-century Britain (the so-called Catholic Revival) and ends his book with two studies dedicated to de Maistre and Bismarck, that is, to the two ideologists of the parties at war in the continental *Kulturkampf* [culture war] around political Catholicism. The studies show the self-refuting attempt to build the sovereignty of the state *against* the group personality of other associations, be these churches or labour unions. Bismarck's defeat in the *Kulturkampf* 'simply demonstrated that men belong not to one all-inclusive group, the State, but to a variety of groups, and that in the last resort they will follow the demands of their conscience' (Laski 1968, 263). In hindsight, Laski's study appears as the first exercise in proving the impossibility of political theology.

As Laski writes in the appendix to *Studies on the Problem of Sovereignty*, 'it is clear that sovereignty of the State does not in reality differ from the power exercised by a Church or trade union. The obedience the Church or trade union will secure depends simply on what measure of resistance the command inspires' (Laski 1968, 270). His conclusion is lapidary: if sovereignty is neither unitary nor omnipotent, then the state can be viewed 'as an organization that in essence is not distant from a federation even if in name it be different. We begin to see the State as akin to that medieval empire which was above all a *community of communities*' (Laski 1968, 274).

Given that the discussion of English pluralism takes up an entire chapter of *The Concept of the Political*, Schmitt must have hardly considered it a matter of indifference. When compared to *Political Theology* and *Roman Catholicism and Political Form*, *The Concept of the Political* adopts the language of Gierke and the English pluralists by speaking of 'groupings' or 'associations' of all kinds, be they religious, economical, or otherwise, as the fundamental building blocks of a society. His thesis is that any such grouping becomes a 'political' grouping whenever it orients itself by distinguishing between friend and enemy. 'This grouping is therefore always the decisive human grouping, the political entity. If such an entity exists at all, it is always the decisive entity, and it is sovereign in the sense that the decision about the critical situation, even if it is the exception, must always necessarily reside there' (Schmitt 2007, 38). Schmitt neatly folds the 'concept of the political' back into the conceptual scheme of sovereignty defended in *Political Theology*, and even the idea of representation is implicit here, for it can only be one representative of the political unity who is charged with deciding the 'critical situation' of war and peace.[69]

More striking, Schmitt's language is entirely taken from Laski's way of understanding sovereignty pragmatically, as a function of the state's ability to encounter the least resistance ('counterforces') to its laws and commands: 'The force of a command of the State is not, therefore, bound to triumph, and no theory is of value which would make it so. When Germany orders its subjects to refrain from discussion of peace terms it may enforce its rule when only Rosa Luxemburg or Liebknecht is concerned, it could not do so were the Socialists as a whole to rebel' (Laski 1968, 270). Nearly twenty years later, Schmitt responds to Laski by using his same vocabulary: 'if in fact the economic, cultural or religious counterforces are so strong that they are in a position to decide upon the extreme possibility [war] from their viewpoint, then these forces have in actuality become the new substance of the political entity' (Schmitt 2007, 39). Schmitt even gives up the internal connection

---

[69] The continuity of pluralism as the polemical object in *The Concept of the Political* is a decisive textual argument against those interpretations of Schmitt that wish to establish a major break between that work and the earlier *Political Theology*. On this question see (McCormick 1998; 2010).

between sovereignty and absolutism, writing, 'In the orientation toward the possible extreme case of an actual battle against a real enemy, the political is essential, and it is the decisive entity for the friend-or-enemy grouping; and in this (*and not in any kind of absolutist sense*), it is sovereign' (Schmitt 2007, 39, emphasis mine). Schmitt concedes that Laski's critique of the illusions of sovereignty operative in both de Maistre and Bismarck 'is largely *justified*. The juridic formulas of the omnipotence of the state are, in fact, only *superficial* secularizations of theological formulas of the omnipotence of God' (Schmitt 2007, 42, emphasis mine).

But Schmitt is unwilling to go the last step with Laski and admit that there is no 'fact of the matter' to sovereignty. The reason is that Laski's analysis does not offer an answer to the question, 'which social entity . . . decides the extreme case and determines the decisive friend-and-enemy grouping? Neither a church nor a labor union nor an alliance of both could have forbidden or prevented a war which the German Reich might have wanted to wage under Bismarck . . . such an opposition would have risked being treated as an enemy. . . . These considerations are sufficient to establish a reasonable concept of sovereignty and entity' (Schmitt 2007, 43). For Schmitt, only 'the ever present possibility of a friend-and-enemy grouping suffices to forge a decisive entity which transcends the mere societal-associational groupings' (Schmitt 2007, 45). There must exist a representative who gives to the society its political 'unity', that is, its form, and thereby makes this representative into a separate 'entity' with regard to all associations of civil society. Schmitt's answer to pluralism is always based on the basic axiom of Hobbes' theory of representation, namely, that the unity of a people is given by its representative and not by the represented.

Schmitt versus Peterson: The turn toward democratic political theology

Schmitt's treatment of political theology began with the study of the transfer of theological concepts to the field of politics and jurisprudence. After the Hobbes book and the critique of English pluralists, Schmitt reverses his thinking on political theology: now it is the transfer of political and juridical concepts on to theological ones that becomes of paramount concern for him. It is as if, in the roughly four decades separating *Political Theology* from *Political Theology II*, he reinterprets Hobbes's decisive sixteenth chapter of the *Leviathan* moving *backwards* from the problem of the political representation of the people in the state to the problem of the political representation of God in the Trinity. Schmitt looks to the Christology of the Trinity to help give a more democratic, less authoritarian formulation of Hobbes's conception of sovereignty. This re-orientation of the problem of political theology towards democracy is entirely motivated by Schmitt's response to Peterson's critique of political theology.

Schmitt wrote *Political Theology II* as a belated response to Peterson's 1935 treatise entitled *Monotheism as a Political Problem*. Peterson argued that Christian theology could not possibly be 'secularized' in the form of a political theology, as Schmitt had proposed, because the essence of Christian theology was Trinitarian. The three persons of God (Father, Son, and Holy Spirit) do not match with the one-to-one analogy between God as King of the universe and the human king. This analogy, according to Peterson, defined political theology since its first development in Judeo-Hellenistic conceptions of divine monarchy.[70] Adopting the groundbreaking work of Erwin Goodenough on Hellenistic kingship, Peterson argued that political theology began as a pagan politico-philosophical discourse. Philo then adopted it for the purposes of working out a Jewish conception of theocracy based on Mosaic legislation.[71] The Church Father Eusebius smuggled it into Christian theology in order to legitimize Emperor Constantine's foundation of a *Christian* Roman Empire. Finally, Augustine's doctrine of the Two Cities banned political theology due to its Gnostic implications.[72] 'Only on the basis of Judaism and paganism can such a thing as a "political theology" exist. . . the peace that the Christian seeks is won by no emperor but is solely a gift of him who "is higher than all understanding"' (Peterson 2011, 104–5).

---

[70] Peterson argues that the God who reigns over the world like a Persian king rules over its empire is the pseudo-Aristotelian image that turns monotheism into a 'metaphysical-political problem' (Peterson 2011, 71ff). More precisely, for Peterson the 'political problem' is that God as King of the world 'reigns, but he does not govern': if one applies the analogy to the human monarch, then this monarch becomes endowed with *auctoritas*, over and above the *potestas* of the intermediary agents which actually 'govern' (without being kings). In the Gnostic interpretation of this model, the intermediary agents are the 'demiurgic forces' in the universe that govern everything in it, and they are 'evil' or 'sinful'; whereas only God as King (who does not govern, and is not identical with the Creator) is truly 'good'. Peterson believes that Augustine's *City of God* is intended to refute this Gnostic rejection of political power as always already 'sinful' and to offer a different articulation between *potestas* and *auctoritas*.

[71] See (Goodenough 1928). I discuss this genealogy of political theology in more detail in *Living Law*.

[72] For a reprise of this thesis, yet without referring to the discourse of political theology, see now (Oakley 2010).

The Christian Gospel announced the advent of a new Kingdom that put an end to the age of human kingdoms (the age of Leviathan and Behemoth). This new Kingdom, at whose head was the resurrected Jesus, brings about a Christian idea of 'peace' that is guaranteed not by any human emperor but exclusively by the charismatic power of Jesus the Christ and the 'gift' of grace. As Peterson argues at length in his lectures on the *Letter to the Romans*, the charisma of Christ is experienced by all Christians prior to their consent since it is granted them exclusively by the sacrament of baptism.[73] This sacrament, consequently, makes all those who accept Jesus as their King into *a people endowed with full powers*, an *ekklesia* as opposed to a *synagogue*. On this account, the *plenitudo potestatis* (fullness of powers) is an endowment of the mystical body of the Church, whose Head or King is Jesus Christ, the Son of God. The bishop of Rome as much as the Holy Roman emperor are granted plenitude of powers only 'vicariously' over the 'children' of God and only until the Second Coming of the King when all the children shall be, like the Son of God, also themselves kings (i.e., will attain the same glory of the resurrected body).

Peterson's point is that, were a Christian political theology to be possible at all, then it could only take a 'democratic' and anti-monarchical form centred on the political and juridical interpretation of the Trinity.[74] Peterson's thesis, instead, is that Augustine's *City of God* rejected Eusebius' attempt to place Christianity at the service of the Roman Empire and, later, of the Byzantine Empire by giving an anti-imperial meaning to the Gospel's injunction to leave to Caesar what belongs to Caesar and give to God what belongs to God. Augustine rids Christian monotheism of its monarchical valence, and, on

---

[73] (Peterson 1997).
[74] The discussion of Peterson's alternative Christian political theology was first put forward in several essays in (Taubes 1983), then discussed at length in (Nichtweiss 2001), and in (Schmidt 2009). This reading of Peterson is motivated by the phrase found in his article "Der Fürst dieser Welt", in which he says that 'the concept of the political cannot be determined from out of the idea of earthly rule [*der irdischen Herrschaft*] but must include the idea of the heavenly angelic rule [*himmlische Herrschaft der Engel*]' cited in (Schmidt 2009, 134). Christoph Schmidt explains that for Peterson the crucial event is Christ's taking up the Throne after His resurrection, and that this event is what determines the anti-political position of the Church (Schmidt 2009, 115–117). However, Schmidt downplays the juridical and political understanding of Christ's kingship in Peterson, essentially reducing the legitimate political action by the Church to an 'apocalyptic intervention of martyrdom' (Schmidt 2009, 123). To Schmitt's political exception of the fight against the enemy Peterson merely opposes 'the absolute exception of the love of the enemy' (Schmidt 2009, 123). Entirely missing from this perspective is the idea that the dualism of Church and Empire conform the 'concrete order' of Jesus' Kingdom and that their 'law' is the law of the people of Jesus Christ. Meier dedicates to the entire question of Peterson's 'theopolitics' one footnote in which he merely states that the treatise on monotheism 'is a highly political treatise, by a political theologian of high rank, as any unbiased reader of his work can see' (Meier 2011, 172, n. 145).

the basis of its Trinitarian doctrine, places the Christian Church in a permanent, but productive tension with the state.[75] To understand this tension or struggle between Church and state, everything depends on how the faith of the subjects that God wants only for Himself is politically interpreted.

Peterson argues that Christian peace required the Christian Church to resist any unification with the political state. In 1935 this meant that Christian churches ought to reject any compromise with the Nazi regime. This did not come to pass. In hindsight, Schmitt says that Peterson's strategy had to fail because 'the traditional "walls" [between Church and state/MV] . . . have been successfully challenged by a revolutionary class' and the political, or the decision on who is friend and who is enemy, is no longer the 'monopoly' of a state (Schmitt 2008c, 44). Reflecting back on the revolutionary mass movements of Bolshevism, Fascism, and National Socialism, Schmitt believes the 20th century had already shown that the state had lost its monopoly on the political. This required the Church—and its role as the restrainer of anarchy—to reject the old model of the Two Cities and the 'wall' of separation between spiritual and political powers and position itself in the world otherwise.

In this context, Schmitt refers to his early book on *Dictatorship*, which he claims first proposed the possibility that a dictator, as the representative of the unified and mobilized masses, would displace the old constellation of both Church and State in the *respublica Christiana* (Schmitt 2013). Schmitt suggests that this possibility was anticipated by the Puritan revolution, which truly brought down the walls of separation between Church and State in a fight against *both* Throne and Altar. For Schmitt, only Hobbes's Leviathan offered the most rational jurisprudential and politico-theological response to the Puritan revolution.

Fundamentally, Schmitt argues that Hobbes constructs a conception of a Christian people, that is, a people organized around the '*unum necessarium*' of belief that 'Jesus is the Christ', whose representative is nevertheless authorized to decide 'Hobbes' all-deciding questions: *Quis judicabit? Quis interpretabit?*' (Schmitt 2008c, 51). As Schmitt argued in the *Concept of the Political*, the entire legitimacy of the sovereign does not rest on being an attribute of a given state, rather sovereignty belongs to that 'political' entity or

---

[75] For other discussions of the Schmitt-Peterson polemic see (Geréby 2008; and Hohendahl 2008). Neither discusses the politico-theological presuppositions of Peterson's rejection of the Roman Empire and its *pax romana*, which are based on the claim that Jesus Christ is the king of a new people. Where my reading distances itself from Hohendahl is also on the point of democracy, which is a dimension missing in his interpretation of the polemic.

grouping of individuals that give their representative a monopoly on the authority to decide between friend and enemy. Only by grouping around such a sovereign does a people effectively become 'Christian' because it brings about peace by *containing* the breakout of wars.

Thus, Schmitt contests Peterson's claim that a Christian people cannot group themselves around a sovereign representative. The fundamental analogy in political theology, for Schmitt, is not that between One God and One King, which he agrees with Peterson belongs with paganism and Judaism, but between One God, composed of Three Persons, and One People. Christian Trinitarianism is essential in providing that *divine representative* of the One God, namely, Jesus the Christ, around which a multitude of individuals can become *one people* and attain *the unity of a political or sovereign entity* (Schmitt 2008c, 72). Schmitt's real problem was that Peterson connected the formula 'One God–One People' to none other than Philo Judaeus, arguably the most important Jewish Hellenistic philosopher. If Peterson's suggestion had some truth, then it would mean that the kind of democratic political theology Schmitt pursued would have to be developed, paradoxically, in the form of a *Jewish* political theology. To parry this possibility, Schmitt finds no other argument that to claim Philo's formula is purely a 'Jewish slogan', since Philo supposedly does not take up the idea of a 'divine democracy' (Schmitt 2008c, 72).[76] In reality, the ideal of a 'divine democracy' was anything but an 'empty slogan' in the philosophical and mystical developments of the Jewish tradition.

Instead of pursuing the path disclosed in Philo's thought, Schmitt claims Hobbes offers another path towards democratic political theology via a more literal interpretation of the theory of personation found in Chapter 16 of the *Leviathan*. This literal reading shows that in order for a people to find a representative that grants them political unity, the analogy with the personation of God in His three historical representatives (Moses, Jesus, and the Holy Spirit) is necessary. These three divine personations, in their political representative functions, made possible three *sovereign peoples*, not three forms of monarchy.

By appealing to the doctrine of the Trinity to ground his idea of sovereignty, Hobbes showed that he was already aware of a crucial shift away from the divinization of human kings and towards the divinization of the political body that took place in the development of medieval political thought.

---

[76] This is incorrect, as I show in the discussion of Philo found in *Living Law*.

In *Constitutional Theory*, Schmitt explains that the principle of monarchism requires that the dynasty be the actual representative of the realm. Through dynastic succession, the realm is physically transferred from one human body of the king to the next. The principle of monarchism therefore calls for the divinization of human kings. But with the rise of Christian doctrine as a source of political theology, the contrary trend emerges and eventually wins out with the progressive humanization of the king's physical body and the parallel divinization of the body politic and its representatives, who are 'elevated' above death. The divinization of the political Body, of the People, as opposed to the divinization of their king, is an idea that only makes sense under the assumption that this political Body is somehow 'eternal' by virtue of the sacraments that tie it to the salvational acts of its Head or King, Jesus the Christ. The 'eternal life' granted to the Body of the congregated believers by virtue of the incarnation of God in the person of Jesus becomes the decisive point in this democratically inflected reading of Christian political theology. This is the very development that would become the topic of Kantorowicz's narrative.[77]

For Hobbes, the '(*Unum Necessarium*) Onely Article of Faith' required by the Leviathan is that 'Jesus is the Christ' (Hobbes 2010, 325/356). Schmitt and Peterson both agree that the Christian understanding of this formula means that Jesus did not come to earth in order to announce a future Kingdom of God, for Jesus is not simply another Jewish prophet. To the contrary, it is the Apostles who announce the 'good news' that Jesus is *already* the King by virtue of His death on the Cross, passage through Hell, and Resurrection to Heaven. This 'event' puts an end to one age (of sin) and opens another age (of grace). It represents the transition from God's personation through Moses's divine law to God's personation through Jesus's divine law. The role of the Christian Church is to spread this 'good news'. But the real question is

---

[77] I therefore disagree with Victoria Kahn's thesis who sees a major distinction here between Schmitt and Kantorowicz (Kahn 2009, 84–86). The centrality of the idea of the mystical body for Schmitt's re-interpretation of political theology in a democratic sense explains Schmitt's claim, in a 1969 letter, that 'the problem of political theology concerns an inherently Christian problem, which, only through the Reformation (namely, through the battle for the *jus reformandi*) reached the historically concrete stage of reflection on which I operate. Expressed theologically, it is a Christological problem and immanent to Christian theology of the Trinity as such: the two natures of the actual God-Man as a single person. Those you named (beginning with Varro and Augustine . . .) did not know it', cited in (Meier 2011, 202, n. 48). The reason why this Christology attains a burning point in the Reformation is because of the Puritan attempt to realize the Kingdom of God on earth in and through a democratic revolution that accelerates the End of history, putting out of play both Church and Empire. This is the spectre against which Voegelin and Löwith write their critiques of secularization, and against which Schmitt is belatedly reacting to as well.

what the analogy with the *actual Kingdom* of Jesus Christ means for the *civil kingdom* of the Leviathan.

The answer is that it depends how seriously one thinks Hobbes took the theory of personation. For Brian Garsten, Hobbes understands the Persons of the Trinity (Moses, Jesus, and the Holy Spirit) more as a function of impersonation than as incarnation. Thus, for him, 'to personate God was closer to playing a role or occupying an office than it was to embodying the divine essence. Hobbes's account suggested that there was no relation of identity between the one God and three members of the Trinity, but instead relations of representation' (Garsten 2010, 538). Such an understanding of representation brings the sovereign representative close to the figure of the impostor. It massively downplays the liturgical, sacramental origin related to the impersonation of the mystical body of Christ central to medieval political theology, as I discussed earlier.[78] For that reason it is difficult to follow Garsten's conclusion that Hobbes meant to show the civil sovereign as an impostor, a fake impersonator.[79]

Garsten's interpretation assumes that Hobbes did not believe in the reality of the Kingdom of Jesus Christ. Yet Hobbes is entirely clear in asserting that there can be no political action by God in history apart from His personations. Hobbes understood all too well that the Trinity, in Christian political theology, refers to God's knowable praxis (as opposed to His unknowable essence). It is only because God is *actually present* in history through His representative Persons, and these Persons, *as a matter of historical fact*, gave rise to two sovereign peoples independent from kings—the Jewish and the Christian peoples—that it makes sense for Hobbes to say that the People are present in history through their representative Person, that is, the civil sovereign.

Contrary to Garsten, James Martel takes Hobbes's claims about the personation of God by both Moses and Jesus Christ seriously. He sees that Hobbes's

---

[78] 'The "mortal God" of the commonwealth was neither a real God nor his lieutenant, but an artificial creation designed to play the political role of the immortal God at a time when that God had receded from direct intervention in politics' (Garsten 2010, 539). There is little evidence in Hobbes's discussion of political representation for Garsten's deflationary conclusion: 'To worship a representation as if it were real was, according to Hobbes, to commit the sin of idolatry. How could citizens obey a sovereign representative without idolizing it? By keeping in mind that it was only a representation' (Garsten 2010, 540).

[79] 'The eschatology in Leviathan helped Hobbes insist that the sovereigns who "represented God's person on earth" during the present time of "quiet waiting" were not in fact speaking for God, and so could not be challenged on the grounds that they did not accurately reflect God's will. These sovereign "representatives" of God were, in Hobbes' account, only temporary place-holders for God; they spoke not on behalf of the divine but in light of its temporary absence' (Garsten 2010, 535).

problem in the *Leviathan* is explaining how the human, artificial sovereign is the sole legitimate government for a Christian people (Martel 2007, 150ff). However, like Garsten, Martel also thinks that the contraposition of God's personation with that of the People's personation in the sixteenth chapter of *Leviathan* has an ironical and subversive intention. Hobbes wants to say that the sovereign person may be an idol when compared to the real personations of Moses and Jesus (Martel 2007, 129). But this is not because the device of personation is an imposture as such. On the contrary, for Martel the reason that Hobbes ironically undermines the sovereign personation is because he understands the real personations of God (in Moses, Jesus, and Holy Spirit) as 'a completely alternative notion of representation set amid the discussion of terrestrial sovereignty' (Martel 2007, 133).

The real problem concerns the relation between civil sovereign and the Third person of God, the Holy Spirit. Martel suggests that Hobbes undermines the absoluteness of the sovereign representative of the Christian people in order to leave room for the action of God's third person, the Holy Spirit, as a symbol of the 'kingdomless' realm of rhetorical persuasion. The age of the Holy Spirit opens up the interpretation of the Bible to an anarchic plurality of interpretations (Martel 2007, 192). This is actually a pluralist reading of Hobbes according to which a Christian people, analogous with the Holy Spirit, will seek to liberalize their practices of faith as much as possible and give rise to a plurality of religious denominations equally protected by the civil sovereign.[80]

But for Schmitt the function of the personation of the Holy Spirit in Hobbes can only be understood in light of the problem of how to reconcile Jesus's commandment to 'love thy enemy' with the fundamental authority of the civil sovereign to decide on who is friend and who is enemy. After all, as

---

[80] Martel 'sees subversion, not of church by king but of king by God's person (in this case, in the form of the church)' (Martel 2007, 188). Another interpretation of Hobbes's political theology is found in (Foisneau 2007), who argues that Hobbes intended to undermine the traditional Christian distinction between God's absolute and ordinate powers that is the basis of the 'political theology' of James I. But Foisneau does not offer a positive picture of what 'political theology' Hobbes was after to replace that of James I. The only hint he gives is that Hobbes's denial that God (or the sovereign who represents Him) has an obligation to Himself and His promises because of His omnipotence means that Hobbes intended to show God's 'abandonment of the promise made to men in the kingdom of God by nature', that is, God abandons his commitment to His Kingdom on earth and thus to the Church as well. Hobbes's eschatology would then merely be 'the theological condition of the legal sovereignty of the modern State' (Foisneau 2007, 285), that is, supposedly, of a state that is not founded on theological orders but on a self-referential system of norms. Foisneau in other words construes for Hobbes a political theology of legal positivism, something that Kelsen would consider self-contradictory.

already discussed, Schmitt is convinced that peace can only be maintained if the sovereign can command a Christian people to wage war against their 'true' enemies. In *The Concept of the Political*, Schmitt's way around this apparent contradiction is to argue that the meaning of 'enemy' in the Gospel and in the theory of sovereignty is different. Jesus taught that one must love one's enemies in the 'private' sense of enmity [*inimicos*], where the enemy is internal to the concrete juridical order and belongs within 'private' right. But this does not exclude the necessity for a Christian people to fight one's 'public' enemies [*hostes*; sing., *hostis*], where the enemy is external to the concrete order and is therefore a matter of 'public' not 'private' right.[81] But this solution does not satisfy Peterson for the obvious reason that he understands all the main concepts of the Gospel as composing a new 'public right' because they all necessarily refer to the elevation of Jesus the Christ to the Throne of the Father as the founding event of a new order of public law.

Schmitt knew that his distinction between *inimicos* and *hostis* begged the question once it was assumed that the age of earthly kingdoms had come to an end as the new age of Christ's Kingdom inaugurated a 'universal' public right that no longer permits 'heathens' to stand outside of God's Kingdom. In *Political Theology II*, he makes one last attempt to show how a Christian idea of peace is inseparable from the sovereign function of declaring war on the enemy. He begins by pointing out that the doctrine of the Trinity teaches the necessary *conflict* (*stasis*) between the three Persons of God. The reference is to claims made by the Church Father Gregory Nazianzus, in *Oratio Theologica* III, 2, according to which in the Trinity God finds Himself in a condition of *stasis*.[82] Then, as if explaining what the real stakes are in this

---

[81] (Schmitt 2007, 29). On the problem of the different senses of 'enemy' and the tension with the Christian commandment to love one's enemy, see (Schmitt 1996a; Derrida 1997; Meier 1998; Taubes 1993; Balakrishnan 2002; and Anidjar 2003), among others.

[82] In Schmitt's rendition: 'The One is always in rebellion against itself', cited in (Blumenberg 2007, 41). The phrase is usually translated as 'one person at variance with itself'. Agamben discusses this moment of Schmitt's argument at some length in (Agamben 2011, 12–14). See also (McLoughlin 2015). The concept of *stasis*, which refers both to a settled state of being and to a social conflict or civil war, is notoriously complicated; see (Vardoulakis 2009). Gourgouris has recently developed Agamben's reading further by claiming that the Trinity, despite Peterson's protestations to the contrary, remains 'political', and ultimately also 'monarchical', in defending the Christian conception of monotheism against both pagan polytheism and Jewish conceptions of monotheism. Gourgouris claims that Schmitt's political theology is 'monarchic' because it is based on the idea of rule as *arche*, whereas the Aristotelian conception of politics is deemed to be 'democratic' or 'anarchic' because the ruler must also be capable of being ruled (Gourgouris 2016, 147). Unfortunately, this is to miss the Aristotelian defence of monarchy and of natural right on which Peterson rests his claim that political theology has an Aristotelian origin. Gourgouris's typology also eliminates a priori the possibility of a 'democratic' political theology, both on the side of Christianity as well as of Judaism.

hypothesis, he concludes his discussion with a cryptic reference to Goethe's motto *Nemo contra deum nisi deus ipse*, 'no one can fight God except God himself'.[83]

The motif of a civil war within the Trinity adds a politico-theological dynamic to the Hobbesian account of the Trinity. The Father's love for the human species first takes the political form of selecting a 'chosen' people as incarnation of God's law with the personation of Moses. This political form imposes a 'tyranny' of the divine law on His people. In response to His people's protest against this yoke and their desire for a human sovereign, God sends His second personation, Jesus as Christ. The Kingdom of Christ both fulfils and abolishes the ancient divine law in the form of the new commandments of universal love. There is, evidently, a conflict between the Father's love for His people and the Son's love for all peoples. This is the conflict alluded to by Goethe's formula. The question for Schmitt, then, is: what is role of the third personation of the Holy Spirit, and to what politico-theological formation does it correspond?

Some interpreters suggest that Schmitt understood Goethe's dictum to mean that the Son unleashed an anarchic force in the world against the Father in an attempt to topple Him from His Throne. Thus, Jesus now needed to be restrained by His own Church in conjunction with a civil sovereign, in the spirit of the Grand Inquisitor's critique of Jesus' teaching in Dostoevsky's *Brothers Karamazov*.[84] But this kind of interpretation does not sit well with what is known about Schmitt's adherence to Christianity: he had no sympathy either for the Marcionite, Gnostic idea of the unworldly saviour, nor did he take the side of the Jewish conception of God as Father.

However, there is an alternative reading of Schmitt's 'stasiology' that fits better with the fundamental jurisprudential purpose of the discourse of political theology and illustrates two reasons why the doctrine of the Trinity is not only a teaching of universal peace, but also of the necessity of war undertaken under the banner of Christ. The first reason Jesus must fight the Father's initial personation is that Moses' teaching in *Genesis* is open to a Gnostic interpretation according to which Nature is the creation of an evil demiurge. If Nature is evil, then power and order are also evil. To Schmitt, this belief inevitably leads to revolutionary and anarchic political consequences, which are captured by the idea of the Anti-Christ (he who brings chaos and disorder

---

[83] I offer an interpretation of this motto and its significance for the discourse of Christian political theology in the Conclusion.
[84] See (Meier 2011; and Hohendahl 2008) for examples.

under the auspices of peace). The Christian must therefore wage a struggle against the Nature created by the Father in order to avoid accelerating the arrival of the Anti-Christ. A third personation, the Holy Spirit, is then required to guide this Christian struggle against Nature to its End in the final redemption of Nature. This guide takes the form of a teaching of divine providence through which what appears to be evil and irrational in the world in reality conforms a higher good.

Still, the development of Schmitt's thought on political theology touches an internal limit with the idea of the Trinity as 'stasiology'. Kelsen attempted to develop a theory of the state based entirely on legality rather than legitimacy, while acknowledging the anarchic core of his thinking. He drew two basic consequences from it: the first required the development of a new form of cosmopolitanism that outlawed the use of war between democracies; the second required the development of the world economy towards a socialist form. By comparison, Schmitt sought to oppose what he perceived as the global spread of anarchy that would follow from the legal abolition of war; thus, he argued that the theory of the state found its legitimacy in a theory of sovereignty as the authority to wage war. However, the Christian and Trinitarian basis he accorded to political legitimacy produced a contradiction. On the one hand, Schmitt argues against pluralists that only a sovereign state could prevent the reduction of political decisions to economic or aesthetic calculations of value. On the other hand, when his political theology takes a 'democratic turn' forcing him to acknowledge the global shift towards democratic legitimacy, Schmitt underwrites this shift by adopting a Christian idea of providence according to which order in the world arose 'spontaneously' from disorder. This latter idea brought him in proximity with the emerging *ordo*-liberal doctrine. On Schmitt's account, the idea of sovereignty might not have a liberal basis, but its 'strong state' fits neatly with the demands of a capitalist economy driven by crisis.[85]

The second reason why the Son must fight the Father has to do with the ground of legitimacy for the Kingdom of Christ. If Moses had to impose the law of God the Father on His 'chosen' people in a 'tyrannical' fashion, then, by opposition, Jesus the Christ could not impose His Kingdom on all other peoples in the same way. The Kingdom of Christ requires the consent of all the peoples of the world. The role of the third personation refers to the

---

[85] On Schmitt's proximity to neoliberal thinking, see (Cristi 1998; and Vatter 2018). On Schmitt's engagement with value pluralism, see now Jorge Dotti's Introduction to (Schmitt 2009).

historical and global shift from monarchic to democratic foundations of sovereignty initiated by Christianity, according to which, to cite the phrase of John Adams, 'all governments rest on opinion' will become in the course of time an evident truth.[86]

As discussed at the start, Kelsen already understood that the adoption of Christology into the theory of state legitimacy left this legitimacy hostage to the believer actually having faith. As Kelsen puts it: the sovereign, just like God, exists only insofar as He is believed in. Schmitt registered the force of the English pluralist argument according to which, if the state depends on the credit its citizens afford it, just like any other church, then there is no reason it should a priori be believed in more than any other church or association. This requires Schmitt to ground his shift to the consensual basis of sovereignty by adopting the theological doctrine according to which Jesus is elevated to the 'glory' of the Throne based on the theurgical power ascribed to his believers' prayers. In so doing he latched onto Peterson's discovery that the Christian liturgy was a transposition of pagan imperial acclamations to the case of Jesus as Christ Emperor. Christ can ascend to His glory only through the glorification of His person as Emperor by His people. Schmitt used this finding in his early writings on direct democracy, which sought a way to give a populist, plebiscitarian legitimacy to the *Führer* of modern mass movements. But this path also ends in a contradiction. For if the Kingdom of Jesus Christ can be 'imposed' on earth only by the power of prayer (and perhaps the imagined terror of Hell), the modern *Führer* imposes his *Reich* through real terror and the recitation of ideology.

Taking stock of Kelsen's critique, in *The Kingdom and the Glory*, Agamben proposes the alternative thesis that Christian democratic political theology requires evacuating sovereignty of all meaning and instead embracing the legitimacy of liberal government. In the Kingdom of Christ, all power and authority rests exclusively on the category of glory or *doxa*, in other words, it rests exclusively on the glorification afforded by popular opinion. Far from being 'neutral' with respect to religion, liberal democracy is the realization of the 'democratic' character of Christ's Kingdom. Agamben's argument takes off from Schmitt's stasiological interpretation of the Trinity, which posed two problems: on the one hand, the need to achieve a reconciliation with created Nature in the form of a doctrine of divine providence, and, on the

---

[86] Paradoxically, these motifs are also found in philosophical and mystical developments of Jewish theocracy. They are central to the discourse on Jewish political theology in the 20th century.

other hand, the need to realize Christ's Kingdom on earth only on the basis of prayer or acclamation. Translated into secular terms, Agamben takes this to mean that the realization of Christ's Kingdom on earth rests on the rule of public opinion and on the providential order of the economy (the free market), the twin pillars of liberal governmentality. But at this point one has definitely left behind the Schmittian precincts of political theology as a legitimation discourse of sovereignty. If Agamben is right, then the requirement that political theology become democratic can only produce a legitimation discourse for liberalism. To explain how and why this happens is the task of the next chapters.

2
Eric Voegelin and Representation

Christian political theology and totalitarianism

By the late 1960s, the opening to a democratic formulation of Christian political theology made possible by Peterson's critique of Schmitt was so established that Schmitt felt the need to respond, obliquely, to the rise of liberation theology that sought an alliance between the Church and Leftist politics, most significantly in the 'new political theology' of Johann Baptist Metz and Jürgen Moltmann.[1] The Second Vatican Ecumenical Council had shifted the emphasis in the liturgy from the Pope as head of the Church to the assembled people of the Church. Additionally, it had taken some steps towards addressing the problem on Christian 'enmity' towards Jews by subsuming anti-Semitism within the Church's rejection of all forms of persecutions against individuals.[2] Christian political theology was no longer proposing itself as the foundation of a theory of sovereignty but as the ground for an 'open' and democratic postmodern society.

The hypothesis that I discuss in this and the following chapter is that Eric Voegelin and Jacques Maritain represent two significant way stations in this development. From the late 1930s through the 1950s, Voegelin and Maritain appropriated the discourse of political theology from Schmitt and subverted its function. They did so by deconstructing Schmitt's reliance on a theory of representation and on the mystical body of the People to prop his adoption of absolute sovereignty. Voegelin and Maritain worked out novel forms of political representation and ideas of the body politic that were anti-sovereign.

---

[1] See (Schmitt 2008c; Metz, Moltmann and Oelmüller 1970). For a discussion of liberation theology as anti-Schmittian, see (Rodríguez 2018).

[2] 'Although the Church is the new people of God, the Jews should not be presented as rejected or accursed by God, as if this followed from the Holy Scriptures. . . . Furthermore, in her rejection of every persecution against any man, the Church, mindful of the patrimony she shares with the Jews and moved not by political reasons but by the Gospel's spiritual love, decries hatred, persecutions, displays of anti-Semitism, directed against Jews at any time and by anyone' (Montini, Battista, and Antonion 1965).

Their significance for contemporary democratic theory, and in particular in relation to the phenomenon of populism, rests on this point.[3]

To ascribe a democratic character to Voegelin's political thought may perhaps sound paradoxical given the usual association of his name with conservative political thought. Yet the paradox partially dissolves if one realizes that, starting in the 1930s, the term 'democratic' received its meaning in the west principally by being set in opposition to the term 'totalitarianism', which was first introduced in Italy in the late 1920s in relation to Mussolini's Fascist movement.[4] The opposition between democracy and totalitarianism occupied a central role in thinkers as diverse as Voegelin, Strauss, Maritain, Arendt, and many others after the end of World War II, when they came to believe that Stalinism was as 'totalitarian' as Nazi-Fascism.[5] Voegelin and Maritain mobilize a Christian political theology in the struggle of 'democracy' against 'totalitarianism'. Conversely, totalitarianism also receives a theologico-political treatment in Voegelin and Maritain through the concept of 'political religion'.[6]

The focus on totalitarianism persists even in post-1968 French democratic theory inaugurated by Claude Lefort and Cornelius Castoriadis, who were eager to rid themselves of the Althusserian legacy.[7] My interpretation of Voegelin and Maritain recovers part of its interest by being placed within the genealogy of the post-Marxist development of radical democratic theory. I argue that, more than Schmitt, it is Voegelin's thought on political representation that resurfaces in Ernesto Laclau's theorization of populism, just as it is Maritain's problem of the relation between democracy and natural law that ultimately orients the 'radical universalism' of Alain Badiou.

---

[3] There are not too many works comparing Voegelin and Maritain, and none that I am aware that think of them as political theologians. For an attempt at comparison, see (Thompson 1988; and Maier 2004).

[4] For the history and meanings of the concept 'totalitarianism' see (Forti 2003) and for a recapitulation of the current debate, see (Traverso 2017). On the debate with regard to the need to renew political philosophy in the face of totalitarianism, see (Opitz 1994).

[5] A critical engagement with this hypothesis of an 'identity' between Stalinism and Nazism is worked out later in the German *Historikerstreit*, see (Peacock 2001) among others.

[6] For the best treatment of the relation of Voegelin to political theology, see (Gontier 2013). Gontier argues that 'for both authors, political order revolves around a pole of transcendence' but that in Voegelin the latter is figured not by a nominalist theology of God's 'absolute power' but of 'a theology of Platonic inspiration' (Gontier 2013, 35). However, Gontier misses the key guiding thread between the two political theologies, which is that of the problem of representation. On the term 'political religion' see (Gentile 2006).

[7] This vein has been productively mined by Samuel Moyn in a series of articles on contemporary French democratic theory, the most important of which is (Moyn 2004). For a recapitulation of his theses see (Moyn 2006). For Lefort's own analysis of his relation to French communism and democratic theory, see (Lefort 1999).

The interpretation of Voegelin and Maritain that I propose here diverges from the usual treatment offered in the literature where these two authors are considered to belong within the tradition of 'Catholic political philosophy'.[8] It is true, of course, that Voegelin and Maritain often identify political theology with 'political religion' and do so in order to distinguish their own discourse as being a 'political philosophy'. But my thesis is that they do so only for polemical reasons, because they want to associate Schmitt's political theology with what they construe as the 'political religion' of totalitarian regimes, and not because their thought has in any way overcome political theology. On the contrary, I shall argue that their thought is central to the development of Christian political theology.

There are two main reasons why the classification as 'Catholic political philosophers' does not quite do justice to thinkers like Voegelin and Maritain. The first reason is that Voegelin and Maritain, in agreement here with Martin Heidegger and Arendt, acknowledge that the main tradition of western political philosophy (by which I mean essentially Aristotelianism in its varied shapes and forms) came to an end during the 20th century. The belief in a 'crisis of tradition' was a premise generally shared by all politico-philosophical thought at the start of the 20th century. As a consequence, when Voegelin and Maritain argue for the need to recover the legacy of Aquinas or Augustine or Plato, this recovery is of an entirely different nature than, say, Aquinas' own engagement with the tradition (i.e., with Aristotelianism) and is much closer to a post-Heideggerian strategy of 'deconstructing' the tradition.

Another reason why one should resist placing Voegelin and Maritain within 'Catholic political philosophy' is the evident polemical character of their theologico-political thought. My hypothesis is that their thought is organized around the same polemical aim adopted by Schmitt: this is the (philosophically) irreconcilable opposition between 'representation' (turning around the figure of Christ) and 'theocracy' (turning around the figure of Moses). Christian political theology is essentially anti-theocratic. Ultimately, this standpoint means that Voegelin and Maritain must reject an alternative

---

[8] For treatments of Voegelin and Maritain that place their thought within the tradition of 'Catholic political philosophy', see (Hittinger 2001; 2003; McKnight 2005; and Colvert 2010). For some of the recent literature on Voegelin's religious and political thought, see (McAllister 1996; Ranieri 2009; and Trepanier and McGuire 2011), and for commentary on being interpreted as a Catholic political philosopher, see (Emberley and Cooper 1993).

source of the western political tradition that is linked to the reception of Judaism and Islam, and that gives pride of place to the figure of the prophet.[9]

Lastly, my attempt to even *try* to think together Voegelin and Maritain with Laclau and Badiou, respectively, may sound like a provocation. Obviously, the radical understandings of democracy in Laclau and Badiou are very different from those of Voegelin and Maritain. However, there exist some striking similarities between them that bear thinking about. Laclau's reconstruction of a post-foundational theory of populism turns on the recovery of the symbolic idea of representation that Voegelin sought to contrast with the liberal idea of democratic representation tied to elections. Likewise, in his book on St. Paul, Badiou argues that radical democracy can ultimately be thought only in terms of a Christian political theology. Badiou also takes it for granted that the philosophical tradition is at an end; and no one represents this end better than Paul, the first real 'anti-philosopher'. Just as in Voegelin and Maritain, the political thought of Laclau and Badiou is radically *polemical*, where the polemical object is the difference between representation and theocracy. In a sense, one can say that for both Laclau and Badiou, 'democracy' is still understood in opposition to 'totalitarianism'. Except that for them what is 'totalitarian' is the conjunction of capitalism with liberalism that prescribes to politics the one-way street of neoliberalism, all the more so after the collapse of the Soviet Union effectively brought to a close the 20th century Marxist-Leninist experience in the west.[10]

An Augustinian response to Schmitt

Voegelin's key work, *The New Science of Politics*, is probably the first significant work in 20th-century political theory that explicitly takes up Peterson's refutation of 'political theology' as a political monotheism.[11] Voegelin accepts

---

[9] This claim needs to be taken with a grain of salt. Voegelin and Maritain adopt some aspects and motifs of Jewish prophetology as is inevitable for Christian political theologians. For instance, Voegelin has much to say about the Jewish prophets in (Voegelin 2001). But he develops an anti-theocratic picture of the Jewish prophets, as discussed in (Sandoz 1998). However, Ellis Sandoz does not mention at all Voegelin's radical critique of Moses found in his earlier works that I discuss later in this chapter.

[10] For an exemplary recognition of this 'end' of Marxism, see (Badiou 1985). For the '*pensée unique*' rhetoric applied to neoliberalism, see now (Micocci and Mario 2017). For a hyper-rhetorical adoption of Stalinist 'totalitarianism' on the side of a 'democratic' struggle against the 'new' totalitarianism of neoliberal capitalism, see (Žižek 2009).

[11] Political monotheism is defined by Voegelin as the belief that 'one *basileus* [king] on earth represents the one God, the one King in Heaven, the one Nomos and Logos. It is a return, indeed, to the imperial representation of cosmic truth' (Voegelin 1952, 104).

Peterson's central claim that Augustine's solution of the Two Cities brings about 'the end of political theology in orthodox Christianity ... [because] the spiritual destiny of man in the Christian sense cannot be represented on earth by the power organization of a political society; it can be represented only by the church. The sphere of power is radically de-divinized; it has become temporal' (Voegelin 1952, 106). Augustine puts an end to ancient political theology because he demonstrates that salvation is no longer achievable in and through a politically organized society like the Roman Empire. Political power has no access to what Voegelin calls the 'philosophical' and 'soteriological' concept of the representation of truth. Political society must remain at the level of what he calls 'existential' representation. By introducing the distinction between truth and existence in the sphere of political representation, Voegelin admits that 'our own analysis follows Peterson closely' (Voegelin 1952, 102, n.76).

Voegelin wrote these words more than a decade before Schmitt responded to the 'myth' of the 'end' of political theology propagated by Peterson's *Monotheism as a Political Problem* with his own work *Political Theology II*. But Schmitt's shrewd response to Peterson, namely, that every 'refutation' of political theology is itself necessarily politico-theological, applies to Voegelin as well. To oppose Eusebius with Augustine is not the same as opposing political theology *tout court*. Voegelin argues that the Augustinian interpretation of Christian revelation in the doctrine of the Two Cities, with the consequent separation of political realities from soteriological truths, is the only way in which immanence can be kept distinct from transcendence and the spectre of a 'political religion' avoided. But 'transcendence' here remains figured in a politico-theological way because it refers to 'a *source of order* superior in rank to the established order of society'. Only in reference to this meta-political order of rank is there a salvational and emancipatory 'opening of soul'. The meta-political order of rank is at the same time theological: it is anchored in the 'idea of a universal God as measure ... [and it entails] the idea of a universal community of mankind beyond civil society, through the participation of all men in the common measure, be it understood as the Aristotelian *nous*, the Stoic or the Christian *logos*' (Voegelin 1952, 156). Voegelin's political theology is Christian—or, in Badiou's sense of the term, 'universalist'—because it aspires at establishing a 'universal community of mankind' beyond all national and party divisions. It is also Christian—in Taylor's sense of the term—because the reference to a meta-political order of rank is designed to 'open' political society by preventing its closure in an 'immanent order'.[12] In what follows I shall explain how both features of this Christian political theology are cashed out in terms of an account of representation as symbolical social agency.

But it is not only by adopting the problem of representation as central to political theology that Voegelin's critique of Schmitt remains within the discursive horizon of Christian political theology. Voegelin's attempted refutation of Schmitt's political theology remains Schmittian because it is characterized by a 'political' motivation: it is based on the identification of the 'true enemy'. In Voegelin's discourse, the moment of theological enmity appears when he contrasts his reconstruction of the unity of pagan philosophy and Christian truth (granted by 'the common measure' of 'Aristotelian *nous*... or Christian *logos*') to what he sees as the nefarious unity of Judaism and Modernity in the form of Gnosticism. For Voegelin, the 'de-divinization' of the world in Augustine means that human destiny, which reaches beyond political history, depends on 'the grace of world-transcendent God' (Voegelin 1952, 107). In contrast to Augustine, the project of Modernity, on his account, stages an anti-Christian 're-divinization' of the world. Unlike Burckhardt and Nietzsche, who identified the seeds of a modern reaction against Christianity in the Renaissance rebirth of paganism, Voegelin identifies this reaction in a dialectic that is internal to Christianity itself: Christianity turns against itself in the form of Gnosticism. But according to Voegelin, the roots of the modern self-critique of Christianity are found in 'the Jewish messianic moment' (Voegelin 1952, 107). In so many words, Voegelin recapitulates Löwith's thesis on philosophy of history as secularized *Heilsgeschichte*—itself drawn from Peterson's intuitions—according to which the real root of political theology in Modernity is none other than the rebirth of Jewish messianism.[13]

The Gnostic turn that constitutes Modernity is blamed on the vicissitudes of the Christian reception of Jewish messianism because—on Voegelin's view—this messianism teaches that the Kingdom of God is to be realized *within* history, not after its End. By way of contrast, Voegelin argues that Christian eschatology is from the start constructed around the concept of

---

[12] In *A Secular Age*, Taylor does not recognize Voegelin's paternity of the Catholic disembedding thesis.
[13] Voegelin explicitly relies on Löwith's interpretation of the authentically Christian idea of history in order to construct his identity between modern secularization and Gnosticism (Voegelin 1952, 120–21).

the *katechon* (the earthly power which is said to 'hold back' the advent of the Anti-Christ, which heralds the Apocalypse). By setting up the Catholic Church as separate from the political state, Augustine's aim was for the Church to represent the *non-happening* of the *Parousia* of God *within* history. Repeating the orthodox doctrine of a Christian 'surpassing' of Judaism, Voegelin says that 'the [Christian/MV] church *actually evolved* from the [Jewish/MV] eschatology of the realm in history toward the eschatology of transhistorical, supernatural perfection' (Voegelin 1952, 108, emphasis mine). Voegelin's thesis is that the Christian *katechon*, precisely because it expresses the fundamental idea that Christ's (the Messiah's) kingdom is 'not of this world', is term for term opposed to Jewish messianism which depends on the 'this-worldly' character of the messianic age.

Christendom's fall away from Augustinianism, and its slow decay into Modernity, begins—according to Voegelin—with the medieval inclusion into Christian teachings of 'the *revolutionary* annunciation of the millennium in which Christ would reign with his saints on earth' (Voegelin 1952, 108, emphasis mine). Construing the meaning of Christian salvation in such revolutionary terms sanctioned 'the permanent effectiveness within Christianity of the broad mass of Jewish apocalyptic literature'. This apocalyptic literature cast into question Augustine's anti-historicist construal of the role of the Church in the millennium. This temporal expression does not give the Christian Church a specific historical shelf life. Rather it means that the Reign of Christ 'in his church in the present *saeculum* that would continue until the Last Judgment and the advent of the eternal realm in the beyond' (Voegelin 1952, 109). For Voegelin, paradoxically, it was only the obsession of Augustine with identifying the 'true enemies' of Trinitarian orthodoxy that made it possible, during the Christian Middle Ages, for 'Jewish chiliasm' to be 'excluded along with polytheism, just as Jewish monotheism had been excluded along with pagan, metaphysical monotheism'. Jewish monotheism and Jewish messianism had to be excluded politically, that is, as theological enemies, for the same reason that they unduly politicized God's relation to the world and to man.[14]

---

[14] It is striking, but hardly surprising, that Voegelin completely avoids mentioning Schmitt in the very passages where he develops a clearly Schmittian conception of the *katechon* by employing theses of Löwith, Peterson, and even Jacob Taubes. Taubes's *Abendländische Eschatologie*, published in Bern in 1947, is cited in (Voegelin 1952, 108, n. 3). In Voegelin's *The New Science of Politics* there is one other evident borrowing from Schmitt's polemical articulation of political theology. This is found in his claim that whereas the West remained Augustinian until the advent of modernity and adhered to a picture of society in which state and church were separate, the same did not happen in Eastern Christendom with the development of Byzantine Caesaro-Papism. Voegelin writes that the idea of

The New Science of Politics therefore recycles Löwith's claim, in *Meaning in History*, that Jewish messianism re-enters into Christian teaching with the 12th-century visionary Joachim of Fiora, whose prophecies attempted to 're-divinize' the secular space by 'applying the symbol of the Trinity to the course of history' (Voegelin 1952, 110).[15] On this reading, Joachim is the first Christian mystic who attempts to map the dispensation of divine providence—the 'economy of mysteries'—onto the historical progression. Previously understood as an intermediate stage between Creation and Redemption, the divine order of history now becomes the divine order *in* history. With modern philosophy of history, world history finally becomes identical to the providential divine order. At that point, Redemption takes the form of a 'closed' and homogeneous society, a 'brotherhood of persons' led by a *Dux, Duce, Führer* (leader) and inspired by a new prophet of revolution. This prophet is the revolutionary intellectual who not only perceives the divine order in history (the so-called Laws of History) but also attempts to realize it socially and politically (Voegelin 1952, 112).[16]

The symbolic conception of political representation

The New Science of Politics is intended to provide the groundwork for a new Christian political theology that will re-establish Augustine's solution on a more secure footing and immune to any Gnostic appropriation. My claim is

---

Constantinople as a 'Second Rome', that was to be followed by a millenarian 'Third Rome' or 'Third Reich', then migrated to Russia in the medieval period. 'Transcendentally Russia was distinguished from all Western nations as the imperial representation of Christian truth' (Voegelin 1952, 116). According to Voegelin, this accounts for why the idea of a 'dictatorship of the proletariat' as advent of the Third Rome occurred in Russia, thanks to the mediation of Dostoevsky's mis-archism. Readers of *Roman Catholicism and Political Form* will immediately hear the echo of its opening sentence '*Nous vivons sous l'œil des Russes*'. For these motifs, see (Palélogue 2004; and Forti 2014). Writing in the middle of the Cold War, Voegelin connects his discourse on Russian Orthodox Christianity as basis of an imperial political theology with the identification of Stalinism with Nazism as the two most perfect forms of political religion in late modernity.

[15] Voegelin does not mention the work of Eugen Rosenstock-Huessy, whose *Out of Revolution* was among the first to draw back the internal connection between modernity and revolution to Joachim's prophecies as they were articulated by Saint Francis and his followers. Agamben articulates his own conception of political messianism in his interpretation of Peter Olivi, a particularly radical Franciscan Spiritualist.

[16] In his *Thoughts on Machiavelli*, echoing Gramsci's idea of the Communist Party as civil prince, Leo Strauss argues that Machiavelli's theory of the armed prophet as civil prince rolls both figures of the leader of the masses and revolutionary intellectual into one. For a standard reading of Voegelin's critique of modern philosophy of history which misses its Schmittian and Petersonian presuppositions, see (Sandoz 1998).

that the new ground on which Voegelin establishes Christian political theology is a theory of political representation alternative to the one proposed by Schmitt. Voegelin attacks Schmitt over the identification between sovereign and the authoritative representative of a theologico-political unity. He denies that sovereignty belongs to a human being in virtue of an institutional setting, namely, in virtue of juridical considerations of office. Instead, he proposes that sovereignty is not a human attribute but belongs exclusively to God, and that the divine ground of order is expressed as 'Word' or *logos* and is humanly accessible through reason or wisdom [*nous*], whose proper representatives are Platonic philosophers and Hebrew prophets.[17] In turn, the philosopher and the prophet stand in another representative relation to a people than the one of the sovereign.[18]

The New Science of Politics argues that representation is 'the central problem of a theory of politics' (Voegelin 1952, 1). Following Schmitt's definition of representation as *Repräsentation* rather than *Stellvertretung*, Voegelin says that by representation he means the 'symbols by which political societies interpret themselves as representatives of a transcendent truth' (Voegelin 1952, 1). However, Voegelin breaks with Schmitt when he claims that there exist *two orders of representation* (in the sense of *Repräsentation*) that are politically fundamental. The first order of representation is the 'existential' one, roughly corresponding to Schmitt's theory of sovereignty, although Schmitt remains unmentioned throughout *The New Science of Politics*, for obvious reasons. This idea of 'existential' representation turns on the principle that there must exist 'rulers who can act for the society, individuals whose acts are not imputed to their own persons but to the society as a whole'. Such rulers are the 'representatives of a society' (Voegelin 1952, 37).

Voegelin's crucial intuition—which still follows Schmitt—is that without a representative who 'articulates' society for its members, that is, without a representative who allows society to represent itself to itself, such a society cannot become a unified people with the power to select its own representatives and, thus, cannot be considered democratic. Voegelin claims that the fundamental principle of democracy is that 'articulation is the condition of representation' (Voegelin 1952, 41). In this formula, 'representation' means

---

[17] See the definition: 'The consciousness of being caused by the Divine ground and being in search of the Divine ground—that is reason. Period.... That is why I always insist on speaking of "noetic" and use the term *nous*', cited in (Sandoz 1998, 74).

[18] For an interpretation of the 'political' role of the philosopher in Voegelin that abstracts from the context of political theology, see now (Sandoz 2009).

democratic electoral representation, representation 'from below', what Schmitt calls *Stellvertretung*. Electoral representation, in turn, requires as its condition of possibility another kind of supra-political 'representative' who is capable of 'articulating' a transcendent ground of order in a symbolic form.[19] Voegelin therefore subsumes democracy under the logic of representation, whereas Schmitt maintains that democracy and representation are based on two opposed principles, respectively those of substantive equality and sovereignty, which are found in every existing constitution.

Voegelin gives a striking illustration of his conception of symbolic representation by interpreting the meaning of Abraham Lincoln's iconic formula for democracy as a 'government of the people, by the people, for the people'. For Voegelin this pathos formula of democracy should be parsed as follows. A government that belongs to the people ('of the people') is a government that belongs to an 'articulated political society'. The *articulated people* can be said to be governed 'by the people' only in the sense that it is governed by the *articulating representative* of the people. Lastly, this articulated people is governed 'for the people' because government is for the sake of that 'membership ... [which] is bound by the act of the representative' (Voegelin 1952, 40). Voegelin's interpretation of Lincoln's formula turns the principle of democratic representation around, in a rather Hobbesian way, so that the symbolic representative of the people becomes the effective constituent power, and the people who nominally have the power to select their political representatives become in turn the constituted power.

The proper significance of Voegelin's thesis comes to light by bringing it in relation with the current debates on constituent power. Whereas some contemporary theorists like Antonio Negri and Andreas Kalyvas ascribe constituent power directly to the people prior to their representative articulation, others like Philip Pettit and Hans Lindahl deny that this is possible.[20]

---

[19] Voegelin distinguishes between ideological symbols of political reality—he gives as an example the 'contract theory of government' or the 'theory of sovereignty'—from theoretical symbols that explain the political reality. 'If the theorist, for instance, describes the Marxian idea of the realm of freedom to be established by a Communist revolution as an immanentist hypostasis of a Christian eschatological symbol, the symbol "realm of freedom" is part of reality ... while such terms as "immanentist" "hypostasis" and "eschatology" are concepts of political science' (Voegelin 1952, 29). Thereby, Voegelin gives a perfect illustration of why his 'political science' corresponds, point by point, to Schmitt's political theology for they both share the belief that political concepts are secularized theological concepts. Voegelin claims that theoretical symbols, unlike political ones, are not polemical. In so doing he incurs in a performative contradiction since his own 'new science of politics' is itself structured polemically, as I discuss later.

[20] For a brief discussion of the issues, I refer to (Vatter 2015). On the history of the concept and its relation to the problem of representation, see (Colón-Ríos 2014; and Rubinelli 2018).

In particular, Lindahl has defended the thesis that a people *cannot* constitute itself 'on its own terms' *as a people* endowed with a political unity. The reason is that for Lindahl 'we' cannot say about ourselves that we are a 'we'.[21] Instead, every group must rely on some representative—who necessarily cannot be an elected official—to take the 'initiative' to designate a given group as a 'we' by opposing antagonistically this group with regard to an alterity and exteriority: 'there can be no gathering together of a multitude into a collective subject without acts that seize the initiative to include and exclude'.[22] This kind of argument is strikingly similar to Voegelin's argument for the primacy of the symbolic representative. The difference is that for Lindahl the constituent role of the symbolic representative is explicitly polemical: 'the emergence of a novel collective always involves an element of conquest; it is never a project of "love" ' (Lindahl 2013, 216). Whereas, in Voegelin's Augustinian vision of symbolic representation, every collectivity is in the last instance a function of love of the divine ground: legitimate political order is based on *ordo amoris* rather than on *amor mundi*.[23]

Articulating the mystical body of the people

If Voegelin adopts an idea of representation that is Hobbesian in order to understand what he calls 'existential' representation, this does not mean that he accepts Schmitt's claim that Hobbes always trumps Augustine. It means, instead, that Voegelin needs to reformulate political Augustinianism in such a way that it takes into account Schmitt's Hobbesian critique of Augustine. Schmitt's critique was simply that any division between church and state will always require some representative person to decide the inevitable conflict of competences, and this sovereign representative has the authority to decide in virtue of representing a unified people. Voegelin's strategy is to focus on what kind of representative can represent a unified Christian people. Hence the central importance that he assigns to John Fortescue's critique of Augustine. Fortescue, an English medieval political philosopher, is often credited as the spiritual father of the English mixed constitution.[24] Voegelin suggests that Fortescue took Augustine to task for having left the Christian church

---

[21] See now the arguments in (Menga 2018) that follow Lindahl's lead.
[22] (Lindahl 2013, 216).
[23] On this motif in Augustine, see (Heyking 2001; and Gregory 2008).
[24] I return to a more detailed discussion of Fortescue in the chapter on Kantorowicz.

(*ekklesia*) without an effective king. According to Fortescue, this had the consequence of turning the mystical body of Christ into an acephalic body, incapable of worldly, political action.[25]

Voegelin does not want to follow Fortescue's suggestion on how to repair Augustine's blunder. For he believes that Fortescue is a precursor of modernist secularization who transferred the idea of Christ's mystical body (*corpus mysticum*) to the secular realm, thereby re-divinizing the political world (Voegelin 1952, 42–43). Voegelin considers that the Paulinian idea of the church as *corpus mysticum* ultimately serves the function of turning the office of the king into a sacral function (Voegelin 1994, 61). The sacralization of kingship is precisely what Voegelin wants to avoid at all costs. This is what Frederick II von Hohenstaufen achieved when he conceived of the Emperor as someone who would put an end to the dualism of Empire and Church and thus opened the way to a conception of salvation that is purely political. It is Frederick II who is seen as 'the messiah-king . . . the pagan god-man' because he assumes in himself, in his state, the functions of the Church and is thus the first example of an 'innerworldly political religion' (Voegelin 1994, 69).

Voegelin discusses Fortescue in order to address the same problem that Kantorowicz would later call 'the King's Two Bodies'. This is the problem of the 'mystical' constitution of the People's body politic. Voegelin's entire discourse of representation is from the start oriented by the problem of the 'mystical body' that corresponds to Christ as Head of the Church. If one is to succeed in separating authentic Christian political theology from modern political religions, a new answer to this problem is required: 'Fortescue quotes St. Thomas: "The king is given for the realm, and not the realm for the king"; and then he goes on to conclude: the king is in his realm what the pope is in the church, a *servus servorum Dei*; and as a consequence, "all that the king does ought to be *referred to his kingdom*"—[this is] the most concentrated formulation of the problem of representation' (Voegelin 1952, 45, emphasis mine).

Unlike Schmitt, the problem of representation for Voegelin does not only mean that the sovereign is representative of the realm because in the absence of this head, the political body lacks all articulation and thus agency. By replacing Fortescue's critique of Augustine within a Thomistic framework, Voegelin wants to show that if the sovereign is to count as the representative of the realm or society, then it is also necessary that everything the sovereign

---

[25] On the motif of a 'headless' Church, see (Heyking 1999).

decides and does 'be referred to *his kingdom*'. The expression 'his kingdom' is overdetermined: it can mean God's Kingdom as much as the reign made up of the People of God, since the king is 'servant of the servants/people of God'. For Voegelin, the problem of representation necessarily opens the problem of the relation between the sovereign, the people, and God. There is no political representation unless the representative can articulate the relation between the human, secular realm and God's Kingdom. The problem of representation in Voegelin is therefore another name for the politico-theological foundation of democracy.[26]

The rise of totalitarianism explains the urgency and importance of having the correct conception of the 'mystical body' of the People. Voegelin was one of the first political theorists in the first half of the 20th century who identified the *internal* connection between the Fascist and National Socialist movements based on the mobilization of the People/*Volk* and a form of 'biopolitics' based on modern state racism.[27] In his books on race and racism, Voegelin attempted to work out an alternative conception of what he called the 'body idea' of a polity. Through this conception of a 'body idea', Voegelin, somewhat implausibly, acknowledged the existence of a racial and ethnic basis of community, the biopolitical ground of modern community,[28] while maintaining the political body 'open' to transcendence in accord with Plato's doctrine of the ideas, culminating in the 'idea of the Good'. The political body is 'mystical' because it cannot be articulated in the absence of reference to this dimension of Platonic 'ideas'. This is the core of Voegelin's attempt to respond to the Hitlerian reduction of the 'body idea' to its 'biological' basis.[29]

---

[26] I share many intuitions with Roberto Esposito's reading of Voegelin as a critic of Schmitt, but I disagree on two fundamental points. The first is that Esposito considers Voegelin to be an 'anti-representative' thinker simply in virtue of his rejecting Schmitt's primacy of 'existential' representation. But this is not to see that Voegelin retains, in very Schmittian ways, the primacy of (symbolical) representation. Second, I cannot follow Esposito when he claims that Voegelin's critique of Roman civil religion and support for the Augustinian 'de-divinization' of temporal power is a sign that Voegelin 'objects to every form of political theology' (Esposito 1988, 93).

[27] The terrain has since been mapped in (Foucault 2003). On Voegelin's writings on race, see (Voegelin 1998a; 1998b).

[28] Contrast with Helmuth Plessner's contemporary rejection of community based on supposed shared physical, racial or ethnic characteristics (Plessner 1999).

[29] On the efforts of philosophers affiliated with Nazism to employ Plato to their racist cause, see (Forti 2006). On the reduction to the body in totalitarian regimes, see also the early text by (Levinas 1990) and, for commentary in relation to the motif in Heidegger, see (Derrida 1991). The theme becomes central again in Lefort's later analysis of modern political regimes (Lefort 1986). For a discussion of Voegelin's constant opposition to Hitlerism, see (Trepanier 2018). Trepanier's discussion of Voegelin's conception of race does not mention its biopolitical and its politico-theological contexts. However, he does show that Voegelin's critique of Nazi race theory is itself based on a politicized conception of race that ties it with the notion of 'body ideas' whose exemplar is the Christian *corpus mysticum*. 'Different races existed, but they all belonged to a universal humanity rather than one race

In order to explain his conception of 'existential' or sovereign representation, and its relation to ideas, in *The New Science of Politics* Voegelin does not refer to Schmitt directly. Instead, he cites the French jurist Maurice Hauriou's *Précis de droit constitutionnel*: 'to be a representative means to guide in a ruling position, the work of *realizing the idea through institutional embodiment*; and the power of a ruler has authority in so far as he is able to make his factical power representative of the idea' (Voegelin 1952, 48, emphasis mine). Hauriou's legal institutionalism was also often cited by Schmitt, and for the same reason that Voegelin refers to it. Hauriou's Platonic-sounding formulation of political representation makes clear that 'the authority of a representative power *precedes existentially* the regulation of this power by positive law' (Voegelin 1952, 48).[30] In other words, for Hauriou just as for Schmitt, the ruler's 'authority', based on their capacity to 'realize' the juridical idea, is superior to the rule of law. Additionally, for Hauriou 'the origin of law cannot be found in legal regulations but must be sought in the decision which replaces a litigious situation by ordered power' (Voegelin 1952, 48). Voegelin makes Hauriou a stand-in for Schmitt's decisionism, which the latter precisely identifies as crucial to political theology.[31]

Through their theories of 'existential' representation, Hauriou and Schmitt were both undermining the constitutional rule of law. Voegelin follows suit: 'In order to be representative, *it is not enough for a government to be representative in the constitutional sense . . . it must also be representative in the existential sense of realizing the idea of the institution*. And the implied warning may be explicated in the thesis: if a government is nothing but representative in the constitutional sense, a representative ruler in the existential sense will sooner or later make an end of it' (Voegelin 1952, 49, emphasis mine).[32] Like for Schmitt, Voegelin also considers that the 'existential'

representing all of humanity. Furthermore, these thinkers approached the subject of race as a spiritual expression of a community rather than a biological one: the race idea was not about biological purity but the spiritual purity of a concept that could unify members into a singular community' (Trepanier 2018).

[30] On the use by Schmitt of Hauriou's theories, see (Schmitt 1995; Cristi 1984; and Bates 2005; 2006). On Schmitt's use of another well-known Italian theorist of legal institutionalism, Santi Romano, see now (Wilde 2018).
[31] There is not in Voegelin's reading of Hauriou a clear distinction between the Schmitt of decisionism and the Schmitt of 'concrete orders'. Voegelin at the time may not have read or registered Schmitt's 1930s texts in which he announces his turn away from legal decisionism and towards the idea of 'concrete legal orders'.
[32] This is probably the reason why Kelsen directs a very strong critique against his old student in his late work (Kelsen 2004).

representative of the 'idea of the institution' stands above the constitutional order. The crucial difference between Voegelin's and Schmitt's political theologies is that for Voegelin the existential representative must realize in the state an 'idea of the institution' which is at once Platonic and Christian, corresponding to the primacy of the Good and to the Christian idea of the Kingdom of God. Voegelin's Christian political theology is defined by this shifting of Schmittian premises towards a more Platonizing conception of tyranny.

Christian political theology and the paradox of democratic dictatorship

Voegelin's 'critical' political science defines the concept of representation in a philosophico-existential sense. The representative decides on the existence of society as a whole when it decides on order, but this order is not the 'concrete order' of a state or church, as in Schmitt, but it is the order of an idea, hence a Platonic political order (Voegelin 1952, 50).[33] The concept of representation cannot be reduced to the juridical signification that it has in Schmitt because for Voegelin it is not only a matter of whether the sovereign articulates the human realm, but it is also a matter of whether the sovereign works for God's Reign. The crucial question is whether the existential, political representative can also be representative 'of something beyond itself, of a transcendent reality' (Voegelin 1952, 54). Voegelin's answer is affirmative: there is no existential representative unless the representative also reflects the 'cosmic order'. What Voegelin calls 'political theology' is the moment of existential representation in which the sovereign presents himself as the representative of cosmic order. Since cosmic order can also be taken as the order established by God, existential representation is 'political theology' as defined by Peterson (Voegelin 1952, 56). When Voegelin uses the term 'political theology' he does so polemically. The term refers to the reduction of political theology to a form of cosmic theology, which is intended to stand for the Judeo-Hellenistic motif of the divine kingship that was supposedly overcome by Augustine.[34]

---

[33] For a discussion of the Platonic philosopher as an 'anti-tyrant' in Voegelin, Strauss, and Kojève, see (Cooper 2011), who misses the politico-theological context of the turn towards Platonism in Voegelin.
[34] See (Goodenough 1928). For an alternative interpretation of this Hellenistic conception of kingship and its relation to Jewish political theology, I refer to the discussion found in *Living Law*.

In his earlier book *The Political Religions*, Voegelin argued that the idea of cosmic order depends on 'the symbol of the ray of light that begins at the divine apex in order to cast itself over all the hierarchy of sovereigns and of their offices down to the most humble subject' (Voegelin 1994, 55). One of the first to adopt Sigmund Freud's hypothesis of an Egyptian origin of Moses, Voegelin connected Judaism with the Egyptian emperor Akhenaton and his introduction of the Sun-God Aton. Political theology is born when Moses adopts and modifies Akhenaton's theology by giving monotheism an explicitly 'political' application in the foundation of a new people (Voegelin 1994, 42).[35]

Voegelin connected this sacral use of the symbol of the sun in the constitution of a hierocracy with Plotinus and Philo, both of whom he considers to be 'Egyptian' philosophers. Even Maimonides falls in this lineage thanks to his doctrine of the 'sacred emanation'. Voegelin calls Maimonides 'the Jewish thinker of the Egyptian court' (Voegelin 1994, 56).[36] According to his genealogy, the tradition of cosmic political theology passes into Christendom through Dante's *Monarchia* and reaches up to Bodin's reworking of the French conception of monarchy into the modern idea of absolute sovereignty (exemplified by Louis XIV, the Sun-King) (Voegelin 1994, 57).[37] In this genealogy, the absolute conception of sovereignty falls under an existential idea of representation based on a Egyptian-Hellenistic-Jewish cosmic theology.

But the real point of Voegelin's Petersonian attempt at liquidation of the term 'political theology' is to establish the discourse of political theology at a higher level. The political theology of monarchism, or existential representation, corresponds to a concept of 'imperial truth' to which Voegelin opposes the idea of 'theoretical truth' that comes from a concept of 'political science' (rather than 'political theology') in which it is philosophy (together with theology), and not the cosmic king, who is the veridical representative of God. Voegelin's rhetorical opposition between 'political philosophy' and 'political theology' is internal to a post-Schmittian development of the discourse on

---

[35] Following Voegelin's lead, Jan Assmann argues that Moses 'the Egyptian' creates a concept of 'religion' based on the distinction between 'true' religion and 'idolatry' in order to make theology 'political' in the friend/enemy sense of Schmitt (Assmann 2000; 2002). He also claims that the Mosaic tradition assigns the worship of the true idea of God to elites, leaving polytheism for the masses as a form of civil theology. Assmann identifies this idea of *duplex religio* as the core of the Enlightenment critique of revealed religions. Thus, for him the Enlightenment is caught up in the Mosaic distinction and thereby also in political theology. Assmann's thesis in the end reinforces the Petersonian idea that Judaism is at the origin of political theology.

[36] The intended slight to Philo and Maimonides is evident.

[37] Bodin is assumed by Voegelin to be a Jewish political thinker.

political theology in which the true representative of God is no longer the human sovereign *simpliciter*, but the philosopher-king.

Voegelin articulates the opposition between existential and veridical forms of representation in terms of Henri Bergson's distinction between an 'open' and a 'closed' society.[38] Existential representation is 'closed' to the theoretical truth of philosophy, and ultimately leads to the Gnostic belief that salvation is only to be found in and through the state and its 'immanent order'. In so doing, existential representation is part of a 'political religion' of sovereignty. Veridical representation maintains society 'open' to a transcendent truth. Voegelin defends Plato as the representative of an 'open society'—pace the contemporary attacks on Platonism by Karl Popper and others who saw in him the original 'totalitarian' thinker.[39] For in the *Republic* Plato argued that the order of the city must be modelled on the order of the human soul or *psyche*, whose truth is placed higher than the cosmic order. The 'true order of the human psyche' becomes the first principle of this new 'political philosophy'. This 'true order' gives way to a 'true' typology of human beings, where the philosopher-king's soul becomes 'the standard for measuring and classifying the empirical variety of human types as well as of the social order' (Voegelin 1952, 63).[40]

More salient than the peculiarities of Voegelin's interpretation of Aristotle and Plato is the fact that he orients anti-sovranist political theology back to classical political philosophy. Voegelin illustrates a movement that is shared by most political theologies without sovereignty of the 20th century. All of them embark upon a return from modern political philosophy back to classical political thought, emphasizing either the Aristotelian side, as with Maritain, or the Platonic side, as with Voegelin and Strauss. It is a remarkable coincidence that all three political theologians first presented their

---

[38] For an excellent discussion of Voegelin's relation to Bergson, see (Gontier 2015). Gontier argues that Voegelin develops the dualism open/closed society prior to his reading of Bergson. I am not convinced of this hypothesis on the basis of the textual evidence he provides. In *Faith and Knowledge*, Derrida re-proposes Bergson's idea of an 'open' society as fundamental to the current return of political theology. I discuss this further in the chapter on Habermas.

[39] (Voegelin 1952, 61). On the opposition between Platonism and the 'open' society, see (Popper 2013).

[40] Voegelin identifies Plato's philosopher-king with Aristotle's figure of the noble person [*spoudaios*] who develops to the fullest their 'philosophical life' [*bios theoretikos*]: 'hence the science of ethics in the Aristotelian sense is a type study of the *spoudaios*' (Voegelin 1952, 64). Although Voegelin pretends to have left behind the political theology of monarchism, the discussion of Plato and Aristotle in *The New Political Science* is not far from the problem of the legitimate ruler as a 'living law', just as in Aristotle's *Nicomachean Ethics* the *spoudaios* is described as being a law unto themselves (*Nicomachean Ethics* III, 5 1113a, 30ff). I return to the complexities of the Aristotelian idea of the 'living law' in the chapter on Kantorowicz.

signature main works, back to back, in the form of the Walgreen Lectures at the University of Chicago in the late 1940s.

Plato's 'anthropological' principle of the *psyche* can be assumed as standard for the best political order *because* 'through the opening of the soul the *philosopher finds himself in a new relation to God* . . . the differentiation of the psyche is inseparable from a new truth about God' (Voegelin 1952, 67, emphasis mine). The veridical representative of a new political order presents a philosophical truth about God. This is the truth that God cannot be identified with the cosmic order, as was the case with the monotheistic and monarchic 'political theology', but can only be approximated through philosophical symbols.[41] Voegelin's Platonic political philosophy is, therefore, another name for a new Christian political theology: both turn on 'the idea of a man who has found his true nature through finding his true relation to God'.[42] As Voegelin puts it, 'the truth of man and the truth of God are inseparably one. . . . This is the great subject of the *Republic*' (Voegelin 1952, 69).[43] Voegelin's 'new political science' is now entirely a function of a political theology of a Platonic type. This hypothesis receives confirmation when Voegelin adorns the veridical representative with messianic attributes: Plato modelled Socrates' martyrdom for truth at the hands of democracy as 'the suffering servant Socrates—if we may use the symbol of Deutero-Isaiah' (Voegelin 1952, 74).

As a representative of divine truth, the Platonic philosopher maintains political society 'open' by keeping it from falling into the Gnostic belief that human salvation is to be achieved exclusively in the form of political salvation (Voegelin 1952, 122–24). But Voegelin understands the philosophical struggle for the 'open' society as radically polemical. The 'open' society requires an ongoing culture war, a struggle to the death against those 'ideological' forces that threaten to 'close' society onto itself as opposed to 'opening' it up to God. Voegelin identifies English Puritanism and its ideal of a 'society of saints' as the paradigmatic modern Gnostic movement that seeks to establish the 'immanent framework' of modernity. 'The saint is a gnostic who

---

[41] For the extended interpretation of Plato and Aristotle, see (Voegelin 1999). On Voegelin's idea of the symbol, see (Hughes 2014). For an approach to the relation between ontology and political philosophy through the analysis of symbols, see (Schürmann 1979).

[42] Voegelin cites from Plato's *Laws* 716c where God is said to be the measure of human beings. On Voegelin's attempt to unite Platonic political philosophy with Christianity, see the correspondence with Leo Strauss in (Emberley and Cooper 1993).

[43] Plato, not Hobbes, becomes the authentic political theologian: 'the validity of the standards developed by Plato and Aristotle depends on the conception of a man who can be the measure of society because God is the measure of his soul' (Voegelin 1952, 70).

will not leave the transfiguration of the world to the grace of God beyond history but will do the work of God himself, right here and now, in history' (Voegelin 1952, 147). When he thematizes the best way to fight such a culture war and engage the 'enmity' posed by the 'society of saints', Voegelin's discussion of the Platonic philosopher-king recovers its tyrannical traits. It is in this context that Voegelin develops an alternative, and highly paradoxical, discourse on dictatorship as a legitimate instrument to preserve democracy from sliding into totalitarianism/Gnosticism.

Voegelin contemplates three strategies to engage 'immanentist' revolutionary movements in modern liberal democracies. He associates the first strategy with the name of Averroes, in what seems a side reference to Strauss's recovery of Arabic medieval political thought. On Voegelin's reading, Averroes advocates an esoteric or elitist conception of philosophy: he makes the 'anthropological and soteriological' truth inaccessible to the 'vulgar' by turning theology into an esoteric discourse to be pursued by philosophical sages, while leaving for the masses only 'a simple fundamentalism, the truth as it is symbolized in Scripture' (Voegelin 1952, 141). But Voegelin does not think this 'Islamic solution of confining philosophical debate to esoteric circles' is practicable in modern western society after the victory of Puritanism and the social realization of Protestantism in modern secularized society.[44]

Voegelin considers a second solution that is quite close to the idea of a 'constitutional dictatorship' developed at that time by Clinton Rossiter and Carl Friedrich.[45] In the context of the English 'Revolution of the Saints',[46] Voegelin names Richard Hooker as the first thinker to give a positive construal to dictatorship as a way to deal with 'Gnostic revolutionaries'. Voegelin argues that dictatorship can be legitimately employed by an 'open' society 'if through inadvertence such a [Gnostic] movement has grown to the danger point of capturing existential representation by the famous "legality" of popular elections' (Voegelin 1952, 144). Clearly, Voegelin has in mind here not only Hitler's 'electoral' rise to power, but also the postwar attempts to transition to socialist regimes through Communist and Socialist parties gaining control of the state by winning democratic elections. In both cases, Voegelin says that 'a democratic government is not supposed to bow to the "will of the

---

[44] Voegelin wrote these lines much before the 'success' of the Islamic Revolution in Iran and the rise of radical Islamic fundamentalisms.
[45] 'For Voegelin, sometimes it was necessary to adopt undemocratic measures to preserve democracy' (Trepanier 2018, 175). On the concept of constitutional dictatorship, see (Agamben 2003).
[46] See (Walzer 1965).

people" but *to put down the danger by force and, if necessary, to break the letter of the constitution in order to save its spirit'* (Voegelin 1952, 144, emphasis mine). Here Voegelin's political theology serves to legitimize the need for 'constitutional dictatorship' and what in our days has been called 'militant' approaches to the defense of democracy against 'extremism' and 'populism'.[47]

The third approach to the combat against modern revolutionary/Gnostic movements considered by Voegelin brings him even closer to Schmitt's political theology, since it calls for a return to Hobbes. As I showed earlier, Voegelin begins his reflection on political theology by defending Augustine against Hobbes. But the English philosopher is later revalorized and recuperated, to a degree, as the ideological enemy of the Puritan Saints. Voegelin thus proposes an interpretation of Hobbes's theory of sovereign representation as a way to unite veridical representation, in the form of natural law, with existential representation, in the form of the sovereign's authority to determine the public religion of the realm in accordance with the doctrine that 'Jesus is the Christ'. The sovereign's control of public religion shows 'Hobbes' intention of establishing Christianity [*theologia supernaturalis*] (understood as identical in substance with the law of nature) as an English *theologia civilis* in the Varronic sense' (Voegelin 1952, 155).[48] Like Schmitt, Voegelin now considers that the Augustinian separation of state and church requires a Hobbesian supplement: the absolute sovereign must turn Christianity into the civil theology of the state.

Unlike Schmitt, Voegelin is not convinced that the Hobbesian solution can be successful in the long run. The problem with Hobbes's solution is that by reducing Christianity's truth to the political function of resisting revolutionary movements and the spread of modern Gnosticism, the state ends up denying 'the existence of a tension between the truth of the soul and the truth of society' (Voegelin 1952, 160–61). The *Leviathan* in the end is nothing but 'the correlate of order to the disorder of Gnostic activists'. Hobbes's conception of sovereignty remains a 'component of the totalitarianism' inherent in Modernity (Voegelin 1952, 184).[49]

---

[47] On militant democracy, see, for example (Kirshner 2014).

[48] Here Voegelin anticipates the reading of Hobbes as advocate for 'civil religion' recently espoused by (Beiner 2011).

[49] Voegelin's reading of Hobbes's theory applies to it a solution he developed to resolve a similar problem he encounters in Plato. The problem with the political vision of the *Republic* is that it is too radical: by imposing on society the standard of order of the *psyche* embodied by the 'veridical representative', Plato ended up doing away with the 'existential' dimension of representation based on the value of physical security. Voegelin believes Plato moderated his vision of the philosopher-king by reintroducing 'civil theology' in the *Laws*. These laws 'mirrored the order of the cosmos', not the order

Political religion and the Jewish Question

Voegelin's interpretation of Hobbes in *The New Science of Politics* is considerably more moderate than the one he published in the years prior to World War II in his book on *Political Religions*.[50] In this earlier work, Hobbes was simply identified as the thinker responsible for the 'closure' of politics from divine transcendence: he was the (liberal) initiator of totalitarianism. Voegelin called Hobbes the Paul of the 'innerworldly *ecclesia*'.[51] Whereas Schmitt thought that Hobbes was a political theologian because he preserved the principle of Catholic representation in modernist garb, Voegelin believes that Hobbes turned the modern state into its own church in order to wrest it free from the dual controls of the 'divine kingdom' exercised by the universal Church and the Holy Roman Empire. 'The state is at the same time the church with the sovereign as head of the church, immediately under God, without the intermediary of the Vicar of Christ' (Voegelin 1994, 80). Hobbes sacralized the People as the mystical body of the sovereign representative.

In *Political Religions*, Voegelin construes Hobbes's 'political religion' as an anti-Christian return to biblical theocracy. 'It is through the force [of the Leviathan] that *the religious power of Jewish theocracy* penetrates in this way the world of English Reformation in order to unite itself with national consciousness in the symbol of the sacral person of the community' (Voegelin 1994, 80, emphasis mine). Most troubling, Voegelin suggests that Hobbes's recuperation of Jewish theocratic motifs, above all his claim that God personated Himself as Moses, prepared the way for the sacralization of the *Volk* that climaxed in the modern totalitarian and racial supremacist state. By way of contrast, Schmitt believed that Hobbes adopted Jewish theocratic motifs in order to set up the modern state on the liberal basis of the protection of the freedom of conscience.

Voegelin's attempt to identify in Hobbes's discourse the meeting point between liberalism and totalitarianism was not unique. To a degree, it was a belief also shared by Arendt and Strauss.[52] However, Arendt rejected Voegelin's

---

of the soul, and in that way 'embodied as much of the spirit [of the truth of the soul/MV] as was compatible with the continued natural existence of society' (Voegelin 1952, 157).

[50] Voegelin's book appeared in Vienna in April 1938.
[51] For a suggestive study of English sovranist preferences for Paul over Peter in the late Renaissance, see (Lupton 2012).
[52] On Arendt's reading of Hobbes in *Origins of Totalitarianism* as a thinker of 'terror' in politics, see (Keedus 2012)

interpretation of totalitarianism as a political religion, and rejected his connection of the rise of totalitarianism with a secularization of Christianity because 'there is no substitute for God in totalitarian ideologies'.[53] The reason may very well be that Arendt suspected Voegelin's 'functional' understanding of the role of religion in Modernity because it carried with it the anti-Jewish claim according to which it was the adoption of 'Jewish theocracy' that first 'secularized' Christian theology into inner-worldly, revolutionary/Gnostic activism.

Voegelin's discourse on political religion reaches a certain paroxysm when he compares Hobbes's sovereign to Abraham as the spiritual leader of a people on the basis of the argument that Abraham is the 'bearer of the personality of his people' and that is why God addresses Abraham directly (Voegelin 1994, 80). He then argues that 'following the example of *the Jewish theocratic idea*, the symbol of Leviathan gains the traits that recall those of *the religion of empire* in Akhenaton' (Voegelin 1994, 81, emphasis mine). The Leviathan's control over public religion deprives his subjects of access to God in public, leaving them with no choice but to follow the sovereign's commands as if they were divine commands. Thus, in 1938, Voegelin expands Peterson's identification of Judaism with Aristotelianism into an exorbitant signifying chain that links Abraham with Hobbes's Leviathan and the latter with the kind of 'political religion' resurrected by the German *Führer* and the Italian *Duce*.[54]

In conclusion, one can say that Voegelin's contorted and overdetermined engagements with Hobbes indicates that the defence of an 'open society' against anti-religious totalitarianism in the discourse of Christian political theology is underwritten by a polemical construal of the 'enmity' between Jews and Christians. For this discourse, 'true' Christians are those who remain 'open' to the transcendent character of truth and its veridical representatives, while 'true' Jews are those who remain 'closed' to this transcendent truth, resist the true universality of the Church, and propose a spurious universalism that is revolutionary and atheist. The ideal of an 'open society'

---

[53] (Voegelin 1953, 82); for commentary on their exchange and new material, see (Baehr and Wells 2012).

[54] It is interesting to note that in some of his texts that led to the German *Historikerstreit* the German historian Nolte argued that Hitler based his interpretation of Bolshevism as a 'Jewish' phenomenon on his idea of Moses as a 'Bolshevik leader' of the Egyptian underclasses. See (Nolte 1961) and for Nolte's ambivalent discussion of the Nazist construal of 'Jewish Bolshevism' see (Nolte 1997; and Peacock 2001, 102–3). For a more objective analysis of the participation of Jews in the European Marxist movements, as well as in the Soviet revolutions in Russia and Germany, see (Traverso 1994). Voegelin's later analysis of Hitler makes no mention of these issues. See (Voegelin 2003).

proposed by Christian political theology crashes against the barrier erected by Paul's claim that God set 'enmity' between Jews and Christians. All forms of Christian political theology in the 20th century grant some form of credence to the belief that Christian universalism comes at the price of a necessary enmity with Judaism. But in accepting this enmity, Christian political theology inevitably runs the risk of 'closing' itself in the form of a Hobbesian 'political religion'.

The only way to address this problem, which is perhaps the most fundamental one in the discourse of political theology, would be to start anew and to think the universalism of the Jewish and Greco-Roman traditions outside the Christian perspective. This alternative universalism was first proposed by Philo in his conception of 'divine democracy'. Precisely that Jewish philosopher whom Voegelin calls the philosopher of the 'Egyptian court' and of whom Schmitt denied that he ever thought of a democracy (as opposed to sovereignty) that is divine.

From Voegelin to Laclau: On the political theology of populism

Voegelin's central idea that electoral representation is itself based on a more primordial symbolical idea of representation anticipates the recent 'Representative Turn' in political science and the emergence of a new 'populist reason'.[55] Proponents of this turn take Hannah Pitkin's classic treatise *The Concept of Representation* as one of their foundational inspirations. Not by accident, Pitkin's book begins with a critique of Voegelin's idea of symbolic representation. Pitkin contrasted Voegelin's premodern conception of representation, in which the representative 'stands-in' or 'symbolizes' the represented, with the modern idea of representation initially devised during the North American Revolution, according to which the representative 'acts-for' the represented, as their 'advocate'.[56]

As Sofia Näsström has shown, Lefort coincides with Pitkin's reading of the break effected by modern ideas of representation: 'To Lefort, the fact that the revolution deprives society of both a natural and mystical body reveals the

---

[55] On the representative turn, see (Urbinati 2008; and Näsström 2011) and for the relation to populism (Saward 2010).
[56] (Pitkin 1967; and Urbinati 2000).

unprecedented nature of modern representative democracy. . . . The locus of power becomes linked to an empty place, by which is meant that who has power and therefore counts as the appropriate incarnation of the people now turns into the very question of democracy' (Näsström 2015, 3). Like Pitkin, Lefort argues that it is the loss of the politico-theological project to give a 'body' to the collectivity, that is, to the sovereign's reign, that is the source of modern representative democracy. Modern democracy can only be 'representational' in an electoral sense precisely because there is no longer a 'nature' or 'substance' to the People for the symbolic representative to personate. On this hypothesis, the empty space of symbolic representation can only be filled contingently by elected officials. However, the real question is whether symbolic representation has been rendered superfluous by electoral democracy. The contemporary resurgence of populism seems to indicate otherwise. Populist reason offers an account of why the modern, democratic *peuple introuvable* can always find an 'incarnation' in a Part of the indeterminable People.[57] This is the Part that stands for the whole by identifying itself in polemical opposition to the 'elites'.[58]

Voegelin's political theology acquires its true relevance only when it is understood as a response to the so-called paradox of representation.[59] It is a basic axiom of modern political philosophy that one cannot presuppose the existence of a 'people' as a political unity. This unity is never given; it must be constructed through some form of representation.[60] This axiom leads directly to the formulation of the paradox of representation: the people need to be 'present' for there to be something to represent and, at the same time, the people must also be 'absent', otherwise there would be no need to represent them. The paradox is simply a 'secularized' version of the problem of representation that Schmitt discussed in relation to the political form of the Catholic Church, in which it is God (not only the People) who needs to be *both* 'absent' and 'present' and therefore *must* be personated. One of the fundamental reasons why political theology perdures in modern democracy is precisely because Lefort's hypothesis of the 'empty place' of the People as a Whole is not an absolute posit, but merely the initial gambit of a dialectical process. The 'emptiness' of the People is always and only a condition

---

[57] For the idea of an 'absent' people in modern democracy, see (Rosanvallon 1998).
[58] For a recent critical review and typology of contemporary discourses on populism see now (Möller 2017).
[59] For a recent formulation of the paradox, see (Runciman 2007). Of course, Schmitt and Voegelin were entirely aware of this paradox.
[60] See the arguments in (Laclau 2006).

of possibility of its 'agonistic' or 'political' representation as a populist (and 'constituent') Part that 'stands in' for the (inevitably absent) Whole of the ('constituted') People. This, at least, is Laclau's standpoint.[61]

In *Disagreement*, Jacques Rancière postulated that the excluded *plebs* or *demos*—when they finally are capable of participating in the political life of the community—do not just seek to be recognized as one of the many countable parts of the state, but instead aspire to represent the entire *polis*, the whole *populus*.[62] For Rancière, such 'equivalence' of a part (the *demos*) for the whole (the *polis*) is in response to the injustice suffered by the plebs in the process of instituting the political state. Justice becomes the token under which the antinomy between order and law, police and politics, state and people, is overcome in a theory of radical equality.[63] Perhaps that is why Rancière's conception of an 'original' wrong or tort done to the plebs by the very existence of a city or state still carries the echo of Augustine's idea that all political life is correlated with the concept of an 'original' sin.

The fundamental question posed by these populist interpretations of radical democratic equality is whether this equality of *plebs* and *populus*, Part and Whole, is functional to the establishment of a new state and a new sovereignty, or whether it has the more anarchic aim of abolishing the division between rulers and ruled. In their interventions on the debate on populism, Žižek and Laclau have argued for the former option. Thus, for instance, Žižek calls the desire for the equalization of the plebs with the people nothing other than the 'totalitarian excess' of radical democracy (Žižek 2009). Laclau thinks of it as the core of a 'populist' construction of the people: 'the *plebs*, whose partial demands are inscribed in the horizon of a fully-fledged totality—a just society which exists only ideally—can aspire to constitute a truly universal *populus* which the actually existing situation negates' (Laclau 2005, 94).[64]

Laclau is the theorist of populism that makes most explicit use of the symbolic idea of representation. For Laclau, the claim to justice inherent in the equalization of *plebs* with *populus* is always already realized in and through

---

[61] For a recent attempt to read populism from a politico-theological perspective informed by Laclau's theory, see (Bergem and Bergem 2019).
[62] (Rancière 1995).
[63] See the discussion in (May 2010; and Chambers 2012).
[64] Rancière has moved to an understanding of equalization that is more an-archic: 'the only remaining title is the anarchic title, the title specific to those who have no more title for governing than they have for being governed. This is what of all things democracy means. Democracy is not a type of constitution, nor a form of society. . . . It is simply the power peculiar to those who have no more entitlements to govern than to submit' (Rancière 2009, 46).

the interpretation given to it by the 'civil' or hegemonic 'sovereign', that is, what Voegelin would call the 'symbolic' representative of the plebs. Laclau's 'populist reason' is an attempt to theorize the 'constituent', and no longer merely 'constituted', role that the symbolic representative plays in a democracy. Taking distance from the purely antinomian constructions of communism, such as the ones found in Badiou and Agamben, Laclau argues that an account of political representation is absolutely essential to achieve what he calls the 'equivalential ruptures' that are constructive of a people and that transform liberal democratic politics into (authentically democratic) populist politics (Laclau 2005, 93). Following very closely Voegelin's analysis of democracy, yet without ever mentioning it, Laclau argues that the fundamental distinction between a liberal democratic politics and a populist democratic politics rests on a difference in their forms of representation. Whereas liberal democracy depends on 'a movement from represented to representative', populist politics depends on a correlative movement 'from representative to represented. The represented *depends on the representative* for the constitution of his or her identity' as a people (Laclau 2005, 158, emphasis mine).

Laclau's central thesis is that a true conception of democracy consists in the construction of a *populus* that becomes unified as a function of the equivalences between diverse social demands of the *plebs*. As is well known, for Laclau these equivalences are constructed, first, *against* an (internal) 'enemy'; second, *under* the name of an 'empty signifier' of justice; and, third, *in* the proper name of a leader (Laclau 2005, 96–97). A social movement is not properly populist unless it adopts the name of its leader: Lenin-ism, Mao-ism, Peron-ism, Trump-ism. This name is what opens the 'immanent' demands of the multiple groups to the 'transcendent singular moment' thanks to which the multiple groups identify to themselves the 'unity of the group with the name of the leader'.[65] Thus, Laclau constructs populism exactly on the same politico-theological opposition between immanent and open society that Voegelin introduces into his discourse on symbolic representation. It is no surprise that Laclau admits that with populist reason 'we are in the situation comparable to that of Hobbes's sovereign' (Laclau 2005, 100). Neither the reference to singularity nor that to Hobbes are accidental in Laclau's

---

[65] 'An assemblage of heterogenous elements kept equivalentially together only by a name is, however, necessarily a singularity. The less a society is kept together by immanent differential mechanisms, the more it depends, for its coherence, on this transcendent, singular moment. But the extreme form of singularity is an individuality. In this way, almost imperceptibly, the equivalential logic leads to singularity, and singularity to an identification of the unity of the group with the name of the leader' (Laclau 2005, 100).

discourse. The former denotes a 'theocratic' and yet nominalist conception of God, very close to Hobbes's theory of divine personation. The claim that the populist leader must rely on personating this singularity in order to become the sovereign representative of the equality of *plebs* and *populus* follows directly from Schmitt's and especially Voegelin's reworking of Catholic and Hobbesian conceptions of political representation.

Like Laclau, Žižek also acknowledges the importance of a Schmittian conception of political representation. 'What *kind of representation should replace* the existing liberal-democratic representative state?' is for him a decisive matter (Žižek 2009, 375, emphasis mine). The distinction between *plebs* and *populus*, between an excluded 'multitude' and a constructed 'people' that has state power, reappears in Žižek's *In Defense of Lost Causes*, and in particular in his critique of Negri's multitude (Žižek 2009, 351–64). Žižek's main contention is that post-Marxist thinkers like Negri have given up on two essentials of Marxism: first, the centrality of class struggle (opting instead for hegemonic identity-politics); second, the conquest of state power (opting instead for social movements in civil society).[66] Žižek rejects Negri's proposal of a constituent power that rules or governs without the intermediary of a constituted state. He sees Negri's Spinozist idea of an 'absolute democracy' as tributary to a mistaken opposition between the 'logic of political representation' tied to the state and the 'logic of expression' tied to the multitude and to social movements (Žižek 2009, 364). For Žižek, a society without representation is an illusion because 'the very flourishing of movements of the multitude always-already had to rely on some *dispositif* of Power which structures and sustains the very space within which they operate.... Today, the movements of gay rights, human rights, and so on, all rely on state apparatuses, which are not only the addressee of their demands, but also provide the framework for their activity (stable civil life)' (Žižek 2009, 371).[67] Žižek is more sanguine about the prospect that such a 'necessary' constituted power take the form of 'the "stronger" (upper-case) Party (as in Communist Party) ... [which] considers the formal procedure of democratic elections secondary as regards the real political dynamics of movements "expressing" their force ... [the Party] does not negotiate with movements, it is a movement transubstantiated into

---

[66] For this claim, see (Butler, Laclau, and Zizek 2000; Laclau 2008; and Žižek 2009, ch. 6).

[67] Žižek is repeating a point that Althusser's reading of Machiavelli had already made in the 1970s, namely, that constituent power is unthinkable outside of its internal relation to constituted power. See (Althusser 2001) and for discussion (Vatter 2004; and Balibar 2008).

the form of political universality, ready to assume full state power, and which, as such, *ne s'autorise que de lui-meme*' (Žižek 2009, 377).

Thus, for Žižek the constituent power of the *plebs* does not stand in need of the constituted power of a republican state, which depends on the authority of law. It need only rely on the constituted power of a one Party-State, which, since it is self-authorized, stands above the law. Following Schmitt's dictum, *protego ergo obligo*, this Party-State will protect the social movements against their 'class enemies' and in this way gain its legitimacy. The state that Žižek defends, therefore, is not the republican one, but the one Party-State whose new pastoral politics is meant to realize Marx's 'dictatorship of the proletariat'. What separates Žižek's idea of communist politics from Stalinism, according to his own lights, is that the 'totalitarian excess of power' accumulated by the one Party-State shall be employed 'on the side of the "part of no-part", not on the side of the hierarchical social order' (Žižek 2009, 379). But this standpoint is basically identical to Voegelin's advocacy of a dictatorial employment of Christianity as 'civil religion' in order to preserve democracy against its internal dissolution occasioned by the adoption of immanentist social movements. The only difference is that Žižek thinks Marxism-Leninism is a better civil religion than Christianity to achieve democracy.

In conclusion, my analysis of the appropriation of Voegelin's politico-theological conception of representation in some of the leading theorists of contemporary populism presents two interesting and perhaps unexpected results. The first result is that it would be a mistake to think that contemporary formations of populism are to be identified with new 'Gnostic' social movements, with the return of a new 'society of saints', as has been typically argued by recent commentators on populism.[68] On the contrary, if my analysis is correct, populist movements represent a climax of sorts of the 'culture wars' unleashed by Christian political theology after World War II as a way to manage the 'enmity' against what it perceives as the disorder and anarchy occasioned by the secularization of Jewish messianic motifs in liberal democracy and its struggle for ever-widening rights.

The second result follows from my claim that the politico-theological interpretations of the Marxist-Leninist tradition articulated by Laclau and Žižek depend on their appropriation of Voegelin's idea of symbolic representation (it is indifferent whether the symbolic representative is personated by the singularity of the Leader—as in Laclau—or by the singularity of the

---

[68] For an example of this trend, see (Müller 2016).

Party, as in Žižek). This claim means that, paradoxically, Voegelin has made it possible for a discourse that used to be associated with 'totalitarianism' (whether this be associated with the Marxist-Leninist tradition or with the Fascist tradition is again indifferent) to be internalized in defence of 'democracy' and, conversely, the very system of electoral liberal democracy comes to occupy the 'totalitarian/gnostic' pole that contemporary populism sets out to combat 'by any means necessary'.

3
Jacques Maritain and Human Rights

Democracy and the universality of human rights

During the second half of the 20th century, democracy came to be associated with the struggle for universal human rights. For some theorists of democracy this development meant having to work out a robust cosmopolitan foundation for human rights.[1] For other post-Marxist democratic theorists it led to ask whether the new politics of human rights was compatible with democracy.[2] According to the recent historiography of the Universal Declaration of Human Rights (UDHR), contemporary political theory took a turn towards cosmopolitanism roughly in the decade of the 1970s when the politics of human rights began to gather traction as a governance mechanism in the emerging neoliberal world order.[3] However, the theoretical connection between democracy and universal human rights had already been established several decades before in the work of the Catholic philosopher Jacques Maritain, who was one of the earliest philosophical proponents of universal human rights, and himself played a non-trivial role as leading intellectual advisor to the drafters of the UDHR.[4] This historico-political constellation suggests the two main questions addressed

---

[1] One thinks of (Habermas 1996) and those theorists who followed his footsteps.

[2] For an exemplary case, see (Brown 1995; 2004). For another example, see (Douzinas 2000).

[3] See (Moyn 2012; 2018b). Much of the interest in post-Rawlsian liberal theory is due to the cosmopolitan turn taken by liberal theories of justice. For some examples, see (Rawls 2001; Pogge 2002; and Benhabib 2011). On some early formulations of cosmopolitanism as a principle of global legal order, see (Held 2010; and Archibugi 2008). For post-Marxist critiques of the new focus on cosmopolitanism based on a politics of universal human rights, see (Negri 2001; Badiou 2003; Hardt 2005; and Douzinas 2007), among others.

[4] For a general discussion of Maritain's role in this Declaration, see (Glendon 2002, ch.5). Moyn argues that 'it was most clearly in early 1942 that Maritain transformed into the philosopher of human rights that he had never been before. In *Natural Law and Human Rights* Maritain took what would be a fateful step for postwar intellectual history as a whole, making the claim that a revival of natural law implies a broad set of pre-political human rights' (Moyn 2010, 94). I show below that the ground for Maritain's turn towards human rights was prepared before 1942, and it had other politico-theological motivations. Moyn is aware of the paradoxical attempt to root human rights in Thomistic natural law, given that most accounts of the emergence of subjective rights date these from Ockham onwards (Tierney 1997), but he does not offer an explanation of why Maritain nevertheless engaged and succeeded in this gambit.

Divine Democracy. Miguel Vatter, Oxford University Press (2021). © Oxford University Press.
DOI: 10.1093/oso/9780190942359.001.0001.

in this chapter. How did *Christian* political theology give the basis for the internal connection between democracy and universal human rights? Furthermore, why did this connection find its expression in a *neoliberal* global legal order?

Understood as a legitimation discourse of the emergent institutional global order, the focus on universal human rights came accompanied with a new and increasing respect afforded to 'world religions' in the liberal public sphere.[5] Additionally, the democratic inflection of the discourse on universal human rights has given a new lease on life to the old category of 'human dignity'. In its recent incarnation, 'dignity' has detached itself from its previous connection to metaphysical or theological conceptions of the human 'person' in order to attach itself to human life as such.[6] These two developments gave rise to two puzzles that retain the interest of political theorists. The first puzzle concerns the relative ease with which, in the last decades, neoliberalism has been coupled with neoconservatism, despite the fact that unleashing the powers of the free market and of individual entrepreneurship do not share, prima facie, much relation to the defence of traditional religious values and the 'sacredness' of life.[7] The second puzzle concerns how the *liberal* effort to provide a cosmopolitan foundation to the discourse of universal human rights became the vector for the development of *postsecular* justifications and critiques of liberal democracy. The political thought of Jacques Maritain remains of interest today because his discussion of universal human rights sheds light on these two puzzles.

Why did 'world religions' become protagonists in the new politics of universal human rights? A cosmopolitan perspective requires that individuals understand themselves first as 'citizens of the world' and then as citizens of a state or members of a nation.[8] It is sometimes claimed that the UDHR, de facto, functions as the 'basic law' of a world civil society.[9] Whoever acts in such a way that they understand themselves as being authorized directly from such a global constitution can be considered a 'world' citizen.[10] Considered

---

[5] On public religions see (Casanova 1994; and Hurd 2017).
[6] On the increasing importance of human dignity in the global legal order, see (McCrudden 2014). On the connection of dignity with democracy, see (Waldron 2015). For a view that connects personalism, dignity, and human rights, see (Esposito 2012). In my opinion the connection between dignity and human rights does not pass through a theory of personalism, not even in Maritain.
[7] For recent discussions of the puzzle see (Cooper 2017; and Brown 2019).
[8] The literature on political cosmopolitanism is enormous. For some recent discussions, see (Appiah 2006; and Nussbaum 2019). For one survey of the current debates on cosmopolitanism and global justice, among many, see (Tan 2010).
[9] See the essays in (Dunoff and Trachtman 2009).
[10] For an overview of the main arguments, see (Brunkhorst 2005; and Thornhill 2018).

in this global-constitutional way, one important normative question arises as to how citizens of nation-states can understand themselves as following directly the 'basic law' of the UDHR. What kind of comprehensive world views afford them an 'overlapping consensus' with the world views of citizens from other nations such that they both understand each other as citizens of this global 'constitution' and thus as 'world citizens'?

Not surprisingly, this difficult question is at times answered by appealing to the supposed 'universalism' associated with 'world religions'.[11] The idea of a 'world religion' is a discursive construct of late modernity, much like the idea of 'world literature'.[12] In their discursive construction, world religions are characterized by the conscious effort to transcend barriers of ethnicity, nationality, class, race, and gender in the name of a common 'human family' or 'brotherhood'. The UDHR contains a reference to 'all members of the human family' in its Preamble, and a reference to 'a spirit of brotherhood' in its Article 1. In her celebrated history of the UDHR, Mary Ann Glendon argued that such language was inserted precisely to fashion a consensus over the Articles on the basis of the various world religious traditions.[13] The basic idea is that whatever in a world religion can appeal to individuals of different races, sexes, ethnicities, nationalities, or classes must overlap with whatever in another world religion functions in the same way. To distil these points of overlap in the form of universal rights is one of the things the drafters of the UDHR were aiming at. On this hypothesis, the very cosmopolitan structure of universal human rights facilitates the re-entry of religions into the national public spheres in order to re-orient their citizens towards their new status as world citizens. In other words, the legitimacy of universal human rights is dependent on a politico-theological

---

[11] For the contested origins of 'world religion' see (Masuzawa 2005). Masuzawa argues that the term emerges as a way to export to other religions the 'universalism' originally ascribed only to Christianity. This occurs less controversially in relation to Buddhism, Hinduism, or even Confucianism, and much more controversially in relation to Islam and Judaism. In general, the question in this early 20th-century debate was whether any given religion had a 'national' substrate or whether it could range across the whole 'world'.

[12] For a critical approach to the world religions paradigm, see (Cotter and Robertson 2016), and with respect to the 'Axial Age' hypothesis, see (Bellah and Joas 2012).

[13] (Glendon 2002, chs. 9,12). Indeed, if one follows Glendon's account, the drafters of the UDHR consciously sought out advice from major representatives of such world religions on what, in these religions, could be seen as offering a support to a charter of universal human rights. This may, of course, simply reflect Glendon's assumption that the idea of world religion can fit under the idea of universalism associated with Christianity. However, one should not discount the fact that, for instance, Sukarno's doctrine of 'Pancasila' and the constituent debates in 1945 in Indonesia also seem to work with the recently developed idea of world religions. For the reference to world religions in non-Christian constitutions, see (Lerner 2013).

approach to these rights. It is not surprising that in the last decade there have been many attempts to show that cosmopolitanism and human rights are not a Eurocentric doctrine, but that their roots are found in all major religious traditions.[14]

The other important normative question raised by cosmopolitan democracy concerns the problem of motivation. Why should someone care about the injustice that happens to another human being thousands of miles away with as much or more passion and 'indignation' than they would experience an injustice done to their fellow compatriot? A few decades ago Henry Shue offered an answer to this question through his reformulation of human rights as a function of 'basic rights'.[15] Theorists like Shue, followed by Thomas Pogge, point out that the indignation with regard to violation of human rights in faraway parts of the world has two mirror components. The first has to do with the fact that human rights violations are always the result of actions or omissions of the nation-states (and of multinational companies) to which these 'compatriots' belong and often support (even if tacitly or passively). Thus, one's national citizenship is directly involved in such violations. This may explain the feelings of 'guilt' felt by those who watch such atrocities at a distance, and the practices of 'naming and shaming' that are linked with the politics of human rights in global civil society. Second, massive violations of human rights often occur to people who have lost their own citizenship, either because they belong to 'failed' states or because their political, indeed democratic aspirations are sacrificed on the altar of other national or ethnic interests. In other words, the object of sympathy and indignation that motivates a world citizen is not simply the suffering of 'precarious life' but, more specifically, the frustration of the *democratic aspirations* of this life.[16] What motivates a national citizen to go against the 'national self-interest' of his or her compatriots and uphold the 'basic rights' of strangers in faraway lands is ultimately the belief that this stranger is the bearer of a (future) *democratic* life. That is why Shue insists that 'basic rights' cannot only be rights to security and subsistence, but must also entail some minimal political rights to 'participation and movement', that is, must entail something like a 'right to democracy'. On this hypothesis, the very cosmopolitan structure of universal

---

[14] An example among many is (Sen 2007), but the problem also explains why Rawls was keen to tolerate, within one 'law of peoples', also 'decent' yet not liberal societies. For an introduction to the role of religion in human rights discourse, see (Witte and Green 2011).

[15] See the criticism of the 'priority to compatriots' thesis in (Shue 1980, 132ff). For a defence of human rights from an ethnocentric perspective, see (Rorty 2001).

[16] On the idea of 'precarious life' and human rights violations see (Butler 2006).

human rights requires that 'life itself' be endowed with a function of legitimation of these rights.[17]

To sum up, one can say that the new democratic cosmopolitanism based on universal human rights depends at some basic level on the shared belief in the intrinsic value of human life or on the sacredness of life itself.[18] Already Arendt thought that the emergence of liberal, secular society characterized by individual rights and free markets was somehow deeply connected with the principle of the sacredness of life. 'The reason why life asserted itself as the ultimate point of reference in the modern age and has remained the highest good of modern society is that the modern reversal operated within the fabric of a Christian society whose fundamental belief in the sacredness of life has survived, and has even remained completely unshaken by, secularization and the general decline of the Christian faith' (Arendt 1958, 314). World religions function as sources of legitimacy for the universality of human rights insofar as they are believed to share, in one form or another, the intuition that human life as such is sacred. This sacred life is also biopolitical in the sense that it grants to every human being, merely in virtue of their humanity, a minimum of constituent power, a law-making power. This insight is nowadays formulated through the idea that universal human rights entail a basic 'right to democracy'.[19]

In this chapter I claim that Maritain's articulation of democracy and universal human rights is perhaps the first theoretical formulation to join together elements of Christian political theology with elements of biopolitics. Maritain explicitly connects universal human rights and the sacredness of life in his explanation of their legitimacy: 'The worth of the person, his liberty, his rights arise from the order of the naturally sacred things.... A person possesses absolute dignity because he is in direct relationship with the absolute.... His spiritual fatherland consists of the entire

---

[17] For life itself as basis of legitimacy, see (Rose 2007; and Fassin 2009). It is indicative that, in order to explain the universal appeal to the UDHR, Glendon cites the following words from a Human Rights Watch/Asia representative: 'Whatever else may separate them, human beings belong to *a single biological species*, the simplest and most fundamental commonality before which the significance of human differences quickly fades.... The *great religious traditions ... take for granted the principle of common humanity*. Islam, Buddhism, Catholicism, Protestantism, Judaism, Hinduism, Taoism, and most of their variants share a recognition of the human condition' (Glendon 2002, 233). Here one can clearly see both the politico-theological and the bio-political approach to the universality of human rights.

[18] Dworkin places this principle on a par with the liberal belief in the dignity of an autonomous life, and does so precisely in order to achieve an overlapping consensus between believers and nonbelievers (Dworkin 1994, 82–83, 90–91).

[19] I refer here to the kinds of arguments found in (Forst 2010; and Benhabib 2011).

order of things which have absolute value, and which reflect, in some way, an Absolute superior to the world and which draw our life towards this Absolute' (Maritain 2011, 67). This connection of human rights with political theology in Maritain's thought may appear paradoxical at first sight if one reduces the discourse of political theology to the thought of Carl Schmitt.[20] For Schmitt expressed mere disdain for universal human rights, seeing them as a tool for the imposition of a new post–World War II Anglo-American form of empire.[21] But the apparent paradox expressed in the idea of a political theology of universal human rights vanishes as soon as one acknowledges the possibility that the discourse of political theology took a 'democratic turn' in the 1930s. Maritain's formulation of the struggle of democracy against totalitarianism as a function of the establishment of a doctrine of the universality of human rights exemplifies such a 'democratic turn' of Christian political theology.

The enabling function of religion in the liberal democratic public sphere organized around the legitimacy of universal human rights is often missed or discounted by both contemporary liberal political philosophers and their post-Marxist critics. Mainstream liberal political philosophy believes that it is possible to justify and implement the UDHR in a new global legal order without recourse to the discourse of political theology, whereas much post-Marxist theory employs aspects of Schmitt's political theology in order to cast into question the universalist claims of global human rights discourse. Neither standpoint is particularly helpful to understand the politico-theological foundation of the neoliberal and neoconservative implementations of universal human rights that was brought to light in the recent critical historiography of human rights. This is one reason why it is important to reconsider Maritain's politico-theological foundation of universal human rights.

---

[20] For another discussion of political theology in Maritain and Schmitt see (McCormick 2013). McCormick points out that Maritain distinguished the 'German', namely, Schmittian idea of political theology from his own 'French' 'théologie politique' already in (Maritain 1968), but he fails to connect this political theology to Maritain's discourse on human rights. Instead, McCormick believes that Maritain's political theology simply refers to the traditional Catholic project of determining the 'theological' or 'spiritual' value of politics, while acknowledging the Aristotelian-Thomist point that politics also has a 'natural', as opposed to super-natural, ground that can be analysed in terms of 'political philosophy' rather than political theology. According to McCormick, 'Schmitt's political theology ... grants politics no such autonomy from theology' (McCormick 2013, 189), which betrays a confusion about the meaning Schmitt's political theology.

[21] See the discussion of this point in (Habermas 2001a; and Hardt and Negri 2000).

Already before his 1942 book *The Rights of Man and Natural Law*, Maritain prepared the groundwork for a democratic conception of universal human rights by putting forward two fundamental theses. The first thesis equates sovereignty with the condition of possibility of totalitarianism. Against this backdrop, his task becomes that of explaining how universal human rights offer the condition of possibility of a cosmopolitan democracy beyond the sovereignty of the nation-state. I shall argue that this thesis allows his approach to the universalism of human rights to waylay Shue's problem of the priority of compatriots. The second thesis has to do with Maritain's attempt to ground universal human rights in natural law. This move is often dismissed as a lapse into a 'metaphysical, not political' justification of human rights. Properly understood, however, Maritain's understanding of natural law means that the normative order based on universal human rights is the true figure of a 'providential' order of history. I argue that this reference to providence contains a theory of liberal governmentality that explains the sense in which the implementation of the UDHR fits within both neoliberal and neoconservative ideals of governance.

Multitude versus Empire:
A motif of Christian political theology

In 1939, Jacques Maritain wrote the pamphlet *The Twilight of Civilization*. It is one of the first attempts to understand philosophically the nature of totalitarian governments ruling both in Italy and Germany and in the Soviet Union.[22] Maritain holds the thesis of the structural equivalence between Stalinism and Nazi-Fascism because both show an anti-Christian essence.[23] What is anti-Christian about these totalitarian regimes and ideologies is

---

[22] For the prehistory of Maritain's adoption of the opposition of democracy and totalitarianism from Waldemar Gurian and his early engagement against Schmitt's political theology, see (Chappel 2011). Chappel plays down the democratic character of Maritain's Christian political theology, emphasizing instead its 'personalist' dimension. See below for my contrary view.

[23] (Maritain 1943, 17–26). For the extended argument, see (Maritain 1939). 'Our time offers to homicidal demons unheard-of feasts. Stalin has given them the kulaks; Hitler has given them the Jews. And each of them has given them Christians. The vast outcry which rises from the concentration camps is not perceptible to our ears, but it penetrates the hidden fibers of the life of the world and tears these apart' (Maritain 1939, 168). Maritain mentions explicitly 'one of the most intelligent theoreticians of National Socialism, Carl Schmitt' and his definition of the political as 'the relationship with the friend against the enemy' (ibid., 162).

not only their 'materialist' rejection of the spiritual roots of the human person. For, after all, these ideologies are also 'spiritual' in the sense that they follow the 'spirit of the world' as opposed to believing in the 'spirit of Christ' (Maritain 1939, 166–67). Rather, what is anti-Christian about them is that both reject 'a *political* ideal of brotherly friendship' (Maritain 1943, 32, emphasis mine). It is only because totalitarian regimes reject this ideal of fraternity, which is *both* a Christian *and* a political ideal, that they can turn politics into its own religion, and the political leader into a god.

For Maritain, totalitarian ideology has two distinct roots. The first root is an 'existential' conception of humanism.[24] Reprising ideas that he had formulated a few years before in *Integral Humanism*,[25] Maritain rejects an 'anthropocentric' or existentialist conception of the human being, which he defines as the idea of 'human nature as closed in upon itself or absolutely self-sufficient' (Maritain 1943, 11). To this 'closure' of the human being onto itself, Maritain opposes the idea 'of an *open* human nature and of an *open* reason' open to the Christian Gospel and to what is 'suprarational' (Maritain 1943, 5). Like Voegelin, Maritain made an early use of the Bergsonian distinction between open and closed societies, employing the adjective of a 'closed' society to describe, essentially, the idea of reason and society worked out by the Enlightenment, what Charles Taylor and John Milbank now call the 'immanent frame' of Modernity.

On this picture, Fascist and Nazi totalitarian ideologies are an 'irrationalist' reaction against the modern closure of reason onto itself (Maritain 1943, 7). They are 'irrationalist' because, in order to oppose the lack of openness to authentic religion found in late modern rationalism, Fascist and Nazi ideologies rely on false idols drawn from myth and racial ideologies. Stalinism, on the other hand, is a fruit of the closure of modern reason because it claims that 'man alone and by himself alone achieves his destiny and works out his salvation' (Maritain 1943, 10). This is analogous to Voegelin's characterization of Modernity as 'Gnosticism'. Maritain and Voegelin both reject as 'Gnostic' the kind of radical humanism in Marx which understands that the full development of the human being as a 'social species-being' will make religious belief in a supranatural God superfluous.

---

[24] Maritain's standpoint turns on a recovery of an alternative sense of humanism than the one given by early existentialists according to which humanism is defined 'in such a way as to exclude from it all that is ordained to the supra-human and as to forswear all considerations of transcendence' (Maritain 1943, 4).

[25] See (Maritain 1968), which first appeared in 1936.

Against both anti-Modern irrationalism and Modern rationalism, Maritain proposes his own position of 'Christian humanism'. This humanism is characterized by a *rational* openness to the suprarational (viz., God as presented in the Gospel) (Maritain 1943, 12). Maritain calls this a 'humanism of the Incarnation', and he understands it as the only way in which to bring together 'the vertical movement towards eternal life . . . and the horizontal movement through which are revealed progressively the substance and creative forces of man in history' (Maritain 1943, 13). This claim is particularly interesting because it confirms that Maritain does not seek to oppose the City of God against the City of Man, but to bring them together in a productive, political, and historical relation, despite their radical difference. This is Maritain's step beyond Augustine.

By 1939, however, Maritain also developed the view that totalitarian ideologies exhibit a second root: totalitarian societies are 'closed societies' not simply because they reject God's transcendence, but because of the way in which they construct a people as a 'collective body, which, attracting to itself all human substance, would claim for itself the power of achieving the divine call of man' (Maritain 1943, 35). For Maritain, totalitarian politics are nothing but the politics of 'the Pagan Empire, as the Apocalypse describes it; and this is the Empire against which Christ took His stand' (Maritain 1943, 35). A politics that is closed to God is a politics in which a people divinizes its political leader, just like the Romans did with their emperors. Maritain believed this pagan practice of apotheosis re-emerged in the 1930s in Europe with Mussolini, Hitler, and Stalin. Conversely, and here is the real novelty of this text, Maritain thinks that to fight successfully against such inner-worldly political religions, the rebellion of Jesus against the Roman Empire must be given a new political form. Only a Christian *political* theology can defeat the political theology of totalitarian regimes. Thus, Maritain argues that the Gospel's rejection of politics is a qualified rejection of politics; it is a rejection of 'politics only *in so far as* it claims to regulate entirely by itself alone the lives and destinies of men and to set itself apart from the truth of God Who has made man according to His image' (Maritain 1943, 34, emphasis mine).[26]

Peterson's critique of Schmitt's political theology is the undisclosed source of Maritain's interpretation of totalitarian regimes as inner-worldly political

---

[26] For an early defence of Christian political theology in very similar terms, but without referring to Schmitt or Maritain, see (Schall 1975).

religions.²⁷ Maritain adopts Peterson's critique of Schmitt's political theology and of sovereignty, but unlike Peterson he argues for the need to develop a *Christian* political theology without sovereignty. This would be a Christian politics that stands for democracy and against the return of Empire. By 1939, Maritain identifies totalitarian political theology with a particular politicization of enmity which he associates with 'one of the most intelligent theorists of National Socialism, Carl Schmitt' and his concept of the political: 'for the politics of the Pagan Empire, hatred of the enemy, within and without, on the part of the community, flows concurrently and from the same impulse as love for the community itself' (Maritain 1943, 35–36). Maritain tacitly rejects Schmitt's claim that the concept of the political can only mean the application of the distinction between friend and enemy because 'if Christ is the Saviour of the world then politics, too, can be saved' (Maritain 1943, 36).²⁸

Maritain is trying to bring together a (redeemed) 'concept of the political' together with the Christian Gospel into a new constellation. He was not taken in by Schmitt's unconvincing rationalization according to which Jesus's commandment to love one's 'enemy' referred to a private conception of enmity, not to the political enemy or *hostis*. For Maritain, pagan politics is a politics based on the 'mystical law' that 'one should really love *one's own* only to the extent that one hates *the others*' (Maritain 1943, 38). But the new 'law' of Christian politics, which shall defeat the pagan Empire, is based on the belief that 'love has primacy over hate and that love radiates out equally to all men, since all men are children of God' (Maritain 1943, 39).²⁹ The point is that for Maritain it is possible to constitute a new politics that does not have the friend/enemy distinction as its primary law. This Christian politics is an inner-worldly politics of universal 'love' that is radically cosmopolitan, since it is directed to 'all men'; and is also radically 'democratic' because it assumes as true the Pauline theologeme that, through faith in Christ, 'all men are sons of God' (Galatians 3:26, Romans 8:14).³⁰

---

²⁷ Maritain wrote the preface to the French translation of Peterson's treatise *The Church from Jews and Gentiles* in 1935 (Crane 2010, 46).

²⁸ In an interesting footnote in *Twilight*, Maritain criticizes an essay by Pierre Klossowski of 1938 in which Klossowski accepts as true the opposition between Schmitt's conception of the political and the Gospel.

²⁹ There follow citations from John 13:34; Matthew 22:39 and 7:40; and Luke 10:29 having the same 'commandment' in mind: 'love thy enemy'.

³⁰ The same year in which Maritain publishes *Twilight of Civilization* he also publishes in New York, in French and English editions, a presentation of Saint Paul's thought: *La pensée de Saint Paul, textes choisis et présentés* (New York: Éditions de la Maison française, 1941) and *The Living Thoughts of Saint Paul*. Tr. Harry Lorin Binsse (New York: Longmans, Green, 1941). In the concluding section I address the remarkable similarity between Maritain's cosmopolitan standpoint and the kind of universalism that Badiou has recently tried to formulate in relation to Saint Paul's theology.

The last chapter of the 1939 book is entitled "Christianity and Democracy". In it Maritain announces that this new Christian political theology should take the form of a 'Christian democracy' (Maritain 1943, 54).[31] At the eve of World War II, Maritain believes that it is no longer in Europe, but in the United States where 'Christian democracy' finds its destiny.[32] The United States is the beacon of the struggle against totalitarian regimes because it defends democracy on the basis of Christian values (Maritain 1943, 53). In this context Maritain quotes Walter Lippmann, an early proponent of what is now called neoliberalism, from a 1939 article in the *New York Herald* in which he calls for 'the reconciliation ... between patriotic freedom, democracy and religion' (Maritain 1943, 55). Lippmann's point is that this reconciliation is only possible if one can '*recognize religion as the source of democracy*' (Maritain 1943, emphasis mine).[33] *Twilight of Civilization* ends by sketching what would become the program of his most famous work of political theory, *Man and the State*: to work out a 'political philosophy which must be called democratic' that is equidistant from Right and Left (Maritain 1943, 57). To show the rootedness of cosmopolitan democracy in a Christian political theology in the form of a doctrine of universal human rights: this becomes Maritain's overriding philosophical project. This internal connection between democracy and religion bridged by a doctrine of universal human rights is the crucial innovation that will later allow for the overlap between neoconservatism and neoliberalism with respect to the function of universal human rights in post–World War II Western liberal democracies.[34]

Christian democracy and the critique of sovereignty

Among interpreters of Maritain's thought there exists a debate as to how one ought to understand the internal connection between Christianity and democracy. The traditional view is that, once in the United States, Maritain

---

[31] His famous text, *Christianity and Democracy*, is from 1943 (Maritain 2011).
[32] Although Maritain could not have foreseen that his proposed reconciliation between democracy and Christianity would take the neoliberal and evangelical forms that it did in the United States, beginning in the early 1980s. See here (Connolly 2008).
[33] On Lippmann and the early stages of neoliberal thought, see (Foucault 2008; and Slobodian 2018).
[34] For this history in postwar Europe, see now (Duranti 2017). In this sense, the approach to the question of the compatibility or incompatibility of democracy with the 'world's religious systems' popularized by theorists of democratization like Alfred Stepan and Juan Linz remains entirely within the framework developed by Maritain. See (Stepan 2000).

folded the concepts of democracy and human rights into his pre-existent discourse on Christian personalism.[35] On this view, modern democracy is secularized Christianity. By contrast, Daniele Lorenzini has recently advanced the argument that, while in the United States, Maritain's discovery of the American republican basis to human rights allowed him to gain a distance from his previous orthodox approach to Christian political philosophy, to its doctrine of personalism and, even, to his problematic interpretation of Judaism.[36] Although I am sympathetic to the latter approach, in my opinion Maritain ultimately arrives to a thinking of democracy that is relatively autonomous from Christian personalism because of the systematic need to fashion an anti-Schmittian Christian political theology characterized by the *absence of sovereignty*. This requires him to adopt a doctrine of human rights as a discourse that contrasts the sovereignty of the modern nation-state and *a fortiori* rejects the forms of nationalism and anti-Semitism congenital with it.

In 1939 Maritain is unable or unwilling to give more precise contours to his conception of Christian democracy, and in particular to the connection with what would become the system of Christian Democratic political parties that ruled for great part of the post–World War II period in many parts of Western Europe as well as in Latin America.[37] What Maritain meant then by 'Christian democracy' and what would become the de facto politics of the Christian Democratic political movement and political parties are not the same things. Maritain's Christian democracy, in fact, is a far more flexible ideological construction, because its two fundamental pillars are, first, the recognition of 'inalienable rights of the human person'; and, second, the principle that 'those invested with authority' are not vicars of God, but 'vicars of the multitude, as Thomas Aquinas said' (Maritain 1975, 98). It is not difficult to see why, only a few years later, Maritain could envision the drafting of a "Universal Declaration of the Rights of Man" as the climax of his new Christian political theology of the Multitude, a sort of new 'gospel'

---

[35] For an excellent overview, see (Schall 1981). For critical interpretations of personalism in Maritain see (Moyn 2010; Deweer 2013; and Esposito 2012; 2015a).

[36] See (Lorenzini 2012). Lorenzini argues that by 1939 Maritain 'abandons' the 'traditional Catholic teaching on natural law and the rights of the human person ... [as] a way of reaffirming the exclusive authority of the Catholic Church ... [instead] arguing that the inalienable human rights that stem from natural law coincide with the rights defined in the eighteenth century during the American and French Revolutions' (Lorenzini 2018, 537).

[37] For the different reception of the human rights agenda in Western Christian Democracy see the indications found in (Moyn 2015; and Invernizzi-Accetti 2018). For Christian Democracy in Latin America, see (Mainwaring and Scully 2003); and globally, see (Shepherd 2009).

that could serve as the basis for the struggle against totalitarian, authoritarian, Marxist-Leninist and Maoist politics.[38]

Maritain's Christian political theology depends on the opposition of the multitude against the sovereignty of the state, a thought that he ascribes to Thomas Aquinas's political theory. The main thesis of *Man and the State* is that 'political philosophy must get rid of the word as well as the concept of sovereignty' because the latter is 'intrinsically wrong' (Maritain 1951, 29). The error contained in the concept of sovereignty consists in thinking that the legislative authority in a society is an *ab-solute* authority, something entirely separate from the political body and standing *over and above it*, as if 'the sovereign . . . transcends the political whole just as God transcends the cosmos' (Maritain 1951, 34); as if he were 'a full-dress political image of God' (Maritain 1951, 37). Sovereignty is entirely the result of a false political theology.

Maritain argues that the concept of sovereignty presents a false image of the nature of the political body. The concept of sovereignty has two components that come to stand in opposition with one another. According to the first component, sovereignty posits that the political body or society possesses a natural right to govern itself, and that this natural right is exercised by a delegated authority or representative. This is, roughly, the medieval understanding of sovereignty. However, the second component of the concept of sovereignty, which emerges in early modernity with Bodin and Hobbes, turns itself against the first component. With Bodin, sovereignty becomes the 'contradictory' notion that the supreme authority in society, that power which has 'superiority' in matters of right, is an *ab-solute* authority, entirely separate from the political body and standing *over and above it*. The modelling of jurisdictional authority on the (pseudo-)Aristotelian depiction of the separateness of God is what Maritain, like Peterson and Voegelin, attacks as 'political theology'.

---

[38] Moyn argues that the new 'gospel' of universal human rights first took root in the form of struggles for national liberation and the extension of independence and social welfare to ex-colonies of the European and British empires. Thus, for him the first form of cosmopolitan democracy was a variant of nationalism. Although I do not disagree with this claim, it seems to downplay the crucial role played by new political interpretations given to world religions in the different national contexts of anti-colonial struggle. This politico-theological foundation of the UDHR is far from exhausted even in the second, post-nationalist implementation of the cosmopolitanism of universal human rights, as I argue below. In any case, the use of nationalism to put an end to the reality of Empire is, arguably, one of the oldest strategy employed by the medieval Christian Church in order to establish its hold on secular powers.

Maritain's standpoint is therefore explicitly anti-Schmittian, and, given what I argue in the first chapter, it comes as no surprise that Maritain situates himself in the lineage of Laski's pluralism, against whom Schmitt had thundered already in *The Concept of the Political*.[39] The Schmittian construal of Christian political theology is rejected by Maritain because it is based on a false conception of the separation of the state from society, as if these were two separate entities analogous to the separation between God and the cosmos. For Maritain, the human body politic is a whole, and it is deprived of sovereignty. The latter belongs solely to God. The human political body merely has the right to autonomy, to self-rule. The state, as a part of this body politic, is not ab-solute with respect to the whole body but functions as its 'instrument', whose primary purpose is that of establishing the rule of law or constitutionalism (Maritain 1951, 12–13).[40]

Maritain denies precisely the claim of Schmittian political theology according to which *only the single representative of the community* (be it a king, pope, emperor, or president) is considered to be the vicar of God, making possible a transposition from God's sovereignty to human sovereignty. 'There is *no valid use* of the concept of sovereignty. Because, in the last analysis, no earthly power is image of God and deputy of God. God is the very source of the authority with which the people invest those men or agencies, but they are not vicars of God. They are vicars of the people; then they cannot be divided from the people by any superior essential property' (Maritain 1951, 50). The relation of power between God and the people is not mediated by 'representatives', as if these representatives were the 'Sons' of God. Maritain gives a democratic reading to the fundamental notion of the vicariate in the sense of a political representation: 'the very right of the people to rule themselves is exercised by the officials whom the people have chosen' (Maritain 1951, 130). If kings and princes are vicars, they are so only as images or representatives *of the people*, not of God. The faith in Jesus as Christ, so Maritain's

---

[39] In his critique of sovereignty in *Man and the State* Maritain cites (Laski 1968).
[40] For Maritain this 'instrumentalist' theory of the state is 'the genuinely political notion of the state' (Maritain 1951, 13). At the same time, Maritain understands his rejection of the absoluteness of the state as a rejection of Hegel, who is the 'prophet and theologian of the totalitarian and divinized state' (ibid., 17). In perfect consonance with the medieval conception of the political, Maritain asserts that 'the concrete function of the state—its principal function—is to ensure the legal order and the enforcement of the law. But the state is not the law' (ibid.). Maritain, though, does not deal with the problem of application, which is what leads medieval political thought in the direction of sovereignty, as I discuss in the next chapter. Another point to consider is the important connection between Maritain's defence of the subsidiarity of the state and the Schmittian idea of sovereignty, as shown in (Cristi 2000a; 2000b).

reading of a particularly complex passage of Saint Paul's Romans 13, turns every believer into an equal 'son of God'. Thus, the authority to rule comes down from God to all people equally, to *all of his sons*, and not directly to the monarchic head who in Persian-Hellenistic fashion thinks of themselves as the only 'Son' of God. I shall call this Maritain's *charismatic* conception of democratic authority.[41]

Maritain's Christian political theology takes up several motifs from the Hebrew political tradition precisely because it considers that human sovereignty, as a political 'image' of God, as the sacralization of worldly power, is a form of idolatry.[42] Maritain's starting point is that no human being or human institution has 'by virtue of its own nature a right to govern' (Maritain 1951, 43). Society is therefore composed of free (undominated) human beings. The right to govern or rule comes to a part of society, i.e. government, only on condition that this part be at the 'service of the common good', that is, the good of society as a whole (Maritain 1951, 44). This common good is related to justice, and thus is ultimately rooted in natural law, and it is always mediated by God's gift of rule to the people as a whole. Once the people receive charismatic authority, they govern themselves always by way of establishing the political body as a legal corporation. Society is a legal order before being a political unity; society is law before becoming a state.[43] This feature of medieval political and social thought is expressed by Isidore of Seville's neo-Ciceronian definition of law: *lex est constitutio populi*. This 'common' or 'customary' or 'ancient' legal order is the very 'common good' that elected representatives must guard as their highest duty. It in this context, that Maritain cites Lincoln's formula for democracy (Maritain 1951, 25). Thus, Maritain identified a direct relation between the medieval Christian understanding of *ascending* representation and Lincoln's 'government of the people, by the people, for the people'. A few years later, as discussed previously, Voegelin offered a reading of Lincoln's formula based on a *descending* conception of representation.[44]

---

[41] For the Christian reception of the Jewish idea of charismatic leadership, see (Hengel 1968).

[42] However, Maritain would deny other doctrines that are crucial for the Jewish tradition of political thought. For instance, he would reject Philo's claim according to which Moses offers a mediation between God and human beings, permitting the *homoiosis* of human beings with God by way of their reason (*logos*). For Maritain, instead, Moses is simply a vicar of the Jewish people, not of God (Maritain 1951, 138). For a general reflection on the employment of Jewish motifs in Christian political thought see now (Yelle 2015).

[43] For an overview of medieval ideas on law, see (Grossi 2004). I discuss medieval constitutionalism in more detail in the next chapter.

[44] Maritain gave this reading of Lincoln's dictum already in (Maritain 1944).

However, as Maritain admits, the authority to rule itself comes to the people from *outside* of their political body, from a transcendent source, in the form of a 'gift of rule' from God understood as 'Author of nature' (Maritain 1951, 127). For Maritain, therefore, democracy is dependent on divine providence. Democracy depends on the grace of God as Creator of nature. Taking up a point from Maimonides, Maritain argues that the government of God is visible in the natural order of things, more specifically, in the fact that all rulers must rule according to natural law or justice if they wish their government to last. Thus, even in Maritain the problem of government comes to stand higher than the principle of the rule of law. As I discuss next, this priority of government is ultimately expressed in his doctrine of universal human rights as the content of natural law.

In sum, it is not difficult to find traces of the Hebrew Republic model in Maritain's political thought, in which theocracy connects to democracy through the exclusion of sovereignty from the political body, but they are encased within a Thomistic understanding of the separate functions of state and church, and within a Thomistic reading of divine providence, that brings back the problem of governmentality. This may explain why Maritain's turn to medieval constitutionalism fits in very nicely both with neoconservative ideologies of the subsidiary character of the political state, as well as with the neoliberal ideologies that see the essence of liberty in preserving the autonomy of the economical and of the legal sphere from the interventions and planning of the political state.

Christian democracy in Maritain is therefore *both charismatic and constitutional.* As he discusses at length in *Man and the State*, the politics of universal human rights can only be achieved by the efforts of 'prophetic' social and political actors who struggle for the democratic representation of the multitudes without and against political sovereignty.[45] For Maritain, this struggle must be combined with the establishment of a global legal order that is effectively supra-national and imposes a neo-medieval rule of law without absolute sovereigns. This new conception of cosmopolitan democracy is dependent on a *democratic* 'gift' that God extends to all peoples in virtue of His being the Creator of nature. For him, this grace or gift of democratic rule, therefore, is visible in two theatres of international relations. First, it is visible

---

[45] Maritain's conception of prophetic democratic actors who struggle for human rights against national governments seems to anticipate the rise of NGOs like Amnesty International or Médecins Sans Frontières. In this sense, Maritain is the most important precursor of the turn to human rights in the French *nouveaux philosophes*. On this theme, see (Whyte 2012).

in the struggle for self-government and independence (struggle for democracy) of all peoples in the world, with special emphasis on anti-colonial and anti-imperial struggles of liberation. Second, and much more important, the democratic grace of God must be visible in the workings of nature itself, more specifically, in the fact that all governments are forced, of necessity, to govern according to natural law or justice. The embodiment of natural law are universal human rights. A global legal order based on universal human rights brings together natural necessity with human freedom in a way that can only be made sense of by appealing to divine providence. If such an interpretation of Maritain's democratic political theology is correct, then it may be necessary to revise the claim in the recent critical historiography of human rights according to which there is a fundamental opposition between a first wave of human rights politics centred on the nationalist struggles for independence and anti-colonialism, and a second wave of the politics of human rights that takes a neoliberal form.[46]

Democracy and divine providence: Why universal human rights need natural law

Maritain attacks the political theology of sovereignty centred on the figure of the king as vicar of God in order to propose a political theology of democracy based on the divine gift of rule distributed evenly to the multitudes. But the connection between democracy and universal human rights passes through his interpretation of natural law. As in Aquinas, natural law is understood to be the reflection in human reason of the divine law. In the recent literature on the philosophical foundations of universal human rights, Maritain's foundational strategy has seriously fallen out of favour.[47] In part, this is due to a commonly shared belief by proponents of the Rawlsian 'political, not metaphysical' view of human rights that if the claim to universality of human rights is given a Christian theological foundation, then it will run afoul with the reality of value and cultural pluralism. No theological foundation of human rights consequently can be used in order to establish the UDHR as the centrepiece of a global or cosmopolitan understanding of public reason.[48]

---

[46] For this opposition, see (Moyn 2018c; and Whyte 2018).
[47] Somewhat sympathetic to aspects of Maritain's natural law foundation of human rights are (Donnelly 1982; and Tasioulas 2011).
[48] For an interesting discussion of the political versus the natural-law views, see now (Valentini 2012).

On another front, today many advocates of cosmopolitan democracy prefer to adopt Kelsen's legal positivist route and identify the UDHR as a 'basic law' for a (coming) global civil society.[49]

For these prevalent views, Maritain's attempt to offer a metaphysical or philosophical foundation to human rights is to misunderstand what the UDHR really is, and is at best a counterproductive strategy. However, the generally accepted definition of universal human rights is that they are rights that ought to be recognized and respected in all human beings simply in virtue of 'being human'. In other words, belief in the universality of human rights all too easily relies somewhere down the line on the assumption that there exists a common 'human nature' or 'humanity' that underlies the variety of cultural identities and values that individuals or peoples adopt during the course of their histories. It is this widespread intuition that accounts for why the identification of the UDHR with a new form of 'natural law' persists in the literature.[50]

Additionally, Maritain himself seems to have anticipated the 'political view' of human rights for he did not think that the UDHR required a 'philosophical' foundation. As he said in a speech to the UNESCO Second General Conference of 1947, the aim was to achieve a consensus 'not on common speculative notions, but on common practical notions, not on the affirmation of the same conception of the world, man, and knowledge, but on the affirmation of the same set of convictions governing action.... Assuming they both believe in a democratic charter, a Christian and a rationalist will, nevertheless, give justifications incompatible with each other, justifications to which their souls, minds, and blood are committed, and over which they will fight.... They remain, however, in agreement on the practical affirmation of that charter, and they can formulate together common principles of action'.[51] This is as clear a statement of a 'political, not metaphysical' approach to the UDHR as any available today. Indeed, the entire debate on whether an 'overlapping consensus' should be achieved on a minimalist or maximalist list of universal human rights falls entirely within the perspective opened

---

[49] For example, see (Lafont 2015). For a discussion of the varieties of foundational and anti-foundational strategies for universal human rights, see (Parekh 2008).

[50] See (Griffin 2008; and Tasioulas 2013). For a critique of this natural law assumption, see (Moyn 2018a). The so-called Asian values debate also gives rise to a discussion on a common underlying humanity that is not culture-specific. See (Langlois 2001).

[51] (Maritain 1951, 77–79). See the discussion on this strategy in (Munro 2003). But Munro distinguishes Maritain's 'political, not metaphysical' grounding of human rights from his foundation of these on his doctrine of natural law. Munro misses the link between the politics of human rights and the role played by the appeal to divine providence in Maritain.

up in Maritain's quotation.⁵² So the real question is the following: given that Maritain already had a conception of the system of universal human rights that is 'political, not metaphysical', why did he still think it of essential importance to pursue their 'foundation' in natural law and in a concept of divine providence?

My hypothesis is that Maritain's interest in finding a connection between human reason and divine law through a doctrine of natural law (or human rights) that is the functional analogon of a doctrine of divine Providence or divine Government is not a lapse back into 'metaphysics'. Rather, it is *part and parcel* of a 'political, not metaphysical' understanding of universal rights. To see why, it is important to recall that, within the discourse of political theology initiated by Schmitt and Peterson, 'divine providence' refers to the problem of God's *existence* in the human world of history and politics; it is not an attribute of God's essence.⁵³ The discourse on divine providence, in other words, is an answer to how human beings can come to know God *despite* the fact that His essence or truth remains shrouded in 'mystery' and is unattainable by human reason. Now, Maritain advances the thesis that God rules over the human world through His Providence in two distinct forms. First, God provides every human being with a modicum of constituent power: this is His universal 'gift' of democratic rule. Second, God providentially *disposes* political, economic, and social matters as a necessary order of human things, in such a way that all people will eventually be able to enjoy the gift of democracy. Maritain identifies this disposition or, in more current terminology, this dispositive with the global normative order of universal human rights.

Christian political theology posits that God's rule, the kingdom of Christ, is the opposite of the kingdom of the world in which humans rule over one another.⁵⁴ Since human rule is the rule of a sovereign power, it follows that God's rule has to be, simultaneously, *destructive of state sovereignty* while at the same time providing for the *security and development* of the life of human beings and the recognition of their dignity. For Maritain, the only form of rule that is both anti-sovereign and yet protects human dignity and life is a global system of legal and economical rules. These rules are not positive legal rules established by sovereign states, but, rather, they function as if they were 'natural laws' that steer sovereign governments, behind their backs and even

---

⁵² I refer to the discussion in (Cohen 2006; and Forst 2010; 2011).
⁵³ See the discussion of being versus acting in relation to the Godhead in (Agamben 2011, 53–67).
⁵⁴ For Maritain, as discussed above, 'closed' or 'totalitarian' societies are those that deny this distinction, whereas 'open' or 'democratic' societies are those that accept it.

against their sovereign wills, towards policies that will implement the universality of human rights.[55]

Maritain leaves no doubts that this kind of deduction of human rights from natural law is entirely dependent on the belief in divine providence: natural law is 'looked upon in an ontological perspective as conveying through the essential structures and requirements of created nature the wisdom of the Author of Being' (Maritain 1951, 84). Like Taylor today, Maritain expressly rejects the foundation of rights in the early modern interpretations of natural law found in Grotius, Pufendorf, and Hobbes. For this way of thinking about natural law leads straight to a theory of sovereignty, which, as he shows in *Man and the State*, is the antithesis of universal human rights. That is why human rights must be interpreted in accordance with an idea of natural law as divine providence. Providence is the belief in a natural law of created natures or essences which contains what is good for each creature, and from which derive the rights or liberties of each creature. The 'nature' or 'natural law' which corresponds to the essence of each created being is called by Maritain the '*normality of its functioning*, the proper way in which, by reason of its specific structure and specific ends, it "should" achieve fulness of being' (Maritain 1951, 84). Natural law is 'the *ideal formula of development* of a given being' or its 'ideal order' (Maritain 1951, 88).

On this providential interpretation, the doctrine of universal human rights seeks a *return* to the state of nature as the truly *political* condition of human beings. In Maritain, this means that politics ought to follow those normative standards that allow every individual being to enjoy the full development or normal functioning of their capabilities. The list of universal human rights specifies what these normative standards and natural-human capabilities are. These standards and capabilities describe the 'pure nature' of humanity as a biological species endowed with sacrality or dignity, what Jean Porter identifies, in Thomistic terms, as the perfection of nature through grace.[56] Maritain's point is that only a human government that adheres in its policies to this understanding of human nature and its flourishing (i.e., in Thomistic terms, its perfection) is therefore legitimate government.[57]

---

[55] The so-called phenomenon of 'norm cascade' is a typical example of what I am calling the providential dispositive associated with the politics of universal human rights. The concept of 'collateral damage' could be another one; see (Whyte 2017).

[56] (Porter 2005, 382–91).

[57] The neo-Aristotelian 'capabilities' approach to universal human rights found in Amartya Sen and Martha Nussbaum reveals itself to be in proximity to Maritain's neo-Thomistic approach to the same rights. See (Nussbaum 2000; 2013). The difference between Nussbaum and Maritain is

In the context of working out the meaning of natural law and providence for the system of universal human rights, Maritain rejoins some of the principal tenets of neoliberal governmentality that were being developed by Friedrich Hayek and others roughly during the same years.[58] According to neoliberal doctrine, government refers to the regulation of the actions of human beings endowed with free, rational choice not by means of external coercive laws, but by spontaneous normative orders that work through the polarity normality/abnormality.[59] Thus, all legal regulations or government policies are legitimate or good if they maintain or restore the 'normal' functioning of these normative orders, for instance, the spontaneous order of the free market. State planning of the economy, on the other hand, produces 'abnormal' development of the economy. Natural law, as Maritain understands it, is but another name for the idea of normal functioning, self-regulating spontaneous order in neoliberalism.[60]

Seen in this context, one can better understand why Maritain is keen that universal human rights be founded upon natural law rather than positive law. Universal human rights are unlike the rights (and duties) that emerge from human positive law, for the validity of human rights is not dependent on a positive legal constitution nor can they be deduced from such a legal constitution. To the contrary, universal human rights are such because they can *only* be realized *outside* of republican constitutional laws, bypassing the classical or republican understanding of the citizen as author of its laws. The normative order of universal human rights, in this sense, is analogous to the spontaneous normative order of the free market, which is also a normative order that is not created by the concerted action of human beings. For this reason, universal human rights are intrinsically the object of what Foucault calls 'police' regulations rather than 'political' legislation. The universality of

---

analogous to the difference between Aristotle and Aquinas on natural law, and this ultimately turns on the different role played by divine providence in each account.

[58] I refer to my governmental reading of Hayek in (Vatter 2014a) and on the motif of divine providence in Hayek, see now (Whyte 2019a).

[59] For a discussion of the literature on this point, see (Vatter 2018).

[60] Agamben explains how the belief in Christian divine providence underlies the 'naturalized' conception of self-steering social systems, exemplified by neoliberal ideas of the free market, by saying that 'theology can resolve into atheism, and providentialism into democracy, because God has made the world just as if it were without God and governs it as though it governed itself' (Agamben 2011b, 286). But this explanation misses the fundamental role played by the connection between human rights and natural law in order to achieve the transition from providentialism to (Christian) democracy. For examples of the coincidence of neoliberal and neoconservative support for universal human rights in the aftermath of World War II that Maritain makes possible, see (Duranti 2012), and for the argument connecting human rights discourse with neoliberalism, see now (Whyte 2019b).

human rights, on this view, can only be established panoptically, when everyone who is victimized by state violence becomes in turn an instrument for the 'policing' of this state, sovereign violence, reporting on its infringement of human rights, punishing its perpetrators through judicial instances that depend directly from the United Nations, and so on.

In his counter-history of universal human rights, Moyn points out that there was a lag of several decades between the declaration of these universal rights and their effective implementation in a full-blown 'politics of human rights'. On Maritain's terms, this lag can be explained as the time it took to set up the instruments and dispositives of a global panopticon sensitive to the interventions of state sovereignty in violation of the natural rules of human dignity, analogous to the global panopticon that makes possible a global free market and is sensitive to all violations by state sovereignty of the natural rules of economic value.

My thesis is that Maritain's apparently metaphysical or theological grounding of human rights in natural law is misinterpreted if it is understood to offer an alternative *moral* foundation to human rights, for example, an anti-constructivist or a metaphysical foundation. Maritain does not appeal to natural law in order to offer a 'metaphysical' foundation of human rights, since he was as aware back in 1947 as we are today that universal human rights do not need such a foundation. To the contrary, his interest in a natural law grounding to universal human rights intended to offer a way to understand these rights as *an instrument of global governance or governmentality*, whereby 'governmentality' is taken in the Foucauldian sense of the term, meaning the ways of controlling the conduct of free individuals ('persons' in Maritain's sense of the term) otherwise than by the rule of law, but through a panoply of control mechanisms, policing functions, and securitization policies that allow for the 'free' development of each person's 'nature' or capabilities, for their 'normal functioning'. Only when seen from this governmental perspective can one understand why Maritain insisted that universal human rights had to require new social and economic rights (biopolitical rights, rights to 'quality of life'), and why he also placed great emphasis on the universal human right to choose one's conception of sacredness or religious belief. Maritain does not insist on a human right to religion for the sake of theology, but only for the sake of politics: the belief that God exists must be safeguarded, but only because the very structure of universal human rights depends on a providential conception of natural normative orders. God's providence or existence is manifest in history only as a function of the spread of recognition of the universality of human rights.

Maritain identified another advantage with grounding universal human rights onto such a conception of natural law. The natural law foundation allows to separate the question of how best to protect these universal rights from the sphere of positive legislation of the state and its coercive power. Since natural law is inscribed in the natural order of things, it is an unwritten law. Unlike human positive laws, natural law does not depend upon being posited by a sovereign authority. This claim leads to the obvious question: how is anyone to know what is natural law, what are universal human rights, if these rights are not first found in written legal codes, and are not interpreted by authorized judges and legislators?

Maritain claims that there are two ways in which natural law comes to be known. The first is through God's 'revealed positive law'. Apart from revealing some aspects of God's essence, religiously revealed positive laws also give the basic contents of the natural law, for example in the form of the Decalogue (Maritain 1951, 90). This is a crucial part of Maritain's argument because it permits the founding of a cosmopolitan regime of human rights on the basis of an overlapping consensus between rational, comprehensive world views, which is precisely what world religions—when appropriately re-interpreted in light of this end—are able to provide.[61] As I mentioned in the beginning of the chapter, Maritain was one of those theorists who argued that any viable cosmopolitan legal arrangement had to work through an overlapping consensus on the basis of a new 'democratic charter'. This charter, in turn, calls for new political actors, new representatives of the universality of human rights who shall be like 'democratic prophets' among elected officials. Here Maritain anticipates the contemporary fascination with non-elected representatives of the multitudes fighting in the 'cause' of universal human rights.

The second way to come to know the contents of the natural law is entirely secular, disconnected from any positive revealed religion. This way consists in letting human reason track the 'inclinations of human nature' (Maritain 1951, 91). Knowledge of the 'natural inclinations' of human nature is a gradual acquisition. Principles of natural law must be revealed throughout

---

[61] It is interesting to note how quickly, after 1947, proponents of the major world religions have undertaken the effort to re-interpret these religions so as to make them adequate candidates for an overlapping consensus on universal human rights. In turn, these re-interpretations have since been locked in battle with fundamentalist interpretations of the same religions. Part of these efforts, especially with regards to Islam and Catholicism, are registered in Rawls's *Law of Peoples*.

history because they cannot be deduced theoretically, at one go (Maritain 1951, 93). At the same time, history does not reveal these principles in a linear, predictive, and progressive fashion: historical development can also experience moments of 'regression', a return to 'barbarism', such as occurred in the middle of the 20th century. Natural law is revealed in the providential structure of human history, but since providence is related to the 'eternal law' of divine wisdom or omniscience, the result of this encounter of time and eternity is that providential order endows historical progress with the character of 'mystery' and 'unfathomability'. 'It is because we are enmeshed in the universal order, in the laws and regulations of the cosmos and of the immense family of created natures (and finally in the order of creative wisdom), and it is because we have at the same time the privilege of sharing in spiritual nature, that we possess rights vis-à-vis other men and all the assemblage of creatures. In the last analysis, as every creature acts by virtue of its Principle, which is pure Act; as every authority worthy of the name (that is to say, just) is binding in conscience by virtue of the Principle of beings, which is pure Wisdom: so too every right possessed by man is possessed by virtue of the right possessed by God, Who is pure Justice, to see the order of His Wisdom in beings respected, obeyed and loved by every intelligence. . . . Natural law is law only because it is participation in Eternal Law' (Maritain 1951, 95–96). For Maritain, human freedom—that is, universal human rights—is a function of God's government as this is shown providentially in the structure of the natural order ('every right possessed by man is possessed in virtue of the right possessed by God . . . to see the order of its Wisdom respected in beings, obeyed and loved by all intelligence'). How can one make sense of this seemingly wild extrapolation from human rights to divine wisdom?

As recently explained by Agamben, providence in Christian theology has two related but distinct meanings.[62] On the one hand, providence refers to an 'economy of mystery'. Here the 'mystery' refers to the gift of salvation that God gives to the human species. Since God does not give this gift all at once, He must employ an 'economy' of dispensations symbolized by the Trinitarian personation of God's essence. In Maritain, clearly, the 'economy of mystery' corresponds to the 'gift of rule' that God distributes *equally among all peoples* and that determines history as the stage of a repeated, sometimes victorious other times defeated, struggle for the emergence of democracy as the only global legitimate form of government. Agamben and other interpreters

[62] (Agamben 2011, 17–49).

of the 'economic theology' of Christianity miss the democratic meaning of the 'economy of mystery' and leap, too quickly in my opinion, to a politico-economical, secularizing interpretation of this mystery.[63]

The second meaning of providence in this Christian context is captured by the expression of the 'mystery of the economy'. Agamben, correctly, shows that this second meaning refers to the idea that God's government or providence operates indirectly, in 'mysterious' ways, because it is an effect of the unintended consequences and secondary causes that constitute the interrelations between the different natures in the world order that give rise to what I called earlier, using Hayek's terminology, a spontaneous normative order.[64] Divine providence is an emergent pattern, an order that develops out of chaos and communication. My hypothesis is that Maritain's interpretation of this second sense of providence, that is, providence as the 'mystery of the economy', comes into play in order to solve the serious problem of how humanity comes to know what is natural law, what is 'naturally good' for each and every individual, when it is not established by sovereign legislations.

Maritain believes that the human knowledge as to what is 'natural law', what is the good of each nature or person, is something that is mysterious to each individual, and can only be computed by an economy of freedom as a whole. Once again, Maritain's intuition with respect to natural law is related to Hayek's transformative idea that useful knowledge is the best distributed thing in the world. The idea of an economy of knowledge allowed Hayek to posit that prices, for example, are best set by the free market understood as a medium of computing, gathering, and processing the perfectly distributed knowledge as to what anything is worth to any given individual, a knowledge that necessarily informs the decisions of how much to supply and demand of that thing.[65] If one expands these intuitions to the field of human rights, then one can begin to comprehend why Shue insists that 'basic human rights' cannot be merely rights to security and subsistence, but they must be also basic rights to 'participation and liberty of movement'. Shue assumes this neoliberal idea of access to and participation in a global network of knowledge, in this 'world wide web' of information, which, as I showed above, is an essential element of the pan-optical structure of the implementation of the universality of human rights. Likewise, Shue's human right to 'liberty

---

[63] See here (Leshem 2016).
[64] For further discussion of this aspect of divine providence see now (Heron 2018).
[65] For a critical view on these ideas, see (Mirowski 2007).

of movement' refers to the liberty of communication and flow of peoples, things, information in this world wide web or global world order. Only these kinds of freedom generate true knowledge of what natural law really is. This is one way to make sense of what Maritain says about divine providence as the root of universal human rights.

From Maritain's Paul to Badiou's Paul: Christian democracy and the Jewish Question

Just as in Christian theology the question of the 'mystery of the economy' is inextricable from the so-called Mystery of Israel, so the emergence of a global legal order based on universal human rights is closely linked with the awareness of the horrors of Hitler's 'Final Solution' to the so-called Jewish Question and the imperative to avoid any new Holocausts in the future. With the creation of the State of Israel, and its assumption of the task to protect Jews from persecution, the new system of universal human rights became increasingly connected with 'multiculturalism', referring to the approach developed by liberal democracies to deal with what Taylor calls the 'politics of difference' associated with national, religious, and ethnic minorities that reject 'assimilation' to the majority nation, religion, or ethnic group and demands, rather, 'recognition' for its identity. In what follows I show how Maritain's controversial and complex, lifelong struggle with the significance of Judaism for Christian political theology, once again, anticipated later trends.

This far, I have proposed an interpretation of Maritain's politico-theological foundation of universal human rights that accounts for the way in which the UDHR and its implementation could function as a meeting point for neoliberalism and neoconservatism, and provide a lever on which to erect a 'new world order' that would itself begin to emerge in the late 1970s. However, since the fall of the Berlin Wall and the collapse of the Soviet Union, cosmopolitanism or universalism has become a discursive vector also for some proponents of post-Marxist thought.[66] That some of these thinkers have proposed their own versions of post-Marxist political theology lends support to my hypothesis that Maritain's inscription of democratic universalism within the discourse of Christian political theology left an important legacy. One of the most radical versions of post-Marxist political theology is

---

[66] For a paradigmatic case of these kinds of debates, see (Butler 2000).

Alain Badiou's *Saint Paul: The Foundation of Universalism*, which I propose to read as another treatise, this time coming from the Left, of Christian political theology.[67]

An additional reason for concluding this chapter with Badiou's political theology is that he is quite explicit in inscribing his approach to universalism within the development of the 'Jewish Question'. If at the start of the 20th century the revolutionary Left was confronted with the anti-Semitic construction of 'Jewish Bolshevism', by the end of the 20th century the post-revolutionary Left was haunted by another, complex and overdetermined construction of anti-Semitism that responds, this time around, to the foundation of the State of Israel and the consequent creation of the 'Palestinian Question'. In this new construction, the Muslim immigrant in the Christian democracies of Europe can appear as the 'new communist', whereas the post-1967 occupation by the Israeli state of the territories in the West Bank and Gaza Strip can appear as a form of 'totalitarian' domination that systematically violates the human rights of the Palestinian population.[68] Badiou's version of Christian political theology is a symptomatic response to this last constellation of anti-Semitism. My hypothesis is that Maritain's path from anti-Semitism to anti-anti-Semitism can shed some light on the field of problems later faced by Badiou and others in the European Left.[69]

Maritain's thought is marked by what Richard Crane calls 'ambivalent philosemitism'.[70] Early in his career, Maritain was close to Charles Maurras's anti-Semitic and fascist movement of Action Française. During the 1930s he broke with Maurras and became an 'anti-anti-Semite'. This move coincided with his adoption of a discourse of democracy and human rights that opposed totalitarian ideology and anti-Semitism. The important question for my purpose is to understand the role assigned to Judaism in Maritain's Christian and democratic political theology. I shall argue that this is a dual role. On the one hand, with respect to the democratic component of Christian political theology, Maritain's 'philo-semitism' is in evidence with the recuperation of

---

[67] I do not thereby wish to reduce Badiou's oeuvre to the theses expounded in this book. For a wide-ranging discussion of the complexities of Badiou's thinking of democracy, see the essays in (Hallward 2004).

[68] For the Muslim immigrant as 'new communist' see (Moyn 2015). For the current debate on Israel, Palestine, and anti-Semitism, see (Butler 2014).

[69] For Badiou's own reading of the recent debate on rising anti-Semitism in France, see (Badiou, Hazan, and Segré 2013). For the current debate on the anti-Semitism and anti-Zionism in the Left in France, see (Segré 2017; and Trom 2019).

[70] (Crane 2008, 409). Apart from the many works by Crane, see also the essays on Maritain's relationship to Judaism in (Royal 1994).

motifs from the Jewish political tradition, above all the idea of charismatic leadership of the prophets. On the other hand, with respect to the cosmopolitan aspect of this political theology tied to the universality of human rights, Maritain's 'philo-semitism' is in evidence with the belief that this universality is necessarily open to an overlapping consensus with other religions and is, therefore, *not* the exclusive fruit of Christianity and its secularization.

As Crane has shown, in an early essay from 1921 entitled *À propos de la question juive*, Maritain adopts what I call the *katechontic* approach to the 'Jewish Question'. This approach turns around the so-called doctrine of the 'Mystery of Israel', which finds one of its deepest formulations precisely in the theology of Peterson. According to this doctrine, Judaism maintains its 'eternal' significance for the Christian Church for a dialectical reason: the resistance of Jews to accept Jesus as the Christ or Messiah is a permanent reminder to Christians that the Kingdom of Christ is *not* the 'kingdom of the world' because it shall be realized only at the End of history, and not in history. The continued existence of Jews and Judaism prevents Christians for falling in with the Anti-Christ. Conversely, and this is the aspect of the doctrine that retains an indelible element of anti-Semitism, the Jewish people function as this reminder precisely because for them the Messiah is an inner-worldly political leader that brings peace unto all nations. 'It is necessary to add that an essentially messianic people such as the Jews, from the instant when they reject the true Messiah, inevitably will play a subversive role in the world . . . because of a metaphysical necessity, which makes of messianic Hope, and a passion for absolute Justice, when they are brought down from the supernatural to the natural level, and are falsely applied, the most active ferment of revolution.'[71] In 1921, entirely taken up by the French Catholic, nationalist, and reactionary culture war against liberal democracy, Maritain rejects the 'natural' realization of messianic hopes. This will all change in the 1930s when he begins to intuit the 'providential' meaning behind the 'revolutionary' realization of democracy and universal human rights in the world heretofore described.

As discussed, by 1939 at the latest Maritain is convinced that in order to defeat the totalitarian Empire, the Christian multitudes must become politically militant in favour of democracy and human rights. This fundamental change of attitude from his early anti-Semitism to his later anti-anti-Semitism is crystallized in his 1937 article on the Jewish Question, entitled *L'impossible*

---

[71] Maritain cited in (Crane 2008, 389).

Antisémitisme.[72] In this article, Maritain still holds on to Peterson's critique of political theology and reading of the 'Mystery of Israel' in order to argue that any attempt to 'solve' the Jewish Question in the world, such as Hitler was proposing, was to be categorically rejected.[73] For Maritain, however, this also meant that Christians had the obligation to 'accept Jewish distinctiveness in the framework of a common humanity' based on human rights. This is a step beyond Peterson because it is the first time that human rights are figured as the correct, 'multicultural' response to cultural/ethnic/religious difference, embodied paradigmatically by the Jewish people in its refusal to assimilate to Christendom and Christian salvation.[74]

Badiou argues that Saint Paul is the founder of what he calls 'universalism'. In his book, universalism is a synonym for a radical egalitarianism.[75] There are three features of universalism or radical egalitarianism that are crucial for him. First, universalism is opposed to multiculturalism as truth is opposed to relativism (Badiou 2003, 61). The defence of a univocal, universal 'truth' that has to 'fight' its way against the opinions of the many in order to gain its final recognition in the world has always distinguished Badiou's thought from other post-Marxists.[76] What seems to have escaped many commentators is that this kind of opposition is structurally analogous with the one mobilized by Voegelin, Maritain, and Strauss against 'liberalism' and its inherent 'relativism' (by which they understood a precursor of multiculturalism).[77]

Second, Badiou understands universalism as building on the foundation of a thorough critique of positive law. This feature of Badiou's egalitarianism

---

[72] See (Maritain and Vidal-Naquet 2003) with the important essay by Pierre Vidal-Naquet, "Jacques Maritain et les juifs: réflexions sur un parcours".

[73] For Maritain, Christians could become anti-Semites only 'in obeying the spirit of the world, not the spirit of Christianity' and so it was 'impossible' for Christians to be anti-Semitic and remain Christian. Cited in (Crane 2008, 406).

[74] This is why Maritain also opposes Christianity to racism: 'racialism to an unimaginable degree degrades and humiliates reason, thought, science and art, which are henceforth made subservient to flesh and blood and are stripped of their natural "catholicity"'. Cited in (Crane 2008, 408). The connection that (Gauchet 1998) makes between Christianity, democracy, and multiculturalism follows from Maritain's ideas, though Gauchet acknowledges neither the influence of Maritain nor the underlying politico-theological discourse on Judaism.

[75] 'The subject constituted by charisma through the gratuitous practice of the universal address necessarily maintains that there are no differences' (Badiou 2003, 78). The connection between this egalitarianism and a radical conception of democracy in Badiou is a complicated question. Obviously, Badiou's universalism cannot be identified with a liberal form of democracy nor with a liberal politics of human rights (ibid., 57). For a general discussion of post-Marxist ambivalence towards human rights, see (McLoughlin 2016). However, Badiou's interpretation of Saint Paul is 'democratic' in a more radical sense that is close to Maritain's, as I discuss below.

[76] For an overview, see (Bosteels 2011).

[77] On Badiou's thought as a re-activation of Platonism, see (Bartlett 2011).

places it in continuity with Christian political theology, which is also structured around a critique of legal positivism. More precisely, what Christian political theology questions is the claim that a people is constituted through law. Christian political theology believes that a people is constituted through a representative (the resurrected Christ), and this representative stands-for the advent of a transcendent truth (which must be spoken-for and spoken-out, hence the centrality of the Gospel). Roman and Jewish political thought, instead, and despite their great differences, share the premise that political community is based on the givenness of law. Saint Paul's theology, as Badiou highlights, is structured around the dual rejection of Roman and Jewish positive law.

Third, like Maritain, Badiou also argues that for Saint Paul, universalism or radical egalitarianism means that everyone is the 'son of God' in virtue of their faith in the 'truth' that is the event(s) of the Crucifixion and Resurrection of Christ. Badiou also figures Saint Paul as the radical antagonist of all 'political religions', which he associates to both nation-states and empires. These political religions, as I have discussed, assume that only 'the king' can have the status of being the Son of God. On Badiou's reading, Saint Paul understands Christ's Resurrection to signal the end of political monarchism. Christ is that Son of God who delivers all humankind from kingship. After the advent of Christ, there can be no more divine monarchs, for in virtue of faith, everyone becomes of equal rank as an equal participator in the 'sonship' of God. 'One must depose the master and found the equality of sons' (Badiou 2003, 59).

By using the categories bequeathed by Jean-Jacques Rousseau's analysis of civil religion at the end of the *Social Contract*, one can identify the sense in which, on Badiou's reading, Saint Paul is the founder of a Christian political theology. First, Badiou argues that Saint Paul's epistles do not reveal a particular attachment to or care for the actual words and deeds of Jesus, as much as to the meaning or truth of the event of Christ's Resurrection. In this sense, Badiou distinguishes Saint Paul's political theology both from the 'religion' of Jesus (what Rousseau calls 'natural divine right') and from the Jewish and Roman *theologia civilis* (what Rousseau calls 'positive divine right'). Badiou does not consider Saint Paul to be the founder of the Catholic Church, a role that falls on Saint Peter. Thus, Saint Paul's political theology is also not the same as what Rousseau calls the 'religion of the priest'. For Badiou, universalism does not find its 'political form' in the Church. In this sense, Badiou's Christian political theology is anti-Schmittian because it is entirely anti-institutional. Badiou envisages the construction of a community or *ekklesia* of those who strive for universalism, or radical equality, beyond positive law.

Saint Paul's Christian theology is anti-institutional (in the sense of being anti-nomian) but its opposition to Empire does not remain at the abstract level expressed by Jesus's sayings ('give to Caesar what is Caesar's', 'my Kingdom is not of this world', and so on). Rather, on Badiou's interpretation Saint Paul's Christian theology is also a *democratic* political theology because the event of the Resurrection of Christ should be understood as a function of grace (Badiou 2003, 63). The gift or grace of Christ's Resurrection means that either 'everyone' must rule (as equal sons of God) or nobody rules. The supra-rational 'truth' content of Christ's Resurrection, therefore, is that no 'one' must rule. Rule no longer belongs to the order of the One: 'the One is that which inscribes no difference in the subjects to which it addresses itself. The One is only insofar as it is for all: such is the maxim of universality.... Monotheism can be understood only *by taking into consideration the whole of humanity*' (Badiou 2003, 76, emphasis mine).[78] This egalitarian articulation of universalism is very close to the conception of the charismatic 'gift of rule' that Maritain set at the basis of his synthesis of democracy and human rights.

Badiou's interpretation of Saint Paul moves within the initial opposition between divine monarchy and divine democracy that was set up in the Schmitt-Peterson polemic, and, indeed, hardly makes any sense outside of this context.[79] It is remarkable that, in the above citation, Badiou does not bother to define 'humanity'. But the fact that his universalism requires a reference to 'humanity' is precisely what places his egalitarian thought in continuity with the 'integral humanism' of Maritain and his politics of universal human rights. For these universal human rights are in tension with the civil rights of citizens because they *must* be applicable to *everyone, without exception*, if they are to be applicable to *any one* at all.[80]

---

[78] For Badiou, in fact, the formula for the State as 'police' is the rule of the One. For the debate on the conceptions of equality in Badiou and Rancière, see (Watkin 2013).

[79] However, Badiou's interpretation does not mention either Schmitt, Peterson, or, for that matter, Taubes (not to speak of Maritain). It is Agamben who situates the post-Marxist interpretation of Saint Paul as a thinker of universalism within the context of 20th-century political theology in (Agamben 2000a). On the debate between Badiou and Agamben over Saint Paul, see (Baker 2013). For other interventions on Saint Paul as a political theologian, see (Milbank 2008; and Milbank, Žižek, and Davis 2010).

[80] Undoubtedly, Maritain's Christian political theology was the first to give an interpretation of the 'universality' of human rights which is in direct opposition to the 'rights of the citizen'. This opposition—which is the crucial issue of what nowadays is known as 'cosmopolitan' or supra-national

The other fundamental pillar of Badiou's interpretation of Saint Paul's Christian political theology also takes off, probably unawares, from Maritain's opposition between the Christian and the 'pagan' understanding of the political relationship of friend and enemy. By 1939, Maritain already was arguing that Schmitt's political theology must be opposed by a new Christian political theology that gives a *political* (no longer a 'private') meaning to Jesus' 'commandment' to love the enemy. Badiou takes this same indication and develops it as follows. For Saint Paul, the pagan 'law' that prescribes hatred towards the enemies of one's city or nation depends on the primacy assigned to law over faith. On the contrary, the Christian 'law' enjoining love of one's enemies is only possible given the primacy of faith in the Resurrection of Christ and the Coming of His Kingdom on earth. However, Badiou reads the classical Pauline opposition between faith and law ('works') in a way that does *not* de-politicize this messianic faith. An extremely clear indication that Saint Paul interpreted Christ's new and revolutionary reformulation of the friend/enemy distinction in 'political' rather than in 'private' terms is his belief that Jesus Christ does not simply break with all divine right (whether positive or natural) but also *establishes a new law*. This is a 'living' or 'spiritual' law of love or charity.[81] As Badiou glosses this *nomos pneumatikos*: 'love names a nonliteral [i.e., not positive/MV] *law*, one that gives to the faithful subject his consistency, and effectuates the post-eventual truth in the world' (Badiou 2003, 87, emphasis mine).

It has escaped the attention of both Badiou and Agamben (but not Milbank) that the term 'spiritual law' (*nomos pneumatikos*) is taken by Saint Paul from the very language used in the formulation of the Judeo-Hellenistic conception of the divine king as living or spiritual law.[82] In other words, the universalism that Badiou reads into Saint Paul's 'law of love' is entirely caught up with the 'political problem of monotheism'. The reference to the Hellenistic conception of divine kingship is still very much present in the

---

democracy—was never contemplated in the original formulation of the "Droits de l'Homme et du Citoyen." In the latter document, 'man' and 'citizen' were still understood as forming a continuum. Along with Maritain, Arendt is the other major political theorist who, during the same years, comes to appreciate the meaning of the 'crisis' of human rights, that is, the constitution of a 'universal' humanity that is not rooted in a 'nation' or 'people' because it no longer has an internal connection with 'citizenship'. Badiou's 'universalism' should be understood as a response to this same crisis.

[81] The reference is to the expression *nomos pneumatikos* in Romans 7:14.

[82] Milbank is made aware of this provenance by (Blumenfeld 2001). Neither Milbank nor Blumenfeld, though, connects this fact with the discourse carried forward about political theology by Goodenough and Peterson. I refer to the discussion of the Judeo-Hellenistic conception of *nomos* in *Living Law*.

Pauline idea of 'law of love'. The difference between the Hellenistic and the Pauline conception of divine kingship is that Christ's 'law of love' denies that this divine kingship belongs to one royal person because it now, in virtue of faith in the Resurrection, belongs to *all* the sons of God. After Saint Paul, all pagans can become kings by becoming equal sons of God in professing their faith in the Resurrection of the Son of God (and King of the Jews). Badiou's reading of Saint Paul's political theology in terms of a rather abstract opposition between the radical equality proclaimed by the Son and the Law established monarchically by the Father is ultimately untenable because it does not recognize that Saint Paul's *nomos pneumatikos*, far from transcending the terms of the Judeo-Hellenistic debate on the 'political problem of monotheism', merely offers the basis for an egalitarian and universalist declension of its politico-theological terms.[83]

The 'spiritual law' of loving the enemy is the common kernel of Christian political theology shared by Maritain and Badiou. What makes 'love' the substance of a Christian *political* theology is precisely the fact that its law is the formula for (political) *militancy*: 'Theorem 7. The subjective process of a truth is one and the same thing as the love of that truth. The real militant of this love is the universal address which constitutes it. The materiality of universalism is the militant dimension of every truth' (Badiou 2003, 92, translation modified).[84] As in Schmitt, so too for Badiou there is no truth which is not polemical. That is why fidelity to 'the subjective process of a truth' transforms, automatically, the believer into a militant. The militant is here someone disposed to make the distinction between friend (of the truth) and enemy (of the truth), and to fight a 'life and death' struggle in its name, as Badiou clearly states in his discussion of the 'antidialectic of death and resurrection'. Like Voegelin and Maritain, Badiou's political theology also rejects the belief of 'political religions' according to which salvation is found in the individual's willingness to die for their Fatherland or Motherland. Yet, Badiou's conception of salvation is also, evidently, not an apolitical or impolitical matter: individual salvation remains a function of the 'political' struggle between friend and enemy understood as the struggle for or against 'universalism'.

---

[83] See the discussion of God's becoming-son in Chapter 5 (Badiou 2003, 59ff) and Chapter 6 (Badiou 2003: 69ff), which attempts an unconvincing and forced separation between Paul's theology and what would become, from Origen onwards, orthodox Trinitarian theology.

[84] On Badiou's idea of a militancy for truth, see (Barbour 2010).

The climax of Badiou's Christian political theology is found in his reading of Pauline 'hope', which comes after the 'faith' in the event of Resurrection, and after the 'love' which is the law that commands fidelity to the truth of that event. Badiou's understanding of hope contains the same signature of Christian political theology found in Maritain and Voegelin. This signature is the category of the 'openness' of society to a truth that transcends its immanent ordering: 'faith would be the *being-open* to the truth; love the universalizing effectiveness of its trajectory; and hope, lastly, a maxim enjoining us to persevere in this trajectory' (Badiou 2003, 93). For Badiou, hope is 'perseverance' in the universalist faith that everyone is equal, despite all the setbacks and sacrifices to which this law of love exposes the individual. One needs this hope, as Badiou says, because 'the work of love is still before us, the empire is vast' (Badiou 2003, 95).

So far, Badiou has parsed in a politico-theological fashion the classical theological virtues (faith, charity, hope). However, the real content of Badiou's understanding of Christian hope is not only the struggle against the pagan Empire. What a real Christian militant must also hope for is that even those peoples who reject in principle the faith in Jesus Christ—foremost among them the Jewish people who do not renounce the Mosaic law—will still be saved at the End of history, despite their 'enmity' to Christ. The content of hope is the 'Mystery of Israel' linked with Saint Paul's claim in Romans 11:28: 'As regards the gospel they [the Jews] are enemies of God, for your sake [Gentiles]; but as regards election they are beloved for the sake of their forefathers'. As commentators have pointed out, in Romans Saint Paul constructs his political theology strictly in view of the strategic goal of spreading the Gospel to the Gentiles.[85] The point is to 'universalize' Christianity beyond the narrow circle of Jewish converts to Christianity found in Jerusalem. Thus, for Saint Paul there is no need to 'hope' for the conversion of the Gentiles. That such a conversion is both possible and necessary is simply the *a priori* of Saint Paul's political theology.

The proper object of Christian hope is whether Jews (and later Muslims, and still later First Peoples who adhere to so-called polytheistic or animistic religions) will also follow the Gentiles along this path of salvation. Thus, the primary meaning of the adjective 'open' in Christian political theology has an inherently and unavoidable polemical content. Christians are, by definition, pagan multitudes who are 'open' to the truth that Christ is the Messiah, while

---

[85] See, for example, the discussions of theological enmity and universality in (Anidjar 2003; 2014).

Jews are, by definition, believers in One God who are 'closed' to that same truth. On this Pauline construction, Jews become the paradigmatic opponents of universalism. Schmitt and Peterson were centrally aware of this motif of theological enmity at the heart of Christian universalism, and so were Voegelin and Maritain. This motif equally underlies Badiou's treatise on universalism. The great problem for all of them is how to figure the 'necessary' enmity to Judaism within the Christian universalistic teaching of equality.

Badiou's solution is stated in the tenth chapter of his book, when he replaces the enmity between Christians and Jews with the struggle between the universalism of radical equality and the claims made on behalf of 'differences' characteristic of late modern 'politics of recognition'. Badiou displaces the problem of the Pauline enmity towards Judaism on to the problem posed by 'multiculturalism' for radical egalitarianism. And it is here that Badiou, again following Maritain's anti-anti-Semitism, rejects in principle any 'totalitarian' 'Final Solution' in order to propose the tactical path of 'compromise' with particularity (again, for him this means tolerance for cultural diversity) in the consecution of the final victory of universalism.[86] For Badiou, the militants who struggle for radical equality must come to accept the 'necessity' of those who defend the 'right to be different', namely, they must come to terms with the fact that not everyone will accept the truth of the resurrected Christ, that is, the truth that all human beings are equal. The name for this tactical compromise is the democratic politics of human rights. However, whereas for Maritain this politics was the only possible 'solution' to the politically and historically 'irresolvable' Jewish Question, for Badiou human rights are merely a 'compromise' in an ongoing struggle between the claims of radical equality and the claims of difference and differential treatment.

In conclusion, I have proposed an interpretation of Maritain's politico-theological foundation of universal human rights that accounts for the way in which the UDHR and its subsequent implementation could function as a lever that could be used by both neoliberal and neoconservative movements in order to 'derail' the Soviet 'locomotive' of history, and impress a new direction to world politics, an orientation towards the establishment of a 'new world order'. The key move in this complex strategy depends on giving a natural-law interpretation to the universality of human rights in order that the politics of human rights may subsume the drive to cosmopolitan

---

[86] 'Christian militantism must traverse worldly differences indifferently and avoid all casuistry over customs' (Badiou 2003, 100).

democracy under a governmental understanding of divine providence. Furthermore, I have shown that the anti-Schmittian political theologies of Maritain and Badiou based on universalizing the Christian 'love for the enemy' retain a fundamental dimension of 'enmity' when it comes time to confront the resistance posed to the 'truth' of Jesus Christ by Judaism and, in my opinion, also by non-revealed forms of religious law associated with polytheism and animism. Both of them give a qualified approval to employ democracy and human rights as the best way to manage the 'Mystery of Israel'.

But what are the reasons of this unsurmountable scandal posed by Judaism for Christian political theology? In *Living Law* I venture the hypothesis that the root of the problem originates in the fact that, contemporary with Saint Paul, there existed another, messianic form of universalism based on an alternative idea of 'divine democracy'. This expression seems to have appeared first in Philo's interpretation of Mosaic law. It reappears in Spinoza's *Theologico-Political Treatise* as the first, early modern attempt to re-found democracy on non-Christian bases. To do justice to the idea of divine democracy that Maritain and Badiou have shown to lie at the basis of universalism, it may be necessary to return to this other, Judeo-Hellenistic source of cosmopolitanism. Its influence on the history of revolutionary republicanism puts into question Maritain's Christian interpretation of divine providence and brings out the existence of another possible way to connect cosmopolitanism and providence, which is also to be found in Spinoza and in Kant.[87] This other genealogy of divine democracy clarifies the fundamental distinction between two forms of cosmopolitanism and two forms in which to understand the universality of human rights. Either, as in Maritain and Badiou, a cosmopolitan democracy and matching politics of universal human rights as the last mutation of God's pastoral government over human beings; or, as in the republican tradition, another conception of divine providence as a democracy of world citizens for whom the love of the world trumps the love of Christ.

---

[87] On an alternative republican idea of divine providence compare (Lloyd 2008; and Vatter 2011a; 2013).

4
Ernst Kantorowicz and Government

'The king reigns but does not govern': Democratic government from Voegelin and Maritain to Kantorowicz

What is the nature of liberal government? From Foucault to Agamben, contemporary attempts to capture its essence have focused on a 19th-century formula, apparently coined by Adolphe Thiers, a French liberal historian and politician: 'the King reigns but does not govern'. For these theorists, the division between sovereign and government expressed in the formula indicates the basic hypothesis that liberal governmentality operates in ways that are autonomous, and perhaps even antithetical, with respect to the sovereign power of the state.[1] Curiously, in the early 1930s, Peterson employed the same formula in order to render the Hellenistic idea of sacral kingship, which he identified as the source of the political theology of sovereignty in the West. Many years later, Schmitt rejected Peterson's suggestion on the ground that it was patently anachronistic. He could not countenance the possibility that a formula for liberalism could capture the politico-theological character he had assigned to absolute sovereignty.[2] Despite Schmitt's dismissal, Peterson's use of the formula opens up the question of what the political theology of liberal governmentality looks like.

Perhaps less well known is that the formula was also employed by Charles Howard McIlwain in his 1940 classic *Constitutionalism, Ancient and Modern*, not in order to capture the essence of modern liberal government, but as the formula for modern constitutionalism.[3] McIlwain's hypothesis is that modern constitutionalism finds its roots in medieval royal law as interpreted by the 13th-century English jurist Henri Bracton, in his work *De*

---

[1] See (Agamben 2011, 70–108; and Foucault 2009, 76). For commentary of the formula in this context, see (Whyte 2013; and Dean 2013, 87, 123–24, 193–95). For its use in 19th-century French liberalism see (Jaume 1997, 158–69, 186–92).

[2] See (Schmitt 1996b, 41–45).

[3] See (McIlwain 1947).

legibus et consuetudinibus Angliae. On this view, Bracton theorized that the monarch must abstain from governing in order that he may bind his reign to a legal constitution. In this way, the separation of reign from government would give rise to sovereignty in the modern form of constitutional or limited government. Hardly a decade later, Kantorowicz developed in *The King's Two Bodies. A Study in Medieval Political Theology* a new interpretation of Bracton that assigns constitutionalism a major role in the creation of an unlimited liberal governmentality within which a limited state sovereignty is embedded. This chapter puts forward the hypothesis that Kantorowicz's contribution to the discourse on democratic political theology consists in showing how sovereignty and constitutionalism both became instruments of liberal governmentality.

Kantorowicz's masterpiece has recently attracted the sustained interest of political, literary, and cultural theorists. Their discussions focus on two motifs that are addressed throughout *The King's Two Bodies*. On the one side, the idea of the 'mystical body' of the sovereign and its application to modern popular sovereignty. On the other, the 'fictional' character of political and legal constructions and the role played by artists in their creation.[4] However, to date these discussions leave more or less untouched the way in which Kantorowicz brings the method of political theology, namely, the study of the transpositions of concepts from theology to jurisprudence, to bear on these motifs and their role in the emergence of liberal constitutionalism and government. In this chapter I begin by situating Kantorowicz's approach to both the problems of the mystical political body and of the 'spiritual' sovereign in relation with his attempt to work out a Christian political theology of government that subsumes both sovereignty and constitutionalism.

Generally speaking, the medieval political world was a world of law, not of the state. Its fundamental problem was that of *iurisdictio*, the authority to say what is given law, which had to be distinguished from *legislatio*, the power to make 'positive' law and decrees.[5] Society was conceived as a community

---

[4] See (Kahn 2009; and Santner 2011; 2015) as well as (Lupton 2012). See also (Raulff 2006; and Lane and Ruehl 2011) for the idea of the artist as political founder in relation to the literary group of Stefan George (*George-Kreis*) of which Kantorowicz was a member in his youth. Kantorowicz's interpretation of the 'two bodies' found a fertile reception earlier in French political theory, starting with the debates between (Lefort 2000; Gauchet 1999; and Rosanvallon 1998) on the absence/presence of the body of the People in popular sovereignty.

[5] See (Grossi 2004). For a brief treatment of the idea of jurisdiction, see (Tierney 1983, 30ff), who defines *iurisdictio* both as 'the judicial authority of a magistrate to settle legal cases' and the 'broader meaning of ruling power in general'. This overlapping of two entirely distinct concepts is precisely what is at stake in political theology.

structured by law, where law originates from the consent of the *societas* or *populus*, not from the commands of the state or government. What characterizes western medieval political thought is precisely the widespread belief that law is given (either by God or by Nature), as well as the marked absence of anything like a modern state endowed with sovereignty, that is, with 'all the power to appoint and dismiss officers and to give laws to everyone'.[6]

The problem of government, in the technical sense I shall use it in this chapter, emerges during the late medieval period, when the concept of *iurisdictio* begins to undergo a major change in its meaning that climaxes with the modern conceptions of sovereignty and reason of state.[7] While initially *iurisdictio* refers to the priority of pre-political, often unwritten divine/natural laws and their interpretation by those presumed to know about such laws, such as philosophers and prophets, by the 13th century the term begins to refer to the power to rule through legislation wielded by secular princes and their court of jurists.[8] As Brian Tierney says, 'the typical process that occurred was the assimilation of a text of Roman private law into church law, its adaptation and transmutation there to a principle of constitutional law, and then its reabsorption into the sphere of secular government in this new form' (Tierney 1983, 25).[9] Kantorowicz's masterpiece offers a politico-theological interpretation of the transition from the first sense of jurisdiction that presupposes the priority of law over state, to its later sense that absorbs law into the state in a theory of government.

In the medieval worldview in which fundamental law is already given, the basic political activity is that of interpreting this law (*iurisdictio*), rather than

---

[6] Jean Bodin, *République* book II, chapter 7 (1576 ed., 281) cited in (Tuck 2016, 19).

[7] As a first approximation, I refer to the discussion of the medieval 'arts of government' in (Senellart 1995). Senellart's discussion is informed by Foucault's, at the time unpublished, lectures on the history of governmentality. Yet, despite few exceptions, there is a generalized disconnect between Foucault's research on governmentality and the historiography of medieval political thought, even on the part of French researchers; see, for example, the otherwise meritorious discussion in (Boureau 2006). For an alternative approach to the history of governmentality that follows the *Begriffsgeschichte* school of Reinhart Koselleck, see (Duso 2006).

[8] Tierney says that the original meaning of *iurisdictio* is connected with the belief in the divine origin of law as expressed in *Digest* 1,3,2: 'Law is something that all men ought to obey for many reasons, and especially because every law is a device and gift of the gods [*inventum ac munus deorum*], a decree of learned men [*decretum vero prudentiam hominum*], a restraint of those who either voluntarily or through ignorance are guilty of crime. It is also a common engagement of the state [*communis sponsio civitatis*] by whose rules everyone in the state ought to regulate his life'.

[9] Interestingly, Tierney does not remark on the relation between this process of transposition of concepts from different spheres and the discourse of political theology. This is all the more curious given that Tierney concludes one of his main works with a citation, left unanalysed, from George Lawson (arguably, the origin of a democratic or republican conception of constituent power): 'Politiks both civil and Ecclesiastical belong unto Theology, and are but a branch of the same'. See (Tierney 1983, 99) citing from Lawson's *Politica*, chapter 4, section 1.

making decrees (*legislatio*). In such a world, the fundamental political question is posed by Schmitt's question: *quis judicabit?* who interprets? Who is the ultimate judge of what the given law says? In *Political Theology II*, Schmitt raised three basic problems linked with this question, but he left them without answers. These three problems form the backbone of Kantorowicz's at times convoluted narrative in *The King's Two Bodies* and they provide the structure for my interpretation in what follows.

The first problem emerges with Schmitt's belated concession that the transposition of concepts between theology and jurisprudence was made possible because of an analogy between God and People, rather than between God and King. In the western medieval period, the only concrete exemplar of such an analogy was given by the conception of the Christian Church as the 'mystical body' of Christ. In 1 Corinthians 10:17–18, Saint Paul suggests that individual believers become united with Christ in a single 'mystical' body by the ingestion of the sacrament of the Eucharist. In partaking of Christ's 'body', the faithful become themselves a 'mystical' body with Christ as their 'head'.[10] The question for political theology is how this conception transitioned into the idea of the modern state as an immortal corporate body whose existence transcends any one individual ruler or officeholder.

The second problem concerns the conflict of competences with respect to who has ultimate jurisdictional authority to interpret given law. In the western medieval world there existed two pretenders to this role: the Pope and the Emperor. Early on, Pope Gelasius assigned the highest authority to the Church because its institution harboured God's Spirit or *Logos*, and its priests were modelled in the Pauline image of the 'spiritual man' who judges all but cannot in turn be judged (1 Corinthians 2:15). For Saint Paul, this 'spiritual man' is sovereign insofar as he is an intermediary between human being and God, as befits the vicar of Jesus the Christ. At the end of the medieval period, and having Hobbes's Leviathan in view, Schmitt argued that peace could be assured only when the role of the last judge, originally taken up by the Pope as vicar of Christ, shall belong to the sovereign as vicar of God. Yet this left open the question of how Hobbesian absolutism could dress itself with the robes of Papal absolutism, as Kantorowicz puts it. By what means and under what logic was the secular sovereign capable of understanding himself as the 'spiritual man'?

---

[10] See the discussion in (Lubac 2007).

The third and last problem concerns the relation between political theology and secularization. For Schmitt, Hobbes's conception of sovereignty preserved and transmitted the legal wisdom of the Church to modern European public law (*jus publicum europaeum*): modern political concepts were secularized theological concepts. But this claim begged the question, Was it not possible for Modernity to develop its own 'secular' political theology? After all, just as the Church tried to preserve its supremacy by transposing its theological concepts into secular law, was it not possible for secular princes to assert *their sovereignty* by transposing Roman legal concepts into Christian theological form? As it happens, this is Kantorowicz's central hypothesis in *The King's Two Bodies*. His book traces how the judges who were to pronounce over matters of *iurisdictio* came to understand themselves as the 'priests' of new *religio iuris* [religion of law] that turned around the 'mystical body' of the People with an absolute emperor at its head.[11] The prince who first worked out this 'secular' political theology is none other than the Emperor Frederick II, the subject of Kantorowicz's extremely controversial book of mytho-poetic history.[12]

Unlike in his Weimar bestseller, the solutions that Kantorowicz offers to these three problems after World War II in the much less readable *The King's Two Bodies* take into account the development of political theology after Schmitt. Voegelin and Maritain had already postulated that a Christian political theology must somehow be linked with the divinization of the People and not with the human king. As discussed earlier, the divinity of the People was prefigured by the Christian idea of the Church as a *corpus mysticum*. However, Voegelin and Maritain were critical of how this idea of the *corpus mysticum* was adopted in secular form in the modern concept of the nation. For them, modern nationalism ultimately led to the deification of the head of state in those 20th-century 'political religions' that were responsible for 'totalizing' the role of the state in society.

In *The King's Two Bodies*, Kantorowicz nonetheless defends the political use of the idea of *corpus mysticum* as the central route through which the western political tradition recovered the idea of an immortal sovereignty that could provide humankind with the conditions for its worldly salvation

---

[11] The origin of the expression is found in *Digest* 1,1,1 where jurists are called 'priests' of Justice because 'we worship Justice and profess the knowledge of what is good and fair' (Kantorowicz 1997, 120).

[12] See the discussion of Kantorowicz's early historiography and its relation to the ideological debates in Weimar Germany in (Mali 1997; and Greiert 2017).

in and through history.¹³ Central to Kantorowicz's reconstruction of the political, state-building application of a theological conception of community is the work of medieval civilian lawyers like Bartolus and Baldus, who recovered the Roman law of corporations in order to give a juridical personality to the association of individuals that was not merely the result of the singular consent of each of its members.¹⁴ But where Schmitt relied on this same tradition to bolster his conception of absolute sovereignty, Kantorowicz is preoccupied with answering Gierke's pluralist objection to Hobbes's social contract. As Gierke put it, by conceiving of a 'single contract by which each pledges himself to each to submit to a common ruler who, on his side, takes no part in the making of the contract... [Hobbes] had destroyed, in the very germ, any personality of the People' (Gierke 1934, 60). In reconstructing the link between the idea of a *corpus mysticum* and the fictional person of the modern state, Kantorowicz seeks to determine the ultimate ground of unity of a People. He seeks to unify the fundamental medieval opposition between the claim that power and authority 'descend' to the people from the hierocratic representatives of the divine and the contrary claim that power and authority 'ascend' from the people's consent to these representatives.¹⁵ In this chapter I show how Kantorowicz's reconstruction of Christian political theology bridges over both alternatives because the conception of liberal government unifies a democratic understanding of the rights of the People with a hierarchical construction of the mystical body of the State.

Voegelin and Maritain were also responsible for rethinking the nature of political representation through a democratic construal of Christian political theology. Their basic claim was that vicariate representation could not be appropriated by the political sovereign. The background to their discussion of representation is given by the Pauline concept of the 'spiritual man' (*pneumatikos*). Whereas Schmitt identified the vicar of God with the Hobbesian sovereign that reunites spiritual and temporal powers, Voegelin and Maritain employ this Pauline figure in order to make

---

¹³ See the discussion of Kantorowicz's reliance on de Lubac's canonical discussion of the mystical body in (Rust 2012). In de Lubac, the idea of the mystical body is conjured up precisely in order to construct a picture of the Church that is not dominated the doctrine of Papal authority. Thus, de Lubac's project is in sympathy with that of Maritain. Although Jennifer Rust is correct to point out that in Schmitt's political theology the vicariate representative plays a more crucial role than the idea of mystical body, she does not see that Kantorowicz's use of the mystical body to support sovereignty as a separate and absolute part of the body politic goes in the direction of Schmitt's project, not against it. On the political ideas linked with the doctrine of the *corpus mysticum*, see (Oakley 1981).
¹⁴ For a discussion of civilian understandings of Roman corporation law, see (Canning 1987).
¹⁵ For this classic formulation, see the papers in (Ullmann 1980).

a distinction between a 'spiritual' form of sovereignty and political sovereignty.[16] Voegelin assigns the role of the 'spiritual man' to those Platonic philosophers and Christian theologians that maintain society 'open' to its transcendent source and thus deprive the king or emperor from the opportunity to usurp this highest of all dignities. Maritain upholds the Gelasian division of authority and power between Church and state as a function of the spiritual, but not temporal, 'sovereignty' of the Catholic Church as universal society based on the respect of human dignity and the democratic aspirations of the poor. Both Voegelin and Maritain want to maintain this 'sovereign' function of the *pneumatikos* separate from the figure of the *politicus*, that is, from the statesman, and in this way hold on to the Augustinian Two City model.

By contrast, in *The King's Two Bodies* Kantorowicz explores the political use of the 'spiritual man' in medieval legal thought in view of establishing a government-based conception of sovereign law and of the administration of justice. In fact, the theological formula for the 'spiritual man' who judges all but cannot in turn be judged corresponds to the medieval legal formula for sovereignty according to which the prince is 'absolved from law' [*princeps legibus solutus*]. According to Tierney, the relation between sovereign and 'spiritual man' passes through the need of the sovereign to be the last judge, and the last judge, in turn, by definition can have no superior judge: 'the very act of setting up a supreme magistrate necessarily removed the chosen person from the sphere of coercive jurisdiction since, by definition, there was no equal or superior who could lay down the law to him with coercive sanctions' (Tierney 1963a, 303).[17] For Tierney this is the essence of Bracton's understanding of the identity of king and judge that defines the king's 'superiority' or sovereignty. It is a thoroughly legalistic conception of the function of the king as last judge, which merely means that 'no judge could dispute his acts. No writ ran against the king. He was indeed *sub lege* in that he had the duty to live according to the laws ... but

---

[16] 'One may even say, in a purely moral sense, that the sage and above all the spiritual man have a kind of sovereignty because they possess supreme independence from above (from Spirit) in relation to the world of passions and the world of law, to whose coercive power they are not subject since their will by itself and spontaneously is in accord with the law [*Summa Theologiae* I–II, 96,6]. They are furthermore "separate in order to rule", that is, to say the truth. And the spiritual man, "judges all and is not judged by anyone" [1 Corinthians 2:15]' (Maritain 1983, 62).

[17] Tierney follows Accursius's gloss to the *lex digna* referring to *Digest* 4,8,4 and 4,8,51 according to which 'a man could not act as arbiter in his own case since he could not issue coercive commands to himself', that is, one cannot be both judge and party of a case since one cannot coerce one's own will.

his observance of the law could be ensured by his own good will, not by judicial coercion' (Tierney 1963a, 303).

Mutatis mutandis, the same paradox of the last judge is repurposed in the establishment of modern public law as that jurisprudential doctrine according to which 'no concept of fundamental law that binds the state can exist' because the absolute state is 'itself the source of law' (Loughlin 2010, 209). The fundamental question that modern public law inherits from medieval jurisprudence is how to employ law in order to 'constitute' the power of the state that is 'absolute' with respect to law because it is the sole authorized maker of coercive law. How is it possible to 'legally' constitute a supra-legal absolute power?[18] 'How can the king be both *legibus solutus* and *sub lege*?' (Loughlin 2010, 40). Here the formula 'the King reigns but does not govern' illustrates the fundamental paradox contained in Loughlin's conception of modern public law. For the idea that the 'King reigns' refers to the 'legal' constitution of the *absolute* state or sovereignty, while the phrase 'but does not govern' refers to what Loughlin calls the 'constitution of the office of government', namely, the received understanding of modern constitutionalism as based on the creation of written constitutions understood as legal documents intended to check the powers and policies of government, but not of sovereignty (Loughlin 2010, 210).

In this chapter, I propose to employ Kantorowicz's interpretation of the 'spiritual man' in order to displace the tension between Tierney's and Loughlin's interpretations of the relation between medieval constitutionalism and modern sovereignty. Tierney's standpoint is generally legalistic and even Kelsenian: the king is loosed from laws (*legibus solutus*), and is thereby granted an incoercible will, only thanks to an underlying 'basic norm' of the type 'thou shalt abide by the laws' because these laws are recognized by all to be divine origin.[19] On the contrary, Loughlin's standpoint is admittedly Schmittian: his distinction between a 'constitution' of the absolute sovereign

---

[18] I put 'legally' in quotation marks because it becomes clear that for Loughlin 'legally' stands for a concept of 'right ordering' (Loughlin 2010, 91) that seems to be his own rendition of Schmitt's idea of *nomos*. For Schmitt's and Loughlin's discussion of *nomos* I refer to (Vatter 2018).

[19] Thus the unbound command of emperor is not the 'ultimate basis of law in the Roman legal system since his authority to command rested on a preceding law and the validity of that in turn on the principle to which we have been led, "law is what all men ought to obey". The essence of the argument was that law logically preceded sovereignty since sovereignty was a product of law' (Tierney 1963b, 394).

and the written, legal constitution overseeing the activity of government is drawn from Schmitt's *Constitutional Theory*. Indeed, Loughlin's main thesis is that the doctrine of 'political jurisprudence' or 'public law' ought to follow Schmitt in establishing the priority of the first or 'material' constitution of the sovereign over the second or 'formal' constitution of government through the rule of law.[20] I argue that Kantorowicz opens a very different understanding of medieval and early modern jurisprudence that subverts both the legalistic and the sovranist interpretations of modern constitutionalism.

Kantorowicz's story traces how the function of the Pauline 'spiritual man' is given an absolutist construal during the Papacy of Innocent III, when the Pope as 'spiritual man' becomes the statesman (*politicus*) par excellence in virtue of his power to intervene in the temporal affairs of princes and emperors, and establishing 'exceptions' with respect to ancient laws and customs.[21] However, Kantorowicz is fundamentally interested in how the role of 'spiritual man' was translated into the secular sphere by Frederick II, the contemporary of Innocent III and St. Francis. It is Frederick II who proposes a new office for the emperor, no longer as a representative of a mystical People but as the representative of a mystical Humanity which later receives its fundamental formulation in Dante's treatise on world empire. Kantorowicz's genealogy shares the same negative goal as Schmitt, namely, to show the impossibility of maintaining a Gelasian division between Church and Empire, spiritual authority and political power. But Kantorowicz's discussion of Dante's cosmopolitan government suggests that his resolution of the congenital crisis of the Augustinian model of the Two Cities does not sit comfortably with Schmitt's Hobbesian solution.

Kantorowicz does not only radicalize Schmitt's political theology in a democratic and cosmopolitan direction. He also innovates on Schmitt's political theology at the methodological level. In *The King's Two Bodies*, Kantorowicz begins by following Schmitt's methodological definition of political theology as the study of 'a transference of definitions from one sphere to another, from theology to law' (Kantorowicz 1997, 19). According to Kantorowicz, the construal of absolute monarchy in medieval English legal and political thought took initially the form of a genuine 'Royal Christology', for it depended on a parallelism between the King's two bodies and Christ's

---

[20] See now also (Loughlin 2018).
[21] For Innocent III and his significance, see (Prieto 1982; and Tierney 1964).

dual nature as human and divine. However, as Kantorowicz's argument unfolds and political theology gets increasingly articulated in democratic and cosmopolitan terms, so too he begins to *reverse* Schmitt's claim that all political concepts are 'secularized' theological concepts. On the contrary, Kantorowicz's research shows that the jurists of the English court employed the Trinitarian theology of the Church for their own secular purposes, which in many ways sought to return the understanding of politics to neo-Hellenistic and neo-Roman paradigms. Thus, *The King's Two Bodies* proposes a 'secular "political theology"' in which it is Hellenistic and Roman legal-political concepts that are transferred into Christian theology, and not vice versa. In this sense, Kantorowicz anticipates Agamben's later attempt to fix the origins of popular government in the liturgy and rituals of imperial acclamations, which only subsequently were adopted by the Church in order to bolster its absolutist claims in favour of Papal sovereignty, starting with Innocent III.

In order to identify the subsumption of the medieval idea of *iurisdictio* into the modern idea of liberal government, I then proceed to compare the picture of medieval constitutionalism found in McIlwain with that proposed by Kantorowicz. I argue that McIlwain offers an interpretation of Bracton as paradigmatic of the medieval tendency to frame and limit the power of government within the authority of constitutional laws. In contrast, I show that Kantorowicz offers an interpretation of Bracton that points out how liberalism frames and limits constitutionalism within an account of the superior power of government. What unites McIlwain and Kantorowicz is their common rejection of the Schmittian claim that modern sovereignty somehow rises above both the elements of constitution and of government. My reading of McIlwain and Kantorowicz therefore questions the current revival of sovereignty in order to counteract the hegemony of liberal governance.[22] The chapter concludes with a critical discussion of the recent attempts by sociologists of constitutionalism like Hauke Brunkhorst and Christopher Thornhill to identify the origin of the supposed autonomy of western democratic constitutionalism with respect to popular/national sovereignty as well as to liberal governance in the 'legal revolution' brought about by canon law and conciliarism.

---

[22] For a critical discussion of how the opposition of sovereignty and government reappears in recent attempts to bolster the sovereignty of the state against the claims of liberal government like (Loughlin 2010; and Tuck 2016), I refer to (Vatter 2019).

The immortality of the corporate body as unity of democratic and monarchic principles

The King's Two Bodies is the most influential text on the discourse of political theology in the second half of the 20th century. Published in 1957, shortly after the fundamental works of Maritain and Voegelin, the book can be read both as a response to their apparent rejection of Schmittian 'political theology', as well as a belated intervention into the political and constitutional debates in Weimar Germany, to which Kantorowicz had been privy as an active member of the George Circle. The Preface to the book points to this contemporary context when it asserts that its theme are 'certain axioms of a political theology which *mutatis mutandis* was to remain valid until the twentieth century' (Kantorowicz 1997, xviii). Kantorowicz refers to the technical term introduced by Voegelin when he speaks of the 'idols of modern political religions' and of the 'horrifying experience of our own time in which whole nations . . . fell prey to the weirdest dogmas and in which political theologemes became genuine obsessions' (Kantorowicz 1997, xviii). The negative connotations used in conjunction with these technical terms and the reference to Cassirer's *Myth of the State* give the impression that Kantorowicz intends the book as a contribution to the de-mythologization of politics, as a critique of political theology. The reading proposed in the following pages, instead, indicates that Kantorowicz intended to develop political theology in a new direction.[23] This new direction can be discerned by starting from the analysis of the basic novelty of the book, pointed out by all interpreters, which consists in placing the immortality of the political body, namely, the 'second' body of the monarch, at the centre of the discourse of political theology.

Kantorowicz's concern is fundamentally with the genealogy of modern sovereignty as an *immortal* corporation. As both Francis Oakley and John Pocock point out, the relation between political form and divine or natural eternity is a fundamental feature of all western political thought.[24] In his recent defence of the idea of the modern state as fictional corporation, Quentin Skinner points to one of the most obvious sources of interest for such an

---

[23] Kahn advances the thesis of Kantorowicz's ambivalent relation to political theology: '*The King's Two Bodies* is a contribution to the project outlined by Cassirer, he signals his own desire not simply to reproduce or advocate political myths (as he did in his *Frederick II*), but to analyse how they worked. Unlike, Cassirer, however, Kantorowicz was also interested in redeeming myth—including artificial or manufactured myth—for modernity', namely, a 'secular "political theology"' (Kahn 2014, 60).

[24] See (Pocock 1975; and Oakley 1999).

immortal corporation: only such an entity can incur financial obligations that would be unsustainable for mortal individuals and groups.[25]

The idea of an immortal and fictional corporation was developed by medieval civilian lawyers like Bartolus and Baldus for whom a corporation or *universitas* is 'a body composed of a plurality of human beings and an abstract unitary entity perceptible only by the intellect and thus distinct from its human members'.[26] On this conception, an association of individuals is a group of people who have been *incorporated* into a juridical personality that is as distinct from the natural persons involved in the association as spirit is distinct from matter. As I already discussed in relation to Schmitt, this idea of a 'spiritual' corporation as a 'fictional person' lies at the basis of the modern conception of the sovereignty of the nation-state.[27] Kantorowicz's interest, however, lies in understanding the paradoxical *reality* of this *incorporated* aggregate of individuals forming one political *body* or People that is 'perceptible only by the intellect' and that is fictionally 'personated' by the sovereign representative.

The legal construction of such an immortal People is entirely dependent on a political theology. That is why Kantorowicz opens his discussion of the People as the 'second body' of the King by signalling the provenance of the figure of an immortal body from monotheistic political theologies of angels. The king or emperor was considered to be angelical in the sense that he was an intermediary between human beings and God.[28] The monotheistic discourses on angels appropriates the figure of Hellenistic kingship that Peterson had seen fit to identify as the source of political theology. Through this reference to angelical emperors, Kantorowicz's book signals that it is offering a history of the reception of Hellenistic ideas of kingship in medieval Western Christendom as the ground on which modernity would derive its conception of the state. From the very start, *The King's Two Bodies* presents itself as a response to Peterson's critique of political theology. For Peterson, Augustine put to rest the Christian reception of Hellenistic sacral kingship. Kantorowicz shows that this reception continues unabated throughout

---

[25] See (Skinner 2009). Skinner's article reflects the lessons from the last great global financial crisis of 2008 that was managed, in extremis, only thanks to the 'immortal corporation' of the United States government posing as 'lender of last resort' for the entire global financial system (Tooze 2018). It is no coincidence that Kantorowicz shows how the doctrine of the immortality of the corporation first comes into its own in relation to the institution of the fisc.

[26] Baldus cited in (Canning 1987, 186).

[27] On the connection between corporate personality and modern state, see (Canning 1983; and Skinner 2009), among many others.

[28] On the idea of the angelical emperor see (Reeves 1969).

late medieval political philosophy and becomes the source of modern state theory.

The 'second' body of the king is that of a *corporation*, composed of a king who as head of the corporation governs the body composed of its subjects. Kantorowicz's chosen theme, from the start, re-occupies the terrain that Schmitt later identified as the proper field of political theology: not the analogy between One God and One King, but that between One God and One People. Kantorowicz seeks to understand the 'mystery' through which the 'body' of the *representative* (viz., the king's 'body') of the people constitutes the 'body' of the People as a whole. In this way, he attempts to give an answer to the problem set out in Schmitt's constitutional theory: How can a constitution articulate together the monarchical principle of representation and the democratic principle of identity?

Schmitt did not give a persuasive argument as to how this was possible, since, as he admits, the monarchic principle was dependent on the dynastic principle, but this principle rested on the physical mortality of the kings. Likewise, the democratic principle did not offer, of itself, a basis of political unity, since the 'immortal' unity of a political body could not be composed by the aggregation of individual wills through the instrument of the contract, for that would make the political body entirely 'mortal' and dependent on the whim of individuals keeping their promises to each other. Thus, Schmitt asserted that Hobbes's Leviathan could not be fabricated in an 'ascending' fashion, simply on the basis of agreements between individuals. Yet he could not identify an alternative ground for the 'transcendence' of the state vis-à-vis the social contract.

Kantorowicz's thesis is that Hobbes's theory of the state was possible only thanks to the concept of a 'second body' of the King that composes the unity of a People in a 'descending' fashion. The idea of the King's 'Two Bodies' offered what Schmitt was looking for: the unity of monarchical and democratic principles in every legal constitution. This is the reason Kantorowicz takes up in all seriousness the legal fiction of the 'corporation sole' in English common law in order to respond to the critique of medieval corporative thinking in Gierke's *Genossenschaftsrecht* (the law of fellowships) and in the English pluralists, for whom this legal fiction figure had become an object of ridicule.

The intention to unify a democratic body with a monarchic head is visible from the very start of the book, when Kantorowicz writes that the English revolutionaries were 'fighting the king to defend the King', and takes this

'Puritan war cry' as evidence that the legal fiction of the King's 'two bodies' was still alive well into the English civil war (Kantorowicz 1997, 23).[29] This bold and paradoxical claim offers a number of important insights into the character of Kantorowicz's democratic political theology. If Kantorowicz is correct, then his hypothesis lends support to Schmitt's contention that even the Republic sought by the Puritan Revolution requires a monarchic principle, albeit one that is not articulated in a dynastic fashion.

This hypothesis has recently been recycled by some historians of political ideas who argue that a republic (a democracy) not only can be, but somehow also needs to be 'monarchic'.[30] The same reasoning is employed to argue that the modern conception of absolute sovereignty in Bodin and Hobbes was always 'constitutional' and 'republican'. Thus, Richard Tuck and Kinch Hoekstra have tried to show that modern constitutionalism is essentially a by-product of modern sovereignty.[31] Kantorowicz's anti-republican interpretation of the Puritan war cry brings to mind how Schmitt, in *The Concept of the Political*, had cited Cromwell's claim that the Spaniard is 'the great enemy of the National Being' in order to illustrate the inescapable horizon of political theology even for republicanism.[32] Today, the same point is articulated by those pundits who claim that the 'War on Terror' and other such challenges can only be addressed through the supremacy of government (and, in particular, of the executive power). From this belief, it is but a short step to claiming that whoever attacks the (new) monarchic principle of the 'second body' of the King is actually 'anti-democratic' and does not have the *salus populi* as their supreme concern.

---

[29] See the discussion of the Puritan war cry in (Norbrook 1996, 340–47). I agree with Norbrook that Kantorowicz presents an anti-republican rendering not only of Shakespeare but of the English civil war.

[30] See (Hankins 2010) and my critical response (Vatter 2014b). An early version of this thesis can be found in (Mansfield 1989). The claim that revolutionary republics are 'monarchic' contradicts all accounts of modern republican revolutions based on the thesis of a return of neo-Aristotelian and neo-Roman republicanism with Renaissance humanism and Machiavelli, as first outlined by (Baron 1988; and Pocock 1975). It is interesting that Eric Nelson starts his revisionist reconstruction of the American Revolution by adopting McIlwain's thesis that the American patriots began their rebellion in 'a sincere desire to rebalance the English constitution in favour of the Crown' and against Parliamentary sovereignty, only to then argue, against McIlwain, that 'the turn to the royal prerogative was the formative moment in the history of what would emerge as American constitutionalism' (Nelson 2017, 6–7). Nelson's book appears to be framed by the formula 'the king reigns but does not govern'—see the last footnote of the book (ibid., 344, n.14).

[31] Hoekstra, for his part, argues that the Hobbesian conception of sovereignty leads to a modern form of constitutionalism because the emphasis on the unique, not mixed idea of sovereignty defended by early modern absolutism does not contradict, and indeed may call for, a mixed, that is, 'limited', idea of government (Hoekstra 2013, 1082–83). Neither of these historians draws his insights back to Kantorowicz's critique of McIlwain.

[32] See the discussion of Schmitt's use of Cromwell in (Meier 1995, 29).

My hypothesis is that Kantorowicz's interpretation of the Puritan war cry indicates that he solves the problem of unifying democratic and monarchical principles in a constitution by theorizing the freedom of 'liberal' government from constitutional limits as the climax of a 'secular' and 'democratic' political theology. For Kantorowicz, government is the true, veridical, or vicariate representative of the King's 'second body' as the body of the People. Government is representative of the immortality of the People as corporate body: its prerogatives, rather than those of the sovereign, fall under the dictum *salus populi summa lex est*. If this hypothesis is correct, then Kantorowicz's political theology of government overturns what Gordon Wood identified as the most proper creation of the Atlantic Revolutions, namely, the principle of 'representative government' itself, according to which all governments rest on the opinion of the people, and therefore all governments are finite and mortal, not infinite and immortal.[33]

Judge of all, not judged by anyone: Vicissitudes of the 'spiritual man'

In his essay "Mysteries of State. An Absolutist Concept and Its Late Medieval Origins", which slightly anticipates *The King's Two Bodies*,[34] Kantorowicz says that the expression 'mystery of state', which dates back to the 12th century, is nowadays 'designated by the more general term of "political theology"' (Kantorowicz 1984, 79). Without mentioning either Schmitt or Peterson by name, he notes that 'this expression ['political theology'] . . . was discussed at length in the 1930s in Germany'.[35] The essay traces how the expression

---

[33] See (Wood 1969).
[34] (Kantorowicz 1955), later republished in (Kantorowicz 1965, 381-98); I shall refer to (Kantorowicz 1984).
[35] Kantorowicz's relation to Schmitt's thought and, in general, the question of whether he adhered or rejected political theology is thematized in (Boureau 1990, 162-71). Boureau argues that Kantorowicz reverses Schmitt because in his work the centrality of the Incarnation offers to political theology an 'emancipatory fiction that affirms the inalienable and sacred dignity of man before and beyond his natural existence' rather than serve the absolutist aspirations of profane monarchs as in Schmitt. As already mentioned, this is not quite correct. The connection to Schmitt is object of discussion in recent work on Kantorowicz such as (Santner 2011; Kahn 2014; and Rust 2012). Excellent discussions of Kantorowicz's ideological commitments are also found in (Monod 2005; and Norbrook 1996). Overall, the most balanced and in-depth treatment of the contested details of Kantorowicz's biography are found in (Benson 1997; and Lerner 2017), which however do not treat of political theology nor of the relation to Schmitt. None of these works attempts to contextualize Kantorowicz's political theology as an argument internal to medieval jurisprudence and philosophy of law, and in that sense they deprive themselves of the proper context in which to decide the question of the nature of Kantorowicz's relation to Schmitt and to political theology.

arcana ecclesiae (the mysteries of the Church) came to be transferred to the state, giving rise to the *arcana imperii* (secrets of state, the content of 'reason of state'), which since then became a privileged marker of modern state sovereignty.[36]

Following Schmitt, Kantorowicz argues that the motivation for this secularizing transfer of theological conceptions onto political ones comes from the juridical, not the religious or economical, sphere. More particularly, the transfer starts from the reception of Roman law by Canon law with Innocent III. From there it moves to the civilian lawyers like Bartolus and his disciple Baldus, and from these to English common law where they are received principally in Bracton's treatment of prerogative, in order to finally reach modern absolutist monarchs like James I and Charles I, who often employed the idea of 'prerogative' as synonymous with 'mysteries of state'.[37] The point of Kantorowicz's genealogy is to highlight the 'Pontificialism' of modern absolutism, by which he means the development of a 'religion of law' (*religio iuris*) that underpins the early modern construction of sovereignty.

Kantorowicz traces the overlap of jurists with priests, of law with theology, back to the Pauline ideal of the 'spiritual man', already alluded to by Jacques Maritain,[38] found in 1 Corinthians 2:15, where it is said that the spiritual man is judge of all but no one can judge him. As discussed earlier, Saint Paul's figure offers the theological basis of the public law conception of sovereignty as the highest *legal* power that itself stands under no law. With Boniface VIII's bull *Unam Sanctam* the Roman Catholic Church claimed for itself the power of 'universal jurisdiction': *Sancta sedes omnes iudicat, sed a nemine iudicatur* [the Holy See judges all men but cannot be judged by anyone]. Not long afterwards, the authority to be the last judge embodied in the Papal office is transferred to the political sphere by civilians like Baldus, who supports the claims to universal jurisdiction voiced by the Holy Roman Emperor.[39] As a consequence the Emperor receives the title of *Rex, quia alios regit et a nemine regitur* [king, who rules over others and is ruled by no one]. The terminal

---

[36] On mysteries of state and reason of state, see (Senellart 1995), and in reference to Schmitt, see (Vatter 2008).

[37] This lineage conforms to the later history of transmission sketched by (Oakley 1968; and Berman 1983), discussed below.

[38] Interestingly, in this essay Kantorowicz refers to Maritain's own treatment of the spiritual man or super-man in his 1933 *Conversations of a Sage*.

[39] Kantorowicz's reading of Baldus's recognition of the emperor's sovereignty does not mention that Baldus understood this jurisdiction to be merely *de jure*, whereas *de facto* other corporations, like city-states, could not recognize the jurisdiction of the emperor over their territories. On this point see (Canning 1987; and Skinner 1978).

station of this lineage is the absolutist interpretation of the English monarchy found in James I and Charles I.

Kantorowicz points out that in Salmasius's apology of the executed English king, *Defensio regia pro Carlo I*, the identification of the king with the 'spiritual man' is an exemplary application of pontifical theory to a secular state: 'the absolute prince had worn the shoes of the Roman pontiff: he, the prince, became the superman, the *homo spiritualis* that Boniface VIII had attempted so violently to monopolize for the Roman pontiff excluding all others' (Kantorowicz 1984, 89).

Kantorowicz's genealogy is designed to illustrate the attempt on the part of secular kings to wrest the crown that the militant jurist-Popes, emboldened by their own clerical legal revolution, had initially placed on their own heads. The genealogy clearly points backwards in time to the struggles of Frederick II against Papal supremacy, which received a theoretical formulation in Dante, as well as forwards towards the self-crowning of Napoleon. Napoleon's gesture finds its most important theoretical reflection in the anti-Christian polemics of Goethe and Nietzsche. Given this context, it is not surprising that Kantorowicz translates the 'spiritual man' as 'superman' or 'overman', a term that also derives from 1 Corinthians 2:10, but whose connotations brings us much closer to the heroes celebrated in the *George Kreis*, figures like Goethe and Nietzsche, for whom humankind is seen to be the invention of Prometheus, who stands in rebellion against Zeus.

The peculiar association established between emperor and poet-philosopher is only strengthened in another crucial essay that postdates *The King's Two Bodies*, "The Sovereignty of the Artist. A Note on Legal Maxims and Renaissance Theories of Art."[40] Here Kantorowicz again returns to the theological question of the origins of sovereign prerogatives. He locates this origin in a defender of Papal absolutism and disciple of Aquinas, Aegidius Romanus and his *De regimine principum*.[41] Following Schmitt's problem of legal application, Kantorowicz highlights Aegidius' claim that, although the act of making human law must follow natural law, the sovereign is faced with the problem of applying the universal norms of natural law to changing historical situations and contexts, and for this reason it must 'invent' what Aegidius calls 'the particular of positive right' (Kantorowicz 1984, 39).

---

[40] Originally published in 1961 in (Kantorowicz 1961); then taken up in (Kantorowicz 1965, 352–65). I shall cite from the French edition, (Kantorowicz 1984).
[41] It is noteworthy that, for the defenders of the neo-Roman lineage of constitutionalism, the key author is another student of Aquinas, Ptolemy of Lucca.

According to Kantorowicz, this freedom of application (of invention or interpretation) of the given universal norm in the work of the human legislator justifies the analogy between the human legislator and the Creator, since the legislator must effectively 'recreate nature' in his or her interpretation of the given law. This the legislator can do insofar as he is *vicarius Christi* (in the case of the Pope) or *vicarius Dei* (in the case of the emperor or king). Thus, in his reading Kantorowicz undoes the traditional distinction between *iurisdictio* and *legislatio*, the distinction between interpreting and making law, and does so precisely in line with Schmitt's understanding of the problem of *quis judicabit?*, the problem of the 'spiritual man'.

The important advance of Kantorowicz with respect to Schmitt's discussion of juridical personality is that he takes the notion of vicariate representation to correspond to the interpretation of the Decretals given around the time of Innocent III, where the Pope as *vicarius Christi* takes the place or re-presents Christ in virtue of being *both divine and human*. It is only for this reason, in the words of the gloss by Tancred to the decretal *Compilatio III 1,5,3*, that the Pope has the power of 'making something out of nothing' [*Item de nichilo facit aliquid ut deus*]. It is this capacity of *creatio ex nihilo*, in the moment of the application of law, that gets designated by the idea of a 'fullness of powers' or *plenitudo potestatis*, and which justifies the Pope's 'right' to dispense with right and go against it [*quia potest dispensare super ius et contra ius*] (Kantorowicz 1984, 44). The importance of this essay thus lies in offering a genealogy of Schmitt's definition of the sovereign as a power to decide, *ex nihilo*, the state of exception to positive law, and thereby 're-create' the legal order, at one as a jurist-priest and as an artist-inventor of political order.

Faithful to the beliefs of the George Circle, Kantorowicz therefore opens the theological category of 'spiritual man' to the artist and poet and conjoins this creative figure with the jurisdictional powers of the sovereign. The jurisprudential basis for Kantorowicz's novel conjunction between emperor, last judge, and artist/poet is provided by another crucial paradigm that was employed in medieval political thought in order to resolve the paradox of sovereignty, or the paradox of a legal constitution of supra-legal sovereignty. This is the paradigm offered by the idea that God's omnipotence takes two forms, an 'absolute' and an 'ordered' form. The first appearance of this distinction in medieval thought also occurs in Aegidius Romanus, one of Aquinas's students. In his treaty on Papal power, Aegidius argued that the Pope, although standing above positive laws, governs the Church like God governs nature: through his 'ordinate power' or *potestas regulate* that is visible in the 'common course of nature', that is, where divine government operates by way of secondary causes. However, Aegidius' point is to signal that the world can also be governed through the 'special providence of God', or in accordance with 'a "special" law', and this second form of divine government corresponds to God's absolute power or *potestas absoluta*.[42] Kantorowicz seems to have been the first to link this 'absolute power' to create 'ex nihilo' a legal order with the imperial-artistic form of government.

In 1968, Francis Oakley published an important essay on the political theology of this conception of absolute power with the title "Jacobean Political Theology: The Absolute and Ordinary Powers of the King." Oakley begins his treatment by identifying the fact that lawyers for Charles I argued that the King had two kinds of powers: absolute and ordinary. The former power is oriented towards the salvation of the people (*salus populi*) and cannot come under positive law because it is meant to deal with unforeseen emergencies (Oakley 1968, 325). Following Kantorowicz's hypothesis, though without citing him, Oakley then proceeds to argue that the King's absolute powers are essentially jurisdictional powers. The doctrine of absolute powers puts in question the constitutional principle that the king is limited by laws or rights which it receives and which it cannot change.[43]

The novelty of Oakley's approach consists in recovering the Papal doctrine of *plenitudo potestatis* away from the imperial and monarchical appropriations, defended by Kantorowicz, in order to make it the basis of a Christian political theology in sympathy with the outlines previously worked out by Maritain. The background of Oakley's argument is theocratic: of interest to him is the sense in which God is the only 'absolute' sovereign, and what consequences this axiom has when absolute power is lodged in the Church, rather than in the Empire. The project, not unlike that of Maritain, is to offer the lineaments of a Christian political theology that would withstand the claims to absolute sovereignty coming from Empire (the very ones outlined by Kantorowicz). With respect to the Gelasian picture, Oakley strongly defends the unitary conception of the Church as holder of all powers, which are merely 'delegated' to the emperor or king according to the circumstances. On this view, the dualist interpretation of Gelasius is too easily interpreted

---

[42] (*De ecclesiastica potestate* IV,7, 181–82) On this origin of Schmitt's theory of constituent power, see (Ojakangas 2012).
[43] In Oakley's genealogy, it is Bodin who makes use of the distinction between absolute and ordinary powers (*Six livres de la république* I,8) in order to give the king, through his absolute power, the capacity to take exception to positive laws, but not to take exception to divine or natural laws.

in pro-imperial ways.⁴⁴ If the Pope is sole vicar of God, then no emperor can be vicar of God. Like for Innocent III, Frederick II is thereby revealed as Antichrist. Through this genealogy of absolute powers, Oakley seeks to reject all forms of sacral kingship in order to bolster the fundamental political role of the Church as that institution in which the analogy between One God and One People finds its institutional realization in the form of conciliarism.⁴⁵

The political role of the Church is to fight against secular claims to absolute sovereignty. Oakley is perhaps the foremost defender of the Figgisite thesis that modern constitutionalism begins with the decree of the Council of Constance of Pierre d'Ailly and Jean Gerson, *Haec sancta synodus*, whereby the general council asserts its superiority over the Pope.⁴⁶ As with Maritain's notion of employing the idea of the mystical body of the Church against the claims of absolutism, which separates the political body into the King's two bodies, Oakley argues that the fundamental thesis of conciliarism is contained in 'the belief that the Pope was not an absolute monarch ... that the final authority in the Church ... lay not with him but *with the whole body of the faithful* or with their representatives gathered in a general council' (Oakley 1969, 368). In reality, Figgis and Oakley put the discourse of political theology, that is, the transference of theological categories onto juridical ones, at the service of an anti-sovereign politics based on the fundamental priority of the right of resistance, which is something denied by all absolutist theories of sovereignty. On the view of Figgis, the mature fruit of conciliarism is none other than the Monarcomachist classic, *Vindiciae contra Tyrannos*, on which Laski wrote an important study in 1924.⁴⁷ In the *Vindiciae*, in fact, the analogy is drawn between the right of a council to depose a Pope with the right of 'the general Assembly of the Estates of any kingdom, who are the representative body thereof' to depose a king (Oakley 1969, 374).

In later essays, Oakley adds an important element to his genealogy of the distinction between absolute and ordered powers. Assigning God an absolute power signals the belief that the order of nature is radically contingent because it emerges *ex nihilo*. Whereas Albertus Magnus and Aquinas

---

⁴⁴ This was evident in Kantorowicz's claim that Dante exacerbated the dualism between Empire and Church, and is a radical 'dualist'. For a general introduction to this issue, see (Kilcullen 2004).

⁴⁵ On sacral kingship, see (Oakley 2006). On the development of this thesis for medieval and early modern political thought, see (Oakley 2010; 2015).

⁴⁶ On the connection between conciliarism and modern constitutionalism, see the long-running polemic between (Oakley 1995; and Nederman 1996).

⁴⁷ See Laski's introduction to the *Vindiciae* in (Laski 1924). Not by coincidence, Oakley cites Laski: 'the road from Constance to 1688 was a direct one' (Oakley 1969, 376).

considered *in abstracto* the possibility that God had an absolute power prior to His choice of the order of creation, but that He does not employ this power once that order has been created, a different and much more radical interpretation of absolute power begins with the 13th-century canonist Hostiensis and climaxes with the Franciscan Duns Scotus. These theologians apply to God the distinction between legal and supra-legal powers that were established by Innocent III's claim to *plenitudo potestatis*, so that absolute power comes to be understood 'as a *presently-active power of potential interposition* in the established order' (Oakley 1998a, 670, emphasis mine). On this view, God is said to act *de jure* according to ordained power but *de facto* 'he can act apart from and against the law' (Oakley 1998b, 447). In other words, the absolute power of God becomes 'a presently active and extraordinary power capable of operating apart from the order established *de potentia ordinate* and prevailing in the ordinary course of things' (Oakley 1998b, 447). In short, with Duns Scotus God's absolute power comes to have the characters of an extraordinary form of legislation.[48]

In his genealogy, Oakley suggests that the idea of an 'absolute' power of God was developed within canon law in order to 'deflect' the perceived threat posed to Christianity by the spread of Arabic Aristotelianism, mainly in the form of Averroism, within the universities.[49] For Oakley, the problem of Averroism is that it links God and nature under the modality of necessity, rather than of contingency. Oakley does not specify the political 'threat' posed by this change in fundamental modalities, but it is not difficult to discern it. If divine government no longer allows for departures from natural law, or natural right, then there is no longer a ground for the Church to claim spiritual leadership of the secular world. This leadership function is now claimed by the alternative Platonic-Aristotelian possibility of the king and last judge being a philosopher who follows natural right. According to Kantorowicz, this is exactly the path adopted by Frederick II and his courts of jurists in their struggle against the Church.

---

[48] This radical nominalist path to modernity is the one favoured in the grand narratives of secularization in Milbank, Taylor, and others. Taylor calls it the 'Intellectual Deviation' narrative that leads from Christian nominalism to early modern mechanism. Taylor himself adds to this the 'Reform Master Narrative' in which Christianity is directed by Protestantism into an exclusively inner-worldly conception of salvation that constitutes the 'immanent frame' of Modernity. For Taylor 'we need both ID and RMN to explain religion today' (Taylor 2007, 776). Milbank's and Taylor's narratives, however, sidestep entirely the genealogy of medieval jurisprudence put forward by Kantorowicz and Oakley.

[49] On the stakes in the spread of Averroism, see (Flasch 2006).

Trinitarianism and secularization: Frederick II and the beginnings of Modernity

In *The King's Two Bodies*, Kantorowicz argues on two fronts simultaneously. On the one hand, he seeks to disprove Schmitt's secularization theorem that the Church's canon law lies at the source of the modern doctrine of the state. On the other hand, he seeks to disprove Walter Ullmann's claim that neither the Church nor the Empire, but rather a combination of feudalism with the recovery of paganism (Aristotelianism), is responsible for granting the political sphere a semi-eternal duration and stability. *The King's Two Bodies* traces an arc that begins from the Norman idea of the king as vicar of Christ and ends with the idea, exemplified by the legend of Frederick II, and theorized by Dante and Marsilius of Padua, that a worldly messianic redemption can only be brought about by a secular emperor who is entirely victorious over the Church's claims to hold the 'plenitude of powers'.

The most surprising and provocative thesis of this book is Kantorowicz's demolition of Peterson's claim that Trinitarianism made political theology impossible. Kantorowicz defends the claim that it was precisely in and through a juridical adoption of Trinitarianism that secularization was first realized in a conception of absolute, popular government. By intimating that it is secular monarchism, rather than hierocratic Papalism, which is the true inheritor of Trinitarianism in jurisprudence, Kantorowicz also reverses Schmitt's secularization thesis: a pagan ideal of politics used Christian theology to persevere in existence more successfully than the Church used its interpretation of Roman law in order to put an end to the claims of imperial power. This is why for Kantorowicz the western medieval emperor (and later the western medieval king) is more than a copy of the Pope. This is what breaks the specular relation between Pope and sovereign that still underlies Schmitt's political Catholicism.

Kantorowicz is adamant about the need to distinguish the notion of the 'dual person' of the king from the traditional Roman law distinction between person and office. The object of the polemic here is Ullmann's notion of a hierocratic conception of the Papacy that relies on Roman law through the idea of office. For Ullmann, all medieval political thought is fundamentally hierocratic: the power to interpret the given law was originally entirely sacral and followed from the fact that Christ had committed to the Apostle Peter, and later to the other Popes who succeeded him, the power of '*solvere* and *ligere* originally referred to the decision of the judge'.[50] The fundamental source for this divine authorization is Matthew 16:18–19: 'you are Peter, and on this rock I will build my church. . . . I will give you the keys of the kingdom, and whatever you bind on earth shall be bound in heaven, and whatever you loose on earth shall be loosed in heaven'. On this view, it is Christ Himself who establishes the Pope as ultimate judge on earth. The function of emperors and kings is only to act as the 'material sword' of the spiritual power to judge.

Ullmann claimed that the crucial passage from theology to law, from the charismatic 'gift of judgment' to its institutionalization in the form of Papal law, occurs during the papacy of Leo I. What permits this passage is the recovery of a figure or legal fiction found in the Roman law of inheritance. Thanks to this fiction, the Pope is understood as the *indignus haeres* of Saint Peter: 'the heir continues legally the deceased. . . . The Pope, consequently, as heir of St. Peter, steps into his place and acts as if Peter himself had acted' (Ullmann 1980, I,38). Here then is the original model of the vicar of Christ: what each Pope inherits is the *office* of Saint Peter; the Pope himself is not a charismatic leader, but an institutional representative. To the office of the vicar of Christ is entrusted the people (*populus*) as a minor, to be spiritually guided by those who know, who have *scientia* of God's ways (Ullmann 1980, VIII,11). Ullmann stresses the Platonic motif of a *radical separation* between the body of the Church, the faithful, and their guide, the Pope and clergy, which maps onto the absolute distinction between soul and body (Ullmann 1980, VIII,15–19).[51]

For Kantorowicz, conversely, the idea of a 'dual person' has a purely theological, Trinitarian origin, which does not depend on Roman law. Ullmann's conception of the Church is Petrine, whereas Kantorowicz's is Pauline. By rejecting the concept of office, Kantorowicz seeks to diminish the dependence of modern government on Roman law and its inherent constitutionalism or legalism, for reasons that will appear clear in the next section.

Kantorowicz's narrative begins with the 'Christ-centred kingship' theorized by the Norman Anonymous, around 1100. In this doctrine, the Norman

---

[50] (Ullmann 1980, I,37). The reference is first to essay number, then its original pagination.

[51] Strangely enough, Ullmann cites from Spinoza's *Tractatus politicus* X,9 *Anima enim imperii jura sunt* [the constitution is the soul of the state] to explain the notion of the Pope and clergy as *anima* of the Church: 'the *anima* symbolized the idea of a permanent idea of law which could be made known and issued only by those who were in possession of the norms constituting law and justice', that is, by those who had 'knowledge of Christ's own mind' (Ullmann 1980, VIII,20). What is curious about this citation is that, in Spinoza, those who know the mind of Christ do not correspond to one Church, and the contents of this mind are the principles of a civil religion.

king is considered to have two natures: he is king by nature and king by grace. By grace, the king is a *christomimetes*, the stand-in for Christ or the Messiah. In this role, the king becomes 'deified' by grace.[52] Kingship is sacral due to a charismatic quality, namely, God's gift of His power to the king for a brief period. At this early stage of development, the conception of the 'Two Bodies' of the King is still not routinized and does not give rise to any claim to sempi-eternal duration. The Norman Anonymous still employs the analogy between One God and One King in order to sacralize human kingship. But in this way the king remains bound to the Church and its priesthood, which offers the necessary sacraments. By the time that Frederick II introduces a model of 'law-centred kingship', the human king needs to be immortalized, not in the first person, but in his 'second person' or 'body', which represents the incorporation of the People. This development occurs only thanks to the adoption and secularization of Trinitarianism into jurisprudence.

Unlike in Maritain, for Kantorowicz the purpose of government is not to carry out God's plan or providence. Instead, divine providence allows God to retreat from history, leaving His Son free to act in history within an always already secular space of government. Kantorowicz took seriously the widespread belief that Joachim of Fiore's prophecy of an 'Age of Spirit', in which the Gospel's message of liberty, equality, and fraternity would become universal, was actually ushered by the appearance of both Saint Francis *and* Frederick II. Both deeply challenged the Papacy's claims to world government. For Kantorowicz, Joachim's view of providence entails that eternity is itself, so to speak, realized in and through history understood as the secular space for governmental action. Far from eternity and politics needing to be 'bridged' by the miracles of God's absolute power, on this view 'eternity' is always already a political matter. Thus, in what is only an apparent paradox, Trinitarianism is the doctrine that allows for the King's second body (i.e., the state as incorporation of the People) to stand in opposition to the Pope as vicar of Christ, that is, to the Church. From this perspective, the separation of state from Church, the signal achievement of modern liberalism, is a function of the becoming-royal of the People as equal sons of God. This promise made by Jesus Christ was realized only under the rule of the new world emperor first adumbrated in Frederick II as vicar of God the Father.

---

[52] 'The power of the king is the power of God. This power, namely, is God's by nature, and the king's by grace. Hence the King, too, is God and Christ, but by grace' (Kantorowicz 1997, 48).

The recovery of a Hebraicizing analogy between One God and One People, in and through this interpretation of Trinitarianism as paradigm for secularization, rejects the undertones of anti-Judaism found in Löwith's and Voegelin's critiques of Joachim of Fiore and of secularization. For Löwith and Voegelin, Joachim of Fiore opened the door to Jewish messianism and led Modernity on a path to the immanent and materialist realization of the End of history. Kantorowicz's understanding of secularization is entirely different: history becomes 'eternalized' in the sense that the sempi-eternity or immortality of the political body is achieved historically in the form of an eternal empire that is cosmopolitan and democratic in nature. This global empire is *not* a function of the secularization of divine providence in the form of the Hegelian state, as Voegelin and Löwith argued.[53] Rather, it is a function of God becoming the King of History (in the person of His Son), which culminates in the idea of humanity being led by a messianic emperor (as in Dante's theory of empire) in order to destroy the Christian Church's claim that only its mystical body stands in for eternity within history.

Kantorowicz's vision of divine providence is drawn from Dante. The global spread of democracy and the legal and political realization of human dignity makes the political body 'eternal'. This end is not achievable in the form of the Hegelian national state as world-historical actor, but through an empire of cosmopolitan, liberal governmentality. The Kingdom of God on earth is ultimately democratic and cosmopolitan (in the sense given by Dante), and is represented neither by the Church, nor by the Augustinian solution of the Two Cities, nor by the Hegelian national state. In Kantorowicz, the empire of humanity 'returns' to God the Father and 'defeats' the claims of both the Church and the state to be the true Kingdom of Christ, the Son. It is in this sense that one has to understand both Frederick II's claim to be the Messiah in the Jewish sense and the Pope's accusation that Frederick II is the Antichrist. Perhaps only Nietzsche's idea of the *grosse Politik* after the 'death of God' captured the ultimate implications of these medieval slogans thrown about in the never-ending struggle between Empire and Church.

The 'divine nature' of Christ that is impersonated by the Norman king is not an 'office' but rather Christ's being or life. The king can be Christ-like, because Christ became man-like. The Norman *christomimesis* occurs in the same period as the Franciscan call to adopt Christ's form of life and reject the

---

[53] The tendency to identify the postmodern form of global empire with a Hegelian sense of secularization is found also in (Negri 2001; and Esposito 2015b).

priestly conception of office.⁵⁴ In this sense, the philosophy of kingship of the Norman Anonymous is 'liturgical' rather than juridical (Kantorowicz 1997, 59). Ultimately, Christ became human in order to deliver human beings from original sin, and that means, in order to elevate all of them to His Throne.

The Norman king has both eschatological and soteriological meanings, very much in line with the Hellenistic theory of kingship. This is why Kantorowicz emphasized that the Norman Anonymous is a 'passionately anti-hierocratic pamphlet' whose aim is to rescue the 'spiritual strata' from being monopolized by the Church. The goal of the pamphlet is to strip the status of the 'spiritual man' and 'over-man' from the Bishop of Rome in order to place it onto the king's 'second' body of the People. This is the democratic possibility of Christian political theology that horrifies Maritain and that Ullmann never considers. For Kantorowicz, therefore, political theology is always already a secular discourse: it is the instrument of the Emperor in the struggle against the Christian Church. That is why Kantorowicz finds its definitive formulation in Dante's political theology of empire.

The historical conjuncture in which the jurisprudential nature of political theology comes to light occurs with the transition to a model of 'law-centred' kingship that takes place after the so-called Papal Revolution begun by Pope Gregory VII and the Investiture Struggle. This European struggle over sovereignty pitted the lawyer Popes Innocent III and Innocent IV against Frederick II. In this climactic period, the Pope takes over the idea of being sole *vicarius Christi* and having *plenitudo potestatis*, stripping monarchs of this vicariate role. In response, the Norman kings and emperors take up the idea that the emperor is *deus in terris*: the king becomes 'vicar of God'.⁵⁵ This signals a shift towards what Kantorowicz calls a 'theocratic-juristical idea of government', which signifies a move away from the Christology that still underlies the Norman Anonymous. What is essential is no longer the becoming-man of Christ, but rather a more 'Hebraic' understanding of the relation between God and King, mediated by the Law rather than by Christ: 'late-medieval kingship by "divine right" was modelled *after the Father in Heaven* rather than after the Son on the Altar, and *focused in a philosophy of law* rather than in the . . . physiology of the two-natured Mediator' (Kantorowicz 1997, 93, emphasis mine). Here what counts is the Law as mediation between God and

---

⁵⁴ See the account of the Franciscan form of life in (Agamben 2013) and my discussion in (Vatter 2016).
⁵⁵ The Roman law basis for this claim is *Digest* 35,2,1,5; 14,2,9; and *Codex Justiniani* 7,37,3,5.

King. Thus, the rise of government goes hand in hand with the foundation of constitutionalism. This is the most subversive part of Kantorowicz's political theology, as I show in the next sections.

Kantorowicz's hypothesis about the medieval origins of modern government in Frederick II's juridical philosophy passes through the seemingly risqué conjunction between pagan natural right and Christian Trinitarianism. The first aspect is taken into account by adopting a formula found in John of Salisbury: the king is 'the very Idea of Justice which itself is bound to law and yet above law because it is the end of all law' (Kantorowicz 1997, 96). It is through this intimate connection of king to law first formulated in the court of Frederick II that 'jurisprudence now felt invited to create its own secular spirituality' and in that way free itself from the Church's monopoly and superiority with respect to spiritual matters. Therefore, the analogy between theology and juridical science, the claim that juridical science is like a theology in being a universal science, must be understood within the context of a politico-theological program in which the law, and he who 'administers' it (namely, the king), needs to be spiritualized in order to attain sovereignty or superiority in jurisdiction.[56] Seeing God's essence as identical with equity or justice is an essential part of this program.

According to Kantorowicz, without this spiritualization or theologization of the law ('juridical science... as a secular theology'), it would not have been possible for Frederick II to designate himself as 'emperor in his own reign' as he does in his collection of Sicilian constitutions—in the Roman sense of the term: the edicts of the emperor—the *Liber Augustalis*. The path seems to be this one: the theologization of law emancipates the jurists from the priests; then comes the sacralization of he who 'makes' law, that is, the emperor (now in his own Reign, not in God's). Prior to Kantorowicz, other historians of medieval sovereignty like Roberto Calasso and Gaines Post had identified in the formula *rex superiorem non recognoscens in regno suo est imperator* the origins of modern sovereignty, but only Kantorowicz articulated its politico-theological basis.[57]

In turn, this politico-theological, 'secular' sacralization of the figure of the king in Frederick II—which is entirely opposite to the idea of

---

[56] For this reason, Kantorowicz cites from a saying of Albericus de Rosata, who claims that of all the sciences, jurisprudence is the most universal of all of them, since it requires grammar, dialectic, logic, rhetoric, arithmetic, geometry, mathematics, music, astrology, medicine and literature: 'juridical science... appears to be a secular theology' (Kantorowicz 1984, 55). Albericus was a jurist in the first half of the 14th century; he composed a commentary on the Decretals as well as on Dante's work.
[57] See the classic discussion of this formula in (Calasso 1957; and Post 1964).

'secularization' in Schmitt—depends on the secularization of a Trinitarian formula found in the *Liber Augustalis* I,31. Here it is said that that the Holy Roman Emperor has 'both the right to legislate and the *imperium*, that from the same person (ruling... over the people by his Power) there might progress the origin of Justice, from whom also the defence of Justice proceeds.... The *Caesar, therefore, must be at once the Father and the Son of Justice*, her Lord and her minister' (Kantorowicz 1997, 99, emphasis mine). The fundamental move here consists in the unification of the legislative or jurisdictional moment (corresponding to God as Father) and the executive or governmental moment (corresponding to God as Son). In Frederick II one finds the symbiosis between the Aristotelian analogy of God and king (or Caesar) fused together with the Trinitarianism of Christian orthodoxy. Kantorowicz's mature representation of Frederick II's jurisprudence leaves Peterson's critique of Schmitt in tatters. But it also puts into question Agamben's later separation of governmentality from sovereignty, which implausibly assumes that the messianic government of the Son could do without reference to the Justice and Law of the Father (represented by the emperor).

The point is that Frederick II's political theology is not only neo-Aristotelian (as Peterson and Voegelin assumed) but also entirely Trinitarian because God the Father stands as origin of the king's power of jurisdiction, and thus the king is 'above' the law in a legal, not merely in an administrative, sense. But the Father gives over the administration or government of Justice to the Son, Jesus (as) Christ, the 'mortal' God, and as this Second Person, the king comes to stand 'under' law in the sense that the king's sovereignty has as purpose the establishment of the legal order as government. In a formula: there is no legal order without the possibility of the sovereign to take exception from that legality and establish its legitimacy. What Kantorowicz calls 'political theology' in its most specific sense—the *juristic* use of Trinitarian theology in Frederick II—coincides with Schmitt's political theology insofar as both agree that 'political theology' is a discourse that does not belong with theology but with juridical science, and its effects are not religious but political. However, Kantorowicz moves political theology in the opposite direction of Schmitt: whereas the latter wanted to see in the juridification of theological doctrines a way to preserve the legacy of the Church in the modern world of sovereign states, Kantorowicz sees the theologization of law as a way to emancipate forever the modern state from the Church.

Liberal government and the antinomy of sovereignty

There is perhaps no more influential text on the question of the medieval roots of liberal constitutionalism in the second half of the 20th century than McIlwain's *Constitutionalism: Ancient and Modern*. Although this text nowhere mentions Schmitt nor the term 'political theology', it quickly became a polemical object for subsequent discussions of medieval political theory as a political theology, foremost among them Kantorowicz's *The King's Two Bodies*. In particular, what came under critique was McIlwain's central hypothesis that medieval political thought establishes an essential difference and order of rank between 'constitution' and 'government', or, jurisdiction and administration, with the former as superior over the latter.[58] Writing in the years just before the outbreak of World War II, McIlwain repeatedly warned that 'the one great issue that *overshadows all others* in the distracted world to-day is the issue between constitutionalism and arbitrary government. . . . Deeper than the problem whether we shall have a capitalistic system or some other enshrined in our law lies the question whether we shall be ruled by law at all, or only by arbitrary will' (McIlwain 1939, 266–67, emphasis mine). This 'great issue' has only increased in urgency over the last decade with the rise of 'illiberal' democracies.

McIlwain liked to distinguish between the limitation and the control of government: he was an advocate of the former, but not necessarily of the latter. Limited or constitutional government meant preserving 'those bounds beyond which no free government ought ever to go, and make them limits beyond which no government whatever can legally go. We must make *ultra vires* all exorbitant acts of government' (McIlwain 1939, 258). The state or government should always be limited by given law (McIlwain 1947, 9, 21). However, within its jurisdictionally or constitutionally determined limits, the action of government need *not* be tightly controlled by a system of checks and balances that separates and opposes the powers of the legislative and executive branches within one and the same government. McIlwain thought

---

[58] The distinction plays a crucial role still in Lawson: 'the subject adequate of politics was a state or commonwealth, and that the parts of this act are two: [...] constitution [and] the administration' (Lawson 1992, 41). Lawson goes on to assign to each its own 'majesty': to the community the constituent power to make government, to government the constituted power of 'personal majesty'. He clearly opposes the idea of 'real sovereignty' or constituent power to the Roman *lex regia* interpreted according to imperial jurisprudence as the permanent alienation of constituent power to the emperor (ibid., 42–46).

that such checks and balances could hamper the government's effectiveness in the defence of liberty.

For McIlwain, the fundamental division was not that between executive and legislative, but between the judiciary system and government as a whole. In the medieval juridical terms he preferred to use, the fundamental division for liberal constitutionalism is that between *iurisdictio* and *gubernaculum*. This distinction depended on 'three necessary assumptions: first, that there is a fundamental constitution; second, that its interpretation rests with the judiciary; and third, that judges have an authority only, in the words of Lord Bacon, "to interpret Law, and not to make Law, or give Law"' (McIlwain 1939, 279). Government should have the widest latitude for making positive, coercive law, but it must not be the interpreter of this law. Freedom is protected only in a political system in which the monarchic function is uncoupled from the activity of judging what is law. In highlighting the dangers of unlimited government McIlwain was reacting specifically against the rise of totalitarian regimes in which the will of the leader had acquired jurisdictional powers, that is, had usurped the power to 'interpret law' in the absence of a constitution. Fascism had given political leaders the power to make law *ex nihilo*.[59] McIlwain would have subscribed to Walter Benjamin's belief that in totalitarian regimes the state of exception had become the norm. These regimes were only government without any constitution.

McIlwain rested the entire case for liberal constitutionalism on his claim that the medieval priority of law over government was given a definitive formulation in Bracton's theory of royal prerogatives and in the distinction contained therein between *iurisdictio* and *gubernaculum*.[60] The heart of this theory consisted in a complex interpretation of two laws formulated in the late Roman legal corpus (*Corpus Iuris Civilis*): the *lex regia* and the *lex digna*.[61] The former law is sometimes referred to as the 'king-making'

---

[59] In the essay "Government by Law", McIlwain offers a long commentary on the "Penal Code Amendment Law" introduced by the Nazi regime according to which the Courts can punish 'offences' not falling under the code of law but merely if they deserve to be punished 'according to the underlying idea of a penal code or according to healthy public sentiment' (McIlwain 1939, 268).

[60] For a recent discussion of the debates on the reception of Bracton in early modern English political thought, which motivates McIlwain's judgment as to its inordinate importance in the history of western constitutionalism, see (Nederman 2009, 304–22).

[61] The *lex regia* refers to a passage of Justinian's *Institutes* 1,2,6: '*Sed et quod principi placuit legis habet vigorem, cum lege regia, quae de imperio eius lata est, populus ei et in eum omne sum imperium et potestatem concessit*' [Whatever is approved by the sovereign has also the force of law, because by the Lex Regia, from whence his power is derived, the people have delegated to him all their jurisdiction and authority]. The *lex digna* refers to the following passage from the *Digest*: '*Digna vox maiestatis regnantis legibus alligatum se principem profiteri: adeo de auctoritate iuris nostra pendet auctoritas. Et re vera maius imperio est submittere legibus principatum*' (*Digest* 1,3,31; *Codex* 1,14,4).

law; whereas the second law is often thought to give the king 'law-making' powers. These two laws determined the power of the emperor in late Roman public law and became the fundamental underpinning of both canon and civilian jurisprudence in the late middle ages.[62]

A great deal of the historiography of medieval political thought in the 20th century turns on the question of the form in which Roman law was recovered and received in the European feudal systems of common law.[63] In his pathbreaking treatment of medieval law, Gierke argued that modern individual liberties were a product of 'Germanic' feudal law, the so-called *Genossenschaftsrecht* (law of association or trust) (Gierke 1934). Gierke believed this 'German' jurisprudence remained importantly immune to the spread of Roman imperial law, which instead was fundamental to the construction of both the medieval Empire and Church. For Gierke, Roman imperial law informed the main traditions of medieval political thought and impressed upon them an absolutist orientation.[64] As discussed in the first chapter, Gierke's rejection of sovereignty was employed by Maitland and Figgis in order to reconceive the history of English common law away from its absolutist, Hobbesian trajectory codified in Austin's *The Province of Jurisprudence Determined*.

Writing in the late 1930s from Harvard, McIlwain could not accept Gierke's 'Germanic' genealogy of individual liberties. He wanted to trace the origin of these liberties back to English jurisprudence, anchored in the Magna Carta, and given ultimate expression by Bracton's appropriation of Roman law. Additionally, McIlwain did not share the English pluralists' critique of sovereignty. For him the crucial point was that sovereignty was legitimate as long as it was understood as 'the highest authority, not the greatest

---

As translated by Kantorowicz: 'It is a word worthy of the majesty of the ruler that the prince professes himself bound to the law: so much does our authority depend upon the authority of the law. And truly, greater than the *imperium* is the submission of the principate to laws' (Kantorowicz 1997, 104).

[62] For standard discussions of the current understanding of these laws, see the treatments in (Canning 1987; Pennington 1993; and Lee 2016). However, these discussions do not view the relation between these laws and the origins of modern sovereignty through the discourse of political theology.

[63] For a succinct and authoritative introduction to the reception of Roman law in medieval Europe, see (Stein 2007).

[64] Gierke's hypothesis is adopted by (McIlwain 1947, 42; and Tierney 1983, 6). The competitor history of medieval political thought (Carlyle 1903–36), exemplifies a history of medieval thought written from the perspective of an imperial understanding of Roman law. Tierney, Oakley, and Berman exemplify an approach to medieval political theory that is also based on Roman law, although in their case it is informed by a privilege given to canon law as an anti-imperial employment of Roman law.

might'. Sovereignty is 'the highest *legal* power in a state, itself subject to no law' (McIlwain 1939, 28–29). He thought Bracton's understanding of the king-making law and the law-making king explained the apparent paradox of sovereignty as both above and below the law. The solution was to conceive of sovereignty as 'unchecked' but not 'unlimited' because it is established by law and under condition of recognizing pre-given natural or divine rights held by the subjects.

Anticipating the turn to neo-Roman republicanism in Skinner and Nederman as the central framework to interpret late medieval political thought, McIlwain argued that Bracton received and adopted Cicero's 'republican' understanding of law.[65] Cicero was the decisive source of all bona fide (medieval) constitutionalism because he gave voice to the more original or authentic definition of Roman *lex* found in Gaius and Papinian.[66] On this definition, law is what the Roman people (*populus*) establish in their assemblies (McIlwain 1947, 44). Law is a function of the people's consent, not of the emperor's will. The emperor receives the power to rule (*imperium*) only as a function of upholding the people's law (*lex*). According to McIlwain, this is the original, republican meaning of the king-making law, the *lex regia*.

For McIlwain, Roman law is based on the belief that each individual has both private and public rights, and that the assemblies of the people are the defender of these rights as the highest source of jurisdiction (McIlwain 1947, 47). This function of the people as defender of individual freedom or rights is what McIlwain believes to be expressed in the Roman notion of consent or agreement (*sponsio*). Papinian's definition of law states that *lex est communis rei publicae sponsio* (*Digest* 1,3,1). *Lex* is an agreement between two parties and thus presupposes the consent of the individual. From here comes the insight that law is what is consented to by the entire people in common. Additionally, in the case of public laws the *sponsio* is associated to *rogatio*: an act of promulgation by popular vote of a measure that thereby becomes *lex*. This feature is found in Aquinas's claim that there is no real law without promulgation (McIlwain 1947, 50).

Lastly, McIlwain points to a third characteristic feature of Roman law that becomes of utmost importance for medieval jurisprudence. After the *Law of the Twelve Tables* were burnt and lost in the first sack of Rome by the Gauls,

---

[65] For two examples, see (Nederman 1988; and Skinner 2002).
[66] To support this claim, McIlwain followed Rudolf von Ihering's suggestion in *Geist von römischen Rechts* that the connection between imperial will and jurisdiction is merely a late imperial construction of Roman law.

written law, *ius strictum*, became ever more rare in Roman jurisprudence. In place of fidelity to an original written constitution, Roman jurisprudence developed the ideal of *aequitas* (justice as equity) according to which judges were charged with determining what is legally right in any given situation by considering how general norms had been previously applied in other cases. According to McIlwain, this shift to judicial interpretation explains the preponderance of *iurisdictio* (establishing what is right according to standing law) over *legislatio* (the practice of making positive legal statutes and decrees) in both the Roman and English legal traditions. For both traditions, law is for the most part whatever is determined by a judge on the basis of 'legal fictions' rather than of statutes made in parliament (McIlwain 1947, 54). Legal fictions are essential to *iurisdictio*, not to *gubernaculum*. Thus, McIlwain considered that 'limited' medieval monarchy based on the priority of *iurisdictio* with respect to *gubernaculum* is itself a juridical 'fiction', an invention of jurists, not of monarchs. Its pathos formula is precisely 'the King reigns but does not govern' (McIlwain 1947, 55).

McIlwain interprets this pathos formula to mean that jurisdiction (the constitutional or fundamental or ancient law of the realm), which the king must uphold, is beyond the reach of the king's government or administration. He believed that the distinction between *iurisdictio* and *gubernaculum* in 12th- and 13th-century medieval legal thought, particularly in Bracton, was the result of the recovery of the spirit of republican Roman law, where law stems from the people's consent and not from the prince's will. From Bracton, this neo-republican legal spirit made its way into English 'common law', managing to defeat the influence of the 'imperial' construal of Roman law, giving birth to the English 'limited' or constitutional monarchy. Hailed by Montesquieu, and thereafter adopted by the Constitution of the United States, this constitutional ideal is the last and highest exemplar of the 'spirit' of Roman republican law (McIlwain 1947, 68ff). For McIlwain, European fascism was intent on rolling back this history and reasserting the imperial conception of Roman law. Such are the high stakes behind McIlwain's reading of Bracton's interpretation of the formula *princeps legibus solutus est*, and this is the decisive context to understand why Kantorowicz's own interpretation of Bracton stands at the heart of *The King's Two Bodies*.

On McIlwain's interpretation, Bracton defended the king's sovereignty as 'highest' legal authority, and maintained the priority of *iurisdictio*, namely, the priority of given divine and natural legal order that stands before and above the king and limits his 'highest' authority. These two characteristics of the sovereign, encapsulated by the imperial Roman *lex regia* and *lex digna*, seem to be at odds with each other. While in certain of his texts, Bracton not only places God and Law as the 'superior' to the king, but also his *curia*, that is, the counts and barons of his court,[67] in other texts he employs Ulpian's maxim *quod principi placet legis habet vigorem* (*Digest* 1,4,1) in order to defend royal 'prerogative' in ways that seem to point to an incipient ideal of kingly absolute sovereignty.

To solve this apparent contradiction, which in a sense is fundamental to all medieval political thought because it signals what Tierney has called the ambivalence between 'consent' and 'will' theories of jurisdiction, McIlwain distinguishes the reading given to *quod principi placet* (q.p.p.) in Justinian from that offered by Bracton. For Justinian, the emperor's will is law, and q.p.p follows, 'because' the *lex regia* has alienated the people's power of jurisdiction entirely to the emperor. For Bracton, instead, the king's will is law, and q.p.p. follows, 'according to' the *lex regia*, which is a law of the people and 'makes' for the power of the king. Thus, the king's will is always dependent on the people's law: the *lex regia* does not alienate the people from its law-establishing power.[68] In this way, a legal formula that was an expression of absolutism in Justinian becomes a formula for constitutionalism in Bracton, where the king's will is merely an authoritative promulgation by the king of what his council declares to be ancient custom. The king's authority comes from the *lex regia*, and what 'pleases him' is what he authorizes after consulting his council (McIlwain 1947, 71).[69] For McIlwain, the coronation

---

[67] The king cannot change the laws that have been approved by common consent (McIlwain 1947, 70–72, 83–84). The fundamental text here is the so-called *addicio de cartis* (II, 110), according to which: 'The king has a superior, namely God. Also the law by which he was made king. Also his court, namely the earls and barons because earls are so called as being companions of the king, and who has a companion has a master [magister]. And therefore if the king should be without a bridle, that is without a law, they ought to put a bridle on him'. Cited in (Tierney 1963a, 314).

[68] There is an important debate in the literature on the influence of civilian interpretations of these two laws of the *Corpus Iuris Civilis* on the development of the doctrine of sovereignty in Bodin and Hobbes. Ralph Giesey, who was a student of Kantorowicz, argued that the civilian interpretation contained an idea of limited government because it 'had been concerned to establish a workable constitution for independent communes by establishing juridical limitations upon the *segnoria* (the word, by the way, given as the Italian equivalent of *souverainté* in the opening sentence of *Répub.* I,8)' (Giesey 2006, 117). On this view, whatever constitutionalism is still found in the absolutist theories of Bodin and Hobbes is of medieval origin. Conversely, Daniel Lee argues that the civilians and legist interpreters are precursors of modern absolutism, not of constitutionalism. For the case that Monarchomachs were absolutists, see (Lee 2008) and for the case of Hobbes, see (Lee 2012).

[69] Similarly, in a famous interpretation, Ewart Lewis argues that for Bracton 'laws' are whatever 'has its origin and its warrant in the practice of the king's court' (Lewis 1964, 249). For Lewis, Bracton advances a procedural notion of law. The law is worked out on the basis of just principles in the court, and then the king's authority gives it 'the imperative and coercive quality essential to laws' (ibid., 253). The king's will is thus a part of the procedure of law-making, not its origin or source of authority: 'the

oaths of the English monarchs are the functional equivalent of the *lex regia*, and these oaths clearly limit the power of the king, and do not constitute it in an absolute fashion (McIlwain 1947, 72).[70]

Still, McIlwain accepts that Bracton's usage of the *lex digna* is tendentially absolutist. According to the *lex digna*, it is left up to the king's will to feel bound to the laws, and this because no one can judge the king's acts since the king *is* the last judge. According to McIlwain, Bracton gives a constitutionalist reading of the *lex regia* and an absolutist reading of the *lex digna*. This is why McIlwain, famously, identifies an antinomy between the two laws.[71] The resolution of this antinomy is the essential problem of medieval constitutionalism.

McIlwain's influential yet highly contested solution to this antinomy of sovereignty turns on making the distinction between *iurisdictio* and *gubernaculum*. The *lex regia* grants the emperor sole jurisdiction as vicar of God in order that he may fulfil his role to give to each subject their own, namely, to render justice, according to given and standing law. By the *lex digna*, the emperor has also the prerogatives to seek peace and make war (McIlwain 1947, 76). This is understood in terms of the power to govern, *gubernaculum*, to which there corresponds the characteristic that no one can judge the acts of government. Government is absolutist because no one can judge the emperor or king, who is the last judge. Yet government is also limited because it does not include the power of jurisdiction (McIlwain 1947, 78). Hence, in the pathos formula for liberal government, according to McIlwain's interpretation, the phrase 'the king reigns' refers to the function of jurisdiction, which presupposes limitation by law, whereas the phrase 'but he does not govern' refers to the absence of jurisdiction in government. Since jurisdiction refers to giving to each its own, to do justice, for McIlwain jurisdiction presupposes the existence of given rights. Thus, what lies outside

---

ius that is derived from *iustitia* by means of *iurisprudentia* must necessarily be—to use Papinian's phrase—"a *consultum* of prudent men"' (ibid., 255).

[70] It is an irony of history that the other recognized authority on English coronation oaths apart from McIlwain was Percy Schramm, Kantorowicz's close friend and later a secretary to Hitler. Norman Cantor calls Schramm and Kantorowicz the 'Nazi twins' of medieval historiography (Cantor 1991). Schramm is an important source of Agamben's understanding of the method of archaeology (Agamben 2008) but, interestingly enough, he does not make an appearance in Agamben's treatment of the oath (Agamben 2010). Voegelin's late lectures on Hitler are based on his interpretation of Schramm's memoirs of his time with Hitler.

[71] Kantorowicz also speaks of the 'antinomy prevailing between the maxims *princeps legibus solutus* [lex regia] and *princeps legibus alligatus* [lex digna]' (Kantorowicz 1997, 105).

the range of government are private rights, preserved by custom as law (the *consuetudinibus Angliae* of Bracton's title) (McIlwain 1947, 81–82). The pathos formula is understood as a formula for liberal constitutionalism.

Furthermore, with respect to the king's *iurisdictio*, customary law does not merely possess 'directive force' but also carries 'coercive force'. The king can be coerced to fulfil his role in accordance to the terms of his coronation oath, through which the king promises to follow this customary law and to achieve justice, *iurisdictio*, 'according to law'. For McIlwain, Bracton's claim that the king's court could 'put the bridle' on a king who does not respect law is indicative of this coercive dimension. Hence, McIlwain concludes that Bracton's idea of the English constitution was already a *regimen politicum et regale*, as Fortescue would later formulate constitutional monarchy. The republican (*politicum*) dimension of the *regimen* refers to the legal limits of *iurisdictio*; the monarchic (*regale*) dimension of the *regimen* refers to *gubernaculum* and to the absolute degree of discretion it can exercise. Absolute sovereignty, namely *gubernaculum*, is therefore 'limited' by law. This is McIlwain's solution to the antinomy of sovereignty.

Kantorowicz's solution to the same antinomy is radically different. Reversing the terms of McIlwain's solution, Kantorowicz argues that, in accordance with the *lex regia*, the king is 'not legally bound to law' yet, by virtue of the *lex digna*, the king 'bound himself to the Law and lived voluntarily in accordance with the law' (Kantorowicz 1997, 105). McIlwain places the sovereign under law in order to exercise its jurisdictional function of giving justice, and places the sovereign above law in order to exercise its administrative function. Kantorowicz does the opposite: the king's obligation to follow given law, *iurisdictio*, is now left up to the *lex digna*, which, on this reading, says that the king voluntarily places himself under law, thereby making justice an administrative duty. Conversely, the king's being loosed from law, in the function of *gubernaculum*, now belongs to the *lex regia*, thereby making the exercise of absolute power a constitutional duty. The *lex regia* that in McIlwain is supposed to legally bind the king, in Kantorowicz 'legally' unbinds the king from law.

But how can a law (*lex regia*) 'legally' make it possible for the king to be 'not legally bound to law'? This is the very question that frames Agamben's well-known interpretation of Schmitt's 'state of exception' as an *internal condition of possibility* of the legal system itself.[72] Kantorowicz argues that the

---

[72] I refer to (Vatter 2016) and the literature cited therein.

key to understand Bracton's solution to the antinomy of sovereignty is found by adopting the hypothesis that Bracton worked with the same jurisprudence as Frederick II's jurists. In particular, Bracton adopted their way of deploying the Trinitarian motif within a scheme of Hellenistic sacral monarchy.[73] As discussed earlier, from the latter scheme these jurists draw the argument that the king is *legibus solutus* because he is bound to a higher Reason, that is, to natural law, according to which the king is a 'living law' or 'animate justice' (*dikaion empsychon*).[74] Frederick II apparently called himself a living law, *lex animata*, following civilian usage. Kantorowicz mentions a connection between *lex animata* and *nomos basileus*, that is, he establishes the connection between these forms of exception to law or sovereignty of law—also discussed by Agamben—in relation to the question of natural law. This notion of 'the absolute power of legal Reason' (Kantorowicz 1997, 134–35) corresponds to the need for the king to comply with 'Public Utility and changing Necessity' (Kantorowicz 1997, 106). Ruling in and through a 'state of necessity' legitimates the king's loosening himself from positive laws for reasons of state.

The paradox is that 'legal reason' itself states that the king is free from positive law for the sake of establishing the administration of law or dispensation of justice.[75] The novelty here is that Kantorowicz's interpretation of the king as being 'above and below' law is *not* for the sake of constructing a conception of sovereignty. Against contemporary constitutional theorists like Stephen Holmes or Martin Loughlin, Kantorowicz is *not* saying that constitutional

---

[73] It is (Schulz 1945) who first points out that Bracton's titles for the king as 'vicar of God' come from the theory of Hellenistic kingship, and from Philo in particular. This title was passed from Hellenistic philosophy to the Roman emperors (Seneca referred to Nero as *vice deorum*) and then was employed by medieval emperors and kings, until Gregory VII's 'legal revolution' denied them the title, leading to the Investiture Struggle. The title of 'vicar of God' is first re-established by the Bolognese legists Accursius and Azo. According to Schulz, it is through this mediation that the title is adopted by Bracton and applied to the English monarchs. Bracton also adopts the formula *Rex superiorem non recognoscens est imperator in regno suo*. However, unlike Kantorowicz, Schulz does not ascribe to Frederick II any role in this history of transmission. Furthermore, Schulz considers the doctrine that the king is both living law and above the law but as king he must do justice and thus be subject to law, to be a 'scholastic and unworkable' doctrine (Schulz 1945, 165).

[74] Kantorowicz refers to Aristotle's *Nicomachean Ethics* 1132a20ff, and to Aquinas's commentary on the passage of the *Politics* V 1311a, where the king is termed the 'guardian of Justice' and *iustum animatum*.

[75] The analogy between Agamben's notion of sovereignty as being 'outside and inside the juridical order' and Kantorowicz's reading of the king as above and below the law is drawn in (Haverkamp 2004). However, Haverkamp fails to account for the use of the Trinitarian motifs in order to bring together natural law and state of exception. Additionally, in Bracton 'supra legem' does not mean 'outside' of law, since the king is always under God's law. Kantorowicz's point is that the state of exception is construed in Trinitarian terms.

laws are functional to sovereignty.[76] Rather, his point is that a constitutionally articulated sovereignty is itself functional to government through law or administration. Thus, Kantorowicz says that it is necessary for the king to be free of the coercion of law because anything short of that would 'establish that "tyranny of the law" which, in the very days of Bracton, and so often afterwards, *threatened to paralyze the orderly functioning of government*' (Kantorowicz 1997, 148, emphasis mine). On this view, it is the rule of law, paradoxically, that needs to be limited (by placing the sovereign 'above the law' through the *lex regia*) in order to allow for 'the orderly functioning of government'.

To clinch this second part of his argument, Kantorowicz's interpretation claims that Bracton translated Frederick II's Trinitarian motif, of being Father and Son of the law, into the topological distinction of being 'above and under law'. 'Thus a king-making Law and a law-making King mutually conditioned each other, and therewith the well-known relations between the king and the Law reappear in Bracton: the king, Law's son, becomes Law's father' (Kantorowicz 1997, 155). Here the problem of legal interpretation folds in together with the question of the political body. Kantorowicz shows that the sovereign freedom from law is not something that absolves power from its duties towards society, as Maritain criticized. To the contrary, for Kantorowicz only the absoluteness of power makes the body 'political', that is, unitary, but only when absolute power is interpreted according to the Trinitarian scheme.

Interpreted according to Trinitarianism, the formula 'the king reigns but does not govern' means that God the Father and King, who is above the law, surrenders the administration or government of Justice to the Son, Jesus (as) Christ, the 'mortal' God. It is in the form of this Second Person that state power comes to stand 'under' law and becomes a legislative and administrative state. The Father ('who reigns but does not govern') maintains His sovereignty only by sacrificing Himself (as the Son) on the Cross of government. Analogously, the king sacrifices his jurisdictional power by giving up his jurists and lawyers to the autonomous system of law and rights of civil society, which has its finality in 'administering' justice according to positive, statutory law. The sacrifice of government on the part of the sovereign is juridically represented by the employment of the *lex digna*: 'the element of Son-ship to law of prince or emperor is found in the *lex digna*' (Kantorowicz

---

[76] See, for instance (Holmes 2012).

1997, 104).[77] Kantorowicz's point can be expressed as follows: since all law is interpretation, in virtue of the fact that the *lex digna* allows judges to make law by their interpretation, and given that the king must obey this condition as Christ, then he who has the last interpretation, he who is the last judge, becomes the Father of all law.[78] This last interpretation or last judgment is precisely one that decides whether there exists the state of exception, that is, the last judgment is a prerogative of sovereignty. In binding himself to the law (by handing law over to judges, by making all law a matter of interpretation), the sovereign becomes the ultimate legislator through his decision (q.p.p.) and *lex regia*.[79]

Ultimately, the sacrifice of the Father or sovereign on behalf of the Son or government has the purpose of transferring the idea of justice away from the constitutional sphere and towards the sphere of administrative action. This is the remote origin of the curious yet widespread modern belief that citizens should demand social justice from the arbitrary, and always changing nature of government public policy, rather than from the courts of justice. Kantorowicz's genealogy offers an explanation of the dynamics that lie at the basis of the recurrent 'crises of legitimacy' occasioned by the insurmountable conflict between the principles of the welfare state and those of so-called liberal constitutionalism that exercised social theorists in the 1970s.[80] In other words, the 'administration' of justice (what McIlwain calls *gubernaculum* and places under *lex digna*) is in Kantorowicz identical to the dispensation of a 'mystery' of state, that is, of prerogatives to law that establish a permanent state of exception in the form of rule by administrative decrees.[81]

---

[77] Eric Santner cites Kantorowicz on the identity between the second body of the King and the idea of government: 'his Body politic is a Body that cannot be seen or handled, consisting of policy and Government, and constituted for the Direction of the People and the Management of the public weal' (Santner 2011, 35). However, he fails to discuss what kind of jurisprudence permits the emergence of government in the first place.

[78] Kantorowicz makes this reading explicit when he speaks of the 'political Christology' of Bracton (Kantorowicz 1997, 159) and refers to Bracton's calling the king a *quasi vice Dei* because the judges of the royal court are *quasi vice Jesu Christi* (ibid., 161). Compare with the interpretation of Bracton's adoption of Trinitarian motifs in (Post 1971).

[79] As Kantorowicz says, the king regains his ancient position as *rex et sacerdos* 'through the high pretensions of Roman legal philosophy which compared jurisprudents with priests' (Kantorowicz 1997, 118).

[80] See the formulations in (Habermas 1975; and Offe 1982); for a recent recovery of these hypotheses, see (Streeck 2016).

[81] This is the point of Arendt's insight that decrees are the 'mystery' of state because they are resistant to reason. Kantorowicz argues that through this new conception of 'administrative needs the governments arrived at new fiction of a *perpetua necessitas*' (Kantorowicz 1997, 296). Santner correctly identifies in this trend the origin of a process whereby the state of exception becomes permanent (Santner 2011, 54, n. 26).

Administering justice, which in Foucault would entail the machinery of disciplinary powers, requires an essential 'taking exception' to the positive law. That is why, in his article on the 'mysteries of the state', Kantorowicz equates the *ministerium* of law to the *mysterium* of the state. The origins of 'reason of state' are to be located within a providential scheme in that the state becomes itself providential, 'l'État providence'. It is not that Hegel's *Rechtsstaat* 'secularizes' a theological providential scheme as Löwith believes, as if the state carries out God's providence, but rather the state internalizes providence, so that it becomes governmental or administrative for the sake of the People. Government is the hollowing out of the rule of law not through an appeal to a transcendent outside, as the sovereign does in Schmitt, but through an appeal to an immanent interior finality, that of governing a population. What Agamben's interpretation of the connection between government and providence seems not to have taken into account is that the providential scheme, the 'economy' of the mystery of salvation through the state's 'rule of law', is not itself 'economic' in a modern sense of the term but entirely juridical. The mystery of salvation is about 'ministering' to the law, not to the economy. The rule of law, not the free market, lies at the heart of political theology in the West.

Dante and the government of humanity

Kantorowicz concludes *The King's Two Bodies* with his celebrated interpretation of Dante's political philosophy. In the history of western political thought, Dante has long held a privileged position as one of the first proponents of a truly secular vision of politics. It is generally accepted that in *Monarchia* Dante sought to put an end to the long-running civil war in the *respublica Christiana* between Emperor and Pope by establishing the principle that 'perpetual peace' would be attained only if one monarch had absolute sovereignty over the entire globe.[82] In histories of international law, Dante is also always mentioned as the precursor of Kant's cosmopolitan ideal, as the modern source for the idea of a world state. But Kantorowicz's interpretation is mainly interested in how Dante seeks to establish the authority of

---

[82] The literature on Dante's political thought is vast, from classic interpretations like (Nardi 1949; d'Entreves 1952; and Gilson 1968) to more recent treatments in (Woodhouse 1997; and Silvestrini 2013). On the much discussed question of whether Dante was a Thomist or an Averroist, see now (Bianchi 2015).

the Emperor on a basis that is entirely independent from the Church by developing a 'Church-independent secular "political theology"' (Kantorowicz 1997, 92).[83] At stake in his reading of Dante is therefore the political theology of world government.

Kantorowicz's hypothesis is that Dante's secular political theology was based on a new conception of the dignity of humanity. As he wrote in his essay on "Dante's 'Two Suns'": 'Both Pontiff and Emperor are, above all, men. Therefore they must be measured by the standard of man, by the *humanitas* which personally they represent' (Kantorowicz 1965, 325).[84] Dante's enormous achievement was to argue that 'the supreme human authority no longer was vested in the office alone, be he emperor, king or pope. It was vested in man as well or, as Dante would have said with Aristotle, in the *optimus homo* adorned "with mitre and with crown" [*Mon.* III,12; *Purg.* XXVII, 142]' (Kantorowicz 1965, 365). Now, Kantorowicz argued that for Dante there was a third pretender to the role of the *optimus homo* as representative of humanity's sovereignty besides the Pope and the Emperor, and this was the poet. 'The equiparation of poet and emperor or king—that is, of the poet and the highest office representing sovereignty—began as early as Dante' (Kantorowicz 1965, 362).[85] His thesis is that modern, secular, and democratic government places humanity as 'the highest office representing sovereignty' above the offices of Throne and Altar. In so doing, modern democratic politics fashions a secular political theology of its own. What makes it a political theology is that the idea of a world government based on the respect of human dignity becomes the form in which the unity of monarchic and democratic principles, which Schmitt postulated as being the condition of possibility of any durable constitutional regime, is finally realized.

For Victoria Kahn, Kantorowicz's interpretation of Dante can be read 'as a dismantling of political theology, one that points in the direction of liberal constitutionalism' (Kahn 2014, 54). Kantorowicz's discussion of Dante's *Monarchia* establishes 'a model of the relationship between religion and secular life that is in principle antifascist. It is antifascist in part because it is

---

[83] I refer here to the discussion in (Aznar 2010) who places Dante in close connection with Marsilius.

[84] The passage continues: 'As men they have to be referred to the *optimus homo* who is the measure of all others and, as it were, their Idea—whosoever this "best man" may be'.

[85] See also the claim that 'This arrogation of *plenitudo potestatis* was true of the offices of poet and, by transference, of painter and artist at large. It may therefore not have been amiss to raise the question here to what extent and in what respects the artistic theology of the renaissance followed certain trails first marked out by the political theology of medieval jurists' (Kantorowicz 1965, 365).

antinationalist. But it is antifascist as well because it insists on a liberal notion of individual autonomy, even while acknowledging its mythical status' (Kahn 2014, 80). Kahn identifies this liberal and cosmopolitan moment in Kantorowicz's interpretation of the scene in the *Divine Comedy* where Dante is crowned by Virgil with the formula: 'I crown and mitre you over yourself'. For Kahn, this scene reveals the moment where literature (fiction) helps in 'creating the notion of the sovereign subject and restoring the dignity of man.... that, to Kantorowicz's modern readers, sounds very much like a liberal notion of autonomy' (Kahn 2014, 76). In so doing, Kahn diverges from previous interpreters who perceived in Kantorowicz's *homo optimus* the Nietzschean traits of the world legislator as 'super-man', for whom peoples and states are the raw materials for his 'work of art', namely, something to be given shape with the 'fullness of power' and *ex nihilo*.[86]

What is undoubtedly clear is that Kantorowicz believed that in order to establish a secular, world government the *optimus homo* had to destroy the claims that the Universal or Catholic Church alone had the right to exercise spiritual authority over all humankind (Kantorowicz 1997, 456). According to Kantorowicz, Dante's strategy was to identify a *second* 'mystical body' that is not related Christ's mystical body, that is, the Universal Church, but to the natural body of humankind, which finds its origin in Adam and Eve. Dante's universal monarch, then, becomes the head of a mystical body composed by all members of the human species, a body to which every human being inheres independently of their religious faiths (i.e., of their membership in other churches). This monarch is set up as 'guide' (*Dux*) to lead humankind to its natural, as opposed to supernatural, end. As Dante says, 'Man has need of two guides corresponding to his two-fold goal:... the Supreme Pontiff, to lead mankind to eternal life in conformity with revealed truth, and the emperor, to guide mankind to temporal happiness in conformity with the teachings of philosophy.'[87]

This worldly end of the human species is called the 'terrestrial paradise': it is God's Kingdom on Earth, opposed to Christ's Kingdom in Heaven. 'In

---

[86] Thus, commentators see in Kantorowicz's equiparation of the sovereignty of the statesman with the sovereignty of the artist an indication of his continued fidelity to the ideals of the *George Kreis*. For Monod, in his discussion of Dante's ideal ruler, 'Kantorowicz returned here to the image of the ruler presented in his *Frederick II*, albeit in perfected form; more importantly, he reverted to the ideology in which his early career has been soaked. Anyone familiar with the ideas of the George Circle can recognize in these passages a version of the *Führer* principle, embodied in the "Master" himself. It is a small step to imagine the national leader so eagerly awaited by the Circle in the role of Dante's Roman philosopher-monarch' (Monod 2005, 120). A similar point is made in (Norbrook 1996, 331–33).

[87] Dante, *Mon.* III, xvi, 17–18. I cite from the English translation in (Dante 1996).

order to prove that his universal monarch was free from papal jurisdiction, Dante had to build up a whole sector of the world which was independent not only of the pope, but also of the Church and, virtually, even of the Christian religion ... the "terrestrial paradise"' (Kantorowicz 1997, 457). The terrestrial paradise is where the human species attains blessedness 'in this life' rather than in the supernatural 'eternal' life achieved in the resurrection of the individual bodies.

The pastoral overtones of the world emperor indicate that Dante is here harking back to the 'political monotheism' of Hellenistic kingship. Peterson showed that Hellenistic political theology was adopted into Christianity by Eusebius and Orosius on the basis of the conceit that Christ's birth in the reign of Augustus made Christ a Roman citizen and proved that the Roman Empire was part of divine providence. Kantorowicz argues that Dante appropriates this prototypical moment of political theology: 'Only under the perfect emperor, Divus Augustus, was there the perfecta *monarchia*, the empire of the Romans, in a state of perfect peace; and in the "fulness of time" the perfect imperial guide to mortal bliss was no more a Christian than Vergil, the poet of the empire, who finally was the guide of Dante himself to the paradise of this world' (Kantorowicz 1997, 466–67). For these reasons it is not entirely surprising that Voegelin identified Dante as the early modern advocate of a completely immanent world order, and his ideal *Dux* as a precursor of Mussolini's *Duce* and of Hitler's *Führer*.

However, Dante's identification with Virgil, and his appropriation of Hellenistic and Roman political motifs for a secular political theology, is a highly overdetermined gesture because it unites within itself both democratic and monarchic principles.[88] For Dante, the human species achieves its worldly or secular blessedness solely by actualizing its 'proper power'. As Dante says in book I of *Monarchia*: 'The peculiar work of the human species taken as a whole is to actualize always the whole power of the potential intellect'.[89] The philosophical path to human salvation was recovered and spread within Christianity through Latin Averroism. Averroes believed that there was 'a single possible intellect for the entire human race ... an intellectual substance wholly independent of the body ... and he taught that, to

---

[88] This is symptomatically shown by the fact that Schmitt and Arendt both refer to Virgil's Fourth Eclogue as capturing something essential about their own thought.

[89] *Mon*. I, 4, 1: *proprium opus humani generis totaliter accepti est actuare semper totam potentiam intellectus possibilis*. Translation slightly modified. See (Marenbom 2001, 358ff) for a discussion of the arguments supporting the claim that Dante adheres to Averroism.

an individual man, knowing means simply sharing in some part or other of the knowledge possessed by this intellect' (Gilson 1968, 168–69). As Étienne Gilson explains, it was Dante who interpreted Averroes's single separate intellect as consisting in 'that universal community of all individual possible intellects which is constituted by the human race.... When Dante speaks of realizing the intellectual potentialities of the whole of humanity (*potentia totius humanitatis*) it is certainly those of all mankind (*universitas hominum*) which must be understood' (Gilson 1968, 170). Irrespective of how Averroes himself understood the doctrine of the unicity of the material or potential intellect, there is widespread consensus on the thesis that it is Dante himself who argues that this actualization of the one potential intellect of the human species requires the participation of a *multitude* of individuals to the thinking activity. Dante, in other words, *democratizes* Averroes's doctrine of the unicity of the potential intellect.[90] Kantorowicz agrees with Gilson and others that for Dante intellectual beatitude is a goal to be attained by the 'body corporate of Man' (Kantorowicz 1997, 471–72). However, he also emphasizes that the 'intellectual oneness of the human race ... made the oneness of monarchic-philosophic leadership imperative' (Kantorowicz 1997, 472).

Kantorowicz's reading of Dante, therefore, emphasizes the need of an appropriate *guidance* for humanity as a whole in order to attain the 'philosophic beatitude' that is the 'natural' end of humankind. 'Man, if properly guided, could attain to the terrestrial paradise of the first man through his own devices, through the power of natural reason and of the four cardinal virtues alone' (Kantorowicz 1997, 470). The reference here is to the intellectual or philosophical virtues associated with Aristotle and pagan philosophy, as opposed to the theological virtues based on divine grace. Kantorowicz refers in a note that the idea of this human guide as *optimus homo* is derived from Aristotle's *Politics*.[91] These passages are clearly philo-monarchical: they discuss the question of whether it is better for one superior human being or a body of inferior human beings to rule. These texts compose Aristotle's treatment of the idea of a *non-constitutional, but legitimate monarchy* within the

---

[90] For further developments of Dante's Averroism as the source for a non-Christian democratic political theology, see Agamben's claim that 'the diffuse intellectuality I am talking about and the Marxian notion of a "general intellect" acquire their meaning only within the perspective of this experience.... They name the multitude that inheres to the power of thought as such' (Agamben 2000b, 11, 114). See also the extended discussion of Averroism in (Esposito 2015b).
[91] Kantorowicz refers to the following passages: *Politics* III, 11,8 and III,12, 1287b20 and 1288a15ff, as well as *Nicomachean Ethics* X, 5,1176a16 where Aristotle speaks of the 'perfect and supremely happy man'.

Politics. The last of these references points to a famous text in which Aristotle hypothesizes the notion of a king who is so pre-eminent with respect to the human grouping, that he stands as whole to parts: 'if so, the only alternative is that he should have *the supreme power, and that mankind should obey him, not in turn, but always*' (Aristotle, 1288a26–30, emphasis mine). The passage is remarkable because it seems to anticipate the theory of the 'double body' of humankind, where the *optimus homo* is like the whole to the parts composed by all individuals of the human species. Additionally, this superior human being ought to rule over 'mankind' as a whole, as a species, and not simply over this or that social group of human beings.[92] Lastly, such a 'perfect' individual would rule 'always', meaning both that they would rule without regard to the principle of rotation of offices, and that they would rule sempi-eternally. In short, this perfect human being is like a god to other humans, but, at the same time, entirely human. One can say that the *optimus homo* is the Antichrist, taking the expression in its most literal sense: just like Christ is entirely divine, but also like any human being to other human beings, so the 'perfect man' is entirely human but like a god or superman to other humans.

In Dante the universal monarch is a 'supra-individual representative of his species, the incumbent of a personal dignity in which the corporate and generic Dignity of Man became manifest' (Kantorowicz 1997, 460–61). The 'secular' political theology that Kantorowicz reconstructs out of Dante's political thought rejects both the analogy between one God and one King and the analogy between one God and one People that underpins the discourse of political theology according to Peterson and Schmitt. For secular political theology is based on the analogy between one Humanity and one World Government. For Dante, world government is functional to the establishment of human dignity over and above the dignities of those who represent reigns and churches.

In light of these considerations, I now turn to an interpretation of Dante's coronation formula that Kahn considers to be the key scene for a liberal constitutionalism based on human dignity. In order to appreciate the pathos-formula whereby Virgil crowns Dante with the words 'I crown and mitre you over yourself', one has to place it in the context of the sacrament

---

[92] Kantorowicz points out that 'the human race, or *humanitas* quantitatively, appeared to Dante like One Man, a single all-embracing community, a universal body corporate' (Kantorowicz 1997, 467). This would still fit Aristotle's notion that a perfect king is superior to the whole community, in this case, to the One Man of humanity, of which it would have to be the eternal head.

of baptism, through which every natural-born human being is made into a Christian. Loosely basing himself on Peterson's study of divine acclamations, Kantorowicz understands Christian baptism as a becoming-crowned and raised up to a divine plane through acclamations 'comparable to those offered at royal coronations and priestly ordinations' (Kantorowicz 1997, 490). Baptism makes of the Christian 'a member of the body of Christ, the King and High-Priest' (Kantorowicz 1997, 491). Unlike in the traditional formulas for the coronations of kings, where human kings are crowned as representatives of God the King of the universe, and also unlike Christian baptism, where Jesus the King makes of every believer a Son of God, Dante's coronation is entirely a human affair: here it is every individual (represented by Dante as a new Adam), who becomes 'sovereign' by their own hands (i.e., at the hands of Virgil, the poet who sang the praises of the Roman Emperor), not in virtue of some divinity that descends from a super-terrestrial paradise.[93] Just like Christ returned victorious from Hell (indeed, from death itself) in order to found a mystical or eternal body politic, so too 'in the moment when Dante re-enters into the terrestrial paradise like another Adam "crowned with glory and honor", he is "crowned and mitred" by Vergil', by which is meant that Dante's own traversal of Hell leads him to be re-born as 'Adam's fellow-ruler . . . he was invested with Man's body corporate and politic' (Kantorowicz 1997, 491).

Thus, in a first moment, Dante's crowning at the hands of Virgil symbolizes the passage from a Roman, aristocratic sense of *dignitas* as 'noble bearing' (symbolized by Virgil) to a modern, democratic sense of dignity that belongs to every individual human being in virtue of their humanity (symbolized by the mitred Dante). From this moment onwards, the dignity of Man, represented by the crowned Dante, acquires 'supreme jurisdiction over man qua mortal man, *regardless of position and rank*' (emphasis mine). Politically speaking, the 'kingdom' based on human dignity stands above all other political regimes.

The signature of political monotheism is present in this coronation scene and it is this signature that makes it a ceremony of secular political theology. The signature is visible in Beatrice's claim that Christ is also present in the earthly paradise. Beatrice invites Dante to consider that he 'shalt be

---

[93] According to Kantorowicz's interpretation, Dante 'achieved his "baptism" into *humanitas* in a para-sacramental and para-ecclesiastical fashion, with Cato acting as sponsor, and with the prophet Vergil as his Baptist—a Baptist, though, who this time unlocked to man not the heavens, but the paradise of Man' (Kantorowicz 1997, 492).

everlastingly with me/A burgher of that Rome whence Christ is Roman' (*Purg.* XXXII, 100ff). Christ is brought down from the heavenly Jerusalem and re-embodied into 'a transcendentalized Rome' (Kantorowicz 1997, 491). Beatrice's prophecy is that Christ shall return on earth in order to form part of the mystical body of Adam: 'the promise to Dante of his future co-citizenship with Christ as fellow-Roman after having been crowned by the Roman Vergil a fellow citizen and co-ruler of Adam' (Kantorowicz 1997, 492). This claim can receive at least two interpretations. It is possible to interpret Beatrice's prophecy in Rousseauian or Kantian terms, where Christ's Gospel is considered to be a 'natural divine right' that is secularized in modernity in the form of 'natural' human rights. On the other hand, it is also possible to say that Kantorowicz understands Beatrice's prophecy in decidedly more Nietzschean terms, where it refers to the future unity of Christ and Caesar in the *Übermensch*.

The Kantian interpretation of the coronation scene understands the image of 'Dante crowned and mitred over Dante himself' as a poetic expression for the doctrine of "Man's Two Bodies" (Kantorowicz 1997, 493–94), the last mutation of the ideal of the 'spiritual man' who judges all but can be judged by none. Dante's self-coronation expresses the idea that 'humanity' must become sovereign over all human beings. After Dante, it is Kant who will take up this idea of human dignity. For Kant, human dignity is not a predicate of the particular or empirical self but refers to the elevation of *homo noumenon* over *homo phenomenon* in the practical employment of pure reason, which finds its highest manifestation in the Idea of a republican constitution. Only in such a republic, is 'Man' as *homo noumenon*, as the 'humanity' that characterizes the person in each individual, crowned over 'man' as *homo phenomenon* and *animal rationale*. In this way, *humanitas* becomes sovereign over *homo*.

There is, finally, a third, Nietzschean interpretation of the scene of self-coronation, which may be called Gnostic. Dante's crowning by Virgil is not only a prefiguration of the Kantian *elevation of noumenal Man over phenomenal man*; it is not merely the recognition of the superiority of the 'right of humanity' over the 'divine rights' of human kings. The coronation of Dante by Virgil also represents the possibility that human dignity requires the *divinization* of the human species as a whole by human beings. This divinization should be understood as the process whereby the biological species *Homo sapiens*, in the course of time and through their mutual and just cooperation, 'gives birth' to humanity as its own species, by consciously designing or making its own species-being. This self-making by human beings of their species-being is represented by the self-coronation by two poets (or: one poet 'making' another poet), where 'poetry', drawing from its Greek root as *poiesis* (making, production), entails the task of the *auto-poiesis* of the species. On this interpretation, Dante's coronation scene enacts a radical reversal of the Christian idea that Man is 'created in the image of God'. Dante stages the process of *imitatio Dei* in an anti-Christian sense, whereby human beings give birth to their humanity. This is the same formula that Feuerbach employs to designate the end of religion. But the self-creation of humanity can also be read in terms of Nietzsche's conception of the internal necessity for humanity to overcome itself and in so doing give birth to itself as a sovereign (post-)humanity, something that Nietzsche would name the Over-Man, or *Übermensch*.

The Papal legal revolution and the sociology of constitutionalism

Recent work in the sociology of constitutionalism shows the continued relevance of the democratic political theology worked out in relation to the history of medieval constitutionalism. The central hypothesis of this sociology is that western constitutionalism originates in the 'legal revolution' through which the Church established itself as a separate and autonomous legal community from that of the Empire. First suggested by Eugen Rosenstock-Huessy in his 1931 book *Die europäischen Revolutionen. Volkscharaktere und Staatenbildung*, the hypothesis was then elaborated by Harold Berman in *Law and Revolution*, and now by Hauke Brunkhorst in *Critical Theory of Legal Revolutions*.[94] All three identify in the clerical revolution against the Holy Roman Emperor begun by Pope Gregory VII (1075–1122) the origins of the normative idea that modern *legitimacy is legality*. Berman developed Rosenstock-Huessy's hypothesis by arguing that the series of modern 'world' revolutions were not a function of extending Europe's imperial power over the world as much as democratic and pluralist processes that extended democratic constituent power to ever-widening circles of actors

---

[94] See the revised English edition of 1938 (Rosenstock-Huessy 1969). Not much has been written on Rosenstock-Huessy's thought as a form of political theology. For an exception, see (Diamantides 2012) who compares it to Arendt's discourse on revolutions.

and peoples.[95] As Brunkhorst puts it, 'the beginning of the Western legal tradition was Kelsenian and not Schmittian, and it is in the *Dictatus Papae* that the juridification of politics begins'.[96] Although staunchly opposed to Kantorowicz's derivation of modern rule of law out of the imperial struggle against the Church, this new genealogy confirms Kantorowicz's insight that modern constitutional government is underpinned by a political theology of legality.

That the idea of a 'legal revolution', which underlies all modern forms of constitutional government, belongs to the discourse of democratic political theology can be seen from the following reflection. For Schmitt, the secular analogon of theology is a sovereign power that keeps human affairs in their best order or restrains the outbreak of political and social disorder. In contrast, the sociological concept of legal revolution developed by Rosenstock-Huessy and Berman suggests that the evolutionary dynamics inherent within constitutional government drives the order of the state beyond itself, towards a messianic End that is post-sovereign, and that finds its expression in the necessity and continuous nature of both revolution and evolution. In other words, this sociology of law shows that the worship of legality and the drive to constitutionalize political and social arrangements does not reflect the secularization of theological concepts as much as employs secular means towards an end that is itself theological, namely, a post-political and post-historical messianic condition.

In 1075 Pope Gregory VII issued the revolutionary slogan 'Freedom of the Church' in order to assert the radical autonomy of Papal legal authority from the Emperor's exercise of *imperium*. For Berman and Brunkhorst, this Papal 'legal revolution' offered the possibility to found the modern state not only as a *Machtstaat* (based on Imperial 'might' or *imperium*) but also as a *Rechtsstaat* (based on the development of Church 'law' or 'right'). It did so because the Papal revolution gave rise to 'an independent, hierarchical, public authority. Its head, the Pope has the right to legislate.... The church also executed its laws through an administrative hierarchy.... The Church interpreted its law ... it adhered to a rational system of jurisprudence, the canon law' (Berman 1983, 113). By separating itself from the Empire, the Church established the legitimacy of its own concrete legal

---

[95] For a similar anti-Schmittian analysis of the evolution of modern constitutionalism, see also (Thornhill 2013; 2018).
[96] (Brunkhorst 2014, 128).

order as a function of its 'liberty' from the imperial command. It therefore sets at the basis of its jurisprudence (canon law) a doctrine of (individual) 'liberties' or 'rights' and, at the same time, developed a conception of the state based on its capacity for legal autonomy that would later be employed by the early modern national kingdoms to argue for their own freedoms.[97] The Papal legal revolution thus turned the Church into the first exemplar of the modern nation-state in which, as Jürgen Habermas likes to emphasize, all legitimate rule must be carried forward in and through the medium of law.

The messianic assumption of the sociology of legal revolutions stands out if one considers the historiography that underlies its hypotheses. At the height of the struggle between Empire and Papacy triggered by Gregory's clerical revolution, Joachim da Fiore prophesied the coming of a Third Age of Spirit, after the ages of Moses and Jesus, characterized by world peace, but preceded by the coming of the Antichrist before the Last Days. On Rosenstock-Huessy's and Berman's telling, the true content of the Third Age of Spirit prophesied by Joachim da Fiore was first realized by the Papal theocracy in the form of constituent power, the power to make constitutions, and was carried forward by the messianic monastic order of Franciscanism based on the ideal of 'highest poverty'. For Brunkhorst this means that the Papal legal revolution already understood itself in terms of class struggle: it sided with the *pauperes* against the *potentes*, the poor again the nobles. 'The monasteries and the reform monks were the pope's revolutionary party organization, and the Crusades were his revolutionary army . . . the reform monks were obsessed with the idea of law, the idea of justice' (Brunkhorst 2014, 111).

Of course, the opposing interpretation of Joachim's prophecy was advanced by the supporters of the Imperial claims to world government. For some of them, Frederick II was the messiah, the harbinger of the *novus ordo saeclorum* predicted by Virgil's *Fourth Eclogue*.[98] Indeed, Berman identifies the model of Norman kingship defended by Kantorowicz as the antithesis of the Papal legal revolution. The book of Norman constitutions produced under Frederick II, the *Liber Augustalis*, 'departs from the spirit and theory of the Papal Revolution in presenting the king as a person of unlimited authority' (Berman 1983, 427). Berman's point is that the Papal Revolution, by

---

[97] Again, for one history of this development, see (Tierney 1982; 1997).
[98] Note that according to Marjorie Reeves, Frederick II was also called "Leviathan" by Innocent III.

separating Church from Empire, and simultaneously developing its code of law (canon law), effectively separated law from might (kingship), and thus allowed for the creation of a 'rule of law' separate from the power of the sovereign.[99] On this view, the Norman theory of kingship does exactly the opposite. Thus, if on Berman's account the Papal Revolution, based on the separation of spiritual from worldly authority, lies at that origin of 'rule of law' (because law stands higher than might), then the ideal of the 'rule of law' of Norman kingship is radically anti-constitutional in its spirit.

The reason for this judgment is that, for Berman, the most fundamental character of western constitutionalism consists in its 'pluralism'.[100] According to his narrative, through its emancipation from the apparatus of Empire, the rule of law developed by the Church after the Papal revolution forced western conceptions of government to give up the Hellenistic dream of establishing one legal system over the whole globe. Papal theocracy requires giving up on the dream of a single world government by means of a world state. The unintended consequence of this is to favour the alternative idea of a world legal order as a function of a covenant or charter between independent nations and peoples, like the United Nations Charter.[101]

In turn, Brunkhorst articulates Berman's claim of legal pluralism in the terms of Niklas Luhmann's conception of social systems. For Brunkhorst, the Papal legal revolution caused the 'functionally differentiation' of western law, that is, the constitution of a self-referential 'legal system' whose code was the emerging 'legal science' linked with canon law. This dis-embedding of law from society required its 'structural coupling' with the political and economical social subsystems. The revolutionary development of constitutionalism in the West was ultimately due to the need for

---

[99] See also Brunkhorst: 'From the beginning, the separation of *sacerdotium* and *regnum* enabled the corporative pluralization of autonomous legal bodies (cities, universities, guilds, kingdoms, congregations, fraternities villages, etc.) and in particular the functional differentiation of the legal system that presupposed the structural coupling of law and academic science . . . the co-evolution and structural coupling of functionally differentiated systems of law and science' (Brunkhorst 2014, 92). This gives rise to the third 'power of *studium*' apart from *sacerdotium* and *regnum*.

[100] 'In the wake of the Papal Revolution there emerged a new system of canon law and new secular legal systems, together with a class of professional lawyers and judges, hierarchies of courts, law schools, law treatises, and a concept of law as an autonomous, integrated, developing body of principles and procedures. The Western legal tradition was formed in the context of a total revolution, which was fought to establish 'the right order of things' or 'right order of the world'. . . . The dualism of ecclesiastical and secular legal systems led in turn to a pluralism of secular legal systems within the ecclesiastical legal order. . . . The systematization and rationalization of law were necessary in order to maintain the complex equilibrium of plural competing legal systems' (Berman 1983, 118).

[101] This assumption lies at the basis of the post-Kantian discussion on the feasibility and desirability of a world state as instrument for global law. See on this point (Habermas 2001a; 2006).

constitutions to provide for this structural coupling of social systems: the coupling is the work of constituent power. The thesis is that modern pluralist societies can no longer be governed by sovereigns, but only through complex constitutional mechanisms that separate and rearticulate power and authority.[102]

What Kantorowicz means for the contemporary debate between sovranists and globalists

Advocates of the political theology of legal revolutions claim that the Papal legal revolution put an end to the idea of 'divine' kingship as source of legitimacy for sovereignty. Gregory VII was the true initiator of a process of secularization because after he was done, the power of emperors and kings became progressively and irreversibly 'disenchanted'. Kantorowicz's *The King's Two Bodies* remains a monumental refutation of this claim. Whereas Berman and Brunkhorst argue that the Papal claim to sovereignty is from the start *internal* to the self-assertion of the rule of law, Kantorowicz shows that the 'Pontificialism' of Norman kingship was an essential element in the strategy of Frederick II to legitimize sovereign power as a 'living law'.[103] Indeed, Kantorowicz shows that in canon law the 'plenitude of power' of the Pope to create law *ex nihilo* did not thereby justify the Pope to go against either natural or divine law, but only against positive law. Whereas this was *exactly* the kind of power that Frederick II, whom Kantorowicz with his characteristic exquisite and perfidious irony calls 'the most gifted student of the Popes', sought to legitimate through his lawyers. In that sense, one can argue that it was the Emperor, rather than the Pope, who is ultimately responsible for setting up a truly autonomous, self-producing system of positive law, completely emancipated from belief in natural and divine legal orders, that today is associated with the idea of the rule of law.

---

[102] For Brunkhorst 'all great legal revolutions have secularized the difference between transcendence and immanence . . . by a step by step internalization of that difference and its reinsertion into immanence that finally led to a transcendence from within this world back to this world (Habermas). I call this the Berman-Habermas thesis' (Brunkhorst 2014, 102).

[103] 'Papal absolutism from the outset was conceived as absolutism through and of law' (Brunkhorst 2014, 127). Compare with Kantorowicz's claim that the 'extraordinary prerogatives' of the Pope were transferred in the 15th century by French theorists of monarchy to the emperor, and from the emperor back to Christ, who thus 'becomes pope' as Kantorowicz ironically states (Kantorowicz 198, 45).

For the advocates of a political theology of legality, that a legal revolution would be first conceived within the Church is not surprising, considering that, as Berman puts it, Judaism, Christianity, and Islam all share the 'postulate that God is a judge and a lawgiver and that man is governed by divine law' (Berman 1983, 78). However, an additional postulate is called for in order to explore why legal pluralism was supposedly discovered by the Catholic Pope. This additional postulate is Berman's claim that only the Christian *dogma of Incarnation* 'released an enormous energy for the redemption of the world; yet it split the legal from the spiritual, the political from the ideological' (Berman 1983, 78).[104] Only Christian messianism gave a purely legal form (as autonomous legal science), a true inner-worldly realization of the commandment to 'love thy neighbour'.

Also with respect to this thesis, Kantorowicz offers massive objections. For in order that Jesus's Gospel be received, after the 12th century, more as a new treatise on law than a new teaching of brotherly love it was necessary that the dogma of Incarnation allow the Church to present itself as being both 'the concrete mystical *and the abstract legal body* of Christ' (Brunkhorst 2014, 100). However, as Kantorowicz shows, this feat was only possible thanks to the development of the conception of the 'King's Two Bodies', which brought together in one political body the Christian idea of a mystical body with the Roman idea of a legal corpus. But this development occurred only thanks to the struggle of the Empire *against* the pretensions of universal spiritual authority of the Church that emerged during its clerical revolution.

However, Kantorowicz's *The King's Two Bodies* also raises important objections to the post-Schmittian recovery of the discourse of sovereign prerogatives. According to its proponents, liberal governmentality has presided over a veritable crisis of the rule of law, where the use of states of exception and crisis management seem to have become entirely the new norm. This post-Schmittian view of liberal government, nowhere staged more provocatively and brilliantly than in Agamben's *Homo sacer* series, is theoretically dependent on the more arcane and erudite debates over medieval constitutionalism whose analysis lies at the heart of *The King's Two Bodies*, and in particular with the treatments of Bracton and Dante.

---

[104] More precisely, Berman argues that after the Papal legal revolution, 'salvation [is] no longer [understood] as mythical resurrection but as the legal act of crucifixion, hence as performance of divine justice through secular legal procedures' (Berman 1983, 176). Here Berman seems to be relying, perhaps unconsciously, on the political theology of liberation first developed after World War II by German theologians like Metz who were followers of Peterson. I discuss these theologians and their influence on Habermas in the next chapter.

Kantorowicz's interpretation of Bracton purports to show that it is the profane government of the State, rather than the sacred government of the Church, which is the true inheritor of Trinitarianism in law. Seen from Kantorowicz's viewpoint, modern public law appears as a device that makes it possible for the modern state to govern its citizens from within an entirely 'immanent frame', where previous forms of 'governing' human beings in the western tradition, as Foucault's studies on governmentality have shown, turned on a pastoral model that promised to lead each individual to their individual salvation. Through public law, theologians lose their utility as interpreters of the 'mystery' of salvation because this mystery is now a 'mystery of state' and requires the 'ministering' of justice through public policy. The bourgeois revolutions replaced priests with lawyers and jurists, but this, as we begin to realize today, may have been just an intermediary step: the constitutional logic of government requires that lawyers be replaced by economic managers, as occurs with the imposition of a neoliberal economic rule of law.[105]

Contemporary jurists like Loughlin argue that the economicism of liberalism corrodes the tradition of public law and western constitutionalism by undermining the 'public law' conception of sovereignty. What difference does it make if one adopts Schmitt's use of political theology, as Loughlin does, or the one proposed by Kantorowicz, as I propose, to help make sense of neoliberal transformations of the public sphere? For Loughlin, the idea of sovereignty is 'constitutional' because sovereignty can be understood as a 'constituent power', defined as the extra-ordinary power to make the highest law that establishes the absolute sovereignty of the state in its radical separation from government (Loughlin 2010, ch. 8 passim). This key motif in Loughlin's jurisprudence deploys Schmitt's later attempts to render his early conception of sovereignty in terms of the ancient Greek idea of *nomos basileus*, which contains in one formula both the meaning of a power that is absolute with respect to law and the meaning of being a ground of the rule of law.[106] This paradoxical idea of a 'legal power not mediated by laws' is called *nomos* by Schmitt and *droit politique* by Loughlin.

---

[105] See the trend toward a 'managerial mindset' in constitutional and international law discussed by (Koskenniemi 2007).

[106] 'It would appear that state (the political unity), constitution (the status of unity and order) and *nomos* (the order of a concrete spatial unity) are, to all intents and purposes, synonyms.... If state highlights unity and constitution the form of that unity, then *nomos* accentuates the motive forces that shape the form of that unity: it is "the full immediacy of a legal power not mediated by laws"; it is a constitutive historical event—an act of *legitimacy*, whereby the legality of a mere law first is made meaningful' (Loughlin 2015, 83).

However, Loughlin's public law framework might find it more challenging to explain the overlap between the Schmittian conception of *nomos* and the employment of *nomos* by a neoliberal thinker like Hayek in order to designate the 'right ordering' produced by free markets and other such 'spontaneous orders'.[107] To account for this peculiar coincidence one would need to explain how the neoliberal rationalization of state sovereignty, thematized by Wendy Brown in terms of the shift from *homo politicus* to *homo economicus*,[108] comes to embody the idea of justice, and rational choice allocations of goods become synonymous with *iurisdictio*. The interpretation of Kantorowicz offered in this chapter suggests that this phenomenon can best be explained if one reverses the causal story proposed by Loughlin: it is not state sovereignty that employs constitutionalism in order to limit government, but, conversely, government employs constitutionalism, namely, *droit politique*, in order to limit the state and embed it in self-steering, autopoietic normative orders that it cannot possibly hope to control.

Loughlin believes that only an appeal to the Schmittian doctrine of state of exception can keep under check the neoliberal *nomos* of the free markets. Kantorowicz's interpretation of Bracton disallows for such a sovereign solution to neoliberal governance, that is, for a Schmittian conception of a legal ('material') constitution that establishes a supra-legal absolute power (viz., sovereignty). Kantorowicz's reading of the formula 'the king reigns but does not govern' points in an entirely different direction. Rather than eliminating constitutionalism, the onslaught on sovereignty by neoliberal governmentality has rather managed to make sovereign constitution-making an intrinsic part of liberal governmentality. The significance of Kantorowicz's genealogy of constitutionalism lies in having shown how government comes to fuse itself with constituent power, thus preparing the way for liberal form of government to be carried out by something that can be called 'constitutionalism without republicanism'.

---

[107] On the 'neoliberal' aspects of Schmitt's juridical thought see (Cristi 1998); on *nomos* in Hayek, see (Vatter 2018).
[108] See (Brown 2015; and Cooper 2017).

5
Jürgen Habermas and Public Reason

Public reason and the debate on postsecularism

According to some recent studies, around 80% to 85% of the world population is affiliated to some religion. The principles of deliberative democracy require that no one's opinions about matters of general concern can a priori be excluded from an open and fair dialogical consideration in view of deciding what people ought to do and what laws they ought to follow. For this same conception of democracy, coercive laws are legitimate if there is (counterfactual) agreement that the interests and opinions of 'all those affected' by the laws have been taken into consideration in formulating them (viz., that these coercive laws advance 'generalizable' interests), and that they treat everyone with 'equal respect' or 'reciprocity'.[1] These criteria for public deliberation conform what is called 'public reason', namely, the kind of discourse on legitimacy that is conducted through a give and take of reasons that no participant can reasonably veto.[2] Most liberal political philosophers believe that arguments can be reasonably vetoed by participants in a legitimation discourse if these are intrinsically exclusive because their acceptance would require an act of faith that cannot be universally demanded. Yet, paradoxically, it would seem that acts of faith are precisely the most widespread communicative tokens in the world. If this is all correct, then there exists a *prima facie* tension between the requirement to integrate religious believers into the conversation of democratic common sense while, at the same time, 'against religion, the democratic common sense insists on reasons which are acceptable not just for the members of *one* religious community' (Habermas 2003, 108–9). This chapter considers how Jürgen Habermas attempts to navigate

---

[1] 'Norms that bestow or restrict such liberties make the claim to be *reciprocally* demandable and to enjoy *general* legitimacy. . . . Reciprocity then means that one cannot refuse to grant another person certain demands that one makes for oneself (reciprocity of contents) and that one must not assume that others share one's evaluative conceptions and interests—especially not by appeal to "higher truths" which are precisely *not* shared (reciprocity of reasons). Generality ultimately means that all those affected must be able in principle to share reasons for regulations' (Forst 2014, 72).

[2] For a wide-ranging discussion of public reason in liberal political philosophy, see (Gaus 2003).

the tension between the generality of faith and the universality or neutrality of reason. For no one more than Habermas has been preoccupied with the coincidence between the turn to public reason in the political philosophy of liberal democracy inaugurated by John Rawls with *Political Liberalism* with a new global awareness of the 'postsecular' condition, in which 'religious' reasons demand to be integrated together with 'liberal' or 'secular' reasons in the discourse of democratic legitimation.[3]

Habermas defines a 'postsecular society' as one in which 'religious communities continue to exist in a context of ongoing secularization' (Habermas 2003, 104).[4] Modern, pluralist democracy reflects a 'many-voiced public' and for that reason its conception of legitimacy requires 'neutrality' from the possible reasons and arguments adduced in justificatory arguments. At the same time, like other critics of secularism such as Talal Asad and Saba Mahmood, Habermas acknowledges that most of the concepts employed in the legitimation discourse of modern western democracies, concepts like those of person, dignity, subjective freedom, equal respect, etc., themselves derive from religious and metaphysical traditions.[5] Thus, Habermas argues that a democratic society needs to 'remain sensitive to the force of articulation inherent in religious languages' so that the 'search for reasons that aim at universal acceptability not lead to an unfair exclusion of religions from the public sphere, nor sever secular society from important resources of meaning' (Habermas 2003, 109). Habermas's much-discussed proposal is that the only way to address these apparently contradictory demands for religious-neutrality and religious-sensitivity is by embarking on a process of 'translation' of the semantic wealth of religious language into secular reasons, which he refers to as a 'secularizing, but at the same time salvaging, deconstruction of religious truths' (Haberman 2003, 110).

The vast literature discussing Habermas's turn to postsecularism is overwhelmingly focused on his claim that it is necessary for public reason to 'translate' religious insights into 'neutral' reasons as a collaborative effort by both secular and religious individuals for the sake of making democratic legitimacy possible.[6] Predictably, Habermas's proposal has been attacked from

---

[3] See Habermas's wide-ranging discussion of the Anglo-American debate on 'religion in public sphere' in the essay "Religion in der Öffentlichkeit. Kognitive Voraussetzungen für den 'öffentlichen Vernunftgebrauch' religiöser und säkularer Bürger" in (Habermas 2005a, 119–54).

[4] For an alternative vision of postsecularism, see (C. Taylor 2007; 2011).

[5] See this oft-reiterated point in (Habermas 2012). I will discuss it at length below. For a comparison of Habermas and Mahmood, see (Jansen 2011).

[6] See most of the essays found in (Calhoun 2013).

both sides. Those who take up the point of view of religious believers argue that public reason's filtering of reasons is either unfair towards religious beliefs because they are not considered on a par with secular reasons, or they simply deny the existence of 'neutral' reasons.[7] Those critics who take up the standpoint of secular citizens argue that religious reasons require no special treatment, no supplement of translation to make them competitive for public reason, because citizens with religious beliefs are already protected by the subjective rights afforded to them by liberal democratic constitutions.[8]

However, surprisingly little attention has been paid to the theoretical basis of Habermas's demand for the translation of religious content into philosophical argument, and his claim that religious reasons are fundamental for democratic legitimacy in postsecular society. The basis of Habermas's postsecularism is the principle of 'methodological atheism' according to which it is possible to give an *'interpretation* of the religious discourses by virtue of *its argumentation alone',* and see whether this 'permits a joining to the scientific discussion in such a manner that the religious language game remains intact, or collapses' (Habermas 2002, 76, emphasis mine). In this chapter I propose to discuss this principle of public reason *as a topic of political theology.*[9]

---

[7] 'If reasons based on ethical and religious worldviews are ruled out as reasons for the acceptability of laws and political decisions, the resulting conception of political autonomy is biased in favour for citizens with postmetaphysical worldviews' (Cooke 2006, 197). Cooke's answer is that 'revelation does not necessarily rule out argumentation' as long as the content of what is revealed is not 'epistemologically authoritarian' (viz., as long as revelation allows for this content to be 'subjected to critical interrogation in argumentation') (ibid., 199–200). This distinction between authoritarian and non-authoritarian forms of revelation is one that actually presupposes Jaspers's discussion of revelation and authority. Jaspers is crucial for Habermas, but his own thinking is usually not addressed by critics of Habermas. I discuss Jaspers at some length below. For another approach, see (Wolterstorff 2013) who rejects the very idea of a postmetaphysical conception of reason, which he calls 'Kant-rationality', on the basis of which a true dialogue between religion and philosophy is both possible and necessary. For Wolterstorff, philosophy and religion are both species of 'worldviews' lacking any true universality. Wolterstorff does not seem to have understood Habermas's interpretation of Kant, which I discuss below.

[8] See, for example, (Lafont 2013). Habermas's response to this claim is that it 'has no bite. On the one hand, it is trivial, because it boils down to the obvious requirement that every citizen, when contributing to public political debates, should respect the limits laid down by the principles of the constitution. On the other hand, the proposal is empty because it does not speak to the interesting point, namely, whether religious fellow citizens must be taken seriously as such in their contributions to the democratic formation of public opinions, and whether their religious utterances can possess a cognitive potential that the secular state must not ignore' (Calhoun 2013, 373).

[9] Habermas's debt to the discourse of political theology in the 20th century has not been generally recognized. (Accetti 2010) explores the problem of political theology in Habermas with respect to his theory of democracy but he assumes Habermas is external to the discourse of political theology. This is because 'political theology' is only understood in its Schmittian declension, as suggested by Habermas himself in (Habermas 2011). The reality is far more complicated.

I argue that Habermas's 'atheism' is both messianic and materialist. I illustrate the apparent paradoxical character of such atheism by offering a genealogy of its idea in the works of Karl Jaspers and Ernst Bloch. In order for Habermas's proposed translation to work, the standpoint of messianic faith must be shown to be operative in a materialist approach to philosophy. This is the contribution that Bloch's late work makes to the idea of methodological atheism. Conversely, the translation proposed by Habermas requires that the standpoint of philosophy be open to the experience of faith. This is the contribution that Jasper's post–World War II work on reason and faith makes to methodological atheism. At the end of the chapter, I show that this genealogy of Habermas's methodological atheism accounts for the surprising convergence between his approach to the conflict between reason and faith and Jacques Derrida's later reflections on the relation between messianicity and democratic reason.

Habermas himself seems to have gradually come around to the conviction of the centrality of such a genealogical approach to postsecularism, as indicated by his adoption of Jaspers's hypothesis about the 'Axial Age'. According to this hypothesis, circa 500 BC there took place in several civilizations, and in *both* religion and philosophy, a concerted shift from mythology to rationality, from *mythos* to *logos*.[10] This genealogy is what underpins Habermas's belief that 'secular reason' needs to 'take seriously the *shared origin of philosophy and religion* in the revolution of worldviews of the Axial Age'.[11] More specifically, Habermas turns back to the late Hellenistic translations of biblical ideas into Greek, namely, pagan philosophical language that, on this telling, eventually gave rise to all the basic 'secular' concepts with which democratic legitimacy articulates public reason, concepts like 'autonomy', 'individuality', 'emancipation', and 'solidarity'.[12] As shown in previous chapters, this is the

---

[10] 'The religions rooted in this period completed the cognitive transformation from narrative explanations of myth to a Logos that discriminates between essence and appearance in a very similar way as Greek philosophy. Since the Council of Nicea, philosophy has also adopted many salvation-related motifs and terms from monotheistic traditions during the "Hellenisation of Christianity"' (Habermas 2005a, 148). All translations from the German are mine.

[11] (Habermas 2010, 17, emphasis mine). See also (Habermas 2012, 96–119), in which he emphasizes how in Hellenism, philosophy began to translate religious contents into its own concepts.

[12] (Habermas 2005a, 149). I discuss the cruciality of Philo in this Hellenistic process of translation in *Living Law*. For a wide-ranging discussion of Habermas's use of Jaspers in light of determining the use of religion for purposes of democratic public reason, see (Junker-Kenny 2014). Junker-Kenny gives great weight to Habermas's claim in (Habermas 2011, 18–19) that the Axial Age hypothesis required reference to a conception of divine law (*Nomosdenken*) as a way to 'desacralize' power such that the human ruler is no longer considered divine, but a 'representative' of the divine. However, she misses the point that this insight is a staple belief in all the 20th-century democratic political theologians discussed so far. Habermas's appropriation of Jaspers's Axial Age hypothesis has been criticized as counterproductive because, implicit in Jaspers's narrative, there is a civilizational discourse

same context that gave rise to the discourse of political theology as a function of the mutual translation of theology to law and philosophy.

But it is not only for genealogical reasons that Habermas approaches the age-old question of Athens and Jerusalem in his attempt to resolve the tension between the need for neutrality and the need for religious-sensitivity in democratic legitimacy.[13] For the principle of methodological atheism offers an answer to two fundamental normative challenges that arise from the situation of postmetaphysical thinking in the 20th century. The first normative challenge has to do with the 'dialectic' of Enlightenment highlighted by Max Horkheimer and Theodor Adorno. The dialectic of Enlightenment is the claim that the modern rationalization of social relations is itself a new form of domination: science and technology, thanks to which *logos* could claim to have defeated 'myth', turn out to harbor a mythical force of their own in modern, rationalized societies.[14] Habermas is convinced that the project of Enlightenment itself, as paradigmatically articulated by Kant and Hegel, can only be defended 'against' its own inevitable 'dialectic', by returning to the way in which Kant and Hegel resolved the conflict between faith and reason. In order to balance the pathological tendency to 'naturalize' human social relations that follows from 'scientism', Habermas argues that one needs to 'rescue' within the scope of post-Kantian critical theory a conception of transcendence that is withheld by religious traditions.

The second normative challenge for postmetaphysical thinking is posed by the existential dilemma of carrying on the spirit of German philosophy from Kant to Marx as a German philosopher after the Shoah. Habermas is entirely aware that the philosophical solutions to the conflict between faith and reason proposed by Kant, Hegel and Marx contain crucial elements of philosophical *anti-Judaism*. It is no coincidence that in his protest against

---

that undermines any perceived advantage with respect to the goal of 'toleration' of non-secular and non-western reasons, as argued by (Rees 2017). However, Rees correctly salvages Habermas's 'minor genealogical arguments', which refer to the 'atheistic assimilation of religious contents' as this is reflected later in Kant's and Hegel's working out of the tension between faith and knowledge as well as in western Marxism (Rees 2017, 223). But Rees does not contextualize Habermas's discussion of these modern thinkers within the discourse of democratic political theology. On the civilizational bias of toleration discourse, see (Brown 2008).

[13] Eduardo Mendieta has done much to emphasize this theologico-political approach to Habermas, as can be seen from his Introduction to (Habermas 2002). The recent *Habermas-Handbuch*, in its discussion of the "Contexts" of Habermas's philosophy, dedicates its last two sections to "Jewish philosophy" and "Monotheism" (Lafont 2009, 121–32), but it does not offer an extended engagement with the problem of Athens and Jerusalem in Habermas's thought itself.

[14] For another discussion of the 'pathologies of reason' see (Honneth 2007).

German idealism and materialism, Kierkegaard appeals to Abraham as the 'father' of faith. Hermann Cohen and Franz Rosenzweig were among the first to diagnose the significance of the anti-Judaism of German Idealism, and their insights inaugurated the renewal of German-Jewish philosophy in the 20th century. Habermas recognized the philosophical importance of this *agonistic* encounter between the tradition of German Idealism and the philosophical defence of the Jewish tradition from very early on.[15] Even in his late *The Future of Human Nature*, Habermas's critique of naturalism and its biotechnological application in genetic engineering is based on holding on to a secular meaning of the difference between God as Creator and the human creature as articulated by German-Jewish thinkers like Hans Jonas and Hannah Arendt. Habermas is thus extremely sensitive to the need to find a resolution to the conflict of faith and reason that is free from the anti-Judaism that characterized the previous solutions offered by German Idealism.

These two normative challenges to postmetaphysical thinking organize the following discussion of Habermas's postsecularism in light of the principle of methodological atheism. I begin by discussing Habermas's belief that Kant's approach to the conflict between faith and reason already contains the kernel of a postmetaphysical conception of philosophy. For Habermas the role of philosophy in the age of post-metaphysical thought is that of *stand-in and interpreter* of semantic contents that philosophy receives from extra-philosophical sources, be these common sense, religious and legal traditions, or empirical natural and social sciences.[16] In Habermas's later work on postsecularism, the paradigmatic sense of philosophy as interpreter is represented by Kant's 'atheistic' appropriation of religiously revealed contents in the ethico-political form of the realization of the 'highest good' as an 'invisible Church' that worships humanity as an end in itself. This Kantian theological-political ideal functions as Habermas' exemplar for the translation of religious contents into democratic public reason.

Just like Löwith and Alexandre Kojève, Habermas believes that Hegel's translation of Christianity into his system of philosophy radicalizes Kant's attempts to articulate an *atheistic and political realization* of biblical content. Habermas adopts Hegel's belief that the task of philosophy ('Athens') is to appropriate religious substance ('Jerusalem') in a subjective form by translating

---

[15] See the 1961 essay "The German Idealism of the Jewish Philosophers" in (Habermas 1985, 21–43).

[16] See (Habermas 1993, 1–20; 1992a); and for commentary Hauke Brunkhorst, "Stand-In and Interpreter", in (Brunkhorst, Kreide, and Lafont 2018, 349–59).

its theological content into criticizable truth claims. As he says in the *Theory of Communicative Action*: 'the aura of rapture and terror that emanates from the sacred, the spellbinding power of the holy [*die bannende Kraft des Heiligen*] is sublimated into the binding/bonding force of criticizable validity claims [*bindenden Kraft kritisierbarer Geltungsansprüche*] and at the same time turned into an everyday occurrence' (Habermas 1981, 119). This profanation of religious mysteries originally accessible to the initiated few into everyday communication accessible to all is what Habermas refers to as the 'linguistification of the sacred'. Habermas's formulation is clearly meant to recall Hegel's transcription into logical form of both the Eleusinian Mysteries as much as Freud's rationalization of sacred taboos into moral claims. These insights still structure Habermas's claims as to how religious content is operative in the socialization of moral consciousness.

Habermas's conception of methodological atheism is not only informed by German idealism but also by the history of materialism in German philosophy. Ever since his dissertation on Schelling, Habermas has pursued the motif of humanity as an *alter deus* ('another god') that, much like Prometheus, struggles against divine heteronomy by divinizing itself. According to Habermas, Schelling was the first to give this motif a materialist declension, which is taken up by Feuerbach's and Marx's subversion of the biblical motif of God as Creator of Man into the anthropological—Voegelin and Maritain would say 'Gnostic'—motif according to which humanity is the creation of human beings.[17] These different threads converge into Ernst Bloch's later work, appropriately titled *Atheism as Christianity*. I argue that Habermas's demand for an 'atheistic' translation of the Bible into philosophy and its idea of practical reason reflects his reception of Bloch's way of connecting Marxism with a messianic interpretation of biblical religion that gives rise to his 'atheistic (political) theology'. Bloch offers Habermas a conception of an atheistic realization of Kingdom of God in the hope of a future communist society.[18]

However, the post-Hegelian articulation of postsecularism poses a dilemma for Habermas. If the post-metaphysical translation of religious substance into philosophical reason (viz., intersubjectively falsifiable validity claims) is successful, then there is no point in preserving and transmitting

---

[17] See (Habermas 2004).
[18] 'This atheistic appropiation of religious content has experienced vital continuations in western Marxism' (Habermas 2005a, 240).

this substance in the form of authoritative religious traditions. But if this translation is not successful, these traditions may equally be lost given the increased social pressure exerted by scientism and naturalism that fosters a market for reductionist explanations of morality and politics couched in the language of evolutionary biology. It is perfectly plausible to translate what families and societies have traditionally taught as rituals and codes of 'love for the other' into the terms of the theory of evolution and natural selection. However, the outcome of this kind of profanatory translation is not likely to be such that, for example, believers in Christian love and adherents of social Darwinism come together in a mutual understanding of what love means for everyone. On the contrary, the likelihood is that the religious substance of (Christian, romantic, et al.) love will have vanished in the process of translation. Habermas often writes about his concern that such extreme naturalistic translation may also get rid of our common sense understanding of subjective freedom.[19] In any case, what seems quite certain is that all processes of translating religion into philosophy run the risk that the ethical substance itself may get 'lost in translation'.[20]

For Habermas this would be an unacceptable price to pay for the advancement of a secular and technological society. For that reason he says that the post-metaphysical philosopher is *existentially defined* as someone who 'has the experience that intuitions which had long been articulated in religious language can *neither be rejected nor simply retrieved rationally*' (Habermas 2002, 79, emphasis mine). The reception of Kierkegaard propels Habermas outside the orbit of German Idealism. The Danish religious thinker represents the late modern resistance posed by an existential understanding of faith rooted in the experiences of everyday life-world against both the idealistic and materialistic attempts to sublate the faith of the singular into the sociality of reason.

However, it is Gershom Scholem's articulation of this argument for the defence of tradition and the authority of revelation that is of fundamental significance for Habermas. Scholem points out the *hubris* of German philosophy

---

[19] For instance, as in (Dennett 1996). See Habermas's discussion of naturalism in (Habermas 2008).
[20] I originally discussed this motif in (Vatter 2011b). It is found in several critical receptions of Habermas's proposal, such as (Bergdahl 2009; Arfi 2015; and Areshidze 2017), as well as the already cited (Junker-Kenny 2014). None of them, however, are particularly sensitive to the German-Jewish context of tradition within which Habermas is working out his proposal; in particular they miss the central point that what Habermas believes requires translating is related to the messianic aspect of religion and the internal relation that this messianic aspect has with western philosophy since Hellenism.

from Kant through Marx in its claim that it could do justice to the Jewish messianic ideal.[21] Scholem's rejection of the so-called German-Jewish symbiosis informs the crucial motivation behind Habermas's claim that a postmetaphysical translation of the religious substance of tradition cannot run the risk of eliminating the memory of its intuitions, despite their perceived 'irrationality' in the lights of modern scientific beliefs. This has to do with the question raised by Adorno about the *memory of the Shoah* as constitutive for the ideas of public reason in post–World War II German philosophy and theology. I take up these considerations in a discussion of Habermas's sympathetic approach to the so-called critical political theology developed by theologians in the Federal Republic of Germany like Jean-Baptiste Metz and Helmut Peukert, who themselves were adopting insights drawn from Bloch's philosophy of hope and Benjamin's concept of 'anamnestic reason'.

The inclusion of the post-Kierkegaardian standpoint of faith into his conception of 'methodological atheism', together with an awareness that the resolution of German collective guilt and individual responsibility for the Holocaust marks the inadequacy of post-Hegelian Christian political theology, leads Habermas inevitably towards the thinking of Jaspers. Although in his most recent work, Habermas explicitly relies on Jaspers's Axial Age hypothesis, I argue that it is Jaspers's theory of philosophical faith that is most important for him for systematic reasons, since Jaspers holds on to the post-Kierkegaardian goal of unifying reason and faith in such a way that it does not sideline faith nor the authority of revelation. Jaspers's thinking is fundamental for Habermas's discourse precisely because Jaspers offers a solution to the conflict between faith and knowledge in terms of a theory of democratic communication, which was later taken up by Arendt and in this form fed into Habermas's theory of communicative action. Both Jaspers and Habermas see in democracy the political form for an open or infinite communication between self and other that does justice to the importance of faith.

The idea of communication in Jaspers cannot be separated from the *internal relation* between faith and reason, which he establishes in terms of the opposition between a 'philosophical' approach to faith and a 'Catholic' approach to faith. With this dual-track approach to the experience of faith,

---

[21] As Habermas says: 'For us, your [Scholem's] speech of 1966 in which you uncovered the profound asymmetries in German-Jewish relations was a shock. Hadn't we just recognized the stream of Jewish productivity in the best traditions—the only ones that outlasted the corruption [of Nazism]— and hadn't we acknowledged them without reservations for the first time? ... Had we not, thanks to Adorno's and your help, discovered Walter Benjamin?' (Habermas 1985, 200).

Jaspers opens the possibility that, behind the opposition between reason and revelation, there lies a common source in a paradoxical idea of a non-religious, a-theistic faith. In his 1994/1995 famous essay on *Faith and Knowledge*, Derrida pursues the same idea. He puts forward the hypothesis that all communicative action at some basic level entails an 'atheistic' faith that makes religion both possible and impossible.[22] This chapter concludes with a comparison between Habermas's problematic of philosophical faith and Derrida's democratic political theology. The latter is based on the idea of an 'atheistic' faith that, not unlike Habermas, is also a-theistic and materialist because it is associated with the figures of a 'messianicity without messianism' and a conception of creative matter, the Platonic *khora*. Together, they are the condition for both the future and democracy, hence as condition of possibility for a democracy to-come. Derrida is perhaps the most radical proponent of the generality of faith as compatible with the universality of reason.

The post-Kantian understanding of the relation between philosophy and religion

Habermas's longest and most detailed explanation for his claim that postmetaphysical reason requires a 'critical *assimilation* of religious content' is given by his analysis of Kant's philosophy of religion.[23] Habermas's interpretation of Kant turns on the discussion of two general propositions. The first proposition is that Kant's critical system makes it possible to consider morality and law as exclusively human, secular, and intersubjective institutions. Kant's destruction of metaphysics (inclusive of religious doctrines) through the clear, critical demarcation of knowledge (based on sensible objects of experience) from faith (in super-sensuous objects) is meant to 'release an autonomous morality based on pure practical reason' (Habermas 2005a, 217). The legitimacy of human morality and legality requires no

---

[22] The history of the relation between Derrida and Habermas on the question of religion is now told in (Bouretz 2011). But Bouretz's account does not reflect Habermas's path towards a messianic atheism through Bloch and Jaspers.

[23] (Habermas 2003, 110). See the essay "Die Grenze zwischen Glauben und Wissen. Zur Wirkungsgeschichte und aktuellen Bedeutung von Kants Religionsphilosophie", in (Habermas 2005a), where he says: 'I am interested in Kant's philosophy of religion from the point of view of how one can acquire the semantic inheritance of religious traditions without blurring the boundary between the universes of faith and knowledge' (ibid., 218, emphasis mine). Kant's attempt is identified as 'an attempt to rationally appropiate religious content' (ibid., 219).

reference to a transcendent ground, such as the ecclesiastical faiths in God illustrate. 'Neither belief in God as the Creator of the world nor belief in God as the Redeemer with the prospect of eternal life are required to recognize the moral law and to recognize it as generally binding'.[24]

However, Habermas is also interested in the second general proposition put forward by Kant, namely, that this same human practical reason cannot but *hope* that human beings, in striving to fulfil their moral and legal duties, will also attain their *supernatural* happiness or blessedness *here on earth*. This is the content of what Kant calls 'philosophical faith'.[25] Despite the fact that there is ' "not the slightest reason for a necessary connection" between the happiness of a morally meritorious person and the happiness that is actually proportionally attributed to her' (Habermas 2005a, 222), nonetheless Kant believes that the reason one feels indignation at gross injustices is because one hears a voice within that says, 'This is not how it should be [*es müsse anders zugehen*]'.[26] Habermas's point echoes the idea expressed in Bloch's *Das Prinzip Hoffnung* [the Principle of Hope]: 'the Kingdom remains the central religious concept. . . . Hence the eventual transformation of the alien astral-mythical mystery, the chance to crack it into the mystery of a *citoyen* of the Kingdom and of his paradoxical relation to what has come to be. Hence, finally and above all, the greatest paradox in the religious sphere that is so rich in paradoxes: the *elimination of the deity itself* so that religious mindfulness and total hope may have a space ahead'.[27] The Blochian inspiration behind Habermas's reading of Kant on faith and reason is evident once Habermas sets out to explain why the object of this Kantian philosophical faith can be nothing other than the idea of God's Kingdom as reconciliation of nature and morality, necessity and freedom.

---

[24] (Habermas 2005a, 219), referring to Kant, *Religion within the Limits of Reason Alone* AK 6:3: 'So far as morality is based on the conception of the human being as one who is free but who also, just because of that, binds himself through his reason to unconditional laws, it is in need neither of the idea of another being above him . . . nor, that he observe it, of an incentive other than the law itself'.

[25] Bloch cites a passage from Kant's *Dreams of a Ghost-Seer* that beautifully illustrates this point: 'But the scales of the understanding are not, after all, wholly impartial. One of the arms, which bears the inscription: *Hope for the future*, has a mechanical advantage; and that advantage has the effect that even weak reasons, when placed on the appropriate side of the scales, cause speculations, which are in themselves of greater weight, to rise on the other side. This is the only defect, and it is one which I cannot easily eliminate. Indeed, it is a defect which I cannot even wish to eliminate', (AK 2:350) cited in (Bloch 1972, 254). For a wide-ranging discussion of the motif of hope in Kant, see (Fenves 1991).

[26] (Habermas 2005a, 223), citing from *Critique of Judgment* (AK 5: 458).

[27] From *Das Prinzip Hoffnung*, 'Man's Increasing Entry into Religious Mystery', cited in (Bloch 1970, 160).

The first and, ultimately, sole important 'translation' that Kant effects is from the biblical conception of God's Kingdom [*Reich Gottes*] to the 'metaphysical concept of the "highest good"' (Habermas 2005a, 223–24). For Habermas, Kant effects this translation in order to 'expand' his conception of morality. Habermas takes the greatest part of his long discussion of Kant to explain why this 'translation' that supplements practical reason into the concept of the 'highest good', namely, into a concept that is 'laden with eschatological content', is necessary. The importance of this point has been missed or downplayed by nearly all of the interpreters of Habermas' turn towards postsecularism, even the most sympathetic ones. They fail to appreciate that Habermas is committed to showing that the autonomy of practical reason *requires the internal relation to the messianic thought of the Kingdom*, what Bloch calls 'Man's progressive entry into the Mystery'. This is a significant claim given that, on both historical and normative grounds, the messianic idea of God's Kingdom clearly belongs within the discourse of political theology. Thus, Habermas's discussion of Kant's philosophy of religion should be recognized as his contribution to the articulation of a democratic political theology.

The main reason why practical reason must be given this eschatological supplement follows from the *intersubjective* requirements of Kant's conception of morality. Seen from the point of view of the individual agent, duty-bound rule-following is not itself a purposive activity because it is regulative of all teleological activity. By applying the principles of practical reason, the individual can determine whether their purposive activities ought to be pursued or not as satisfying a duty. However, when viewed from an intersubjective perspective, Habermas believes that it is inevitable to ask what *kind of community* is constituted if all individuals were to follow rules out of duty, and not because they are instrumental in the pursuit of certain ends they each deem to be good. What is the *final purpose* of non-purposive moral action? Kant's answer is that when all human beings become ruled solely by their duties towards the law then God's Kingdom is *realized on earth*. Whereas the concept of a 'Kingdom of ends' is a regulative, purely intelligible, and thus unrealizable ideal for the single moral actor, God's Kingdom is a *historically effective*, sensuous ideal that is regulative for all of humanity.[28]

---

[28] "This ideal [in which the 'intelligible realm of ends is transformed into a kingdom of this world'] is not represented as a goal to be pursued cooperatively, but as the hoped for collective result of the singular ends pursued by each individual in accordance with moral laws' (Habermas 2005a, 225).

Habermas suggests that Kant was required to extend his conception of practical reason into the sphere of the messianic in order to counteract the perceived threat of Spinoza's atheism, itself derived from his famous denial of the objective reality of purposiveness. The issue is not the existence of God as such. For Kant, even if one does not believe in God, one would still have the duty to follow the moral law. The real point is that 'ohne allen Zweck kann kein *Wille* sein' [without some end there can be no will].²⁹ Ultimately, for Kant and Habermas it is necessary to connect the belief in doing what is right to the belief that if people act morally, the world will become a better place, 'to strengthen the moral attitude through self-confidence and to shield it against defeatism' (Habermas 2005a, 229). The messianic finality of rightful action is therefore an object of faith or trust, of a '*Vernunftglaube*', or philosophical faith, that being moral will do 'some good' in the overall pattern of things, that it will make a real difference.

The semantic content of biblical images and symbols that indicate 'a God acting in history' who guarantees that 'the idea of the "Kingdom of Ends" is translated from the transcendental pallor of the intelligible world into an innerworldly utopia' must ultimately be preserved because they lend courage and motivation to the moral person (Habermas 2005a, 230–31). Likewise, Habermas's reference to religious traditions as 'storehouse' of symbols should be understood more strictly in terms of storehouse of *messianic* discourse that is required by *democratic public reason*. Adopting motives from Lessing's *Education of Humankind*, Habermas argues that the realization of God's messianic Kingdom in and through the concatenation of moral actions throughout human history takes the form of an "invisible Church" (Habermas 2005a, 232).

Ian Hunter and Daniel Weidner are among the few interpreters who identify in this concept the key to a veritable Kantian political theology of the bourgeois public sphere that is parallel and opposed to Schmitt's Catholic political theology.³⁰ What is undeniable is that through the conception of an

---

²⁹ (Habermas 2005a, 227), citing Kant, *On the Common Saying* AK 8: 279, note.
³⁰ According to Hunter, Kant's and Hegel's philosophies of religion 'rather than being scholarly theories or histories of the confessional churches and their theologies . . . were heterodox rivals to their confessional counterparts, designed to contest and displace them on the shared ground of spiritual pedagogy. In transferring Christian spiritual pedagogy to extra-ecclesial academic subcultures—and in this restricted sense "secularizing" it—Kantian and Hegelian philosophies permitted extra-ecclesiastical philosophers to occupy the illuminated persona of the metaphysician, imbued with prophetic insight into the transcendent structure and destiny of the visible world' (Hunter 2017, 14). The thesis was anticipated in (Hunter 2001). See (Weidner 2016), who does not refer back to Ian Hunter's thesis. Both Hunter and Weidner fail to acknowledge the distinction between religion and messianism.

'invisible Church', Kant is appropriating for republican aims the same problematic of the mystical body of the People that animates, as I have shown in previous chapters, the efforts to work out a Christian democratic political theology.

For Habermas, the idea of an 'invisible Church' refers to a people that has been formed into an 'ethical community' as a function of their belonging to a political world ruled by juridical rules under a republican constitution (Habermas 2005a, 233). This 'invisible Church' has as its strict correlate a constitutional republic, and therefore the 'legitimacy' that such an idea affords is entirely internal to the *legality* it affords. According to Habermas, the idea of an 'invisible Church' allows Kant to give up the dualism of morality and legality, the opposition between inward freedom and external coercion, that already the early Hegel showed to be untenable. Habermas argues that Kant's turn to a philosophical conception of religion allowed him to sidestep this weakness in his moral system and to put forward an idea of 'ethical community' (*Sittlichkeit*) that corresponds to a constitutional republic, in which public happiness is achieved in and through rule-following in accordance to moral principles.

Furthermore, for Habermas the motif of the 'invisible Church' in Kant's discourse is evidence of the attempt to employ the theocratic ideal of God's *Kingdom* on earth in order to criticize the traditional employment of the biblical image of God as Lord and Creator of the world in the establishment of the legitimacy of Empire and Church. Republican civil religion has always countered the political theologies employed to uphold absolute monarchies and Papal sovereignty. As discussed at length below, the emphasis on the messianic Kingdom is tendentially 'atheist' and it therefore offers another basis for a 'neutral' approach to constitutionalism. This messianic *and* atheistic basis for republican constitutionalism matches nicely with Habermas's two requirements for a postsecular conception of public reason. To recall them, the first requirement is to maintain the 'neutrality' of the state without lending a deaf ear to religious reasons. The second requirement is to avoid construing this 'neutrality' as a function of moral and political 'relativism', that is, as a function of denying universal truth claims to all reasonable conceptions of philosophical or religious worldviews. The latter is the conception of neutrality based on moral relativism, which Hunter ascribes to the tradition of German 'religious constitution'. Unlike the republican constitutionalism of Kant and Hegel, this German 'religious constitutionalism' based on reason of state rather than on public reason was 'not to be based on any absolute theological or philosophical truth, even if (or especially if) its role was to secure the maintenance of a plurality of truths within society' (Hunter 2017, 14). For Habermas, on the contrary, a reference to 'absolute' truth in the realm of practical reason needs to be retained. This is done in the Kantian strategy of translating into republican terms the ancient, biblical understanding of *messianism* as the faith in the earthly realization of God's Kingdom.[31] In this way, Habermas suggests that a messianic faith lies at the heart of the democratic system of law. Habermas's thesis that the discourse of democratic legitimation is the result of a secularizing process of translation of religious content therefore retains not a religious so much as a *messianic* condition of possibility or underlying narrative.

Hegel, the linguistification of the sacred, and the tradition of Judaism

In his essay on Kant's philosophy of religion, Habermas mentions Hermann Cohen once in passing. This may have been rather ungenerous of him, considering that Cohen was the first to make the argument that Kant cannot, in one and the same gesture, argue that human reason needs a messianic supplement and demand that revealed religion be treated exclusively 'within the limits of reason alone', as if it were merely the handmaiden for the realization of a subjectivist or individualist liberal morality. For Cohen, taking seriously the messianic ideal that is variously expressed in monotheistic religions entails the task of working out a rational conception of a republican ethical community or *Sittlichkeit* for humankind. When it comes to the proper relationship of priority between revealed religion and critical morality, the neo-Kantian Cohen signalled that a serious engagement with Hegel was unavoidable.

The motif of the 'invisible Church' finds its concretization with Hegel's conception of the 'ethical state' as *Sittlichkeit* that transcends Kantian *Moralität* by radicalizing the translation of religion into philosophy so that God's Kingdom is revealed to be the essence of secular sociality. Already in his early article on *Faith and Knowledge*, Hegel rejected the claim that the experience of the Absolute must remain isolated from human reason, in the 'in itself' accessible only by merely subjective faith, as suggested by Kant's

---

[31] For the genealogy of this effort, see (Vatter 2017).

division of knowledge and faith.³² Hegel argued that if it is true that religion provides the substance of normativity, then it must be possible to appropriate this substance by human reason in a way that is universally communicable. In Hegelian vocabulary, any fundamental separation of the sphere of religion from that of philosophy prevents the underlying moral 'substance' from being grasped also as 'subject'.³³

Habermas's own understanding of the Hegelian project of translating religious content into philosophical form, thereby understanding substance as subject, is deeply influenced by Löwith's interpretations of Hegel.³⁴ For Löwith, Hegel's system is a 'philosophical theology' that brings 'worldly wisdom' or philosophy ('Athens') together with 'knowledge of God' or theology ('Jerusalem') (Löwith 1964, 43). Hegel's system has one overriding politico-theological goal, which happens to coincide with the aim of messianic Judaism, namely, the realization of the Kingdom of God on earth in the form of the Johannine 'invisible Church' understood as 'a reality in which God reigns as the one and absolute spirit' (Löwith 1964, 46).³⁵ The Johannine ideal of the 'invisible Church' traverses Hegel's *Phenomenology of Spirit* insofar as this work translates the Christian *Gottesreich* [Kingdom of God] into a *Geisterreich* [Kingdom of Spirit] on the strength of St. John's claim that God is *Logos* or Spirit (Löwith 1962, 161). Hegel's philosophy of objective Spirit argues that the realization of the Kingdom of God gives rise to an ethical society (*Sittlichkeit*) in which the state can establish its relation to churches in

---

³² See the argument in (Hegel 1977a).
³³ See the famous formula for the Absolute: 'everything turns on grasping and expressing the True, not only as Substance, but equally as Subject' (Hegel 1977b, 10). Hegel's mature writings express the politico-theological basis of his system with more emphasis. See the famous claim in the *Philosophy of Right* : 'the march of God in the world, that is what the state is [*Er ist der Gang Gottes in der Welt dass der Staat ist*]' (§258 Addition). In his reading of Hegel's political theology, "Bemerkungen zum Verhältnis von Staat und Religion bei Hegel", Böckenförde argues that this saying means: 'as the realization of reason, for Hegel [the state is] God's thought and is—concretely and historically—the product of religion' (Böckenförde 2006, 121). Likewise, Böckenförde argues that Hegel's dictum that 'religion is the very substance of the moral life itself and of the state [*die Basis der Sittlichkeit und des Staates*]' (Encyclopaedia of the Philosophical Science §552) means that the state 'rests on the customs and manners [der Sitte und Gesittung] of citizens, which recognize and support the state; as such the state has its source and strength in religion' (ibid., 133).
³⁴ Habermas refers especially to (Löwith 1962).
³⁵ This goal is already apparent in Hegel's early discussion of the 'fate' of Christianity. This 'fate' is determined by the Christian rejection of the Jewish understanding of the Kingdom of God ('the Jewish spirit had not only made itself master of all modifications of life but also had made itself into a law, as a state, in them') that posits the realization of the Kingdom outside of this world. For Hegel this move entails the impossibility of passing from a relationship of love to a relationship of life. Hegel criticizes Jesus for taking flight from 'all living relationships because they all lay under the law of death, because men were imprisoned under the power of Judaism' (Hegel 1971, 284–85). 'This removal of itself from all fate, is just its [Christianity] greatest fate' (ibid., 280).

a 'liberal' way, but always and only on the assumption that 'religion and the state can and must come to agreement on the ground of the Christian spirit' (Löwith 1964, 46).[36]

For Löwith, the philosophical formula of Hegel's *Sittlichkeit* expressed in the iconic formula that 'all that is rational is real' presupposes 'a philosophy which is also a theology'. The formula, in fact, expresses 'God's dominion over the world'—quite in the sense of the Jewish Tradition (and, one could add, also of Islam)—since God is both what is most real and most rational (Löwith 1964, 146). Thus, for Löwith, Hegel's theory of the ethical state is what ultimately realizes the translation of revealed religion into philosophy, and at the same time gives social reality on earth to the messianic promises of monotheistic religions. However, Löwith also shows that this point of Hegel's maximum proximity to the Jewish teaching of divine providence is also the point of his extreme distance from this same teaching. For Hegel understands the possibility of unifying Athens and Jerusalem, knowledge and faith, in the modern age of the absolutization of Christian 'spirit' only on condition of rejecting the 'positivity' or *Gesetztheit* of 'Jewish religion of law'.[37]

Habermas adopts Hegel's conviction that the 'substance' of morality and ethical life has a religious origin, more particularly in a conception of divine reason or *Logos* that unfolds in the form of a history of salvation or *Heilsgeschichte*. In *Postmetaphysical Thinking* he writes: 'I do not believe that we, as Europeans, can seriously understand concepts like morality and ethical life, persons and individuality, or freedom and emancipation, without *appropriating the substance* of the Judeo-Christian understanding of history in terms of salvation.... But without the *transmission through socialization and the transformation through philosophy* of any one of the great world religions, this semantic potential could one day become inaccessible' (Habermas 1992b, 15, emphasis mine). However, unlike Hegel, Habermas argues that it is no longer in the state that subjects can appropriate for themselves the moral substance of religious traditions. Rather, the spheres in

---

[36] Already the young Hegel argues that the duty of the state is the 'defense and maintenance of faith' understood as the defence of the 'right to believe ... a fundamental article in the social contract, of a human right, which cannot be renounced by entry into any society whatsoever' (Hegel 1971, 127). The thesis regarding the Christian ('Protestant') basis of Hegel's liberal understanding of the relation between church and state has now been adopted by Böckenförde in an attempt to argue that political liberalism requires a Christian foundation, not an 'atheistic' one as argued by Habermas.

[37] Otto Pöggeler adds the interesting remark that, by starting from (Christian) faith in order to translate its revealed content into philosophy, Hegel paradoxically remains faithful to the Jewish view of priority of faith while separating the meaning of faith from adherence to revealed law (Pöggeler 1988, 119).

which substance becomes subject are those animated by a post-metaphysical conception of philosophy and by a democratic conception of common sense (what he calls 'socialization' in the above citation). Habermas establishes a mutual and dialectical relation between socialization and philosophy to account for the constitutive role of traditional religious worldviews in making moral consciousness possible within a secular society in which religious authority is waning.[38]

For Habermas post-metaphysical philosophy begins from the analysis of profane communication and can no longer be understood in terms of the Hegelian unfolding of the principle of absolute subjectivity. Philosophy undergoes a linguistic and 'pragmatic turn',[39] so that what is true for the absolute subject in Hegel's logic becomes, in transcendental pragmatics, what could turn out to be true for an indefinite future community of interpreters. The principle of subjectivity has passed over into a principle of intersubjectivity. Habermas does not consider that it is possible for a conception of reason based on intersubjectivity to subsume within itself, in a perpetual present of absolute Spirit, all of the past tradition in a final representation of truth. The critical unveiling of truth through communicative action occurs in the medium of tradition, where one is never 'finished' with what tradition bequeaths to any given interpreter of its content.

To explain this critical rescue of tradition, Habermas refers to Charles Peirce's semiology, the basis of his transcendental pragmatics. Habermas takes Peirce's notion of the sign to show that the 'good reasons' that allows speakers to attain a weak 'transcendence from within' their tradition-determined linguistic contexts are not themselves oriented to the present. Good reasons have both an internal relation to a *future* interpreter and to a *past* referent. This means that communicative reason, at its deepest level, must rely on the previous existence of what is withheld and transmitted, but not universally known, in and through tradition and its authority.

What this means is, at first, quite unproblematic: since according to transcendental pragmatics something is universally valid if and only if it could become—counterfactually—that about which an indefinite community of speakers could come to enjoy an understanding [*Verständigung*] under ideal conditions, it follows that the translation of religious content must be such that it is potentially understandable by all possible perspectives, that

---

[38] The account of this exhaustion of premodern understandings of religion are given by Habermas in chapter 5 of (Habermas 1984b).
[39] For the standard narrative, see (Habermas 1992a, 35–105).

is, it must be a translation that does not exclude non-believers. If religious semantic content is to be appropriated linguistically (communicated intersubjectively), then it must be possible for it to receive an 'atheistic' translation, since otherwise it could not be shared by people who lack faith in divine revelation.

At the same time, if the translation of religious content must be 'atheist' in order to be universally acceptable, this only underscores the requirement that the translated content be connected to a conception of the good and of justice that is not historically relative or contextualized but, to the contrary, comes with an attestation to its divine origin. For Habermas, the 'atheistic' translation of religious substance *must* be attempted for the sake of morality itself. The reason is that 'postmetaphysical philosophy does not trust itself any longer to offer universal assertions about the concrete whole of exemplary forms of life' (Habermas 2002, 70). In pluralist, functionally differentiated modern society, the burden of providing concrete forms of good life necessarily falls back onto ethical forms of life (*Sittlichkeit*), onto substantial ideas of the good, which offer the 'common sense' basis from which to reflexively come to an agreement about what is 'equally good for all', the latter denoting the properly 'moral' standpoint.[40] Without the rootedness in ethical substance, the moral standpoint would have no place from which to transcend the limitations of this very substance. For Habermas the paradigmatic rootedness of life in ethical substance remains best expressed by the Jewish conception of the tradition of divinely revealed law. He therefore rejects Hegel's claim that Christianity offers a 'liberal' realization of the Kingdom of God on earth that makes superfluous the Jewish attachment to divine law and the transmission of its teachings through tradition. On the contrary, as he asserts in his essay on Scholem, 'once the authority of the voice that said "I am the Lord, thy God" no longer holds as unquestionably true, there remains only a (in your terms) transformed tradition that knows no crime but one: Whoever cuts off the living bond between the generations commits a crime. Among modern societies, only those who can bring essential elements of their religious tradition, which points beyond the merely human, into the spheres of the profane will be able to save the substance of the human as well' (Habermas 1985, 210).

---

[40] On the distinction between ethical and moral in Habermas's communicative ethics, see (Habermas 1993).

This ethically laden conception of the continuity of generations in the religious conception of tradition seems to me to be the background of Habermas's claim that 'we acquire our moral intuitions in our parents' home, not in school. And moral insights tell us that we do not have any good reasons for behaving otherwise.... It is true that we often behave otherwise, but we do so with a *bad conscience*. The first half of the sentence attests to the weakness of the motivational power of good reasons; the second half attests that rational motivation by reasons is more than nothing [*auch nicht nichts ist*]—moral convictions do not allow themselves to be overridden without resistance' (Habermas 2002, 81). Habermas here rests his hope of redemption (expressed in Benjaminian language: the weak messianic force of the better argument) on the facticity of processes of socialization at the level of the family that can establish by themselves the solidarity of communication.[41] Socialization plays a crucial role for the success of translating religious substance into profane communication. Habermas, therefore, argues that there are good reasons to be moral, but these reasons find their 'strength' at the level of 'bad conscience' not at the level of motivating good actions, since here good reasons turn out to be 'weaker' than other means to get people to do the right thing. Thus, ultimately, for Habermas an individual's sense of being rational comes from their feeling of guilt whenever they do something that they are not supposed to do, in accordance with the substantive ethical norms into which they have been socialized. Habermas's acceptance of guilt as *index sui* of moral truth is as good an indication as any that his conception of communicative reason draws some of its premises at least from the early 20th-century debate on Judaism as a 'religion of reason'.

The remarkable essay that Habermas writes on occasion of Scholem's 80th birthday is significant on a couple of levels. First, it helps to situate Habermas's methodological atheism in the context of Judaism's own complicated and overdetermined treatment of atheism, with the mystical doctrine of God's nothingness at one extreme, and Spinoza's conception of God as Nature at the other. Second, Habermas's essay on Scholem's treatment of the problem of tradition in Judaism also sheds further light on what I called above the unsublatable pre-supposition of the divine nature of truth harboured by tradition in Habermas's post-metaphysical conception of communicative action.

---

[41] See (Novak 2005) for the claim that the peculiarity of Judaism consists in the idea that God contracts with a family prior to a people: the family, in its philosophical-allegorical sense, is the original site of morality. For a wide-ranging discussion of this motif, see *Living Law*.

Habermas identifies in Scholem's historical reconstruction of the meaning of tradition in Judaism a philosophical effort to 'seek the solution for the problems of how the *fallibility of human knowledge* and the historical multiplicity of interpretations can be *united with the unconditional and universal claim to truth*' (Habermas 1985, 205, emphasis mine). He thinks Scholem's mystical approach to the Jewish tradition approximated this solution by identifying the revelation of (divine, eternal) truth not with the written Torah brought by Moses and imposed as civil law on the Jewish people, but with 'the Torah's process of tradition itself; revelation is intrinsically related to the creative commentary [of the Oral Torah]' (Habermas 1985, 205). By shifting the burden of unveiling revealed truth from the written law to the process of interpreting an unwritten law, Habermas says, Judaism made the 'written Torah' (viz., the exemplar of religious substance) into 'a disputable interpretation' of the 'divine word', while, at the same time, linking truth with 'a mystic notion referring to the messianic state of a future knowledge' (Habermas 1985, 205). In this interpretation of Scholem's theses, it is easy to recognize the very kernel of Habermas's later reading of Kant's 'critical appropriation' of the substance of revealed religion. Habermas believes that Scholem shows in which way one can say that the mystical and messianic approach to the Jewish tradition is already Kantian in spirit, and, conversely, that Kant's a-theistic approach to revelation is also compatible with the Jewish tradition.[42]

In a second moment, Habermas argues that the above account of the Jewish conception of tradition presupposes that it is *the one and eternally same truth* itself that gets transmitted in and through the contest of interpretations. Habermas identifies this eternal truth with the symbol of the 'tree of life', whereas the infinity of contested interpretations of the one truth is symbolized by the 'tree of knowledge': 'only in the state of redemption—when theory and practice, the tree of knowledge and the tree of life, have been joined together—does the Torah enter the light in an unhidden way' (Habermas 1985, 205). Whether consciously or not, this claim places Habermas in much closer proximity with a Heideggerian, and then Derridean problematization of divine revelation and faith, than is usually admitted by commentators, as I indicate at the end of this chapter.[43] Here I merely wish to show that

---

[42] But see the in-depth discussion of Scholem's thought in *Living Law* that departs from Habermas's interpretation.

[43] In his treatment of the debate between Habermas and Derrida on religion, Peter Gordon has argued that Habermas consistently questioned Derrida's proximity and distance from Heidegger as a function of 'a neo-pagan betrayal of, and an ethical loyalty to, the monotheistic heritage', with Habermas siding uncompromisingly with the former stance (Gordon 2014, 125). At the same time,

Habermas's reading of Scholem's messianic thinking is not only compatible with his own reading of Kant's philosophy of religion, but recovers also his interpretation of Peirce's pragmatic understanding of truth: 'The dimension of time—the centuries throughout which the instructional conversation remains unbroken, and which is headed toward the vanishing point of a consensus achieved in the end ("in the long run", as the secularized formula of Peirce has it)—makes it possible to reconcile the fallibilism of the process of knowledge with a view of the unconditional character of knowledge itself', that is, with the messianic hope that knowledge acquisition is progressing toward that messianic 'last day' when the whole truth will appear in 'the bright light of certitude' (Habermas 1985, 205).

Third and last, Habermas takes up Scholem's discussion of the problem of *creatio ex nihilo* in terms of the Kabbalistic conception of God's 'self-negation by which God, so to speak, calls forth the nothing' (viz., self-contraction) out of which the creation of the world occurs. In clarifying the meaning of this Kabbalistic doctrine of contraction, Habermas refers to his own ideas on Schelling's adoption of the Kabbalistic theory of divine contraction as the key step towards the development of historical materialism from out of German Idealism. On this hypothesis, the Jewish idea of God's 'being in exile' and 'in need of being led back and redeemed' is to be understood in terms of a *'materialist dialectic of nature*. . . . The contraction of God is renewed in each process of nature, that in each and every creative process the contact with nothingness is repeated' (Habermas 1985, 207, emphasis mine).

In sum, Habermas's reading of Scholem is subtle and holistic. Thus, in his interpretation he also points out that Scholem considers primarily two other interpretative outcomes of the Kabbalistic doctrine of God's nothingness: one is revolutionary, the other is nihilist. The former takes Habermas straight 'from the early Marx on down to Bloch and the late Benjamin, it takes the form "no resurrection of nature without a revolutionizing of society"' (Habermas 1985, 208). The latter, instead, leads Habermas to link the 'religious nihilism' of the Sabbatian movement with 'the current version of terrorism, which from the standpoint of the participants could well be

---

and somewhat paradoxically, Gordon argues that Habermas always felt uneasy about the way in which the Jewish 'inheritance informs Derrida's work' because of his supposed 'apprehension in the face of a particularistic cultural-religious tradition when the viability of translating its contents into the criticizable language of public reason remains in doubt' (ibid., 130). Gordon's reading of Habermas does not seem to take into account the subtlety and affirmative character of Habermas's treatment of Scholem, nor how this discussion is exceedingly close to the way in which Derrida problematizes Heidegger's approach to revelation and truth, as indicated below.

directed toward saving the pure content of revolution by means of shocking exhibitions of pure destructiveness at the exact moment when the possibility of revolution wanes' (Habermas 1985, 209). Although this text was written in 1978 and referred to the Baader Meinhof and Rote Armee Fraktion brand of terrorism, it also anticipates his own turn to postsecularism that was accelerated after the Al-Qaeda terrorist act of September 11.[44]

Bloch and the atheism of Christianity

How does Habermas deal with the challenge that the translation into the intersubjective language game of argumentation, the give and take of reasons, poses to the transmission of religious substance? The answer comes in the form of two distinct argumentative strategies. The first is that for Habermas it is essential to distinguish between religion and theology in the postmetaphysical age. By religion Habermas means ritual praxis. In ritual praxis the meanings of symbols are not open to interpretation. For instance, seen from the perspective of ritual, the Eucharist is either the body of Christ or a piece of unleavened bread, depending on whether you belong to a certain community of faith or not. But, seen from a theological perspective, the Eucharist may be given a criticizable interpretation: as a symbol, it can be made sense of in such a way that its meaning may, potentially, be understandable to both a believer and a non-believer.[45] This, at least, is how Habermas understands theology, in opposition to religion, once theology takes a postmetaphysical turn, that is, once the experience of the sacred becomes linguistically mediated. In short, the inevitable loss of substance that religion must undergo once it enters into the demythologizing currents of linguistic translation must be made up by theology understood as the conceptual interpretation of religious substance. Habermas's separation of religion from theology has two principal sources of inspiration: Jaspers and Bloch.[46]

---

[44] In this context, see the interviews by Habermas and Derrida collected in (Borradori 2003).
[45] This crucial idea of a symbol is derived from Jaspers's works on the relation between faith and philosophy, such as the 1947 *Der philosophische Glaube angesichts der Offenbarung* [Philosophical faith in the face of revelation] (Jaspers 1994).
[46] It is amusing to note that Habermas, in his philosophical-political profile dedicated to Bloch, refers to the ironical saying circulating in the 1950s in western Germany that spoke of Bloch as the 'Jaspers from the East'. Habermas's early essay on Bloch was written much before the publication of *Atheism in Christianity* and at the time Habermas could not have consciously registered the extent of the conjoint influence that Jaspers and Bloch would exert on his later discourse on postsecularism.

What Habermas calls the 'linguistification' of the sacred and its relation to the doctrine of the Kingdom finds its first real formulation in Philo's doctrine of *Logos* and in the belief that *Logos* is personified in the messianic figure of the 'Son of Man' or *alter deus*. Cohen pointed out that Philo was the crucial thinker for the question of the relation between philosophy and religion in the West, precisely because in Philo a (Jewish) messianic content is given a (Greek) philosophical and mystical form in a way that would influence all subsequent medieval thought about the relation of philosophy to religion. The crucial element of the translation occurs in Philo's fateful conjunction of the Zoroastrian, then Jewish mythical conception of the Redeemer as the Son of Man with the Greek philosophical concept of the *Logos*. This is the proper historico-philosophical context within which Habermas's argument for a messianic supplement to Kantian practical reason must be situated. For Kantian practical reason remains itself the 'translation' of the idea of Christ the Redeemer as *Logos* or *alter deus*. Habermas finds the source for the development of this argument in Bloch's later meditations on biblical religion. It is Bloch who provides Habermas with a model for how a *collaboration between philosophy and theology* gives the proper expression to the Mystery of the communication of human beings with God in the form of a-theism.

Bloch's late work *Atheism in Christianity* contains two exergues that are directly taken up in Habermas's postsecular discourse. The first of these reads: 'only an atheist can be a good Christian; only a Christian can be a good atheist'. This claim stands behind Habermas's conviction that the aspiration to neutrality of the democratic state requires adopting a standpoint of 'methodological atheism' that is at the same time open to the biblical semantic and messianic content. Bloch argues that this paradoxical 'religious atheism' is possible because the biblical religious content that needs to be 'critically saved' turns on the doctrine of the Kingdom, and the realization of the Kingdom is a-theistic. The second exergue reads: 'what is decisive: to transcend without transcendence'. This claim stands behind Habermas's conviction that the context-transcending force of validity claims, without which no moral discourse is possible, does not have a transcendent origin but can be given immanently, within the life-world of democratic citizens. Both claims are contained in Bloch's central politico-theological thesis that Kant's 'invisible Church' should be understood as a function of the 'Utopia of (the Son of) Man'.

For Bloch the Bible contains two types of content, which corresponds, on the one hand, to an idea of God as omnipotent Creator and Lord of the world, and, on the other hand, to an idea of a Promethean divinity, a redeemer figure who stands against the former God and represents 'the hope that lies before-us' (Bloch 1972, 31). The former content lies at the basis of the religion(s) of the Church, which works as 'the opium of the people' and justifies their oppression. For Bloch, the deep connection between Marxism and biblical religion is to be understood in the role that materialism has to play in order to reject this conception of religion as *instrumentum regni*.[47] The name for the hoped-for utopia or 'new heaven and new earth' is the Kingdom of God. For Bloch, this Kingdom can be approximated only in a process of revealing that 'the existence of God—indeed God as such, as a distant being—is superstition; faith is solely the belief in a messianic kingdom of God, without God. Therefore far from being an enemy of religious utopianism, atheism is its premise: without atheism there is no room for messianism' (Bloch 1970, 162).

In order to show that the biblical idea of the messianic Kingdom has atheism as its premise, Bloch argues that within the Bible there exists a 'choked and buried "plebeian" element . . . by virtue of its ever-expansive, explosive antithesis: Son of Man—Land of Egypt' (Bloch 1972, 75). The connection between Marxism and biblical content lies entirely with this mysterious figure of the 'Son of Man' that Bloch *opposes* to the Emperor and Pope as figurations of the politico-theological idea of the 'Son of God'. Although Habermas's article on the transition from Schelling to Marx does not mention Bloch, his interpretation of the figure of humanity as the *alter deus* coincides with Bloch's Promethean interpretation of the 'Son of Man'.

The expression 'Son of Man' (Mark 8:38; Daniel 7:13) is the kernel of what Bloch calls the *Biblia pauperum* or Bible of the poor, the Bible of Thomas Münzer as opposed to Luther's Bible. The *Biblia pauperum* becomes one of the key concepts of Liberation Theology. For Bloch, the Exodus is one of the motifs of this Bible of the poor that contains the all-important internal connection between morality and highest good that Habermas retrieves from Kant: 'the idea of the Creator-of-the-world as well as of its Lord had to retreat continually before that of the *Spirit of the Goal* who has no fixed abode' (Bloch 1972, 94). The other fundamental motif of this subversive Bible is found in Job's lament against the Creator God. More precisely, Bloch draws

---

[47] 'Implicit in Marxism—as the leap from the Kingdom of necessity to that of Freedom—there lies the whole so subversive and so un-static heritage of the Bible: a heritage which, in the exodus from the static order, showed itself far more a pure protest, as the archetype of the Kingdom of Freedom itself' (Bloch 1972, 69). On Bloch's Biblical criticism, see (Boer 2007).

attention to Job's hope for the advent of a 'redeemer' [*goel*, better translated as 'avenger'] in and through which 'in my flesh shall I see God' (Bloch 1972, 114–15). For Bloch, this 'avenger' of Job's cause against the Creator God is the messianic/promethean idea of the Son of Man as a figuration of Humanity itself.

Relying heavily on the mystical tradition of Judaism, Bloch argues that the 'Son of Man' is 'in fact the son of the *Heavenly Man*, of the divine Adam' mentioned in Ezekiel 28: 12–14 and Daniel 7:13. Bloch attempts to *unify* the Christian account of Christ as "Son of Man" (1 Corinthians 15:47) with this mystical Jewish account of Adam Kadmon. In a way, this move is not so distant from one possible reading of Dante's doctrine on Adam as discussed in the previous chapter. Not surprisingly, Bloch refers to Philo (*Legum allegoriae* I, 12) for a way to justify this Judeo-Christian unity: 'the first-born of creation . . . contained within himself the mystery of the Heavenly Adam, of the archetypical Man himself . . . Philo's Logos-Messiah . . . was the "image of the divine essence"' (Bloch 1972, 150). But this interpretation of Philo is in turn overlaid with Bloch's adoption of a Valentinian Gnostic reading of Adam Kadmon as the 'eternal' body of humanity that survives the destruction of the world and comes to rule over 'the new heaven and new earth proper to the Man-hypostasis' (Bloch 1972, 155).

Bloch's virtuoso interpretation of the figure of the Son of Man culminates precisely with Kant's doctrine of the invisible Church of the ethical community of republican citizens whose unity is the mystical body of this Son of Man. Kant adopts 'a purely social Adam Kadmon . . . the Mystical Body and the Kingdom. Kant's mocking [of Swedenborg] was not aimed at this: *indeed, the concept of society in the form of a Great Man—of the greatest of men in the final analysis—is the mystical background of his own ethics.* Society is, for Kant, a community of intelligible worlds, of which man, because of his moral character, is a fellow-citizen. And being the ethico-religious ambience of the human race, society possesses man's intelligible form' (Bloch 1972, 157). For Bloch, Jesus is a Kantian politico-theological actor in so far as with him, *Deus homo factus est* [God became human]. But this becoming-human of God is no longer the speculative Calvary that justifies the (Trinitarian) unity of God as Creator with God as Redeemer. The figure of the 'Son of Man' instead separates forever the Creator God from the Redeemer, so that 'his triumphant Day at the end of days [is transformed] into the unveiling of quite a different face: the face of man' (Bloch 1972, 165). Thus, Bloch clearly anticipates Habermas's thesis on Kant's discourse on messianism as basis for methodological atheism: 'the words "with unveiled face" refer not only eschatologically, but also apocalyptically to our real identity as men: they uncover what was always pointed out and reveal it as the universal Kingdom of the Son of Man ... a figure who stands alone, without Yahweh, a-*Kyrios* and a-*theos*, at once in the true sense of *cur deus homo* [why God became man]' (Bloch 1972, 170).

There is a final element of Bloch's political theology that plays an important part in Habermas's later discourse and is related to the question of naturalism. Like Benjamin and Adorno, Bloch holds on to the biblical utopian belief in the 'resurrection' of the flesh under a Marxist formulation: the naturalization of Man and the humanization of Nature.[48] Thus, Bloch needs to inscribe his utopianism, or weak transcendence, within the radical immanence of a conception of matter. Bloch's strategy turns on an appropriation of Avicenna's and Averroes' theory of the material intellect. According to this reading, medieval Arabic Aristotelianism contains the doctrine of 'the education of forms from a nature that is no longer passive and unqualitative, but is also almost free from the need for a transcendent Father God' (Bloch 1972, 231). I mention this aspect of Bloch's discourse because it has a direct relation to the later affinity between Habermas's and Derrida's turns to messianic discourses based on a related conception of matter, namely, the Platonic idea of *khora*.

Bloch also identifies in this Arabic conception of formative matter a bridge to the Spinozist idea of *natura naturans* and the latter, in turn, with a conception of (eternal) 'life-force' or *conatus* in which he locates the immanent ground of transcendence. He gives two descriptions of this 'eternal' life-force: the first is related to 'that principle within us which makes us *stand up straight*, whether this is understood in an organic or a political or a moral way' (Bloch 1972, 251).[49] The second expression of this eternal life-force is 'finality' (Kant's 'highest good' of humanity) that 'comes to join morality as a second source of life-force: the finality which lay in the courage to break free from this devil's guest house, this world. . . . Mystical sources were called on too: for example, the words of Augustine as Eckhart quotes them: "I am aware of something within me playing before my soul and illuminating it. If it could only come to fulfillment and permanence within me it could not but

---

[48] '[Materialism] agrees with theology where it is most materialistic. Its longing would be the resurrection of the flesh' (Adorno 2003b, 207).

[49] I have discussed the internal relation between conatus, eternal life, and *sui iuris* status (which is how I would understand Bloch's 'stand up straight') in (Vatter 2014a).

be eternal life"' (Bloch 1972, 251). At issue here is what Habermas will call the tension between human dignity and the dignity of life, which I address below in relation to Spinoza and Derrida.

Erinnern, wiederholen, durcharbeiten: Habermas and critical political theology

Accepting the distinction between religion and the theological doctrine of the Kingdom put forward by Bloch, Habermas suggests that in order to 'to save intuitions that have not been exhausted in philosophy' by translating them into philosophical language, the approach to theology that best lends itself for the task of a critical translation of biblical content into secular reasons is the one represented, among others, by Adorno and Metz (Habermas 2002, 74).[50] Adorno and Metz stand for a consciously anti-Hegelian translation of religious semantic potential into conceptual language because they understand this conceptual language in a post-metaphysical fashion. More particularly, Metz wants to recover the religious experience of Covenant and Redemption carried forth by Judaism against Hegel's philosophically Christian translation of religious substance. Adorno, for his part, wants to use concepts in such a way as to think the non-identical 'beyond all non-objectifying concepts'.

Here Habermas introduces another crucial element into his philosophical discourse on religion. This is the concept of the 'rest' or of the radical 'other'.[51] Metz and Adorno, the former in relation to theology, the latter to philosophy, attempted to register at the level of the concept (*Begriff*) the radical caesura entailed by the event of the Shoah, this attempt at the complete annihilation of human difference, of a people who stood apart from other nations ('the

---

[50] The reference to the 'critical political theology' of Metz is found in early Habermas as well: in 'the repoliticization of the biblical inheritance observable in contemporary theological discussion (Pannenberg, Moltmann, Solle, Metz) . . . does not mean atheism in the sense of a liquidation without trace of the idea of God. . . . The idea of God is transformed [*aufgehoben*] into the concept of a *Logos* that determines the community of believers and the real life-context of a self-emancipating society. "God" becomes the name for a communicative structure that forces men, on pain of a loss of their humanity, to go beyond the accidental, empirical nature to encounter one another *indirectly*, that is, across an objective something that they themselves are not' (Habermas 1975, 121). For discussion of Habermas's relation to this critical political theology, see (Arens, Ottmar, and Rottländer 1991; Fiorenza and Browning 1992; and Arens 1997).

[51] For this reason it would be much too quick to oppose Habermas's theological discourse to those developed by Derrida and Agamben, for whom the motif of the 'rest' or 'remainder' is also explicit and essential.

rest of Israel', understood in all of the many senses of this expression). As discussed earlier, the western philosophical tradition has long considered the Jewish people to offer the most perfect exemplar of 'religious substance' and of 'ethical life'. This exemplarity is clearly acknowledged by all modern philosophical critics of Judaism, whether Spinoza and Hegel, or Marx and Nietzsche. This explains why, unless Habermas is able to provide a conception of the translation of religious substance, *in primis* of the Jewish tradition, into philosophical language that fares better than Hegel's attempt (which ends up eliminating the voice of Judaism in the unity of reason),[52] then it is the entire project of a 'communicative ethics' that would fail to live up to Adorno's motto: 'remember, repeat, work through' (*erinnern, wiederholen, durcharbeiten*).[53] This is not to say that Habermas shares Adorno's beliefs with respect to the fate of reason after the Shoah, but it does mean that he cannot afford to minimize the implications of Adorno's motto in his own attempt at re-establishing the public role of philosophy in postwar Germany.

In my opinion, the above point offers the best explanation for why Habermas feels so close to Metz's 'critical' political theology, which turns on the idea of an 'anamnestic reason'.[54] The concept of anamnestic reason is precisely the idea of a rationality that remembers, that is, which brings back into Christian theology, the memory of the Shoah and counterbalances what Metz (here again following Bloch) believes to be the 'original sin' of Christian theology, namely, its having chosen the language of Greek metaphysics rather than of biblical prophecy in order to spread the 'glad tidings', the gospel of Christ's death and resurrection to eternal life.[55] Thus, it is absolutely essential for Habermas that the theology that translates the religious substance into the public sphere (hence 'political' theology in the sense of Metz is synonymous with 'public' theology) must be a theology that brings into the consciousness of the democratic public sphere the memory of the

---

[52] On Hegel's translation of Judaism into philosophical reason, see (Fackenheim 1973; and Yovel 1998).

[53] See "Was bedeutet: Aufarbeitung der Vergangenheit", in (Adorno 2003b).

[54] See the essay "Israel or Athens: Where Does Anamnestic Reason Belong? Johannes Baptist Metz on Unity amidst Multicultural Plurality", in (Habermas 2002, 129–38).

[55] On Metz's political theology, see (Metz 2002). Along the same lines, see Bloch: 'Greek thought, which is being-oriented and anti-historical, instead of with the historical thought of the Bible with its Promise and its Novum—with the Futurum as an open possibility for the definition of being right up to the point of Yahweh himself... hence the difference between epiphany and apocalypse, and between the mere anamnesis of truth (remembering, circular line) which stretches from Plato to Hegel, and the eschatology of truth as of something still open with itself, open with Not-yet-being' (Bloch 1972, 56). In reality, the relationship of the Jewish tradition with Greek philosophy and mysticism is far more complex, ambivalent, and overdetermined.

Shoah, that is, which offers a kind of testimony in favour of the restitution of the exterminated 'rest' of humanity.

The concept of 'anamnestic reason' has a prevailing meaning in post–World War II Germany: it means that the conception of democratic public reason must be such that the memory of the Shoah becomes what is first and foremost for philosophy as such. Post-metaphysical, post-Hegelian reason can no longer pretend that the Jewish faith can be *aufgehoben* by German philosophical *Geist*. That is why Habermas's conception of democratic public reason cannot ever be a conception for which the biblical faith could simply vanish. This consideration helps to explain why the later Habermas has been unwilling to adopt a standpoint of 'pure' universalism, that is, a standpoint according to which, if a particular religious faith cannot be translated into terms that are universally acceptable (and this is clearly the case with the Jewish faith in Israel as God's 'chosen' people), then this should be understood as a loss for that particular faith. 'As long as religious language bears with itself inspiring, indeed, unrelinquishable semantic contents which elude (for the moment?) the expressive power of a philosophical language and still await translation into a discourse that gives reasons for its positions, philosophy, even in its postmetaphysical form, will neither be able to replace nor to repress religion.'[56] The task for Habermas, if one wishes, is how to allow the intuitions that define the Jewish tradition to survive, to live-on in a democratic public reason that must remain 'methodologically' atheist. How to communicate universally what the meaning of Judaism is (namely, universal peace and justice represented in history by a people that separates itself from all others),[57] within a universalistic renewal of the project of Enlightenment?

Habermas's solution to the dilemma just described requires him to inscribe the standpoint of faith in the heart of his conception of communicative reason through the principle of methodological atheism. The example that Habermas chooses to illustrate his proposed methodology concerns the biblical conception of God as that of a 'personified divine power', of God as *Adonai* or Lord. Any theology that wants to translate the religious insight behind this symbolic representation of God into publicly acceptable terms, that is, taking into account of the supreme value of individual autonomy, would have to abandon the idea of God as a heteronomous source of normativity, as

---

[56] (Habermas 2002, 79), where he cites himself in (Habermas 1992a, 60).

[57] This general definition is drawn from Cohen (1924), generally recognized as the source of the renewal of Jewish thinking in the 20th century. For another more recent and 'realist' perspective on the messianic vocation of Judaism, see (Hartman 1998).

the Lord of human beings (and of the World), and in this sense, the theology would be a-theist.

So far, Habermas is still working with a Blochian idea of 'atheism in Christianity'. This idea guides his immanent critique of two possible contemporary theologies that claim to pass the test of methodological atheism. The first is associated with the political theology of Peukert.[58] For Peukert, God is understood atheistically as a reality 'that can connect ourselves beyond our own death with those who went innocently to their destruction before us'— only this reality can keep alive our 'desire to hold on to solidarity with everyone else in the communicative fellowship, even the dead' (Habermas 2002, 77). It is not difficult to see why a German political theology like Peukert's, developed after Auschwitz, would consider as absolutely essential the possibility that those who died innocently be saved, that is, that solidarity must extend not only to the present community or to a future community but also to those of another community who were annihilated as innocents in the past since precisely *this* solidarity vanished in Germany during the Hitler years. The question of German 'guilt', which Jaspers posed as inescapable for German philosophy immediately after the war, and which received a daily, concrete reminder for Habermas himself when Adorno and Horkheimer brought the 'Frankfurt School' (and the memory of Benjamin's 'martyrdom') back from exile to Frankfurt: this is the crucial context for the figure of 'anamnestic reason' with which Habermas is called upon to wrestle.

Remarkably, Habermas does not follow the path of Peukert and other German theologians, probably because he also understood Adorno's other devise: 'extreme asceticism towards any belief in revelation, extreme loyalty to the ban on images, far beyond what it once meant in a particular time and place' (Adorno 2003a, 616). For Habermas, unlike Peukert, a methodological atheism must also do away with the belief in God as what vouches for the resurrection of the dead, that is, for their eternal salvation. In other words, Habermas does not believe that any faith in a redeeming God can ultimately eliminate the guilt incurred for the Shoah. Rather, he adopts the position that this guilt must be 'something that spurs us to fight against the conditions that have produced the guilt'. One does so by holding on to 'our solidarity with all who have suffered and died, now and before' (Habermas 2002, 78).

This conception of solidarity is charged with picking up Benjamin's contribution to critical theory. Habermas conceives of solidarity as that 'weak'

---

[58] For another interpretation of Peukert's importance for Habermas, see (McCarthy 1993, ch.8).

messianic force that animates the struggle against the conditions of evil in this world of which Benjamin speaks in his *Theses on the Philosophy of History*.[59] The weak messianic force is harboured by 'the ideal communicative fellowship'—in other words, it is nothing other than the 'force' of the better argument, and of those conditions of communication that allow for this 'force' to prevail over the force of violence and myth. Habermas's atheist theology places 'ideal communicative fellowship' in the place of the Christian God as what represents best the memory of Benjamin, and, through Benjamin, somehow, the rest of Judaism (Habermas 1988).

But Habermas takes a further step away from the above atheist theology with the principle that his methodological atheism expresses a 'transcendence from within the world' and not from without (i.e., from a transcendent and forgiving God). Yet Habermas is aware that such transcendence contained by the 'anticipation of an unlimited community of communication' necessarily raised by every validity claim (Habermas 2002, 80) cannot by itself offer the hope for the 'deliverance for the annihilated victims' that anamnestic reason wants. This hope depends on a 'transcendence from beyond' that 'is accessible only in the language of the Christian tradition' and is thus not the object of a possible universal understanding because it excludes those who are not Christian. Habermas goes as far along as he can with the anamnestic political theology of Metz, Peukert, Moltmann, and others, but separates himself from their Christian political theology over the question of whether the faith in the crucified Christ can be a political symbol strong enough to do away with injustices in the world.[60] Habermas is not willing to defend the claim that Christian hope (in the universal salvation of all human beings, including those who 'resist' the 'glad tidings' of Jesus as the Christ or Messiah) is a requirement for 'the perspective of living together in solidarity and justice' (Habermas 2002, 80).

Jaspers and the universality of faith

However, there is more to Habermas's methodological atheism than the Blochian legacy. The concern expressed by Habermas for the 'rest' of the Jewish people and its faith does not allow him to adopt Bloch's Gnostic

---

[59] On Habermas's use of Benjamin to traverse the conflict of 'Athens and Jerusalem' see now (Brunkhorst 2010).
[60] For the same theme, see now (Habermas 2005b).

claim according to which the heteronomy of religious substance itself *ought* to vanish in order to uncover a purely anthropological content. Habermas does not wish to replace all theology by atheism because that would amount to *denying a role for faith as such* in post-metaphysical philosophy and in a democratic public reason. A theology that is 'methodologically atheist' still needs to be a *theology*; it must still advance some *faith-based* idea of God, but one that is potentially acceptable by all possible interpreters. Habermas does not want to deny recognition to a religious *faith* that, as faith, allows for its rational interpretation and thus successful integration into public reason. Thus, the conception of a theology that is 'methodologically atheist' requires introducing a 'scientific' or 'philosophical' conception of faith alongside a 'religious' conception of faith. For this philosophical conception of faith, Habermas is in debt with Jaspers's development of the modern philosophical discussion of the theme of faith and knowledge introduced by Kierkegaard and Nietzsche.[61]

Together with Löwith, Jaspers is responsible for bringing to prominence in the German philosophy of the 1920s the critique of philosophy on the basis of faith staged by Kierkegaard and Nietzsche, first in *Psychologie der Weltanschauungen* [The psychology of worldviews] of 1919 and then in *Vernunft und Existenz* [Reason and existence] of 1935. For Jaspers the 'present philosophical situation' after the 'end' of metaphysics is determined by these two postmetaphysical thinkers. Jaspers's concept of a 'present situation' is a technical term through which he rejects post-Hegelian historicism that relativized absolute truth to the 'spirit of the age'. For Jaspers, the contrary is the case: what places one in a 'situation' is the happening or event of a truth that transcends it, that is absolute with respect to the temporal horizon. In *The Spiritual Situation of Our Time* (1931) Jaspers argues that the task of philosophy is not to grasp one's time in concepts, but rather to understand one's present situation as an encounter with what is situation-transcendent (viz., the eternal, truth).

According to *Vernunft und Existenz*, Nietzsche and Kierkegaard allow for a recovery of the context-transcending force of truth because they reject the Hegelian idea of a completed 'system' of absolute knowledge in favour of an understanding of philosophy as a form of life. Life, not knowledge, is directly

---

[61] Habermas's definition of atheistic theology may also be indebted to Heidegger's definition of theology as '*die Wissenschaft des Glaubens*' [the science of faith] found in his very early essay "Phänomenologie und Theologie" (Heidegger 1978, 55). If theology is a 'scientific' treatment of faith, then it is also thereby 'methodologically atheist' in Habermas's terms.

in touch with transcendent truth, and this encounter is the experience of faith. Thus, faith and philosophy (understood as the pursuit of a truthful, authentic, or *redlich* form of living) are by no means contrary to each other. It follows that all knowledge of Being is always a matter of interpretation: all claims to knowledge must be able to be falsified. Lastly, and politically most important, Kierkegaard and Nietzsche understand philosophy as a form of life in terms of the possibility of being an exception to the rule, and both emphasize that this form of life demands individual responsibility for taking a decision for or against claims to validity raised in communication (Jaspers 1994, 39–42).

By bringing metaphysics to an end, Kierkegaard and Nietzsche inaugurate the possibility of a post-metaphysical thinking, which Jaspers formulates as follows: 'to philosophize, without being an exception, in view of the exception' (Jaspers 1994, 51). By the expression 'in view of the exception', Jaspers means the effort of 'seeing the counter-rational rationally'. By the expression 'without being an exception' Jaspers means that post-metaphysical thinking must occur in the medium of communication because 'it considers itself true only if it can be translated into the actuality of the many' (Jaspers 1994, 52). Lastly, post-metaphysical thinking will move in the space demarcated by, at one extremity, the Kierkegaardian origin, namely, faith in the punctual revelation of absolute truth, and, at the other extremity, the Nietzschean origin, namely, faith in the nothingness of absolute truth (Jaspers 1994, 52). Jaspers therefore defines post-metaphysical thinking as a philosophical approach to the priority of faith over knowledge.

Jaspers's central intuition is that the context-transcendent force of *truth* is precisely what signals the internal dependency of post-metaphysical thinking on *faith*. The conception of faith is articulated by Jaspers through the concepts of the exception and of authority, but these are illuminated, in turn, by his communicative conception of truth. For Jaspers there exist three 'meanings' or 'concepts' of truth: truth as scientific knowledge, truth as existential decision, and truth as what is reasonable. Jaspers believes that none of these meanings attains the one absolute or eternal truth. The exception denotes the failure on the part of these concepts to grasp transcendent truth: the exception 'destroys truth as permanent and universally valid', that is, truth as a function of an 'absolute' knowledge (Jaspers 1994, 246).

Jaspers's concept of the exception rehabilitates the idea of authority. Given that absolute knowledge has no access to absolute truth, this truth appears historically only as an exception, in the figure of authority. Here Jaspers is simply formalizing Max Weber's claim that substantive moral ends appear to human beings in the form of charismatic authority. Unlike knowledge, authority is not a function of rule-following, but a function of the exception to rules. Jaspers defines authority as 'that form of truth in which truth is neither exclusively universal knowledge nor exclusively external command and demand, nor exclusively idea of a whole but all of these at once.... Authority is a claim based on transcendence which is obeyed even by the person who at any given time gives commands based on it' (Jaspers 1994, 249).

For Jaspers, authority is the medium of human freedom and reason: it is that background of sense, carried by a tradition, which encompasses all meanings of truth. 'Wherever they occur, truth based on authority and truth uttered by the exception are the most immediate and overwhelming truths' (Jaspers 1994, 251). Here Jaspers is subverting the answer of German Idealism to the dualism of faith and reason. The most authentic truth does not take the form of knowledge as opposed to authority; truth is not the destruction of all positivity in the infinity of the concept (Hegel). To the contrary, truth is that limit-experience in which transcendence breaks through the universality of our concepts and allows for a contact with what is nonidentical, with *singularity*. This limit-experience can therefore manifest itself only in the forms of exception and authority (Jaspers 1994, 252).

The opposition between singularity and universality, transcendence and immanence, allows Jaspers to introduce his conception of 'philosophic truth', which he associates with the standpoint of 'reason' and defines in terms of the will to attain the Unity of 'the One that contains all truth' (Jaspers 1994, 254). Jaspers's language is telling of his historico-philosophical assumptions. The reference to the One is an obvious borrowing from the terminology of neo-Platonism. It is modelled after the Judeo-Hellenistic belief in a rational approach to the Mystery (of God as One) that finds its most exemplary formulation in Philo. For Jaspers, philosophical reason *moves out* from the limit-experience of faith. Philosophical reason is not separated from faith (Spinoza) or opposed to faith as sensible to supersensible (Kant), nor does reason identify the content of faith with that of knowledge (Hegel). Rather, Jaspers defines human reason (or the reasonable) as moved by 'the total will to communicate' the singular truth that manifests itself in faith under the form of exception and authority.

However, Jaspers argues that there exist two paths that human reason can follow when it sets out to communicate the singular experience of faith: on one path, the transcendence and singularity of truth is enclosed by the *immanence of universal conceptual* language. When the communication of the experience of faith takes this path, it becomes a 'catholic' understanding of faith. The other path, which Jaspers calls 'philosophical' or 'rational' faith, entails the communication of the exception and of authority, and the truths to which they testify, through the *practice of translation into the standpoint of other exceptions and authorities.* For Jaspers there are only two options: either an authority claims for itself universal validity, so that one experience of singular transcendence (for instance, the faith in Jesus as the Christ) is claimed to be of universal significance for the entire human species; or, the experience of authority can remain an event that does not become the basis of a philosophy of history, but which is also not of relative value. Jaspers calls the first scenario a case of 'forced historicity' that reduces singular events of transcendence into the basis of metaphysical knowledge of history, into a philosophy of history. The second scenario, instead, allows these events to escape their 'historical relativism' while maintaining their 'original historicity', that is, their capacity to elicit meaning for both believers and non-believers. Hegel's system is the paradigm of catholicity, which 'wants and asserts knowledge of the whole'. But for Jaspers, 'complete universality . . . would abolish communication' (Jaspers 1994, 285–86). Reason maintains open 'the authentic mystery of the transcendent One and its compelling attraction in worldly communication' (Jaspers 1994, 286). The contradiction between catholicity and reason is permanent and irreconcilable: 'it is the deepest tension of being-human' (Jaspers 1994, 284).

It is well known that Arendt's notion of action as disclosure to others in speech acts is an important influence on Habermas's theory of communicative action.[62] As their correspondence shows, Arendt herself adopted a variant of Jaspers's idea of communicative reason.[63] However, what is less often remarked is that Jaspers develops his ideas on communicative reason precisely in relation to the problem of faith and philosophy. Some of these connections are retained in Habermas's discussion of Jaspers's theory of the symbol but the extent of the real influence exerted by Jaspers's treatment of 'Athens and Jerusalem' on Habermas, to my mind, remains to be more fully explored.

---

[62] See the important essay "Hannah Arendt: On the Concept of Power", in (Habermas 1985, 171–85).
[63] On Jaspers's theory of communication seen from an Arendtian perspective, see (Young-Bruehl 1981; and Flakne 2012).

In 1947 Jaspers published *Der philosophische Glaube angesichts der Offenbarung*, in which the opposition between reason and catholicity is given in terms of the tension between a philosophical and a revelational faith. The difference between these two types of faith is what Jaspers calls the distance or proximity with relation to 'the transcendent One': for philosophy, the One (God) remains distant; for faith in revelation, God is proximate. Indeed, the more proximate the impersonal One is experienced, the more it is figured as a personal God. The most important achievement of Jaspers's book is the attempt to treat the relation of philosophy to revelation, and of revelation to philosophy, as an exercise of communicative reason, where the reasons of both parts are listened to in equal ways. Without employing the term of 'public reason', Jaspers argues the same thesis that Habermas would later adopt: a plural understanding of democracy requires the 'reunification' between philosophy and theology. In order to achieve this aim, Jaspers calls on 'the believer in revelation ... to infer the possibility ... that what is absolute for him because it is divine revelation itself is not binding on all men.... The philosophic believer, however, would have to acknowledge the faith that is alien to him as a possible truth emerging from a different source, even if he is unable to understand it' (Jaspers 1994, 472). This requires that both standpoints employ 'the whole critical energy of reason' to see the limits of each position.[64]

The argumentative strategy that Jaspers employs in order to bring about this 'critical' and 'rational' reunification of faith and knowledge, not on the basis of the Kantian transcendental conditions of possible knowledge, but on the basis of a politico-theological priority of faith, turns on a theory of symbolic representation.[65] According to Jaspers, philosophy understands

---

[64] For an excellent treatment of Jaspers's thinking about religion, especially his engagement with German theologians like Karl Barth and Rudolf Bultmann see in general (Thornhill 2002, ch.6). Thornhill mentions but does not discuss how Jaspers offers 'a striking counterpoint to certain more conservative perspectives in Jewish political theology' (ibid., 133) because his approach to translation of revealed truth into philosophical faith is not mediated by law. But in my opinion this claim misses the neo-Platonic dimension of Jaspers's discourse on religion and revealed law, as well as the politico-theological point of the doctrine on exception and authority.

[65] Habermas's discussion of Jaspers's theory of the symbol does not acknowledge how close Jaspers's strategy with respect to faith and knowledge match with his own. For this later essay on Jaspers see (Habermas 2001b, ch. 2). Habermas's early treatment of Jaspers in his 1958 essay "Karl Jaspers: The Figures of Truth" (Habermas 1985, 44–52) avoids entirely the problem of faith and reason in Jaspers post–World War II thought. Instead, Habermas takes issue with Jaspers's distinction between philosophical reason and scientific knowledge. He reads this distinction through Jaspers's Axial Age hypothesis and takes the latter as 'a model of competing powers, each of which witnesses in its representatives to its own historical truth without allowing a knowable truth of the whole. The general questions are no longer to be decided in a rational discussion that is normative for all' (Habermas 1985, 45). In his later reflection on the Axial Age hypothesis, Habermas clearly abandons this early

revelational faith as based on the phenomenon of authority, whether this be the authority of prophets or of a church. Without belief in this authority, the Bible would become poetry. Additionally, philosophy assumes that everything revealed is but a cipher or symbol, a *possibility* of revelation, not an actual fact of revelation. These religious symbols are therefore open to criticism: authority becomes the object of critique (Jaspers 1994, 446).

This religious authority is opposed to 'an authority which we find in ourselves', in freedom and reason, given that 'there is no direct reality of God in the world' (Jaspers 1994, 446). With this distinction, Jaspers is denying that there is an internal connection between the transcendent reality of God and the principle of symbolic representation as argued by Schmitt and Voegelin. From a philosophical perspective, the God 'who manifests himself in the reality of revelation, as measured against the distant God, cannot be God himself' (Jaspers 1994, 447). In revelation, God is re-presented by an authority as being proximate: it is this *representation* of the revealed reality, not the revelation of transcendence itself, that is the object of critique from philosophy's perspective. Jaspers's advocacy of the possibility of a critical appropriation of revealed symbols comes under the biblical commandment not to worship idols as if they were the One God.

From the perspective of revelational faith, philosophical faith is not a faith in God, 'for revelational faith is personal. He confronts us as the Thou with whom, in prayer, communication is possible from person to person' (Jaspers 1994, 447). Here Jaspers adopts motifs from the 'new thinking' of Martin Buber and Franz Rosenzweig. Jaspers's point is that revelational faith responds to philosophical faith by asserting that the God of the philosopher is not the God of Abraham: 'The God of the revelational believer is concrete, proximate, he is the living God of the Bible' (Jaspers 1994, 448) and not a mere thought-entity.

Jaspers does not accept this position as an absolute truth. Rather, for him the proximate God is 'present only in ciphers' and thus, strictly speaking,

---

reading. Additionally, in this early reading Habermas thinks that Jaspers's account of authority remains much too aristocratic: these authorities are 'contemporaries of the eternal, they are eternally contemporaries for us who are mere mortal. The eternal element in the work and life permits the great man (Jaspers does not observe any great women) to become a manifestation that can speak fundamentally any time to anyone' (ibid., 48). Habermas believes that Heidegger's idea of authentic existence returns in Jaspers: 'Jaspers relates greatness expressly to the rank ordering of human existences. But this rationale is not enough. Whoever does not accept judgments about this kind of greatness finds Jaspers imputing to himself instincts that would level off human importance in favour of sorcerers, supermen, and totalitarian leaders' (ibid., 51). Habermas here ignores the democratic strategy that lies behind Jaspers's reunification of faith and philosophy.

there is no revelation of mono-theism but always of poly-theism. True monotheism can only be approximated by philosophical faith, which remains more open to the radical transcendence of the One (Jaspers 1994, 448). Ultimately, Jaspers seems to hold the following position: 'the hearing of revelation qua revelation cannot, as such, be proved.... What is forbidden is to ground it [the fact of revelation/MV] through some kind of *logos* or to turn it into a universally valid cognition' (Jaspers 1994, 459). This position leaves open the faith in the facticity of revelation but prohibits turning this fact into a knowledge of God, and thus into a theology. Jaspers is offering what one could call an a-theist conception of revelation.

Jaspers's own solution to the conflict between philosophical and revelational faith is, from the standpoint of philosophy, to assume that 'the reality of revelation itself, which is maintained by faith, becomes a cipher' (Jaspers 1994, 462). In this way, the 'fact' of revelation is itself turned into an interpretation, rather than presupposing the reality of the 'fact' of revelation, which it is then possible to interpret variously. In this sense, Jaspers adopts the Nietzschean suggestion to turn all facts into interpretations, into ciphers. According to Jaspers's suggestion, 'what is contained in the substance of revelations would become purer and truer through divesting itself of the reality of revelation' (Jaspers 1994, 467).

Jaspers's solution to the conflict between faith and reason relies on what Arendt will call the fact of human multiplicity: 'originally differing ways of conducting practical life and of the faith that goes with it are indeed mutually exclusive: they cannot be actualized in the same person. However, they do not exclude each other if they encounter each in different people in the world. Each historicity can love the other in its existential earnestness and can know to be bound to it in what is overarching' (Jaspers 1994, 474). Philosophical faith and faith in divine revelation can coexist not by reducing the multiplicity into one (mystical) Person representing humanity, but rather by disseminating radically the faith in the One (God) into the irreducible human multitude.

Derrida and the messianicity of public reason

Despite their initial distance and opposition, Habermas and Derrida came to hold much closer positions with respect to postsecularism and the need of a democratic public reason for the reunification of faith and knowledge.[66]

---

[66] See the accounts of (Bouretz 2011; and Gordon 2014), who do not, however, develop their

In 1994 and 1995, Derrida penned his famous essay *Faith and Knowledge*. In 2001, Habermas pronounced his talk "Faith and Knowledge" in which he claims that Derrida, 'a worthy winner of the Adorno Prize also in this respect', held a similar thesis to Adorno. Adorno's thesis is that reason, in order to achieve 'a desublimated earthly realization of the Kingdom of God' needed to secure 'albeit within a purely methodological intention, the help of the Messianic perspective' (Habermas 2003, 112).[67] Yet what unites and what separates Habermas's and Derrida's appeals to an internal messianicity of the public use of reason has yet to be explored in light of the discourse of democratic political theology.

Habermas and Derrida share a starting point in the Kantian approach to faith as a way to productively engage the dialectic of Enlightenment in particular as it affects the preservation of human life. For Habermas, the unrestrained pursuit of technological progress and instrumental rationality runs the risk of endangering the principle of the 'inviolability of human dignity' that stands at the core of the principles of justice considered within democratic public reason. The basis of Habermas's critique of technology consists in the emphatic distinction between 'human dignity' and the 'dignity of human life'.[68] Habermas worries that democratic common sense may be persuaded to justify the manipulation of human genetic code on the grounds that in so doing it may better preserve the 'dignity of human life', for instance, by modifying the genetic endowment of the embryo in view of preventing all kinds of genetically based diseases and malformations. For Habermas, this kind of genetic manipulation may undermine the assumptions about human nature that underlie the respect for 'human dignity', the fundamental assumption being that 'we do not level out the absolute difference that exists between the creator and the creature' (Habermas 2003, 115). Habermas wants to safeguard a minimal transcendence of humanity or human nature within the immanence of the life-process and its technological or mechanical reproduction. He believes this 'transcendence from within' is linked to the biblical conception of Creation and the human being 'made in the image' of the Creator.

---

insights in relation to the question of public reason in conditions of postsecuralism.

[67] Habermas then proceeds to cite Adorno's *Minima Moralia*: 'Knowledge has no light but that shed on the world by redemption'. The derivation of this assertion from Philo is obvious, but Habermas does not remark on it.

[68] See (Habermas 2003, 29–37).

In his attempt to counter the dialectic of Enlightenment, Habermas distinguishes and opposes one Enlightenment project, as parsed by Spinoza's principle of the self-preservation of life (*conatus*), to another Enlightenment project, as parsed by Kant's principle of self-determination, for which the absolute respect for human dignity is the basic ground of moral value. On this view, the Spinozist Enlightenment is absolutely hostile to 'religious truths', whereas, as discussed earlier, the Kantian Enlightenment operates a 'secular' and 'salvaging' translation of them (Habermas 2003, 110, 114). In "Faith and Knowledge", Habermas reiterates his belief that the best means to contrast the totalitarian outcomes of the dialectic of Enlightenment, which take the form of a reductionist scientism and a religious fundamentalism, still remain those offered by the Kantian Enlightenment insofar as it is capable of the critical translation of religious semantic content and, in so doing, strengthen 'the civilizing role of a democratically shaped and enlightened common sense that makes its way as a third party, so to speak, amid the *Kulturkampf* [culture war] confusion of competing voices' (Habermas 2003, 104). For Habermas the current culture wars take place between the 'competing voices' of modern technology and pre-modern religion. In order to dissipate the Babel-like 'confusion' he believes that these voices need to justify their claims in the liberal-democratic public sphere, whose legal-philosophical principles serve as an objective and neutral 'third party' against which to judge the merits of the conflict and thereby bring it to rest.

Derrida's approach to the problem of faith and reason is similarly focused on the internal and paradoxical relation of religion and science, of miracle and machine, within a dynamic of auto-immunization of life. In *Faith and Knowledge*, Derrida identifies the source of the dialectic of Enlightenment in an 'alliance' between Latin Christianity and techno-scientific modernity which he believes is established for the sake of achieving the final immunity, the salvation, of the self against what can be called, using Jaspers's language, limit-experiences of singularity tied with the encounter of radical otherness.[69] Although they appear to be opposed to each other, in reality religious faith and scientific reason have 'the same source' in the experience of religiosity understood as 'the experience of the unscathed, of sacredness or of holiness [*l'expérience de l'indemne, de la sacralité ou de la sainteté*]' (Derrida 1998, 32). At the same time, Derrida argues that both religion and science share a 'second source' in a primordial experience of faith that is irreducible

---

[69] (Derrida 1998, 27–29). In what follows I shall cite the essay by its section numbers.

to both, and that stands prior the opposition between theism and atheism. Derrida approaches this primordial irreligious experience of faith through two rather obscure conceptions of 'messianicity without messianism' and of matter as Platonic *khora*.[70]

Derrida's hypothesis as to how, throughout western civilization, the alliance between faith and reason sought to provide immunity or integrity for the self while unleashing auto-immunitary, self-destructive dynamics is too well known to warrant further discussion in this context.[71] For the purposes of comparison with Habermas, the central point of Derrida's hypothesis is concerned with the motif of the *universality of faith* that underpins, on one side, the faith that Christianity places on science and, on the other, the reliance of modern science and technology on 'this elementary act of faith . . . that structural performativity of the productive performance that binds from its very inception the knowledge of the scientific community to doing, and science to technics' (Derrida 1998, 37). In turn, the standpoint of the universality of faith is recovered and articulated by Derrida in two fundamentally opposed ways: one is the object of deconstruction, the latter is indeconstructible.

The first, deconstructive approach to the universality of faith is formulated by Derrida through his reading of Kant's philosophy of religion. Like Habermas, Derrida also points out that Kant, at first, clearly demarcates morality—giving to one's intention the pure form of law—from the obedient reception of divine commands expressed in divine revelations. Like Jaspers, he identifies in Kant the origin of the distinction between 'reflective faith', which is ultimately based on the universality of the *Faktum* of practical reason, and traditional 'religious faith', which is ultimately based on the belief that divine revelation happened as a matter of historical fact. To be autonomous in the Kantian sense, as Derrida says, 'one must act as though God did

---

[70] Derrida's essay has given rise to much commentary. For Derrida's 'turn' towards religion in relation to post-Kantian philosophy, see (Vries 2001). For the distinction between selfhood and singularity, see (Weber 2014). On whether Derrida's critique of religion and affirmation of singularity means that his standpoint is atheistic, see (Hägglund 2008). For contrary arguments, see (Caputo 2014). In what follows I shall engage mostly with the commentary of the text given in (Naas 2012).

[71] 'The same movement that renders indissociable religion and tele-technoscientific reason in its most critical aspect reacts inevitably to itself. It secretes its own antidote but also its own power of auto-immunity. We are here in a space where all self-protection of the unscathed, of the safe and sound, of the sacred must protect itself against its own protection, its own police, its own power of rejection, in short against its own, which is to say, against its own immunity. It is this terrifying but fatal logic of the auto-immunity of the unscathed that will always associate Science and Religion' (Derrida 1998, 37). Derrida reiterates this view in his interview (Borradori 2003).

not exist or no longer concerned himself with our salvation . . . act as though God had abandoned us' (Derrida 1998, 15).

Like Habermas, but for entirely different reasons, Derrida also argues that Kant does not uphold his own strict separation between reason and revelation. Derrida believes that for Kant there exists one *positively revealed* religion that does fulfil the conditions of a 'moral' religion, namely, Christianity. The reason is that the condition of possibility of Christian faith is precisely the experience of the abandonment, and death, of God in the species of the Passion of Christ: 'The unconditional universality of the categorical imperative is evangelical. The moral law inscribes itself at the bottom of our hearts like a memory of the Passion. When it addresses us, it either speaks the idiom of the Christian—or is silent' (Derrida 1998, 15).[72] Thus, Kant's philosophical faith is not simply opposed to the obedient faith of positive religions. Instead, the act of reflection brackets the existence of God only because it mimetically intends to awaken in each individual, irrespective of their particular confession, something like the 'memory' of the Passion of Jesus on the Cross. Derrida believes that Kant's secularization of Christianity in the form of practical reason offers one illustration as to why Christianity would place its faith in the hands of the tele-technoscientific capacity of modern Enlightenment to carry forth, and spread globally, the Christian Gospel in and as the experience of the death of God.[73]

Derrida's hypothesis of an auto-immunitary dynamic between faith and science calls into question the separation between the 'dignity of human life' and 'human dignity', the separation between the Enlightenment based

---

[72] On this point, Habermas's reading of Kant confirms Derrida's interpretation: 'Kant refused to the let the categorical "ought" be absorbed by the whirlpool of enlightened self-interest. He enlarged subjective freedom to autonomy, thus giving the first great example . . . of a secularizing, but at the same time salvaging, deconstruction of religious truths. With Kant, the authority of divine commands is unmistakably echoed in the unconditional validity of moral duties' (Habermas 2003, 110).

[73] Derrida is here reprising a Christian 'theology of the death of God' and at the same time showing how this 'death of God' functions within Christianity's 'catholicity'. On this North American version of Christian atheism, see (Altizer 2003; and M. Taylor 2007). Agata Bielik-Robson convincingly shows that Derrida attacks the 'kenotic' form of Christianity adopted since Hegel, which is based on the 'memory of the Passion', namely, of God's 'death' on the Cross, because such 'death' still leaves God 'unscathed'. Bielik-Robson instead suggests that Derrida's God is the one of Jewish mysticism, a God that retreats into His Nothingness 'in order to make room for the otherness of the other' (Bielik-Robson 2019, 7). Her reading relies on Scholem's analysis of Jewish mysticism. The productivity of the 'death of God' and 'nihilism' for Christianity is also the theme of Gianni Vattimo's approach to postsecularism. According to Vattimo's standpoint, the 'Word made flesh' corresponds to a progressive hermeneutization of truth in western 'nihilism'—a process that Vattimo celebrates. Here again there is more than one echo to Jaspers's strategy of understanding revelation as symbolic, although for Vattimo the main sources are Heidegger and Nietzsche. See (Vattimo 1999; 2002). On the relation between Christianity, death of God, and globalization see also (Nancy 2002).

on the principle of self-preservation and the Enlightenment based on the principle of self-determination, on which Habermas stakes his response to the dialectic of the Enlightenment. Derrida argues that the drive to self-preservation, and thus the 'dignity of human life' preserved by the alliance between religion and science, makes sense only insofar as one is willing to sacrifice human life for the sake of 'human dignity', which he calls the 'excess of the living': 'The price of human life . . . the price of what ought to remain safe (*heilig*, sacred, safe and sound, unscathed, immune) . . . this price is priceless. It corresponds to what Kant calls dignity of the end in itself, of the rational finite being. . . . This dignity of life can only subsist beyond the present living being. Whence transcendence, fetishism and spectrality; whence the religiosity of religion. This excess above and beyond the living, whose life has only absolute value by being worth more than life,—this, in short, is what opens the space of death that is linked to the automaton, to technics, the machine . . . this death-drive that is silently at work in every community, every co-auto-immunity, constituting it as such in its iterability, its heritage, its spectral tradition' (Derrida 1998, 40). Derrida's point is that the opposition between two Enlightenments, that of Spinoza's self-preservation and that of Kant's moral autonomy, is a dialectical opposition.

The Spinozist principle of self-preservation is ultimately maintained through the auto-immune destruction of what nominally carries forth this principle. Therefore the fundamentalist attack, on the part of religion and in the name of the 'sanctity of life', against its own alliance with technoscience (which is an alliance that preserves religion in and through secularization, modernization, and globalization) is not, as might seem at first, a 'rejection' of the principles of modern Enlightenment, of the forces that embody 'human dignity' and the respect for autonomy. On the contrary, by sacrificing the alliance with these principles, and with the forces of modernization, religion is attempting to preserve 'human dignity' itself. In this sense, one can say that through its auto-immune reaction, religious fundamentalism is acting in the name of the principle of self-preservation (i.e., preservation of selfhood as human dignity) because 'human dignity', the absolute dignity of selfhood, is only recognized by a willingness to commit an (auto-immune) sacrifice of its 'mere' life (i.e., to sacrifice whatever defence-system maintains selfhood 'merely' alive).[74]

---

[74] In this reading of Latin Christianity in Modernity, Derrida seems to appropriate Schmitt's interpretation of Roman Catholicism as a *complexio oppositorum*. Schmitt claims that the survival of the Catholic Church occurs in and through the appropriation of what opposes it. But whereas for

Derrida's auto-immunitary hypothesis shows the self-defeating nature of all attempts to set up a distinction between a 'civilized' West and a 'barbarian' rest of the world. According to his argument, the very possibility of maintaining an absolute respect of human dignity even against the defenders of the 'dignity of human life', the very belief that moral self-determination stands higher than self-preservation, is pragmatically realized in the religious and fundamentalist attacks on the 'civilization of human rights' that helps, by way of its secular translation, to maintain Latin Christendom in life. Enlightenment and counter-Enlightenment here become indistinguishable: by sacrificing its liberal self-defence system in a fundamentalist attack on it, western religiosity reveals the deepest level at which it coincides with the most Enlightened liberalism, namely, the level attained by sacrificing the principle of self-preservation for the sake of preserving the absolute dignity of selfhood, and with that of human autonomy.

At this point one can consider Derrida's second, indeconstructible approach to the universality of faith, where this bare faith is associated to 'fidelity, the appeal to blind confidence, the testimonial that is always beyond proof, demonstrative reason, intuition', rather than to the experience of the unscathed and the holy (Derrida 1998, 32). Prior to the alliance of religion and reason that protects the selfhood of the self, this other sense of bare faith is defined by '*la halte du scrupule (religio)*' before the otherness of the other (Derrida 1998, 34).[75] If there exists a chance of escaping the auto-immune consequences that follow all attempts to immunize the selfhood of the self, then this chance lies with maintaining the *différance* between selfhood (ipseity) and singularity, with valorizing the non-coincidence between 'religion', that is, the experience of salvation, and bare irreligious 'faith', that is, the relation to the other as any other, to the other in general.[76]

The formula for Derrida's second approach to faith is given as 'n + One' (Derrida 1998, 50–52). 'The more than One is this n + One which introduces the order of faith or of trust in the address of the other, but also the mechanical, machine-like division' because 'there are, for the best and for the worst,

---

Schmitt the Christian *complexio oppositorum* is the representation of the overcoming of death in life, the representation of eternal life, for Derrida, the *complexio oppositorum* of Christianity and Enlightenment is the purest expression of a death-drive.

[75] 'Let us remember the hypothesis of the two sources: on the one hand, the fiduciary-ity of confidence, trustworthiness or of trust . . . and on the other, the unscathed-ness of the unscathed (the safe and sound, the immune, the holy, the sacred, *heilig*)' (Derrida 1998, 47).
[76] On the distinction between ipseity and singularity, see (Derrida 2003, 30ff, 196ff).

division and iterability of the source' (Derrida 1998, 50). Interpreters have not acknowledged that Derrida's formula for an indeconstructible faith is actually derived from Philo's neo-Platonic interpretation of divine revelation. The 'One' refers to the Mystery of the living God, which remains shrouded in its withdrawn invisibility. The '+' refers to the 'Stream' of the divine Light or *Logos* that issues forth from the One. And the 'n' refers to the *many* revealed or positive religions that are 'mechanically, automatically' generated as a function of the human reception or interpretation of the Stream of Light.[77] The effect of auto-immunity that Derrida uncovers refers to the temptation for human religion and human reason to claim that 'n = One', namely, to claim that any one revealed religion is *the only true* religion and to adopt an alliance with human reason and technoscience to make good on this belief. This is what Jaspers calls the 'catholicity' of faith to which he opposed the 'philosophical' approach to the primacy of faith in the Mystery.

For Derrida, philosophical faith takes the form of public reason: it means being open to the incalculable effects of the formula of indeconstructible faith 'n + One', that is, to the effects of the irreligious, materialist, and cosmic 'machine' that generates those conceptions of sacred, unscathed life that are called religions.[78] Derrida's formula is Judeo-Hellenistic because it denotes a Greek, philosophical, and a fortiori even 'polytheistic' approach to monotheisms as the result of what Derrida calls the 'division and iterability' (n+) 'of the source' (One). It is to be contrasted with the catholicity of faith, whose ultimate formula is Trinitarian: monotheism as polytheism, rather than the polytheism of monotheisms.

Michael Naas is the commentator who has pursued most clearly this second strategy to conceive of the universality of faith in Derrida's text, but he fails to contextualize Derrida's conceptions of messianicity and *khora* both in the Judeo-Hellenistic context of Philo as much as in the context of democratic public reason. Derrida's indeconstructible idea of 'faith' as fidelity remains 'philosophical' because it is tied to an experience of universality, whereas 'religion' depends on an idea of faith that is 'catholic' according to Jaspers's categories. As Naas shows, Derrida's analyses of his second conception of bare faith rely and engage with Heidegger's own distinction between

---

[77] For this interpretation of Philo see (Goodenough 1969).
[78] The basis of this claim is the following text: 'No to-come without some sort of messianic memory and promise, of a messianicity older than all religion. . . . No promise . . . without the promise of a confirmation of the yes. This yes will have implied and will always therefore imply the trustworthiness and fidelity of a faith. No faith, therefore, nor future without everything technical, automatic, machine-like supposed by iterability' (Derrida 1998, 38).

revelation and revealability, *Offenbarung* and *Offenbarkeit*. Habermas has often contested the proximity of Derrida's 'deconstruction' to Heidegger's *Destruktion* of metaphysics because for Habermas the post-metaphysical turn in Heidegger is motivated by a rejection of biblical monotheism and an adoption of pagan polytheism. But, independent of what might be Heidegger's own 'religious' standpoint, the question of the relation between revelation and reason, monotheism and polytheism, is an extremely complex one within the Judeo-Hellenistic context of Philo, to which both Habermas and Derrida refer in the last instance. For Heidegger's notion of *aletheia* as revealability also refers back to the Mystery of the *Logos* in the Philonic context. Derrida links bare faith, as common source to religion and reason, to the idea that 'light takes place' and he *opposes* this locution to the biblical version: 'Let there be light' (Derrida 1998, 8). Derrida's expression is much closer to Philo's interpretation of the Mystery of Creation than to the orthodox readings of the book of Genesis. This fact alone should give pause to Habermas's belief that Derrida manages to loosen himself from Heidegger *thanks* to referring his conception of 'messianicity without messianism' back to the (orthodox) biblical formulation of monotheism.

The crucial point is that Heidegger's dualism between *Offenbarung* and *Offenbarkeit* itself relies on the priority of the image of *Logos* as Light, which is common to both biblical religion and revelation and to the Greek and Modern Enlightenment. What commentators have failed to signal is that underlying this image of Light is a political theology of Mystery, Oneness, whose Stream of Light is simultaneously rational *and* messianic. Derrida's conception of bare faith is tributary to this tradition of Jewish political theology. For this reason, Derrida acknowledges that he can neither simply accept nor simply reject the Heideggerian distinction between revelation and revealability. In a text cited by Naas, Derrida says that he cannot decide between two possibilities: either the Heideggerian model according to which 'the general structure of messianicity' offers a 'groundless ground' for the existence of positive divine revelations; or the model of Jewish philosophy (exemplified by Cohen and Rosenzweig) according to which 'the events of revelation, the biblical traditions, the Jewish, Christian, and Islamic traditions, have been absolute events... which have unveiled this messianicity'.[79]

Naas's commentary does not contextualize Derrida's discussion of messianicity and *khora* in relation to Habermas's theme of the messianicity

---

[79] Derrida cited in (Naas 2012, 171). See also the discussion of 'atheistic khora' in (Kearney 2014).

of reason, which had been earlier developed by Bloch. Yet the latter context is evident from Derrida's words: 'an invincible desire for justice is linked to this expectation [i.e., to promise].... This abstract messianicity belongs from the very beginning to the experience of faith, of believing, of a credit that is irreducible to knowledge and of a trust that "founds" all relation to the other in testimony. *This justice ... alone allows hope beyond all 'messianisms' of a universalizable culture of singularities, a culture in which the abstract possibility of the impossible translation could nevertheless be announced.* This justice inscribes itself in advance in the promise, in the act of faith or in the appeal to faith that inhabits every act of language and every address to the other. The universalizable culture of this faith ... also permits a "rational" and universal discourse on the subject of "religion"' (Derrida 1998, 22, emphasis mine). Derrida's passage is very close to Habermas's proposal on several fronts. It takes up both Blochian and Jasperian motifs common to both. With respect to Jaspers, it is evident that for Derrida all communicative praxis relies on an extension of faith as trust in the other that is tied up with the promise to tell the truth, that the communication will be truthful, in any of Jaspers's three senses of truth. On the other hand, what Derrida calls a 'universal culture of singularities' is nothing other than what Bloch and Habermas call the Kingdom. Hope in the realization on earth of this Kingdom lies at the basis of what Derrida calls a '"rational" and universal discourse on the subject of "religion"'—that is, a post-Kantian aspiration—which is itself based on 'the abstract possibility of the impossible translation' of faith into reason and vice versa.

In his discussion of Platonic *khora*, Derrida's discussion of bare faith also takes up the Blochian motif of the 'life-force' that propels the a-theistic core of all faith. Although neither Naas nor Hägglund mentions this, the doctrine of *khora* is an essential component of the Greek philosophical doctrine of the Mystery of God as *to on*, the singular Being. For this doctrine teaches that the Stream of Light that comes from the hidden One must make contact with a material that is uncreated and entirely impassive in order for the intelligible world to be formed. This intelligible world is in turn the condition for the Creation of the visible world(s) that comes about as a copy or icon or repetition of the intelligible world. In mythical parlance, the doctrine of *khora* corresponds to the cult of Demeter and Dionysus. The internal connection between faith and 'atheism' thus refers to the material, uncreated matrix of messianicity.

Like Habermas, who attempted to connect a mystical conception of divine self-contraction with the origin of Marxist materialism, and the latter with a democratic conception of humanity as *alter deus*, so too Derrida attempts to connect his atheistic conception of *khora* to a conception of public reason and democracy. Derrida, very abstractly, refers to this context by claiming that the metaphor of light is internally connected to a 'public space' rooted in *khora* (Derrida 1998, 11). 'The chance of this desert [*khora*] in the desert [of revelation] . . . in uprooting the tradition [of revelation] that bears it, in atheologizing it, this abstraction [*khora*] without denying faith, liberates a universal rationality and the political democracy that cannot be disassociated from it' (Derrida 1998, 22). The point of this text is that *khora* a-theologizes messianic faith and the tradition of revelation—much as Bloch's motif of atheism in Christianity—in order to make possible a democratic public reason. Here Derrida sketches, in a way that he will never be able to further demonstrate, the claim that the biblical tradition of divine revelation contains within it a previous, pagan, and philosophical trace, that orients political theology in a democratic and reasonable direction. As I show in *Living Law*, this insight found in late Derrida has been there all along the development of Jewish political theology since Cohen and Rosenzweig.

Furthermore, Derrida's passage also contains an unconscious reference to Bloch's claim that messianic hope cannot be thought independently of the idea of *natura naturans*, of a connection between a Platonically inflected materialism with messianic hope. As it will be remembered, in Bloch the key concept was that of a 'life force' that originates with the a-theological messianic. This idea of a deep connection between God and a form of 'eternal' life is not only mentioned but affirmed by Derrida: 'Judaism and Islam would thus be perhaps the last two monotheisms to revolt against everything that, in the Christianizing of our world, signifies the death of God, the death in God, two non-pagan monotheisms that do not accept death anymore than multiplicity in God (the Passion, the Trinity, etc.) . . . by recalling at all costs that "monotheism" signifies no less faith in the One, and in the living One, than belief in a single God' (Derrida 1998, 15).

On Naas's reading, the reliance of religion with technoscience means that 'a necessary and unavoidable contamination of life by means of a technoscientific supplement that comes to inscribe repetition, duplicity, and death into the heart of life or the living present' (Naas 2009, 196). The 'machinal' aspect of life's autoimmunity, or in-built drive towards death, opens up the question of what Derrida's 'atheism' means. For Hägglund, the internal relation between life and repetition means that our lives are closed to God as source of 'immortality'. For him, human and finite life survives only in and through the ineluctable horizon of impending death. Conversely, the belief that God is immortal actually means 'death' for finite life. As Martin Hägglund says in *Radical Atheism*: 'the logic of auto-immunity is radically atheist' to the extent that 'theism' is linked with an idea of an immortal God.

But Derrida's reference to the 'living One' casts doubt on Hägglund's connection of divine immortality with 'death'. For in this text Derrida turns away from both Latin Christianity and modern Enlightenment in their auto-immunitary attempt to 'save' life and its 'dignity' by incorporating death within God in the form of the Passion. Rather, Derrida explicitly moves towards a certain Islam and a certain Judaism which are characterized precisely by *their rejection of 'death' in God* and which are furthermore joined by a common reception of a certain Platonism, the doctrine of the Mystery, and by a shared resistance to the dynamics of 'mondialatinization', to the alliance between Christianity and Enlightenment:

Derrida explicitly adopts the definition of the Judeo-Greek Mystery of Philo as subversive underpinning to all revealed religion of monotheism: bare faith in the One, and the One as (eternally) living. In contradistinction to Latin Christianity, Derrida says that certain traditions within Judaism and Islam share an adherence to the bare 'faith in the One'. This bare faith lies at the basis of their elective affinity with Pythagoreanism and Platonism, that is, with the basic texts of henology in western culture. From these non-Christian religious and philosophical traditions Derrida draws out the experiences of Oneness shared by Platonic henology and the mystical and rationalistic variants of Jewish and Islamic monotheisms. Their shared 'faith in the One' harbors the experience of a groundless bare faith as a 'link to the other in general. . . . It would link pure singularities prior to any social or political determination, prior to all intersubjectivity, prior even to the opposition between the sacred (or the holy) and the profane' (Derrida 1998, 20). Platonism, Judaism, and Islam multiply the faith in the One and in so doing express the generalized non-coincidence of singularity. These articulations of bare faith are indeconstructible and they harbor the experience of an openness to the other, an 'unconditional hospitality' (Derrida 2003, 204–5), a community of pure singularities, which is systematically unheeded by the alliance between Latin Christianity and modern Enlightenment, and that divides at the source the integrity of western civilization.

In *Rogues: Two Essays on Reason*, Derrida elaborates the idea of a 'democracy to-come' by emphasizing that its peculiar formlessness, as well as its conceptual indeterminacy, should be understood beginning from the Platonic understanding of democracy. Moreover, he remarks that for the medieval philosophers of enlightened Judaism and Islam it is Plato, rather than Aristotle, who offers the essential resources to think about ethics and politics. Indeed, the development of Jewish political theology in the 20th century shows that the non-reception of Aristotle's *Politics* makes all the difference between medieval Jewish and Islamic political philosophy and Latin Scholasticism, the latter serving as a transmission belt from Latin Christianity to the modern Enlightenment ideals of democracy and rights.[80] The radical difference between (divine) justice and (human) law, and the connection established between an irreligious faith which, in being irreducible to religion, is thereby also universally shareable and thus 'alone permits a "rational" and universal discourse on the subject of "religion"' (Derrida 1998, 22), are the two motifs that stand in tension with the foundations of democratic legitimacy worked out in Christian political theology. They reveal Derrida as a theorist of postsecular democracy who is turned around to the beginnings of Jewish political theology in the 20th century.

---

[80] On Plato and democracy, see (Derrida 2003, 43ff); on Islam and democracy, see (Derrida 2003, 51–66).

Conclusion

"Only a god can resist god": Gnosticism and Political Theology

The Gnostic obsession of Christian political theology

An obsession with Gnosticism characterizes all the central authors treated this far. Some of them identify in Gnosticism a threat to the democratic vocation of Christian political theology; others see it as essential in order to articulate its radical democratic potential. That Gnosticism should occupy such a central role in the discourse of Christian political theology is not surprising. Christianity is based on the mystery of the Incarnation of God as a human being in the person of Jesus Christ, the Son of God. The core Gnostic belief is that the Son of God is best understood as the Son of Man, whose mission on earth is to emancipate humanity from the tyranny of God the Father and Creator of nature.[1] Whereas Voegelin and Maritain were repelled by the Gnostic promise that humanity could save itself through its own resources, Kantorowicz and Habermas are fascinated with the motif of humanity as a Promethean 'alien god' (*alter deus*) who leads a revolutionary struggle against the God of orthodoxy who vouches for Throne and Altar. While the former thinkers believe that human self-assertion against God and Nature leads to a disastrous dialectic of Enlightenment, the latter cannot conceive of freedom otherwise than as a function of this self-assertion.

Gnosticism is a convenient way for the discourse of Christian political theology to focus its polemical energies. It allows this discourse to portray the project of Modernity in terms of establishing an immanent framework for human salvation that, in attempting to sideline religion from the public sphere, accounts for the slide from liberal democracy to totalitarianism. Additionally, Gnosticism is seen to underlie all those mass ideologies that foster the belief that government and law are necessarily in the hands of the

---

[1] On Gnosticism and its significance for modern political philosophy, see (Jonas 1958).

rich and powerful, and that as a consequence the salvation of the powerless can only come through the destruction of authoritative institutions. Lastly, for Christian political theology Gnosticism figures the rebelliousness of young against old, children against parents in modern societies, their tendency to identify freedom with disorder, and thus justifies in some political theologians the appeal to dictatorship as a means to save liberal democratic society from its own anarchic disposition.

In *Political Theology II*, Schmitt criticized the Modern project of self-assertion defended by Blumenberg in *The Legitimacy of the Modern Age* on the grounds that human self-assertion against God and created nature still suffered from the Gnostic syndrome, except that in Modernity, it is humanity itself that takes the place of the alien Redeemer. In formulating this critique, Schmitt made a gnomic reference to Goethe's 'famous Latin motto', *nemo contra deum nisi deus ipse* [against a god, only a god].[2] In this motto, Schmitt identified one of the roots of that 'atheistic' reading of Christianity that Bloch and Habermas have brought to prominence, according to which the mysterious figure of the 'Son of Man' in the Gospels refers to the belief that Jesus would eventually be elevated to His Throne and His Kingship established on earth only in and through the elevation of the 'dignity' of Man. In this way, Jesus' Kingdom on earth would be established through democratic forms of government that realize the Rights of Man and Citizen by overthrowing the old privileges of emperors, monarchs, and priests. More than others, Taubes has popularized the idea that Saint Paul's messianism is an 'immanentized' form of Gnosticism that employs its rejection of worldly power towards revolutionary aims.[3] The Christian Gospel, in its Pauline interpretation, leaves itself open to be developed in a Gnostic direction either by interpreting it as a call for the radical renunciation of the world and its government—a species of nihilism—or as a call for humanity (rather than divinity) to redeem itself by getting rid of all institutional religions—a species of anarcho-communism. Both options can figure the desired reconciliation with the true Father, the 'alien' God who is not of this world at all. Taubes's 'Gnostic' (but also 'Schmittian') interpretation of Saint Paul has

---

[2] According to Schmitt, the 'source' of Goethe's motto is to be located in the fragments of a *Sturm und Drang* play by Jakob Michael Lenz, "Catherine of Siena", in which Catherine, running away from her father, exclaims: 'My father looked at me threateningly, like a loving, aggrieved god. But if he had reached out both of his hands—God against god! . . . Save me, rescue me, my Jesus, whom I follow, from his arms!', cited in (Blumenberg 2007, 47). All translations from German are mine.

[3] Taubes proposes this Benjaminian approach to Paul's messianism in (Taubes 2003; 2013).

had considerable influence within the post-Marxist reception of the discourse of political theology.[4]

As a theological doctrine that identifies the monotheistic God as Father and as Creator of the world with a malevolent deity, Gnosticism seems to strengthen the argument according to which the government of the world ought to be in the hands of the Son, of Jesus Christ. Yet the institution that stands and falls on the claim of the government by Sonship, that is, the Christian Church, considered that Gnosticism posed a grave threat to its soteriological mission as the institution that represents in history the *promise* (not the reality) of its End.[5] The reason, as Peterson explains, is that the Gnostic Hidden God, radically transcendent from the world, relinquishes the government of the world to intermediary, 'demiurgic forces' or 'demonic' individuals who have all the power without any of the authority to exercise it (Peterson 2011, 71ff). Goethe penned his motto precisely to describe these charismatic leaders: '[demonic individuals] radiate an enormous strength and exercise incredible power over all creatures, even over the elements, and who can say just how far such influence does extend? All the moral powers in unison can do nothing against them.... They cannot be conquered by anything less than the universe itself, which they have defied. And from such observations may well have arisen that strange but prodigious saying: *Nemo contra deum nisi deus ipse*'.[6]

Peterson believed that the doctrine of the Trinity established a model for the relation between Father and Son that put an end to the Gnostic threat, at the same time limiting the power of worldly rulers in accordance to the authority of the Church, and orienting the universal message of the Son towards the ideal of brotherly love rather than revolutionary class struggle. Schmitt was sceptical that the Trinitarian doctrine could counter Gnosticism because he thought this doctrine harboured the Gnostic teaching of a 'civil war' (*stasis*) between a God of Love, the saviour-God who is not of this world, and the Creator God who lords it over an evil world. What makes the Gnostic dualism a permanent threat or challenge, for Schmitt, is precisely the fact that an all-powerful and all-knowing Creator-God cannot also be a Redeemer-God. 'The Lord of a world that needs to be changed because it is

---

[4] See the discussion of this Paulinian-Benjaminian construal of anarchy found in (Martel 2012).
[5] See the classic presentation in (Harnack 2007). For an extended argument that relates political theology to Gnosticism, see now (Lettieri 2014). I thank Prof. Gaetano Lettieri for sharing with me his unpublished conference paper.
[6] The motto is found in Part IV, chapter 20 of Goethe's autobiographical *Poetry and Truth* (Goethe 1998, 177), English translation given in (Nicholls 2015, 205).

corrupt... and the one who emancipates from this world, the one who brings about a new, changed world cannot be good friends. They are, so to speak, automatically enemies' (Blumenberg 2007, 45). In this sense, Trinitarianism is not an original political theory—it is more like a compensatory device for an inability to deal with the Gnostic challenge to worldly power and politics. Schmitt believed that the task of the Christian Church and its imperial *katechon*, the mysterious figure that restrains the advent of the Antichrist, but, perhaps, also of the 'Son of Man', was to maintain a difficult balance between holding on to the belief that the Kingdom and the Glory belongs to Jesus the Christ, and simultaneously avoid fuelling the Gnostic resentment and hatred against earthly monarchs and governments.[7] Hence Taubes's apt characterization of Schmitt as an 'Apocalypticist of the Counterrevolution'.[8]

For Blumenberg, Goethe's motto was never intended as a subversive commentary on the Trinity. Instead, it reflects Goethe's sustained adoption of pantheistic (Spinozist) and polytheistic (pagan) motifs.[9] Blumenberg argues that Goethe's formula offers a response to the Gnostic challenge by articulating a cosmological idea of the balance of powers that rejects both the idea of an absolute power as much as an other-worldly escape from power. 'Only the entire universe can prevail against a demonic-divine nature, which is able to overpower every individual power within this universe. The universe is the absolute which cannot be shaken, in its power, by what occurs within it' (Blumenberg 1988, 525). Blumenberg's Spinozist reading of Goethe is intended to counter Schmitt's critique of Modern self-assertion. In this conclusion I wish to interpret it also as a response to Agamben's understanding of the struggle between the Church and its inner Gnostic spirit. For Agamben, the rebellion of the Son against the Father, His attempt to garner the acclamation of a free humanity in order to conquer the Father's Throne, does not express the 'hatred of power' of the masses and does not bring about permanent disorder and revolution. To the contrary, Agamben understands the Gnostic *stasis* as functional to the establishment of a global form of liberal governance that works in and through the 'anarchy' and 'disruption' brought

---

[7] For an interpretation of the *katechon* as a function of the instability of the Augustinian solution to the problem of political monotheism, see (Esposito 2015b; and Cacciari 2017), who nicely emphasizes the blurred line that separates the Antichrist from the Son of Man.

[8] See (Taubes 2013) and the brilliant reading of the Taubes-Schmitt relation given by (Rosenstock 2014).

[9] In their correspondence about Goethe's motto, Blumenberg writes to Schmitt: 'You have made a wonderful discovery about this motto that allowed you to give a Christological interpretation of it. My interpretation is polytheistic and brings the motto in connection with the Prometheus-syndrome' (Blumenberg to Schmitt, August 7, 1975) cited in (Blumenberg 2007, 132).

about by normative 'spontaneous orders' like the free market (Agamben 2007a, 126–48). The real teaching of Trinitarianism is that Jesus Christ governs the world not only in the absence of the Father's sovereignty, but thanks to the deployment of Gnostic, revolutionary, and anarchic energies. In what follows I explain why the discussion over Goethe's motto, Gnosticism, and the stasiology of Christianity that Schmitt and Blumenberg engage in at the end of the short 20th century sheds light not only on the problem, indicated by Agamben, of liberal government in the absence of sovereignty, but also on the postsecular 'polytheism' that must characterize a rational democratic public reason, as pointed out by Habermas and Derrida.

Christian political theology, Hitler, and *parrhesia*

In his discussion of Goethe's motto, Schmitt claims that it 'was cited and interpreted by Goethe-knowers [*Goethe-Kennern*] in innumerable secret [*nichtöffentlichen*] conversations' during the Nazi regime.[10] This remark presumably implies that Goethe's motto had become a shibboleth of the so-called internal resistance to Hitler's rule. That the German poet could be cited in this context has to do with an implicit comparison between the 'charismatic' leadership of the *Führer* and those 'demonic' individuals discussed by Goethe. When Schmitt references Goethe's motto in the 1960s, one can sense a self-exculpatory argument: even if some German Christians had wanted to resist Hitler, only the intervention of God Himself could have stopped his 'demonic' character.[11] But lying beneath this layer of meaning, there appears another more obscure and unsettling one, namely that Hitlerism was itself a manifestation of the conflict between the Persons of the Trinity, the Father worshipped by Jews and the Son whom Christians acclaim as their King, thematized by Gnosticism.

To fathom the limits of Christian democratic political theology, one could do worse than reflect on a question posed many times before, and that John Rawls saw fit to thematize in a footnote to *The Law of Peoples*, his treatise on the 'realistic utopia' of human rights and human dignity. The question is,

---

[10] Schmitt, cited in (Blumenberg 2007, 46). Hugh Barr Nisbet points out that at least one German Goethe scholar (Raabe 1942) employed Goethe's motif of a struggle against the demonic to illustrate the war effort of Nazi Germany against its enemies (Nisbet 1971, 277).
[11] On Hitler and Goethe's category of the demonic, see (Pyta 2015). (Nicholls 2015, 206) refers to the exculpatory use of the idea of the demonic made in the Nüremberg Trials by some of the accused. On the 'new demons' of totalitarianism, see now (Forti 2014).

Why did the vast majority of German Christians and their ecclesiastical representatives not stand up to Hitler?[12] Since at least the 1937 Papal encyclical *Mit brennender Sorge*, the Nazi *Führer* of the Third *Reich* was portrayed as a return of the 'pagan' cult of emperors as human divinities (*deus imperator*), and Nazism itself was conceived as an anti-Christian 'political religion'.[13] This was the belief shared by many of the authors discussed in this book. So why was this not enough to keep Christian peoples from acclaiming the new emperors? Maybe the 'democratic turn' of Christian political theology, although in principle intended to prevent the worship of human political leaders as gods, also harbours within it another, contrary dynamic that favours the continued emergence of 'new despotisms' and 'aspirational fascism'.[14]

Agamben's archaeology of modern governmentality suggests that modern democratic legitimacy still relies on the mechanisms of acclamation and glorification of the leader as Head of a mystical Body brought to light in my reconstruction of Christian political theology. Given his hypothesis, Agamben could therefore answer Rawls's question as to why so many Christians went along with Hitler by pointing out that the elevation of Jesus to His Father's Throne through the prayers and acclamations of His people, namely, the key principle of Christian democratic political theology, is a model of the populist acclamation of a leader who incarnates the substantive identity of a people. More insidiously, Agamben also suggests that this principle underlies 'the neutralized state that resolves itself in the communicative forms without subject': liberal and totalitarian forms of government 'are opposed only in appearance. They are but two sides of the same glorious apparatus in its two forms: the immediate and subjective glory of the acclaiming people and the mediatic and objective glory of social communication' (Agamben 2011, 258). Agamben's hypothesis suggests that the liberal exercise of public reason is prey to the logic of democratic political theology based on glorification.

If this is so, then public reason would find itself powerless, as it apparently already is, when confronted with new technologies of manipulation of

---

[12] Referring to 'the prominent Protestant clergyman Bishop Otto Dibelius' defence of the Nazi boycott of Jews in April 1, 1933, Rawls adds: 'It would stand to reason that in a decent society any such boycott organized by the state should be considered a blatant violation of freedom of religion and liberty of conscience. Why didn't these clergymen think so?' (Rawls 2001, 22, n. 16). Rawls points towards the tradition of 'Christian anti-Semitism' as an important factor explaining the acquiescence of the German churches to Nazism. But Rawls also repeatedly refers to Hitler's 'demonic' character (Rawls 2001, 20–21). For the debate on Christianity and Nazism, see (Hockanos 2004; and Bergen 2007).

[13] See (Stowers 2007).

[14] See (Connolly 2017; and Keane 2020).

public opinion in a 'post-truth' political environment. The 'legitimacy' that is currently afforded a new breed of 'strongmen' thanks to the new regimes of democratic political theology that exploit the acclamation and glorification generated on internet social media platforms reveals the weak side of liberal democracy based on public opinion. The current nostalgia for Schmittian-style sovereignty espoused by so many sovranists can perhaps no longer be countered by relying on Kelsen's quip that absolute sovereignty exists only if it is believed in by all. One can no longer rest assured that a liberal government based on public reason and upholding freedoms of conscience and association is enough to contain the resurgence of such a faith in sovereignty.

Blumenberg's interpretation of Goethe's motto is significant for our contemporary situation because it contains a lesson in truth-telling or parrhesia in the face of absolute power. Unlike Schmitt, Blumenberg thought that Goethe's motto gave gnomic expression to the lesson the poet had derived from his famous personal encounter with Napoleon's 'demonic being'.[15] To the 19th century, Napoleon appeared as a new pagan emperor, as the rebirth of the Hellenistic ideal of the 'ruler of the world' (Eckermann 1839, 338). In particular, Napoleon sought the foundations of his liberal governmentality in glory and glorification, and it is in this context that, upon conquering Germany, he sought out an interview with the greatest living German poet, Goethe. Their meeting took place in Erfurt at the start of October 1808.

It is the merit of Foucault's last lectures to have highlighted the role of parrhesia in Plato's rethinking of the relation between philosophy and tyranny. Foucault's reading of the philosopher's speaking truth to power offers a new way to approach the division between sovereignty and governmentality that characterizes Hellenistic kingship, overdetermines Christian political theology, and is exploited by Gnosticism in a revolutionary and anarchic direction. In order to appreciate Blumenberg's reconstruction of the relation between Goethe (the Spinozist philosopher) and Napoleon (the

---

[15] (Blumenberg 2006, 519). 'I dined with Goethe and the conversation turning on Demonology, he said: "The Demoniacal is that which cannot be explained by Reason or Understanding; it lies not in my nature, but I am subject to it." "Napoleon", said I, "seems to have been of a demoniacal sort". "He was so", said Goethe, "so thoroughly, and in so high a degree, that scarce any one is to be compared with him."' (Eckermann 1839, 378). Goethe's expression of the "demonic" [*das Dämonische*] stands for that capacity or energy of certain human beings to do great, perhaps inhuman or superhuman things. Goethe seems to connect the demonic to a violence that rules over the natural elements, and he associates it both to the figure of Jesus (who accomplished miracles) and to that of Napoleon (an anti-natural 'force of nature') (Blumenberg 2006, 522). Walter Benjamin, not mentioned by Blumenberg in this context, was equally interested in Goethe's theory of the demonic. Alison Ross has discussed the strange absence/presence of Benjamin's reading of Goethe and myth in Blumenberg's discussion of Goethe's motto, in (Ross 2015).

French Emperor) and its significance for the theme of political theology and Gnosticism, it is helpful to briefly review Foucault's findings.

For Foucault, philosophical parrhesia is not simply synonymous with *isegoria*, based on the equal right of citizens to speak in public. Foucault's hypothesis is that Platonic parrhesia accounts for the transition from Athenian democratic politics to a novel conception of legitimate government based on a kind of philosophical veridiction that is adopted by Hellenistic ideals of kingship and then transmitted in the tradition of Christian political theology. Once the philosopher enters into the democratic scene as parrhesiast, 'as the person who, in a particular political conjuncture, tells the truth on the political stage in order to guide either the city's policy of the soul of the person who directs the city's policy' (Foucault 2010, 195), democracy is criticized as hopelessly corrupt and badly governed, and the activity of truth-telling is transferred on to the scene of the Prince or tyrant. The problem becomes: 'How is one to address the Prince; how is one to tell him the truth? How, on what basis, and through what training should one act on his soul?' (Foucault 2010, 189). For Foucault, the problem of parrhesia leads to the Platonic motif of the advisor of the Prince, which in turn is essential to 'the genealogy of the art of governing' (Foucault 2010, 197).

The question of the legitimacy of government depends on philosophical veridiction: it is not a question that needs to be raised in democracy, because it makes sense only in the context of princely or monarchic government. Herein lies the deep reason why princes, kings, and emperors tend to surround themselves with philosophers (who are also theologians), at least since Aristotle became the tutor of Alexander the Great. Thus, it is not insignificant for the analysis proposed below, to note that Napoleon set out in his expedition to the Middle East in order to bring back for his empire the entire wisdom of the Orient. The same need for legitimacy that brings kings and emperors to surround themselves with philosophers and poets compels Napoleon to ask for a meeting with Goethe, whose *Sorrows of the Young Werther* accompanied him in his military campaigns.[16]

Conversely, the role of the parrhesiast reveals the increased political importance of philosophy: 'truth-telling in the field of politics can well and truly

---

[16] A point that was not lost on Goethe: ' "See what book Napoleon carried in his field library—my "Werther"! . . . "He had studied it as the judge does his Acts", said Goethe, "and talked with me conformably about it" . . . What is worth noticing in this list [of the books Napoleon took to Egypt] is the manner in which the works are classed, under different rubrics. Under the head *Politique* we find mentioned the Old Testament, the New Testament, the Koran; from which we may judge what Napoleon's view was on religious matters' (Eckermann 1839, 299).

only be philosophical truth-telling. Philosophical truth-telling and political truth-telling must be the same' (Foucault 2010, 217). This helps to explain why philosophers, theologians, and poets are just as attracted to princes and tyrants as the latter are attracted to the former. This element is particularly important in shedding light on why Goethe remained fixated on Napoleon's fate throughout his life, as discussed below. Foucault argues that giving political advice to the tyrant is the only way in which Platonic philosophy can put its reason or *logos* into practice: political advice is the proper 'work' (*ergon*) of the philosopher's art. In this context, Foucault does not mention that this political reading of Plato lies at the source of the Renaissance idea of the state as a 'work of art', as a theoretical and poetical construction. As Kantorowicz showed, throughout the late Middle Ages and then in the Renaissance there emerged the idea of a close connection between the 'sovereignty of the artist' and the 'sovereignty of the state'.[17] Evidently, Goethe's parrhesiastic relationship with Napoleon was, consciously or unconsciously, modelled on this Platonic legacy that sees 'great politics' as a 'work of art', and thus associates the philosopher-poet with the figure of a sui generis legislator. Indeed, in the last instance, philosophical practice and practice of government are 'identical': 'the Prince's soul must be able to govern itself truly according to true philosophy for the Prince to be able to govern others according to a just politics' (Foucault 2010, 295). Foucault omits to mention that such an imperial ideal of the philosopher-king was already prefigured in the Hellenistic idea of monarchy, the root of the discourse of political theology. This last point turns out to be crucial to understand the necessity for Napoleon's confrontation with a philosopher-poet like Goethe: the prince had to measure how far he had been able 'to govern himself according to true philosophy' in order to truly establish his imperial rule over others. The peculiar signature of this Hellenistic idea of monarchy was the idea of the philosopher as a *living law*, as *nomos empsychos*.[18] According to this Hellenistic paradigm, written laws are contraposed to the *living law* that the philosopher's life has become.[19] If one recalls that Napoleon's self-crowning as emperor was preceded by his creation of a new law code (the Civil Code), and that 'from July 1801 he presided over discussions of his Code, often line by line' in order that its meaning would reflect his sovereign will rather than the 'science' of the

---

[17] See (Kantorowicz 1961), who develops intuitions drawn from Burckhardt.
[18] See (Goodenough 1928).
[19] Compare with the recent interpretation of Foucault's 'care of self' found in (Lefebvre 2018).

jurisprudents,[20] then one can appreciate the parrhesiastic context of Goethe's encounter with Napoleon.

Polytheism, the division of powers, and republican civil religion

In *Work on Myth*, Blumenberg approaches the interpretation of Goethe's motto 'only a god can stand against a god' by contextualizing it within his youthful self-identification with the myth of Prometheus' contest with Zeus, the sovereign god.[21] In his autobiography *Dichtung und Wahrheit*, Goethe claimed that his youthful ode to *Prometheus* set off the explosive conflict within the German Enlightenment known as the 'Pantheism controversy' (*Pantheismusstreit*). This was the poem that Jacobi handed to Lessing on his fateful visit asking for a comment about its (Goethe's) Spinozism, and, perhaps, also asking for help in dealing with this Spinozism.[22] To Jacobi's shock, Lessing is supposed to have replied that he shared Goethe's Spinozism: 'there is no philosophy but the philosophy of Spinoza' (Blumenberg 2006, 447–49). For Blumenberg, these (reported) words of Lessing also reflect Goethe's deepest belief.[23]

The details of Goethe's encounter with Napoleon were shrouded in mystery and secrecy from the very start, as if to highlight that the issue at stake in this encounter belonged to the highest 'mysteries of state' (Blumenberg 2006, 510ff).[24] It is known that they exchanged views on the situation of contemporary drama. On this occasion, Napoleon rejected classical French drama based on 'destiny' and formulated his famous politico-philosophical maxim according to which, for the moderns, 'politics is destiny'.[25] As Blumenberg

---

[20] (Kelley 2002, 293, 296).

[21] 'Die Fabel des Prometheus wird in mir lebendig' [the story of Prometheus comes to life in me] (Goethe 1998, 48).

[22] '[T]hat poem became so significant in German literature because it allowed Lessing to declare some important points of his thinking and feeling against Jacobi. This poem served as the spark that ignited an explosion.... The split was so violent that we lost, by a series of chance events, one of our most dignifed men, Mendelssohn' (Goethe 1998, 49). The literature on the *Pantheismusstreit* is immense. For recent work on the philosophical and religious context within which Blumenberg's approach to this critical episode in German philosophy should be situated, see (Rosenstock 2009; and Lazier 2008).

[23] Blumenberg cites an entry from Goethe's diary from October 10, 1786: 'Herder always made fun of me, saying that I had learned all my Latin from Spinoza, since he noticed that that was the only Latin book that I read' (Blumenberg 2006, 586).

[24] For the most recent conjectures on the content of this conversation see (Becker 2010).

[25] (Blumenberg 2006, 511). 'We talked of the Greek idea of Destiny, as exhibited in their tragedy. "It does not suit our way of thinking", said Goethe, "it is obsolete and contradicts our views of religion.

puts it, Napoleon thought that classical Fate had been replaced by imperial Will, and, of course, whatever pleased this Will took the form of law, as Napoleon had recently shown by dictating his *Code Civil*. If Napoleon understands himself as a 'destiny', so that politics takes the place of tragedy in Modernity, for Goethe, instead, Napoleon represents the Fate of Modernity that needs to be 'tragically' confronted and overcome.[26] 'Politics as destiny— that meant originally, and for Goethe always meant (in view of Napoleon), "politics acting *like* destiny"'(Blumenberg 1988, 487).

According to Blumenberg's hypothesis, Goethe's initial self-identification with Prometheus expressed the belief that the poet had to build a new world through poetry, despite the fact that the world always already existed.[27] But after his encounter with Napoleon, Goethe realized the untenability of this identification for the poet, and transfers to Napoleon the traits of Prometheus because of Napoleon's belief that the world is there in order to be remade, not by poetry, but by politics. Goethe himself then occupies an alternative standpoint, one that finds its ultimate expression in his motto. The 'demonic' replaces Goethe's earlier belief in the 'divine' character of human beings because, for the late Goethe, all 'divinity' has been pantheistically absorbed by the universe as a whole: everything is, as such, 'divine' (Blumenberg 2006, 520). Against what is truly 'exceptional', that is, the demonic, Goethe opposes the infinity of the universe itself as captured in the Spinozist pantheist formula, *Deus sive natura*. Goethe therefore transitions from a belief in the Promethean powers of human beings to a belief in cosmic balance. 'Balance, the deeply polytheistic fundamental idea that the restricting counteraction must always be a different power. It is the mythical principle of the separation of powers. But it is also the pantheistic possibility of reconciliation, which sees everything individual and each particular power as, in its turn,

---

If a modern poet introduces those antique ideas into his dramas, he gives them an air of affectation...." "It is better for us moderns to say with Napoleon, "Political Science is Destiny"'(Eckermann 1839, 411). Although Blumenberg does not aver this, it is possible to read this long discussion of Goethe and destiny as a response to Schmitt's claim, made in the 1933 third edition of *The Concept of the Political* that 'the political unity... is "total first because every matter can potentially be political... and second because man is totally and existentially grasped in political participation. Politics is destiny."' Cited in (Meier 1995, 16). The phrase 'politics is destiny' is not found in the second, 1932 edition of *The Concept of the Political*, which is the basis of the English translation. Meier does not pick up its Napoleonic resonance and a fortiori does not comment on Blumenberg's critique of Schmitt in this context.

[26] Again, Blumenberg seems to be employing here themes drawn from Benjamin's understanding of tragedy found in his *Trauerspiel* book, but Blumenberg never cites Benjamin in this context. See Ross cited above.

[27] (Blumenberg 2006, 567).

a specification of the whole, which restricts itself in the process of realizing itself. Spinozism is not replaced by polytheism but tied to it as its manner of both aesthetic and historical self-presentation' (Blumenberg 1988, 530).

Like other emperors before and after him, Napoleon had the effect of re-awakening a long-slumbering Gnostic vein in western political thought that reacts to worldly power through a passionate *mis-archy* or hatred of power. Blumenberg is interested in articulating a convincing response to the Gnostic threat of mis-archy while providing an alternative to Schmitt's political theology of sovereignty. Blumenberg argues that Goethe's motto formulated the gist of the polytheistic and pantheistic insights articulated by Spinozism and the radical Enlightenment, offering a world-affirming form of resistance to the appearance of the 'demonic' in world history.[28]

Goethe's pantheism is therefore also a 'polytheism' in the sense that it contains both the divine—that is everything—*and* the demonic: the exceptional human being (Blumenberg 2006, 521). In a letter to Schmitt, Blumenberg makes explicit the first meaning of the pathos formula: 'Goethe's apothegm seizes upon the generality of the meaning of polytheism as its separation of powers, its prevention of absolute power and of any religion as a feeling of unconditional dependence on this power. Gods, when there are many of them, always already stand one against the other. A god can only in turn be limited by a god'.[29] Blumenberg's formulation gives Goethe's motto an immediate political meaning explicitly directed against the idea of absolute power and, thus, also against any religion that makes the self-preservation or individuals conditional on their dependence to such absolute power. But Goethe's belief that 'A god can only be balanced by another god. That power should restrict itself is absurd. It is only restricted, in turn, by another power',[30] connects his polytheistic ideal of balance to the *republican* political ideal of the 'division of powers'. As Arendt has shown in her celebrated reading of Montesquieu, the republican ideal assumes that power can be checked only through its pluralization, that is, power is checked only through empowerment.[31] Goethe's idea of balance fits closely with the constitutional 'checks and balance' to

---

[28] On Blumenberg and pantheism, see (Lazier 2004) and for a recent excellent discussion of this claim, see (Buch 2017).
[29] (Blumenberg 2007, 133), English translation in (Nicholls 2015, 210). The formulation in *Work on Myth* runs as follows: 'Everything that is itself a god can be against a god—something that it makes sense to speak of only if there is not only *one* god' (Blumenberg 1988, 479, modified translation).
[30] Goethe in 1807, cited in (Blumenberg 1988, 528).
[31] See (Arendt 1990), and in particular her treatment of the Federalist principle that only power can be a check to power.

government that had been recently realized in the American Revolution (and partially also by the French Revolution, at least in its first, constituent phase).[32]

Goethe seems to have interpreted his meeting with Napoleon as 'the moment in which he had withstood the eyes of the victorious conqueror' (Blumenberg 1988, 469). He had stood up to Napoleon 'eye to eye'. Blumenberg cites Heinrich Heine's impression of Goethe's stare as being that of a god, and compares it to Napoleon's stare, which is also deemed to be divine.[33] However, the striking formulation of the encounter also matches that recently employed by Philip Pettit to express the fundamental republican idea of equality, the so-called 'eyeball test' for non-domination.[34] Goethe's belief that he had, so to speak, passed the 'eyeball test' with Napoleon, the 'ruler of the world', is thus both subversive and at the same time ironical, coming from Goethe—who was no admirer of the French Revolution in its excesses—and applied to an emperor who was the creation of the French Republic itself.

Blumenberg's interpretation of Goethe's motto excludes Schmitt's Trinitarian interpretation precisely because Goethe denies that God can limit Himself, for example in the manner that the Father, though One with the Son, is nevertheless limited by the Son.[35] Goethe's perception of being the 'equal' of Napoleon is legitimated neither from a Promethean belief in his own divinity, nor in light of Gnostic-Christian reflections on the Trinity, but on the basis of a Spinozist belief in a 'general divinity': 'There stands a god [*Da ist ein Gott*], and whoever means to oppose him or even merely to stand firm against his gaze must already be "another god". It is no longer aesthetic self-empowerment, but rather a laying bare that resulted from having lived through being faced with something entirely alien' (Blumenberg 1988, 531). From being the expression of a Gnostic formula in which the 'alien'

---

[32] Taking off from Blumenberg's *Work on Myth*, Odo Marquard picks out this connection between republican political theory and polytheism, but, compared with Arendt's formulation of the significance of the idea of 'balance of power', Marquard's reading pales into a liberal paean to diversity, losing entirely its revolutionary implications. See (Marquard 1983) and the replies by (Faber 1983; and Taubes 2010, 302–14), which emphasize the connection between pagan mythology and its Fascist revival. For a new and promising postcolonial approach to the question of Prometheus, polytheism, and cosmic balance see now (Hickman 2016). Jared Hickman argues that 'one must make a distinction between Euro-Christians' Gnostic drama of racialized cosmic warfare in which non-Euro-Christians were identified with an immanent sphere of creation slated for ruin . . . and an encompassing drama of racialized cosmic confrontation in which the shape of the cosmos going forward would be determined by the unpredictable, contingent outcomes of contact' (Hickman 2016, 63).

[33] On Heine as an advocate of Spinozism, just like Goethe, see (Goetschel 2004).

[34] See (Haugaard 2017).

[35] (Blumenberg 2006, 574).

god rejects worldly empowerment, as in Schmitt's reading, Blumenberg sees in Goethe's motto the idea that the 'alien' god is in reality a power that has alienated itself from the balance of the universe, and thus has illegitimately absolutized itself from the whole. Blumenberg rejects the Christian reading of the motto that renders it: against a god (Napoleon) only the One God (Blumenberg 2006, 583). Only the pantheistic and polytheistic interpretation of the motto will do: 'If one god oppresses you, another one helps—but it has to be a god' (Blumenberg 1988, 538).

Thus, for Goethe world history is characterized by a moral world order that is traversed by demonic power, and that such power can itself be overcome by the divinity of Nature.[36] The idea of religion that corresponds to this drama of history is not a monotheistic, revealed religion characterized by apocalyptic and eschatological motifs. Rather, Blumenberg intimates that such an idea of religion would have to be a tripartite one, that would allow people to be 'pantheists in the investigation of nature, polytheists in poetry, monotheists in ethics' [*naturforschend Pantheisten, dichtend Polytheisten, sittlich Monotheisten*].[37] With respect to the relation between his Spinozism and his polytheism, Blumenberg hypothesizes that for Goethe polytheism is an anthropological expression for pantheism: it is the 'rhetoric' of true, namely, Spinozist philosophy (Blumenberg 2006, 599). It is interesting to note that Goethe's tripartite division of religion corresponds quite closely to Varro's conception of civil religion in its distinction of natural, poetical, and civil theologies.[38] The crucial distinction between Christian political theology and pagan civil religion being, precisely, that whereas the former seeks to legitimate an absolute power on earth by referring to a radical transcendence of God from nature, the latter understands religion as functional to the establishment of a constitutional organization of power that abolishes all claims to absoluteness in the relation between free and equal individuals.

The character of the theologico-political thinking behind the United States Declaration of Independence has long been an object of debate. From Arendt to Derrida, the reference to 'Nature's God' contained in this political document that turns on its performative 'We, the People' has been read as an attempt to metaphysically underwrite the abyssal lack of legitimacy of the

---

[36] Blumenberg's final claim is that: 'the principle of mutual adjustment and of the separation of powers, precisely suits his [Goethe's] remarks (in connection with the saying) about the balance of powers within the world, up to the limiting case of this equilibrium that is seen in the fact that the demonic can only be overcome by the universe itself' (Blumenberg 1988, 539).

[37] Citing from Goethe's *Maximen und Reflexionen* 807 in (Blumenberg 1988, 539).

[38] On the idea of civil religion, see (Silk 2004; and Beiner 2011).

revolutionary Declaration itself, as if the signatories could only establish that political subject whose authorization was presupposed to validate the signatures by appealing to a monotheistic, Christian God.[39] But what if this were an incomplete identification? What if the author of the Declaration, Thomas Jefferson, had employed that term 'Nature's God' in order to open, next to the Deistic possibility, a pantheistic and polytheistic conception of the divinity that was far closer to Goethe's sensibility than to any Puritan legacy? In a recent book, Matthew Stewart has indeed argued that 'Nature's God' refers to a Spinozist God.[40] What difference would this make in the understanding of republican constitutionalism?

In *The Royalist Revolution*, Eric Nelson has provocatively argued that the American Revolutionaries began their rebellion in order to re-establish the English king's 'reign' against Parliamentary self-attribution of 'sovereign government' (Nelson 2017). If one assumes, as Peterson does, that the formula 'the king reigns but does not govern' expresses a Gnostic critique of worldly government, the American Revolution as interpreted by Nelson was a Gnostic phenomenon motivated by mis-archy. Constitutional rule, underwritten by the One true God, and with ample prerogatives assigned to the executive power, as secular representative of the divine right of kings, would then be the result of a deep mistrust in the possibility of popular self-government or democracy. This is an interpretation of the American Revolution that might have pleased Schmitt, for whom only a political theology of sovereignty could 'restrain' the permanent state of war between the Gnostic revolutionaries and the supporters of the worldly powers of government.

The interpretation offered here of the parrhesiastic encounter between Goethe and Napoleon proposes a republican, civil-religious reading of the motto. The republican conception of constitutionalism is polytheistic, in the sense that, like Weber, the late Rawls, and the late Derrida, Blumenberg understands the Goethean call for the renunciation of absolutes to mean that political philosophy must assume as its starting point an irreducible plurality of comprehensive doctrines (divinities). An 'overlapping consensus' between these doctrines, in which the different divinities stand 'eye to eye' with each other, becomes possible only on condition that a republican constitution bar a single site of sovereign authority; that it 'divide' power into the constituent

---

[39] See (Arendt 1990; and Derrida 1986). For commentary, see (Honig 1993; and Moyn 2008) and more recently (Lindahl 2013; and Butler 2018).
[40] (Stewart 2014). See also (Bernstein 2013).

power of the people and the constituted power of government; and that it provide 'checks and balances' for all governmental powers. In order to do so, a republican constitution does not need to be underwritten by monotheism (if only in its Trinitarian mode) but can rest on the pantheistic belief in the divinity of the world as it was, is, and always will be. This is what the expression 'Nature's God' refers to. Such a reading of republican constitutionalism allows one to counter Gnostic mis-archy not by appealing to a political theology of sovereignty, but to a civil religion of republican an-archy, or a conception of balanced power as necessary condition for life in a state of non-domination, where everyone can look into everyone's eyes and not have to avert their gaze.

References

Accetti, Carlo Invernizzi. 2010. "Can Democracy Emancipate Itself from Political Theology? Habermas and Lefort on the Permanence of the Theologico-Political." *Constellations 17* (2): pp. 254–70.
Adorno, Theodor W. 2003a. *Kulturkritik und Gesellschaft II. Eingriffe, Stichworte, Anhang*. Edited by Rolf Tiedemann. Vol. 10.2, *Gesammelte Schriften*. Frankfurt: Suhrkamp.
Adorno, Theodor W. 2003b. *Negative Dialektik. Jargon der Eigentlichkeit*. Edited by Rolf Tiedemann. Vol. 6, *Gesammelte Schriften*. Frankfurt: Suhrkamp.
Agamben, Giorgio. 1998. *Homo sacer. Sovereign Power and Bare Life*. Stanford, CA: Stanford University Press.
Agamben, Giorgio. 1999. *Remnants of Auschwitz. Homo sacer III. The Witness and the Archive*. New York: Zone Books.
Agamben, Giorgio. 2000a. *Il tempo che resta*. Turin: Bollati Boringhieri.
Agamben, Giorgio. 2000b. *Means without End. Notes on Politics*. Vol. *20, Theory out of Bounds*. Minneapolis: University of Minnesota Press.
Agamben, Giorgio. 2003. *État d'exception*. Paris: Seuil.
Agamben, Giorgio. 2004. *The Open: Man and Animal*. Stanford, CA: Stanford University Press.
Agamben, Giorgio. 2005. *The Time That Remains: A Commentary on the Letter to the Romans*. Stanford, CA: Stanford University Press.
Agamben, Giorgio. 2007a. *Il Regno e la Gloria. Per una genealogia teologica dell'economia e del governo*. Rome: Neri Pozza Editore.
Agamben, Giorgio. 2007b. *Profanations*. New York: Zone Books.
Agamben, Giorgio. 2008. *Signatura rerum. Sul metodo*. Torino: Bollati Boringhieri.
Agamben, Giorgio. 2010. *The Sacrament of Language: An Archeology of the Oath*. Stanford, CA: Stanford University Press.
Agamben, Giorgio. 2011. *The Kingdom and the Glory. For a Theological Genealogy of Economy and Government*. Stanford, CA: Stanford University Press.
Agamben, Giorgio. 2012. *The Church and the Kingdom*. Calcutta: Seagull Books.
Agamben, Giorgio. 2013. *The Highest Poverty. Monastic Rules and Form-of-Life*. Stanford, CA: Stanford University Press.
Althusser, Louis. 2001. *Machiavelli and Us*. London: Verso.
Altizer, Thomas J. J. 2003. *The New Gospel of Christian Atheism*. Aurora, CO: The Davies Group Publishers.
Anidjar, Gil. 2003. *The Jew, the Arab. A History of the Enemy*. Stanford, CA: Stanford University Press.
Anidjar, Gil. 2006. "Secularism." *Critical Inquiry 33* (1): pp. 52–77.
Anidjar, Gil. 2014. *Blood. A Critique of Christianity*. New York: Columbia University Press.
Appiah, Kwame Anthony. 2006. *Cosmopolitanism. Ethics in a World of Strangers*. New York: W. W. Norton.

Archibugi, Daniele. 2008. *The Global Commonwealth of Citizens: Towards Cosmopolitan Democracy*. Princeton: Princeton University Press.

Arendt, Hannah. 1958. *The Human Condition*. Chicago: University of Chicago Press.

Arendt, Hannah. 1990. *On Revolution*. New York: Penguin.

Arens, Edmund. 1997. "Interruptions: Critical Theory and Political Theology between Modernity and Postmodernity." In *Liberation Theologies, Postmodernity, and the Americas*, edited by David Batstone, pp. 222–42. New York: Routledge.

Arens, Edmund, John Ottmar, and Peter Rottlaender, eds. 1991. *Erinnerung, Befreiung, Solidaritaet: Benjamin, Marcuse, Habermas und die politische Theologie*. Düsseldorf: Patmos Verlag.

Arens, Edmund. 1997. "Interruptions: Critical Theory and Political Theology between Modernity and Postmodernity." In *Liberation Theologies, Postmodernity and the Americas*, edited by David Batstone, pp. 222–42. New York: Routledge.

Areshidze, Giorgi. 2017. "Taking Religion Seriously? Habermas on Religious Translation and Cooperative Learning in Post-secular Society." *The American Political Science Review 111* (4): pp. 724–37.

Arfi, Badredine. 2015. "Habermas and the Aporia of Translating Religion in Democracy." *European Journal of Social Theory 18* (4): pp. 489–506.

Asad, Talal. 2003. *Formations of the Secular. Christianity, Islam, Modernity*. Stanford, CA: Stanford University Press.

Assmann, Jan. 2000. *Moses der Aegypter*. Frankfurt: Fischer.

Assmann, Jan. 2002. *Herrschaft und Heil. Politische Theologie in Altaegypten, Israel und Europa*. Frankfurt: Fischer.

Aznar, Bernardo Bayona. 2010. *El Origen del Estado Laico desde la Edad Media*. Madrid: Tecnos.

Badiou, Alain. 1985. *Peut-on penser la politique?* Paris: Éditions du Seuil.

Badiou, Alain. 2003. *Saint Paul: The Foundation of Universalism*. Stanford, CA: Stanford University Press.

Badiou, Alain, Éric Hazan, and Ivan Segré. 2013. *Reflections on Anti-Semitism*. London: Verso.

Baehr, Peter, and Gordon C. Wells. 2012. "Debating Totalitarianism. An Exchange of Letters between Hannah Arendt and Eric Voegelin." *History and Theory 51* (3): pp. 364–80.

Baker, Gideon. 2013. "The Revolution Is Dissent. Reconciling Agamben and Badiou on Paul." *Political Theory 41* (2): pp. 312–35.

Balakrishnan, Gopal. 2002. *The Enemy: An Intellectual Portrait of Carl Schmitt*. London: Verso.

Balibar, Étienne. 2008. "Historical Dilemmas of Democracy and Their Contemporary Relevance for Citizenship." *Rethinking Marxism 20* (4): pp. 522–38.

Barbour, Charles. 2010. "Militants of Truth, Communities of Equality. Badiou and the Ignorant Schoolmaster." *Educational Philosophy and Theory 42* (2): pp. 251–63.

Baron, Hans. 1988. *In Search of Florentine Civic Humanism*. Princeton: Princeton University Press.

Bartlett, A. J. 2011. *Badiou and Plato. An Education by Truths*. Edinburgh: Edinburgh University Press.

Bates, David. 2005. "Political Unity and the Spirit of Law: Juridical Concepts of the State in the Late Third Republic." *French Historical Studies 28* (1): pp. 69–101.

Bates, David. 2006. "Political Theology and the Nazi State. Carl Schmitt's Concept of the Institution." *Modern Intellectual History 3* (3): pp. 415–42.
Baume, Sandrine. 2009. "On Political Theology: A Controversy between Hans Kelsen and Carl Schmitt." *History of European Ideas 35*: pp. 369–81.
Becker, Rudolf. 2010. "Das Rätsel um Napoleons Kritik an Goethes *Werther*. Skizze einer moglichen Lösung." *Deutsche Vierteljahrsschrift für Literaturwissenschaft 84* (2): pp. 176–85.
Beiner, Ronald. 2011. *Civil Religion. A Dialogue in the History of Political Philosophy*. New York: Cambridge University Press.
Bellah, Robert, and Hans Joas, eds. 2012. *The Axial Age and Its Consequences*. Cambridge, MA: Belknap Press.
Benhabib, Seyla. 2010. "The Return of Political Theology. The Scarf Affair in Comparative Constitutional Perspective in France, Germany, and Turkey." *Philosophy & Social Criticism 36* (3–4): pp. 451–71.
Benhabib, Seyla. 2011. *Dignity in Adversity. Human Rights in Troubled Times*. Cambridge, UK: Polity.
Benson, Robert, and Johannes Fried, eds. 1997. *Ernst Kantorowicz*. Stuttgart: Franz Steiner.
Bergdahl, Lovisa. 2009. "Lost in Translation: On the Untranslatable and Its Ethical Implications for Religious Pluralism." *Journal of Philosophy of Education 43* (1): pp. 31–44.
Bergem, Ingeborg M., and Ragnar M. Bergem. 2019. "The Political Theology of Populism and the Case of the Front National." *Philosophy and Social Criticism 45* (2): pp. 186–211.
Bergen, Doris L. 2007. "Nazism and Christianity: Partners and Rivals? A Response to Richard Steigmann-Gall, *The Holy Reich. Nazi Conceptions of Christianity, 1919–1945.*" *Journal of Contemporary History 41* (1): pp. 25–33.
Berman, Harold. 1983. *Law and Revolution. The Formation of the Western Legal Tradition*. Cambridge, MA: Harvard University Press.
Bernstein, Jeffrey A. 2013. "'Nature's God' as *Deus sive Natura*. Spinoza, Jefferson and the Historical Transmission of the Theologico-Political Question." In *Resistance to Tyrants, Obedience to God. Reason, Religion, and Republicanism at the American Founding*, edited by Dustin Gish and Daniel Klinghard, pp. 65–81. Lanham, MD: Lexington Books.
Bianchi, Luca. 2015. "L'Averroismo di Dante. Qualche Osservazione Critica." *Le tre corone 2*: pp. 71–109.
Bielik-Robson, Agata. 2019. "The Marrano God. Abstraction, Messianicity and Retreat in Derrida's 'Faith and Knowledge.'" *Religions 10* (22): pp. 94–116.
Bloch, Ernst. 1970. *Man on His Own: Essays in the Philosophy of Religion*. New York: Herder and Herder.
Bloch, Ernst. 1972. *Atheism in Christianity*. New York: Herder and Herder.
Blumenberg, Hans. 1988. *Work on Myth*. Cambridge, MA: MIT Press.
Blumenberg, Hans. 1996. *Die Legitimitaet der Neuzeit*. Frankfurt: Suhrkamp.
Blumenberg, Hans. 2006. *Arbeit am Mythos*. Frankfurt: Suhrkamp.
Blumenberg, Hans, and Schmitt, Carl. 2007. *Briefwechsel 1971–1978*. Frankfurt: Suhrkamp.
Blumenfeld, Bruno. 2001. *The Political Paul. Justice, Democracy and Kingship in a Hellenistic Framework, Journal for the Study of the New Testament*. London: Sheffield Academic Publishers.

Böckenförde, Ernst-Wolfgang. 1983. "Politische Theorie und politische Theologie." In *Religionstheorie und Politische Theologie. Band 1. Der Fuerst dieser Welt. Carl Schmitt und die Folgen*, edited by Jacob Taubes, pp. 16–25. Paderborn: Wilhelm Fink Verlag.
Böckenförde, Ernst-Wolfgang. 2006. *Recht, Staat, Freiheit*. Frankfurt: Suhrkamp.
Boer, Roland. 2017. *Criticism of Heaven. On Marxism and Theology*. Leiden: Brill.
Borradori, Giovanna. 2003. *Philosophy in a Time of Terror*. Chicago: University of Chicago Press.
Bosteels, Bruno. 2011. *Badiou and Politics*. Durham, NC: Duke University Press.
Bosteels, Bruno. 2013. "On the Christian Question." In *The Idea of Communism 2. The New York Conference*, edited by Slavoj Žižek, pp. 37–55. London: Verso.
Boureau, Alain. 1990. *Histoires d'un historien: Kantorowicz*. Paris: Gallimard.
Boureau, Alain. 2006. *La Religion de l'État. La construction de la République étatique dans le discours théologique de l'Occident médiéval (1250–1350)*. Paris: Les Belles Lettres.
Bouretz, Pierre. 2011. *D'un ton guerrier en philosophie. Habermas, Derrida & Co.* Paris: Gallimard.
Bragagnolo, Celina Maria. 2011. "Secularization, History, and Political Theology. The Hans Blumenberg and Carl Schmitt Debate." *Journal of the Philosophy of History* 5: pp. 84–104.
Brown, Wendy. 1995. *States of Injury. Power and Freedom in Late Modernity*. Princeton: Princeton University Press.
Brown, Wendy. 2004. "'The Most We Can Hope For . . .': Human Rights and the Politics of Fatalism." *The South Atlantic Quarterly* 103 (2/3): pp. 451–63.
Brown, Wendy. 2008. "Tolerance as/in Civilizational Discourse." In *Toleration and Its Limits. NOMOS XLVIII*, edited by Melissa S. Williams and Jeremy Waldron, pp. 406–41. New York: New York University Press.
Brown, Wendy. 2014. "Is Marx (Capital) Secular?" *Qui Parle* 23 (1): pp. 109–24.
Brown, Wendy. 2015. *Undoing the Demos: Neoliberalism's Stealth Revolution*. New York: Zone Books.
Brown, Wendy. 2019. *In the Ruins of Neoliberalism*. New York: Columbia University Press.
Brunkhorst, Hauke. 2005. *Solidarity. From Civic Friendship to a Global Legal Community*. Cambridge, MA: MIT Press.
Brunkhorst, Hauke. 2010. "All Nightmares Back: Dependency and Independency Theories, Religion, Capitalism and Global Society." In *Crediting God: Sovereignty and Religion in the Age of Global Capitalism*, edited by Miguel Vatter, pp. 142–59. New York: Fordham University Press.
Brunkhorst, Hauke. 2011. "Critique of Dualism: Hans Kelsen and the Twentieth Century Revolution in International Law." *Constellations* 18 (4): pp. 496–512.
Brunkhorst, Hauke. 2014. *Critical Theory of Legal Revolutions: Evolutionary Perspectives*. London: Bloomsbury.
Brunkhorst, Hauke, Regina Kreide, and Cristina Lafont, eds. 2018. *The Habermas Handbook*. New York: Columbia University Press.
Buch, Robert. 2017. "Der Mythos der Gnosis im Streit um die Moderne." *Weimarer Beiträge* 63 (2): pp. 165–86.
Butler, Judith. 2006. *Precarious Life. The Power of Mourning and Violence*. London: Verso.
Butler, Judith. 2014. *Parting Ways. Jewishness and the Critique of Zionism*. New York: Columbia University Press.
Butler, Judith. 2018. *Notes toward a Performative Theory of Assembly*. Cambridge, MA: Harvard University Press.

Butler, Judith, Ernesto Laclau, and Slavoj Žižek. 2000. *Contingency, Hegemony, Universality: Contemporary Dialogues of the Left*. London: Verso.
Cacciari, Massimo. 1977. *Pensiero negativo e razionalizzazione*. Venice: Marsilio Editore.
Cacciari, Massimo. 2017. *The Withholding Power. An Essay on Political Theology*. London: Bloomsbury Academic.
Calasso, Francesco. 1957. *I glossatori e la teoria della sovranità*. Milan: Giuffré.
Calhoun, Craig, Eduardo Mendieta, and Jonathan VanAntwerpen, eds. 2013. *Habermas and Religion*. London: Polity.
Canning, Joseph. 1983. "Ideas of the State in Thirteenth- and Fourteenth-Century Commentators on the Roman Law." *Transactions of the Royal Historical Society 33*: pp. 1–27.
Canning, Joseph. 1987. *The Political Thought of Baldus de Ubaldis*. Cambridge, UK: Cambridge University Press.
Cantor, Norman. 1991. *Inventing the Middle Ages: Lives, Works and Ideas of the Great Medievalists of the 20th Century*. New York: W. Morrow.
Caputo, John D. 2014. "Unprotected Religion. Radical Theology, Radical Atheism, and the Return of Anti-Religion." In *The Trace of God. Derrida and Religion*, edited by Edward Baring and Peter E. Gordon, pp. 151–77. New York: Fordham University Press.
Carlyle, R. W, and A. J. Carlyle. 1903–36. *A History of Medieval Political Theory in the West*. 6 vols. London and Edinburgh: William Blackwood and Sons.
Casanova, José. 1994. *Public Religions in the Modern World*. Chicago: University of Chicago Press.
Casanova, José. 2011. "The Religious Situation in the United States 175 Years after Tocqueville." In *Crediting God. Sovereignty and Capitalism in the Age of Global Capitalism*, edited by Miguel Vatter, pp. 253–72. New York: Fordham University Press.
Casanova, José. 2013. "Exploring the Postsecular: Three Meanings of 'the Secular' and Their Possible Transcendence." In *Habermas and Religion*, edited by Craig Calhoun, Eduardo Mendieta, and Jonathan VanAntwerpen, pp. 27–48. Cambridge, UK: Polity.
Cavanaugh, William T. 2009. *The Myth of Religious Violence. Secular Ideology and the Roots of Modern Conflict*. New York: Oxford University Press.
Cavanaugh, William T., Jeffrey W. Bailey, and Craig Hovey, eds. 2011. *An Eerdmans Reader in Contemporary Political Theology*. Grand Rapids, MI: Eerdmans.
Chambers, Samuel. 2012. *The Lessons of Rancière*. New York: Oxford University Press.
Chappel, James. 2011. "The Catholic Origins of Totalitarianism Theory in Interwar Europe." *Modern Intellectual History 8* (3): pp. 561–90.
Chen, Jianhong. 2006. "What Is Carl Schmitt's Political Theology?" *Interpretation. A Journal of Political Philosophy 33* (2): pp. 153–76.
Clarke, Maude V. 1936. *Medieval Representation and Consent*. London: Longmans, Green and Co.
Cohen, Hermann. 1924. *Juedische Schriften*. Edited by Bruno Strauss. 3 vols. Berlin: C. A. Schwetschke & Sohn.
Cohen, Jean L. 2013. "Political Religion vs. Non-establishment. Reflections on 21st-century Political Theology: Part I." *Philosophy & Social Criticism 39* (4–5): pp. 443–69.
Cohen, Joshua. 2006. "Is There a Human Right to Democracy?" In *The Egalitarian Conscience. Essays in Honor of G. A. Cohen*, edited by Christine Sypnowich, pp. 226–48. Oxford: Oxford University Press.
Colón-Ríos, Joel. 2014. "Five Conceptions of Constituent Power." *Legal Quarterly Review 130*: pp. 306–36.

Colvert, Gavin T., ed. 2010. *The Renewal of Civilization: Essays in Honor of Jacques Maritain*. Washington, DC: Catholic University of America Press.
Connolly, William. 2008. *Capitalism and Christianity, American Style*. Durham, NC: Duke University Press.
Connolly, William E. 2017. *Aspirational Fascism. The Struggle for Multifaceted Democracy under Trumpism*. Minneapolis, MN: University of Minnesota Press.
Cooke, Maeve. 2006. "Salvaging and Secularizing the Semantic Contents of Religion: The Limitations of Habermas' Postmetaphysical Proposal." *International Journal of Philosophy of Religion 60*: pp. 187–207.
Cooper, Barry. 2011. "Voegelin, Strauss and Kojeve on Tyranny." In *Eric Voegelin and the Continental Tradition*, edited by Lee Trepanier, pp. 218–39. Columbia: University of Missouri Press.
Cooper, Melinda. 2017. *Family Values. Between Neoliberalism and the New Social Conservatism*. New York: Zone Books.
Cotter, Christopher, and David Robertson, eds. 2016. *After World Religions: Reconstructing Religious Studies*. London and New York: Routledge.
Crane, Richard Francis. 2008. "Surviving Maurras: Jacques Maritain's Jewish Question." *Patterns of Prejudice 42* (4/5): pp. 385–411.
Crane, Richard Francis. 2010. *Passion of Israel. Jacques Maritain, Catholic Conscience, and the Holocaust*. Scranton, PA: University of Scranton Press.
Cristi, Renato. 1984. "Hayek and Schmitt on the Rule of Law." *Canadian Journal of Political Science XVII* (3): pp. 521–35.
Cristi, Renato. 1998. *Carl Schmitt and Authoritarian Liberalism: Strong State, Free Economy*. Cardiff: University of Wales Press.
Cristi, Renato. 2000a. *El pensamiento político de Guzmán: Autoridad y libertad*. Santiago: LOM.
Cristi, Renato. 2000b. "The Metaphysics of Constituent Power: Carl Schmitt and the Genesis of Chile's 1980 Constitution." *Cardozo Law Review 21*: pp. 1749–75.
Cristi, Renato. 2011. "Schmitt on Constituent Power and the Monarchical Principle." *Constellations 18* (3): pp. 352–64.
Cusa, Nicholas of. 1995. *The Catholic Concordance*. Edited by Paul E. Sigmund, *Cambridge Texts in the History of Political Thought*. Cambridge, UK: Cambridge University Press.
d'Entreves, Alessandro Passerin. 1952. *Dante as a Political Thinker*. Oxford: Clarendon Press.
Dante. 1996. *Monarchy*. Cambridge, UK: Cambridge University Press.
Dean, Mitchell. 2013. *The Signature of Power: Sovereignty, Governmentality and Biopolitics*. London: Sage.
Dennett, Daniel C. 1996. *Darwin's Dangerous Idea*. New York: Simon and Schuster.
Derrida, Jacques. 1986. "Declarations of Independence." *New Political Science 7* (1): pp. 7–15.
Derrida, Jacques. 1991. *Of Spirit. Heidegger and the Question*. Chicago: University of Chicago Press.
Derrida, Jacques. 1997. *Politics of Friendship*. London: Verso.
Derrida, Jacques. 1998. "Faith and Knowledge. The Two Sources of 'Religion' at the Limits of Reason Alone." In *Religion*, edited by Jacques Derrida and Gianni Vattimo, pp. 1–78. Cambridge, UK: Polity.
Derrida, Jacques. 2000. *Foi et Savoir. Les deux sources de la "religion" aux limites de la simple raison*. Paris: Seuil.

Derrida, Jacques. 2003. *Voyous. Deux essais sur la raison*. Paris: Galilée.
Deuser, Hermann. 1999. "Inkarnation und Repraesentation. Wie Gott und Mensch zusammengehoeren." *Theologische Literaturzeitung 124* (4): pp. 355–70.
Deweer, Dries. 2013. "The Political Theory of Personalism. Maritain and Mounier on Personhood and Citizenship." *International Journal of Philosophy and Theology 74* (2): pp. 108–26.
Diamantides, Marinos. 2012. "*On* and *Out of Revolution*: Between public law and religion." *Law, Culture and the Humanities 10* (3): pp. 336–66.
Diamantides, Marinos, and Anton Schütz. 2018. *Political Theology: Demystifying the Universal*. Edinburgh: Edinburgh University Press.
Donnelly, Jack. 1982. "Human Rights and Human Dignity: An Analytic Critique of Non-Western Conceptions of Human Rights." *American Political Science Review 76* (2): pp. 303–16.
Douzinas, Costas. 2000. *The End of Human Rights. Critical Legal Thought at the Turn of the Century*. Oxford, UK: Hart Publishing.
Douzinas, Costas. 2007. *Human Rights and Empire. The Political Philosophy of Cosmopolitanism*. New York: Routledge-Cavendish.
Dunoff, Jeffrey L., and Joel P. Trachtman, eds. 2009. *Ruling the World? Constitutionalism, International Law, and Global Governance*. New York: Cambridge University Press.
Duranti, Marco. 2012. "The Holocaust, the Legacy of 1789 and the Birth of International Human Rights Law: Revisiting the Foundation Myth." *Journal of Genocide Research 14* (2): pp. 159–86.
Duranti, Marco. 2017. *The Conservative Human Rights Revolution: European Identity, Transnational Politics, and the Origins of the European Convention*. New York: Oxford University Press.
Duso, Giuseppe. 2003. *La rappresentanza politica. Genesi e crisi del concetto*. Milan: Franco Angeli.
Duso, Giuseppe. 2006. "La democrazia e il problema del governo." *Filosofia Politica 20* (3): pp. 367–90.
Dvornik, Francis. 1966. *Early Christian and Byzantine Political Philosophy. Origins and Background*. Vol. 2. Washington, DC: Dumbarton Oaks Center for Byzantine Studies.
Dworkin, Ronald. 1994. *Life's Dominion. An Argument about Abortion, Euthanasia, and Individual Freedom*. New York: Vintage Books.
Dyzenhaus, David. 2010. "Hobbes's Constitutional Theory." In *Hobbes, Leviathan*, edited by Ian Shapiro, pp. 453–80. New Haven: Yale University Press.
Eckermann, Johann Peter. 1839. *Conversations with Goethe in the Last Years of His Life, from the German, of Eckermann*. Boston: Hilliard, Grey & Co.
Emberley, Peter, and Barry Cooper, eds. 1993. *Faith and Political Philosophy. The Correspondence between Leo Strauss and Eric Voegelin, 1934–1964*. Columbia: University of Missouri Press.
Espejo, Paulina. 2010. "On Political Theology and the Possibility of Superseding It." *Critical Review of International Social and Political Philosophy 13* (4): pp. 1–37.
Espejo, Paulina Ochoa. 2011. *The Time of Popular Sovereignty: Process and the Democratic State*. University Park: Pennsylvania State University Press.
Esposito, Roberto. 1988. *Categorie dell'impolitico*. Bologna: Il Mulino.
Esposito, Roberto. 2012. *The Third Person*. London: Polity.
Esposito, Roberto. 2015a. *Persons and Things: From the Body's Point of View*. London: Polity.

Esposito, Roberto. 2015b. *Two. The Machine of Political Theology and the Place of Thought*. New York: Fordham University Press.

Faber, Richard. 1983. "Von der 'Erledigung jeder politischen Theologie' zur Konstitution politischer Polytheologie." In *Religionstheorie und politische Theologie. Band 1: Der Fürst dieser Welt. Carl Schmitt und die Folgen*, edited by Jacob Taubes, pp. 85–99. Munich: Wilhelm Verlag.

Fackenheim, Emil. 1973. *Encounters between Judaism and Modern Philosophy. A Preface to Future Jewish Thought*. New York: Schocken Books.

Fassin, Didier. 2009. "Another Politics of Life Is Possible." *Theory, Culture and Society* 26 (5): pp. 44–60.

Fenves, Peter D. 1991. *A Peculiar Fate. Metaphysics and World-History in Kant*. Ithaca, NY: Cornell University Press.

Figgis, J. Neville. 1911. "Respublica Christiana." *Transactions of the Royal Historical Society* 5: pp. 63–68.

Figgis, John Neville. 1960. *Political Thought from Gerson to Grotius 1414–1625*. New York: Harper & Brothers. Original edition, *Studies of Political Thought from Gerson to Grotius: 1414–1625*; Cambridge University Press, 1907.

Fiorenza, Francis Schüssler, and Don Browning, eds. 1992. *Habermas, Modernity and Public Theology*. New York: Crossroad.

Flakne, April N. 2012. "Beyond Banality and Fatality. Arendt, Heidegger and Jaspers on Political Speech." *New German Critique* 86: pp. 3–18.

Flasch, Kurt. 2006. *Meister Eckhart. Die Geburt der "Deutschen Mystik" aus dem Geist der arabischen Philosophie*. Munich: C. H. Beck.

Foisneau, Luc. 2007. "Omnipotence, Necessity and Sovereignty." In *The Cambridge Companion to Hobbes's Leviathan*, edited by Patricia Springborg, pp. 271–90. New York: Cambridge University Press.

Forst, Rainer. 2010. "The Justification of Human Rights and the Basic Right to Justification." *Ethics* 120: pp. 711–40.

Forst, Rainer. 2011. *Kritik der Rechtfertigungsverhältnisse. Perspektiven einer kritischen Theorie der Politik*. Frankfurt: Suhrkamp.

Forst, Rainer. 2014. "Toleration and Democracy." *Journal of Social Philosophy* 45 (1): pp. 65–75.

Forti, Simona. 2003. *Il totalitarismo*. Roma-Bari: Laterza.

Forti, Simona. 2006. "The Biopolitics of Souls. Racism, Nazism, and Plato." *Political Theory* 34 (1): pp. 9–32.

Forti, Simona. 2014. *New Demons: Rethinking Evil and Power Today*. Stanford, CA: Stanford University Press.

Foucault, Michel. 2003. *"Society Must Be Defended": Lectures at the Collège de France, 1975–1976*. New York: Picador.

Foucault, Michel. 2008. *The Birth of Biopolitics. Lectures at the Collège de France, 1978–1979*. Edited by Arnold I. Davidson. New York: Palgrave Macmillan.

Foucault, Michel. 2009. *Security, Territory, Population: Lectures at the Collège de France 1977–1978*. New York: Picador.

Foucault, Michel. 2010. *The Government of Self and Others. Lectures at the Collège de France 1982–1983*. New York: Palgrave Macmillan.

Frank, Stephanie. 2010. "Re-imagining the Public Sphere. Malebranche, Schmitt's Hamlet, and the Lost Theater of Sovereignty." *Telos* 153: pp. 70–93.

Galli, Carlo. 1996. *Genealogia della politica. Carl Schmitt e la crisi del pensiero politico moderno*. Bologna: Il Mulino.

Garsten, Bryan. 2010. "Religion and Representation in Hobbes." In *Thomas Hobbes. Leviathan*, edited by Ian Shapiro, pp. 519–48. New Haven: Yale University Press.
Gauchet, Marcel. 1998. *La religion dans la démocratie*. Paris: Gallimard.
Gauchet, Marcel. 1999. *The Disenchantment of the World*. Princeton: Princeton University Press.
Gaus, Gerald F. 2003. *Contemporary Theories of Liberalism. Public Reason as a Post-Enlightenment Project*. London: Sage.
Gentile, Emilio. 2006. *Politics as Religion*. Princeton: Princeton University Press.
Geréby, Gyorgy. 2008. "Political Theology versus Theological Politics: Erik Peterson and Carl Schmitt." *New German Critique 35* (3): pp. 7–33.
Geuss, Raymond. 2001. *History and Illusion in Politics*. Cambridge, UK: Cambridge University Press.
Gierke, Otto von. 1934. *Natural Law and the Theory of Society 1500 to 1800*. Cambridge, UK: University of Cambridge Press.
Gierke, Otto von. 1902. *Johannes Althusius und die Entwicklung der naturrechtlichen Staatstheorien*. Breslau: Verlag M. & H. Marcus.
Gierke, Otto von. 2002. *Community in Historical Perspective*. Edited by Antony Black. Cambridge, UK: Cambridge University Press. Original edition, *Das deutsche Genossenschaftsrecht*.
Giesey, Ralph E. 2006. "Medieval Jurisprudence in Bodin's Concept of Sovereignty." In *Jean Bodin*, edited by Julian Franklin, pp. 105–22. London: Routledge.
Gillespie, Michael. 2008. *The Theological Origins of Modernity*. Chicago: University of Chicago Press.
Gilson, Étienne. 1968. *Dante and Philosophy*. Gloucester, MA: Peter Smith.
Glendon, Mary Ann. 2002. *A World Made New. Eleanor Roosevelt and the Universal Declaration of Human Rights*. New York: Random House.
Goethe, Johann Wolfgang von. 1998. *Werke. Band 10 Autobiographische Schriften II*. Edited by Lieselotte Blumethal and Waltraud Loos, *Hamburger Ausgabe in 14 Bänden*. Munich: Deutscher Taschenbuch Verlag.
Goetschel, Willi. 2004. *Spinoza's Modernity. Mendelssohn, Lessing and Heine*. Madison: University of Wisconsin Press.
Gontier, Thierry. 2013. "From 'Political Theology' to 'Political Religion': Eric Voegelin and Carl Schmitt." *The Review of Politics 75*: pp. 25–43.
Gontier, Thierry. 2015. "Open and Closed Societies. Voegelin as Reader of Bergson." *Politics, Religion & Ideology 16* (1): pp. 23–38.
Goodenough, Erwin Ramsdall. 1928. "The Political Philosophy of Hellenistic Kingship." *Yale Classical Studies 1*: pp. 55–104.
Goodenough, Erwin Ramsdall. 1969. *By Light, Light. The Mystic Gospel of Hellenistic Judaism*. Amsterdam: Philo Press. Original edition, Yale University Press, 1935.
Gordon, Peter E. 2014. "Habermas, Derrida, and the Question of Religion." In *The Trace of God. Derrida and Religion*, edited by Edward Baring and Peter E. Gordon, pp. 110–31. New York: Fordham University Press.
Gourgouris, Stathis. 2016. "Political Theology as Monarchical Thought." *Constellations 23* (2): pp. 145–59.
Gregory, Brad. 2015. *The Unintended Reformation: How a Religious Revolution Secularized Society*. Cambridge, MA: Harvard University Press.
Gregory, Brad S. 2017. "The One or the Many? Narrating and Evaluating Western Secularization." *Intellectual History Review 27* (1): pp. 31–46.

Gregory, Eric. 2008. *Politics and the Order of Love: An Augustinian Ethic of Democratic Citizenship*. Chicago: University of Chicago Press.
Greiert, Andreas. 2017. "Innovation und Ressentiment. Ernst Kantorowicz im historiographischen Diskurs der Weimarer Republik." *Historische Zeitschrift* 305 (2): pp. 393–419.
Griffin, James. 2008. *On Human Rights*. Oxford: Oxford University Press.
Gross, Raphael. 2005. *Carl Schmitt und die Juden*. Frankfurt: Suhrkamp.
Grossi, Paolo. 2004. *L'ordine giuridico medievale*. Bari: Laterza.
Habermas, Jürgen. 1975. *Legitimation Crisis*. Boston: Beacon Press.
Habermas, Jürgen. 1981. *Theorie des kommunikativen Handelns. Zur Kritik der funktionalistichen Vernunft*. Vol. 2. Frankfurt: Suhrkamp.
Habermas, Jürgen. 1984a. *The Theory of Communicative Action. Volume 1. Reason and the Rationalization of Society*. Boston: Beacon Press.
Habermas, Jürgen. 1984b. *The Theory of Communicative Action. Volume 2. Lifeworld and System: A Critique of Functionalist Reason*. Boston: Beacon Press.
Habermas, Jürgen. 1988. "Walter Benjamin: Consciousness-Raising or Rescuing Critique." In *On Walter Benjamin*, edited by Gary Smith, pp. 90–128. Cambridge, MA: MIT Press.
Habermas, Jürgen. 1992a. *Nachmetaphysisches Denken: philosophische Aufsätze*. Frankfurt: Suhrkamp.
Habermas, Jürgen. 1992b. *Postmetaphysical Thinking: Philosophical Essays*. Cambridge, UK: Polity.
Habermas, Jürgen. 1993. *Moral Consciousness and Communicative Action*. Cambridge, MA: MIT Press.
Habermas, Jürgen. 1996. *Between Facts and Norms*. Cambridge, MA: MIT Press.
Habermas, Jürgen. 2001a. *The Inclusion of the Other*. Cambridge, MA: MIT Press.
Habermas, Jürgen. 2001b. *The Liberating Power of Symbols: Philosophical Essays*. Cambridge, MA: MIT Press.
Habermas, Jürgen. 2002. *Religion and Rationality. Essays on Reason, God and Modernity*. Edited by Eduardo Mendieta. Cambridge, MA: MIT Press.
Habermas, Jürgen. 2003. *The Future of Human Nature*. Cambridge, UK: Polity.
Habermas, Jürgen. 2005. *Zwischen Naturalismus und Religion. Philosophische Aufsätze*. Frankfurt: Suhrkamp.
Habermas, Jürgen. 2008. *Between Naturalism and Religion*. Cambridge, UK: Polity.
Habermas, Jürgen. 1985. *Philosophical-Political Profiles*. Cambridge, MA: MIT Press.
Habermas, Jürgen. 2004. "Dialectical Idealism in Transition to Materialism: Schelling's Idea of a Contraction of God and Its Consequences for the Philosophy of History." In *The New Schelling*, edited by Judith Norman and Alistair Welchman, pp. 43–89. London: Continuum.
Habermas, Jürgen. 2006. "Does the Constitutionalization of International Law Still Have a Chance." In *The Divided West*, edited by Jürgen Habermas, pp. 115–93. Malden, MA: Polity.
Habermas, Jürgen. 2010. *An Awareness of What Is Missing. Faith and Reason in a Post-secular Age*. Cambridge, UK: Polity.
Habermas, Jürgen. 2011. "'The Political.' The Rational Meaning of a Questionable Inheritance of Political Theology." In *The Power of Religion in the Public Sphere*, edited by Judith Butler, Jürgen Habermas, Charles Taylor, and Cornel West, pp. 15–34. New York: Columbia University Press.

Habermas, Jürgen. 2012. *Nachmetaphysisches Denken II. Aufsätze und Repliken.* Frankfurt: Suhrkamp.
Habermas, Jürgen, and Ratzinger, Joseph. 2005b. *The Dialectics of Secularization.* San Francisco: Ignatius Press.
Hägglund, Martin. 2008. *Radical Atheism. Derrida and the Time of Life.* Stanford, CA: Stanford University Press.
Hallward, Peter, ed. 2004. *Think Again. Alain Badiou and the Future of Philosophy.* London: Continuum.
Hamacher, Werner. 2002. "Guilt History: Benjamin's Sketch 'Capitalism as Religion.'" *Diacritics 32* (3/4): pp. 81–106.
Hankins, James. 2010. "Exclusivist Republicanism and the Non-Monarchical Republic." *Political Theory 38* (4): pp. 452–82.
Hardt, Michael, and Antonio Negri. 2000. *Empire.* Cambridge, MA: Harvard University Press.
Hardt, Michael, and Antonio Negri. 2005. *Multitude: War and Democracy in the Age of Empire.* Cambridge, MA: Harvard University Press.
Harnack, Adolf. 2007. *Marcion: The Gospel of the Alien God.* Eugene, OR: Wipf and Stock Publishers.
Hartman, David. 1998. *A Living Covenant. The Innovative Spirit in Traditional Judaism.* Woodstock, VT: Jewish Lights Publishing.
Haugaard, Mark, and Philip Pettit. 2017. "A Conversation on Power and Republicanism: An Exchange between Mark Haugaard and Philip Pettit." *Journal of Political Power 10* (1): pp. 25–39.
Haverkamp, Anselm. 2004. "Richard II, Bracton, and the End of Political Theology." *Law and Literature 16* (3): pp. 313–26.
Havers, Grant. 2013. *Leo Strauss and Anglo-American Democracy: A Conservative Critique.* DeKalb: Northern Illinois University Press.
Hegel, G. W. F. 1971. *Early Theological Writings.* Philadelphia: University of Pennsylvania Press.
Hegel, G. W. F. 1977a. *Faith and Knowledge.* Albany: State University of New York Press.
Hegel, G. W. F. 1977b. *Phenomenology of Spirit.* Oxford: Oxford University Press.
Heidegger, Martin. 1978. *Wegmarken.* Frankfurt: Vittorio Klostermann.
Held, David. 2010. *Cosmopolitanism: Ideals and Realities.* Cambridge, UK: Polity.
Hengel, Martin. 1968. *The Charismatic Leader and His Followers.* Edinburgh: T. & T. Clark.
Hennis, Wilhelm. 2000. *Max Weber's Central Question.* Newbury, UK: Threshold Press.
Heron, Nicholas. 2018. *Liturgical Power. Between Economic and Political Theology.* New York: Fordham University Press.
Herrero, Montserrat. 2015. *The Political Discourse of Carl Schmitt. A Mystic of Order.* Lexington: Rowman & Littlefield.
Heyking, von John. 1999. "A Headless Body Politic? Augustine's Understanding of a Populus and Its Representation." *History of Political Thought 20* (4): pp. 499–567.
Heyking, von John. 2001. *Augustine and Politics as Longing in the World.* Columbia: University of Missouri Press.
Hickman, Jared. 2016. *Black Prometheus: Race and Radicalism in the Age of Atlantic Slavery.* New York: Oxford University Press.
Hill, Christopher. 1972. *The World Turned Upside Down.* New York: Viking Press.
Hittinger, John. 2003. *Liberty, Wisdom, and Grace. Thomism and Democratic Political Theory.* Lanham, MD: Lexington Books.

Hittinger, John, and Timothy Fuller, eds. 2001. *Reassessing the Liberal State: Reading Maritain's Man and the State*. Washington, DC: Catholic University of America Press.
Hobbes, Thomas. 2010. *Leviathan*. Edited by Ian Shapiro. New Haven: Yale University Press.
Hockanos, Matthew D. 2004. *A Church Divided. German Protestants Confront the Nazi Past*. Bloomington: Indiana University Press.
Hoekstra, Kinch. 2013. "Early Modern Absolutism and Constitutionalism." *Cardozo Law Review 34*: pp. 1079–98.
Hofmann, Hasso. 2007. *Rappresentanza-Rappresentazione. Parola e concetto dall'antichità all'ottocento*. Milan: Giuffrè Editore.
Hohendahl, Peter. 2008. "Political Theology Revisited: Carl Schmitt's Postwar Reassessment." *Konturen I*: pp. 1–28.
Hoibraaten, Helge. 2011. "Carl Schmitt, Henrik Ibsen und die Politische Theologie." In *Henrik Ibsens "Kaiser und Galileaer". Quellen-Interpretationen-Rezeptionen*, edited by H. H. Faber, pp. 233–93. Wuerzburg: Verlag Koenigshausen und Neumann.
Holmes, Stephen. 1993. *The Anatomy of Antiliberalism*. Cambridge, MA: Harvard University Press.
Holmes, Stephen. 2012. "Constitutions and Constitutionalism." In *Comparative Constitutional Law*, edited by Michael Rosenfeld and András Sajó, pp. 189–216. New York: Oxford University Press.
Honig, Bonnie. 1993. *Political Theory and the Displacement of Politics*. Ithaca, NY: Cornell University Press.
Honneth, Axel. 2007. *Pathologien der Vernunft*. Frankfurt: Suhrkamp.
Hovey, Craig, and Elizabeth Phillips, eds. 2015. *The Cambridge Companion to Christian Political Theology*. New York: Cambridge University Press.
Hughes, Glenn. 2014. "Symbols of the 'Depth' of Psyche and Cosmos in Eric Voegelin." *Humanitas 27* (1/2): pp. 36–63.
Hunter, Ian. 2001. *Rival Enlightenments. Civil and Metaphysical Philosophy in the Early Modern Germany*. Cambridge, UK: Cambridge University Press.
Hunter, Ian. 2017. "Giorgio Agamben's Genealogy of Office." *European Journal of Cultural and Political Sociology 4* (2): pp. 166–99.
Hunter, Ian. 2017. "Secularisation: Process, Program, and Historiography." *Intellectual History Review 27* (1): pp. 7–29.
Hurd, Elizabeth Shakman. 2017. *Beyond Religious Freedom. The New Global Politics of Religion*. Princeton: Princeton University Press.
Invernizzi-Accetti, Carlo. 2018. "Is the European Union Secular? Christian Democracy in the European Treatises and Jurisprudence." *Comparative European Politics 16* (4): pp. 669–84.
Jansen, Yolande. 2011. "Postsecularism, Piety and Fanticism. Reflections on Jürgen Habermas' and Saba Mahmood's Critiques of Secularism." *Philosophy and Social Criticism 37* (9): pp. 977–98.
Jaspers, Karl. 1994. *Basic Philosophical Writings*. Edited by Konrad Ehrlich, George Pepper, and Edith Ehrlich. Atlantic Highlands, NJ: Humanities Press.
Jaume, Lucien. 1997. *L'individu effacé ou le paradoxe du libéralisme français*. Paris: Fayard.
Jaume, Lucien. 2011. "The Avatars of Religion in Tocqueville." In *Crediting God. Sovereignty and Religion in the Age of Global Capitalism*, edited by Miguel Vatter, pp. 273–84. New York: Fordham University Press.

Jonas, Hans. 1958. *The Gnostic Religion. The Message of the Alien God and the Beginnings of Christianity*. Boston: Beacon Press. Original edition, *Gnosis und spätantiker Geist*, 1934.
Junker-Kenny, Maureen. 2014. *Religion and Public Reason. A Comparison of the Positions of John Rawls, Jürgen Habermas and Paul Ricoeur*. Berlin: De Gruyter.
Kahn, Paul. 2011. *Political Theology. Four New Chapters on the Concept of Sovereignty*. New York: Columbia University Press.
Kahn, Victoria. 2009. "Political Theology and Fiction in *The King's Two Bodies*." *Representations 106* (1): pp. 77–101.
Kahn, Victoria. 2014. *The Future of Illusion. Political Theology and Early Modern Texts*. Chicago: University of Chicago Press.
Kalberg, Stephen. 1980. "Max Weber's Types of Rationality: Cornerstones for the Analysis of Rationalization Process." *American Journal of Sociology 85* (5): pp. 1145–79.
Kalyvas, Andreas. 2005. "Popular Sovereignty, Democracy, Constituent Power." *Constellations 12* (2): pp. 223–44.
Kalyvas, Andreas. 2009. *Democracy and the Politics of the Extraordinary: Max Weber, Carl Schmitt and Hannah Arendt*. New York: Cambridge University Press.
Kantorowicz, Ernst H. 1955. "Mysteries of State. An Absolutist Concept and Its Late Medieval Origins." *The Harvard Theological Review 48*: pp. 65–91.
Kantorowicz, Ernst. 1961. "The Sovereignty of the Artist. A Note on Legal Maxims and Renaissance Theories of Art." In *De Artibus Opuscula XL. Essays in Honor of Erwin Panofsky*, edited by Millard Meiss, pp. 267–79. New York: New York University Press.
Kantorowicz, Ernst H. 1965. *Selected Studies*. Locust Valley, NY: J. J. Augustin Publishers.
Kantorowicz, Ernst H. 1984. *Mourir pour la patrie et autres textes*. Paris: PUF.
Kantorowicz, Ernst H. 1997. *The King's Two Bodies. A Study in Medieval Political Theology*. Princeton: Princeton University Press. Original edition, 1957.
Keane, John. 2020. *The New Despotism*. Cambridge, MA: Harvard University Press.
Kearney, Richard. 2014. "Derrida and Messianic Atheism." In *The Trace of God. Derrida and Religion*, edited by Edward Baring and Peter E. Gordon, pp. 199–212. New York: Fordham University Press.
Keedus, Liisi. 2012. "Liberalism and the Question of 'The Proud'. Hannah Arendt and Leo Strauss as Readers of Hobbes." *Journal of the History of Ideas 73* (2): pp. 319–41.
Kelley, Donald R. 2002. "What Pleases the Prince: Justinian, Napoleon and the Lawyers." *History of Political Thought 23* (2): pp. 288–302.
Kelsen, Hans. 1919. "Zur Theorie der juristischen Fiktionen. Mit besonderer Beruecksichtigung von Vaihinger's Philosophie des Als Ob." *Annalen der Philosophie 1*: pp. 630–58.
Kelsen, Hans. 1973. *Essays in Legal and Moral Philosophy*. Dordrecht: Reidel.
Kelsen, Hans. 1981. *Der soziologische und der juristische Staatsbegriff*. Amsterdam: Scientia Verlag.
Kelsen, Hans. 2004. *A New Science of Politics. Hans Kelsen's Reply to Erik Voegelin's 'New Science of Politics'*. Edited by Eckhart Arnold. Heusenstamm: Ontos Verlag.
Kervégan, Jean-François. 2005. *Hegel, Carl Schmitt: la politique entre spéculation et positivité*. Paris: PUF.
Kervégan, Jean-François. 2009. "¿Qué significa ser un teólogo de la jurisprudencia?" *Deus Mortalis. Cuaderno de Filosofía Política 8*: pp. 91–102.
Kervégan, Jean-François. 2011. *Que faire de Carl Schmitt?* Paris: Gallimard.
Kilcullen, John. 2004. "Medieval Political Theory." In *Handbook of Political Theory*, edited by Gerald F. Gaus and Chandran Kukathas, pp. 338–52. London: Sage.

Kirshner, Alexander S. 2014. *A Theory of Militant Democracy: The Ethics of Combatting Political Extremism*. New Haven: Yale University Press.
Koskenniemi, Marti. 2007. "Constitutionalism as Mindset: Reflections on Kantian Themes about International Law and Globalization." *Theoretical Inquiries in Law* 8 (1): pp. 9–36.
Laborde, Cécile. 2014. "Three Theses about Political Theology: Some Comments on Seyla Benhabib's 'Return of Political Theology.'" *Critical Review of International Social and Political Philosophy* 17 (6): pp. 689–96.
Laborde, Cécile. 2017. *Liberalism's Religion*. Cambridge, MA: Harvard University Press.
Laclau, Ernesto. 2005. *On Populist Reason*. London: Verso.
Laclau, Ernesto. 2006. "Why Constructing a People Is the Main Task of Radical Politics." *Critical Inquiry* 32 (4): pp. 646–80.
Laclau, Ernesto. 2008. *Debates y combates: por un nuevo horizonte de la política*. Buenos Aires: Fondo de Cultura Economica.
Lafont, Cristina. 2013. "Religion and the Public Sphere. What Are the Deliberative Obligations of Democratic Citizenship?" In *Habermas and Religion*, edited by Craig Calhoun, Eduardo Mendieta, and Jonathan VanAntwerpen, pp. 230–48. Cambridge, UK: Polity.
Lafont, Cristina. 2015. "Human Rights, Sovereignty and the Responsibility to Protect." *Constellations* 22 (1): pp. 68–78.
Lane, Melissa S., and Martin A. Ruehl, eds. 2011. *A Poet's Reich. Politics and Culture in the George Circle*. Rochester, NY: Camden House.
Langlois, Anthony J. 2001. *The Politics of Justice and Human Rights. Southeast Asia and Universalist Theory*. Cambridge, UK: Cambridge University Press.
Laski, Harold J. 1924. *A Defence of Liberty against Tyrants, a Translation of the Vindiciae contra Tyrannos by Junius Brutus, with an Historical Introduction by Harold Laski*. London: G. Bell & Sons.
Laski, Harold. 1968. *Studies in the Problem of Sovereignty*. London: George Allen & Unwin.
Lawson, George. 1992. *Politica Sacra et Civilis*. Cambridge, UK: Cambridge University Press.
Lazier, Benjamin. 2004. "Overcoming Gnosticism: Hans Jonas, Hans Blumenberg, and the Legitimacy of the Natural World." *Journal of the History of Ideas* 64 (4): pp. 619–37.
Lazier, Benjamin. 2008. *God Interrupted. Heresy and the European Imagination between the World Wars*. Princeton: Princeton University Press.
Lee, Daniel. 2008. "Private Law Models for Public Law Concepts: The Roman Law Theory of Dominium in the Monarchomach Doctrine of Popular Sovereignty." *The Review of Politics* 70: pp. 370–99.
Lee, Daniel. 2012. "Hobbes and Civil Law." In *Hobbes and the Law*, edited by David Dyzenhaus and Thomas Poole, pp. 210–35. Cambridge, UK: Cambridge University Press.
Lee, Daniel. 2016. *Popular Sovereignty in Early Modern Constitutional Thought*. New York: Oxford University Press.
Lefebvre, Alexandre. 2018. *Human Rights and the Care of Self*. Durham, NC: Duke University Press.
Lefebvre, Alexandre, and Melanie White, eds. 2012. *Bergson, Politics, and Religion*. Durham, NC: Duke University Press.
Lefort, Claude. 1986. *The Political Forms of Modern Society*. Cambridge, MA: MIT Press.
Lefort, Claude. 1999. *La Complication. Retour sur le communisme*. Paris: Fayard.

Lefort, Claude. 2000. *Writing: The Political Test*. Durham, NC: Duke University Press.
Lefort, Claude. 2006. "The Permanence of the Theologico-Political?" In *Political Theologies. Public Religions in a Post-Secular World*, edited by Hent de Vries, pp. 148–87. New York: Fordham University Press.
Lemke, Thomas. 2019. *Foucault's Analysis of Modern Governmentality: A Critique of Political Reason*. London: Verso.
Lerner, Hanna. 2013. "Permissive Constitutions, Democracy, and Religious Freedom in India, Indonesia, Israel, and Turkey." *World Politics* 65 (4): pp. 609–55.
Lerner, Robert. 2017. *Ernst Kantorowicz: A Life*. Princeton: Princeton University Press.
Leshem, Dotan. 2016. *The Origins of Neoliberalism. Modelling the Economy from Jesus to Foucault*. New York: Columbia University Press.
Lettieri, Gaetano. 2014. "Nemo Contra Deum Nisi Deus Ipse. La messa in questione trinitaria del monoteismo in alcuni testi gnostici." Unpublished paper. Colloquio Enrico Castelli—Rome, 6 January 2014.
Levinas, Emmanuel. 1990. "Reflections on the Philosophy of Hitlerism." *Critical Inquiry* 17 (1): pp. 62–71.
Lewis, Ewart. 1964. "King above Law? 'Quod Princeps Placit' in Bracton." *Speculum* 39 (2): pp. 240–69.
Lilla, Mark. 2001. *The Reckless Mind: Intellectuals in Politics*. New York: The New York Review of Books.
Lindahl, Hans. 2013. *Fault Lines of Globalization: Legal Order and the Politics of A-Legality*. New York: Oxford University Press.
Lindahl, Hans. 2015a. "Law as Concrete Order. Schmitt and the Problem of Collective Freedom." In *Law, Liberty and the State: Oakeshott, Hayek, and Schmitt on the Rule of Law*, edited by David Dyzenhaus and Thomas Poole, pp. 38–64. Cambridge, UK: Cambridge University Press.
Lindahl, Hans. 2015b. "Possibility, Actuality, Rupture: Constituent Power and the Ontology of Change." *Constellations* 22 (2): pp. 163–74.
Lloyd, Genevieve. 2008. *Providence Lost*. Cambridge, MA: Harvard University Press.
Löwith, Karl. 1962. "Hegels Aufhebung der christlichen Religion." In *Einsichten. Gerhard Krüger zum 60. Geburtstag*, edited by Klaus Oehler and Richard Schäffler. Frankfurt: Klostermann.
Löwith, Karl. 1964. *From Hegel to Nietzsche*. Garden City, NY: Anchor Books.
Lorenzini, Daniele. 2012. *Jacques Maritain e i diritti umani. Fra totalitarianismo, antisemitismo e democrazia (1936–1951)*. Brescia: Morcelliana.
Lorenzini, Daniele. 2018. "Jacques Maritain on Anti-Semitism and Human Rights. A Conversation with Daniele Lorenzini." *Journal of Human Rights Practice* 10: pp. 536–45.
Loughlin, Martin. 2004. *The Idea of Public Law*. New York: Oxford University Press.
Loughlin, Martin. 2010. *Foundations of Public Law*. New York: Oxford University Press.
Loughlin, Martin. 2015. "Nomos." In *Law, Liberty and State: Oakeshott, Hayek, and Schmitt on the Rule of Law*, edited by David Dyzenhaus and Thomas Poole, pp. 65–95. Cambridge, UK: Cambridge University Press.
Loughlin, Martin. 2018. *Political Jurisprudence*. New York: Oxford University Press.
Löwy, Michael. 2009. "Capitalism as Religion: Walter Benjamin and Max Weber." *Historical Materialism* 17 (1): pp. 60–73.
Lubac, Henri de. 2007. *Corpus Mysticum. The Eucharist and the Church in the Middle Ages*. Notre Dame, IN: University of Notre Dame Press.

Lupton, Julia Reinhard, and Graham Hammill, eds. 2012. *Political Theology and Early Modernity*. Chicago: University of Chicago Press.

Lupton, Julia Reinhard. 2012. "Pauline Edifications. Staging the Sovereign Softscape in Renaissance England." In *Political Theology and Early Modernity*, edited by Graham Hammill and Julia Reinhard Lupton, pp. 212–39. Chicago: University of Chicago Press.

Maier, Hans. 2004. "'Political Religions' and Eric Voegelin." In *Totalitarianism and Political Religions. Volume I. Concepts for the Comparison of Dictatorships*, edited by Hans Maier, pp. 158–74. London: Routledge.

Mainwaring, Scott, and Timothy R. Scully, eds. 2003. *Christian Democracy in Latin America. Electoral Competition and Regime Conflicts*. Stanford, CA: Stanford University Press.

Mali, Joseph. 1997. "Ernst H. Kantorowicz. History as Mythenschau (Myth, Mythology, Nation)." *History of Political Thought 18* (4): pp. 579–603.

Mansfield, Harvey. 1989. *Taming the Prince. The Ambivalence of Modern Executive Power*. New York: The Free Press.

Marenbom, John. 2001. "Dante's Averroism." In *Poetry and Philosophy in the Middle Ages. A Festschrift for Peter Dronke*, edited by John Marenbom, pp. 349–74. Leiden: Brill.

Maritain, Jacques. 1939. "The Pagan Empire and the Power of God." *The Virginia Quarterly Review 15* (2): pp. 161–75.

Maritain, Jacques. 1943. *The Twilight of Civilization*. New York: Sheed & Ward.

Maritain, Jacques. 1944. *Principes d'une politique humaniste*. New York: Maison française.

Maritain, Jacques. 1951. *Man and the State*. Chicago: University of Chicago Press.

Maritain, Jacques. 1968. *Integral Humanism: Temporal and Spiritual Problems of a New Christendom*. New York: Charles Scribner's Sons.

Maritain, Jacques. 1975. *El crepusculo de la civilización*. Santiago: Edición del Pacifico.

Maritain, Jacques. 1983. *El hombre y el Estado*. Madrid: Ediciones Encuentro.

Maritain, Jacques. 2011. *Christianity and Democracy and The Rights of Man and Natural Law*. San Francisco: Ignatius Press.

Maritain, Jacques, and Pierre Vidal-Naquet, eds. 2003. *L'impossible antisémitisme précédé de Jacques Maritain et les Juifs*. Paris: Desclée de Brouwer.

Marquard, Odo. 1983. "Aufgeklärter Polytheismus—auch eine politische Theologie?" In *Religionstheorie und politische Theologie. Band 1: Der Fürst dieser Welt. Carl Schmitt und die Folgen*, edited by Jacob Taubes, pp. 76–84. Munich: Wilhelm Fink Verlag.

Martel, James. 2007. *Subverting the Leviathan. Reading Thomas Hobbes as a Radical Democrat*. New York: Columbia University Press.

Martel, James. 2012. *Divine Violence. Walter Benjamin and the Eschatology of Sovereignty*. London: Routledge.

Marx, Karl. 1975. "On the Jewish Question." In *Early Writings*, edited by Lucio Colletti, pp. 211–42. New York: Vintage Books.

Masuzawa, Tomoko. 2005. *The Invention of World Religions. Or, How European Universalism Was Preserved in the Language of Pluralism*. Chicago: University of Chicago Press.

May, Todd. 2010. *Contemporary Political Movements and the Thought of Jacques Rancière: Equality in Action*. Edinburgh: Edinburgh University Press.

McAllister, Ted V. 1996. *Revolt against Modernity: Leo Strauss, Eric Voegelin, and the Search for a Postliberal Order*. Lawrence: University Press of Kansas.

McCarthy, Thomas. 1993. *Ideals and Illusions: On Reconstruction and Deconstruction in Contemporary Critical Theory*. Cambridge, MA: MIT Press.

McCormick, John. 1998. "Political Theory and Political Theology. The Second Wave of Carl Schmitt in English." *Political Theory 26*: pp. 830–54.
McCormick, John. 2010. "From Roman Catholicism to Mechanized Oppression: On Politico-theological Disjunctures in Schmitt's Weimar Thought." *Critical Review of International Social and Political Philosophy 13* (2–3): pp. 391–98.
McCormick, William. 2013. "Jacques Maritain on Political Theology." *European Journal of Political Theory 12* (2): pp. 175–94.
McCrudden, Christopher, ed. 2014. *Understanding Human Dignity*. Vol. *192, Proceedings of the British Academy*. London: British Academy.
McIlwain, Charles Howard. 1939. *Constitutionalism and the Changing World*. Cambridge, UK: Cambridge University Press. Reprint, 1969.
McIlwain, Charles Howard. 1947. *Constitutionalism: Ancient and Modern*. Ithaca, NY: Cornell University Press.
McKnight, Stephen A. 2005. "Symposium: Eric Voegelin's New Science of Politics: A Reconsideration after Fifty Years." *Political Science Reviewer 34* (1): pp. 22–27.
McLoughlin, Daniel. 2015. "On Political and Economic Theology. Agamben, Peterson and Aristotle." *Angelaki 20* (4): pp. 53–68.
McLoughlin, Daniel. 2016. "Post-Marxism and the Politics of Human Rights: Lefort, Badiou, Agamben, Rancière." *Law and Critique 27*: pp. 303–21.
Mehring, Reinhard. 2009. *Carl Schmitt. Aufstieg und Fall. Eine Biographie*. München: Verlag C. H. Beck.
Menga, Ferdinando. 2018. "Antagonism, Natality, A-legality. A Phenomenological Itinerary in the Democratic Transgression of Politico-Legal Orders." *Ratio Juris 31* (1): pp. 100–18.
Meier, Heinrich. 1995. *Carl Schmitt and Leo Strauss. The Hidden Dialogue*. Chicago: University of Chicago Press.
Meier, Heinrich. 1998. *The Lesson of Carl Schmitt*. Chicago: University of Chicago Press.
Meier, Heinrich. 2011. *The Lesson of Carl Schmitt. Four Chapters on the Distinction between Political Theology and Political Philosophy*. Expanded ed. Chicago: University of Chicago Press.
Meierhenrich, Jens, and Oliver Simons, eds. 2017. *The Oxford Handbook of Carl Schmitt*. New York: Oxford University Press.
Menga, Ferdinando. 2018. "Antagonism, Natality, A-Legality. A Phenomenological Itinerary on the Democratic Transgression of Politico-Legal Orders." *Ratio Juris 31* (1): pp. 100–18.
Metz, J. B., J. Moltmann, and W. Oelmüller. 1970. *Kirche im Prozess der Aufklaerung. Aspekte einer neuen "Politische Theologie"*. München: Kaiser.
Metz, Johann Baptist. 2002. *Dios y tiempo. Nueva teología política*. Madrid: Editorial Trotta. Original edition, *Zum Begriff der neuen Politischen Theologie*.
Micocci, Andrea, and Flavia Di Mario. 2017. *The Fascist Nature of Neoliberalism*. London: Routledge.
Milbank, John. 2006. *Theology and Social Theory*. 2nd ed. London: Blackwell.
Milbank, John. 2008. "Paul against Biopolitics." *Theory, Culture & Society 25* (7/8): pp. 125–72.
Milbank, John, Slavoj Žižek, and Creston Davis. 2010. *Paul's New Moment. Continental Philosophy and the Future of Christian Theology*. Grand Rapids, MI: Brazos.
Mirowski, Philip. 2007. "Naturalizing the Market on the Road to Revisionism: Bruce Caldwell's *Hayek's Challenge* and the Challenge of Hayek Interpretation." *Journal of Institutional Economics 3* (3): pp. 351–72.

Mohler, Armin, ed. 1995. *Carl Schmitt. Briefwechsel mit einem seiner Schueler*. Berlin: Akademie Verlag.
Möller, Kolja. 2017. "Invocatio Populi. Autoritärer und demokratischer Populismus." *Leviatan 34*: pp. 246–67.
Monod, Jean-Claude. 2002. *La querelle de la sécularisation de Hegel à Blumenberg*. Paris: Vrin.
Monod, Paul. 2005. "Reading the Two Bodies of Ernst Kantorowicz." *The Leo Baeck Institute Yearbook 50* (1): pp. 105–23.
Montini, Giovanni, Enrico Battista, and Maria Antonio. 1965. "Nostra Aetate" [Declaration on the relation of the Church to non-Christian religions]. Rome: Holy See.
Mouffe, Chantal, ed. 1999. *The Challenge of Carl Schmitt*. London: Verso.
Moyn, Samuel. 2004. "Of Savagery and Civil Society: Pierre Clastres and the Transformation of French Political Thought." *Modern Intellectual History 1* (1): pp. 55–80.
Moyn, Samuel. 2006. "Antitotalitarianism and After." In *Democracy Past and Future*, edited by Pierre Rosanvallon, pp. 1–28. New York: Columbia University Press.
Moyn, Samuel. 2008. "Hannah Arendt and the Secular." *New German Critique 35* (3): pp. 71–96.
Moyn, Samuel. 2010. "Personalism, Community, and the Origins of Human Rights." In *Human Rights in the Twentieth Century*, edited by Stefan-Ludwig Hoffmann, pp. 85–106. Cambridge, UK: Cambridge University Press.
Moyn, Samuel. 2012. *The Last Utopia. Human Rights in History*. Cambridge, MA: Harvard University Press.
Moyn, Samuel. 2015. *Christian Human Rights*. Philadelphia: University of Pennsylvania Press.
Moyn, Samuel. 2018a. "Human Rights in Heaven." In *Human Rights: Moral or Political?*, edited by Adam Etinson, pp. 69–87. New York: Oxford University Press.
Moyn, Samuel. 2018b. *Not Enough: Human Rights in an Unequal World*. Cambridge, MA: Harvard University Press.
Moyn, Samuel. 2018c. "A Powerless Companion: Human Rights in the Age of Neoliberalism." In *The Politics of Legality in a Neoliberal Age*, edited by Ben Golder and Daniel McLoughlin, pp. 137–60. Abingdon, UK: Routledge.
Müller, Jan-Werner. 2003. *A Dangerous Mind: Carl Schmitt in Post-War European Thought*. New Haven: Yale University Press.
Müller, Jan-Werner. 2016. *What Is Populism?* Philadelphia: University of Pennsylvania Press.
Munro, Bradley R. 2003. "The Universal Declaration of Human Rights, Maritain, and the Universality of Human Rights." In *Philosophical Theory and the Universal Declaration of Human Rights*, edited by William Sweet, pp. 109–25. Ottawa: University of Ottawa Press.
Naas, Michael. 2009. "Miracle and Machine. The Two Sources of Religion and Science in Derrida's 'Faith and Knowledge.'" *Research in Phenomenology 39*: pp. 184–203.
Naas, Michael. 2012. *Miracle and Machine. Jacques Derrida and the Two Sources of Religion, Science and the Media*. New York: Fordham University Press.
Nancy, Jean-Luc. 2002. *La création du monde ou la mondialisation*. Paris: Galilée.
Nardi, Bruno. 1949. *Dante e la cultura medievale: nuovi saggi di filosofia dantesca*. Bari: Laterza.

Näsström, Sofia. 2011. "Where Is the Representative Turn Going?" *European Journal of Political Theory 10* (4): pp. 501–10.
Näsström, Sofia. 2015. "Democratic Representation beyond Election." *Constellations 22* (1) pp. 1–12.
Nederman, Cary. 1996. "Constitutionalism—Medieval and Modern: Against Neo-Figgisite Orthodoxy (Again)." *History of Political Thought 17* (2): pp. 179–94.
Nederman, Cary J. 1988. "Nature, Sin, and the Origins of Society: The Ciceronian Tradition in Medieval Political Thought." *Journal of the History of Ideas 49*: pp. 3–26.
Nederman, Cary J. 2009. *Lineages of European Political Thought: Explorations along the Medieval/Divide from John of Salisbury to Hegel*. Washington, DC: Catholic University of America Press.
Negri, Antonio, and Hardt, Michael. 2001. *Empire*. Cambridge, UK: Cambridge University Press.
Negri, Antonio. 1999. *Insurgencies: Constituent Power and the Modern State*. Minneapolis: University of Minnesota Press.
Negri, Toni. 2015. "A proposito di Italian Theory." In *Differenze italiane. Politica e filosofia: mappe e sconfinamenti*, edited by Elettra Stimilli and Dario Gentili. Rome: DeriveApprodi.
Nelson, Eric. 2017. *The Royalist Revolution. Monarchy and the American Founding*. Cambridge, MA: The Belknap Press.Nicholls, Angus. 2015. *Myth and the Human Sciences. Hans Blumenberg's Theory of Myth*. London: Routledge.
Nichtweiss, Barbara, ed. 2001. *Vom Ende der Zeit. Geschichtstheologie und Eschatologie bei Erik Peterson*. Berlin: Lit Verlag.
Nietzsche, Friedrich. 1982. *Beyond Good and Evil*. New York: Vintage Books.
Nisbet, Hugh Barr. 1971. "Das Dämonische. On the Logic of Goethe's Demonology." *Forum for Modern Language Studies 7* (3): pp. 259–81.
Nolte, Ernst. 1961. "Eine frühe Quelle zu Hitlers Antisemitismus." *Historische Zeitschrift 192*: pp. 585–606.
Nolte, Ernst. 1997. *Der europäische Bürgerkrieg: Nationalsozialismus und Bolshewismus*. Munich: F. A. Herbig.
Norbrook, David. 1996. "The Emperor's New Body? *Richard II*, Ernst Kantorowicz, and the Politics of Shakespearean Criticism." *Textual Practice 10* (2): pp. 329–57.
Novak, David. 2005. *The Jewish Social Contract: An Essay in Political Theology*. Princeton: Princeton University Press.
Nussbaum, Martha. 2000. *Women and Human Development. The Capabilities Approach*. New York: Cambridge University Press.
Nussbaum, Martha. 2013. *Creating Capabilities. The Human Development Approach*. Cambridge, MA: Harvard University Press.
Nussbaum, Martha C. 2019. *The Cosmopolitan Tradition. A Noble but Flawed Ideal*. Cambridge, MA: Harvard University Press.
Oakeshott, Michael. 1996. *On Human Conduct*. Oxford: Clarendon Press.
Oakley, Francis. 1968. "Jacobean Political Theology: The Absolute and Ordinary Powers of the King." *Journal of the History of Ideas 29* (3): pp. 323–46.
Oakley, Francis. 1969. "Figgis, Constance and the Divines of Paris." *The American Historical Review 75* (2): pp. 368–86.
Oakley, Francis. 1973. "Celestial Hierarchies Revisited: Walter Ullmann's Vision of Medieval Politics." *Past and Present 60*: pp. 3–48.
Oakley, Francis. 1981. "Natural Law, the *Corpus Mysticum*, and Consent in Conciliar Thought from John of Paris to Mathias Ugonius." *Speculum 56* (4): pp. 786–810.

Oakley, Francis. 1995. "Nederman, Gerson, Conciliar Theory, and Constitutionalism: Sed Contra." *History of Political Thought 16* (1): pp. 1–19.
Oakley, Francis. 1998a. "The Absolute and Ordained Power of God and King in the 16th and 17th Centuries: Philosophy, Science, Politics and Law." *Journal of the History of Ideas 59* (4): pp. 669–90.
Oakley, Francis. 1998b. "The Absolute and Ordained Power of God in 16th and 17th Century Theology." *Journal of the History of Ideas 59* (3): pp. 437–61.
Oakley, Francis. 1999. *Politics and Eternity. Studies in the History of Medieval and Early-Modern Political Thought*. Leiden: Brill.
Oakley, Francis. 2006. *Kingship. The Politics of Enchantment*. Oxford: Blackwell.
Oakley, Francis. 2010. *Empty Bottles of Gentilism. Kingship and the Divine in Late Antiquity and the Early Middle Ages (to 1050)*. New Haven: Yale University Press.
Oakley, Francis. 2015. *The Watershed of Modern Politics*. New Haven: Yale University Press.
Ober, Josiah. 2010. *Democracy and Knowledge. Innovation and Learning in Classical Athens*. Princeton: Princeton University Press.
Offe, Claus. 1982. "Some Contradictions of the Modern Welfare State." *Critical Social Policy 2* (5): pp. 7–16.
Ojakangas, Mika. 2012. "*Potentia absoluta et potentia ordinata Dei*: On the Theological Origins of Carl Schmitt's Theory of Constitution." *Continental Philosophy Review 45*: pp. 505–17.
Opitz, Peter J., ed. 1994. *Eric Voegelin, Alfred Schütz, Leo Strauss, Aaron Gurwitsch. Briefwechsel über die Neue Wissenschaft der Politik*. Freiburg: Karl Alber Verlag.
Paléologue, Théodore. 2004. *Sous l'oeil du grand inquisiteur. Carl Schmitt et l'héritage de la théologie politique*. Paris: Cerf.
Parekh, Serena. 2008. *Hannah Arendt and the Challenge of Modernity. A Phenomenology of Human Rights*. New York: Routledge.
Peacock, Mark S. 2001. "The Desire to Understand and the Politics of *Wissenschaft*: An Analysis of the *Historikerstreit*." *History of the Human Sciences 14* (4): pp. 87–110.
Pennington, Kenneth. 1993. *The Prince and the Law, 1200–1600*. Berkeley: University of California Press.
Peterson, Erik. 1997. *Der Brief an die Römer*. Edited by Barbara Nichtweiss. Vol. 6, *Ausgewählte Schriften*. Wuerzburg: Echter Verlag.
Peterson, Erik. 2011. *Theological Tractates*. Stanford, CA: Stanford University Press.
Pettit, Philip. 1997. "Freedom and Antipower." *Ethics 106*: pp. 576–604.
Pitkin, Hannah. 1967. *The Concept of Representation*. Berkeley: University of California Press.
Plessner, Helmuth. 1999. *The Limits of Community. A Critique of Social Radicalism*. Amherst, NY: Humanity Books.
Pocock, J. G. A. 1975. *The Machiavellian Moment. Florentine Political Thought and the Atlantic Republican Tradition*. Princeton: Princeton University Press.
Pogge, Thomas. 2002. *World Poverty and Human Rights*. Cambridge, UK: Polity.
Pöggeler, Otto. 1988. "Between Enlightenment and Romanticism: Rosenzweig and Hegel." In *The Philosophy of Franz Rosenzweig*, edited by Paul Mendes-Flohr, 107–23. Hanover, NH: University Press of New England.
Popper, Karl. 2013. *The Open Society and Its Enemies. New One-Volume Edition*. Princeton: Princeton University Press.
Porter, Jean. 2005. *Nature as Reason. A Thomistic Theory of the Natural Law*. Grand Rapids, MI: William B. Eerdmans Publishing.

Post, Gaines. 1964. *Studies in Medieval Legal Thought: Public Law and the State 1100-1322*. Princeton: Princeton University Press.
Post, Gaines. 1971. "Bracton as Jurist and Theologian on Kingship." In *Proceedings of the Third International Conference of Medieval Canon Law, Strasbourg 3-6 September 1968*, edited by Stephan Kuttner, pp. 113-30. Rome: Biblioteca Apostolica Vaticana.
Postema, Gerald J. 2011. *Legal Philosophy in the Twentieth Century. The Common Law World*. Vol. 11, *A Treatise of Legal Philosophy and General Jurisprudence*. New York: Springer.
Prieto, Alfonso Prieto. 1982. *Inocencio III y el Sacro-Romano Imperio*. León: Colegio Universitario de León.
Przworski, Adam, Susan C. Stokes, and Bernard Manin, eds. 1999. *Democracy, Accountability, and Representation*. Cambridge, UK: University of Cambridge Press.
Pyta, Wolfram. 2015. *Hitler. Der Künstler als Politiker und Feldherr*. Munich: Siedler.
Raabe, August. 1942. *Das Erlebnis des Dämonischen in Goethes Denken und Schaffen*. Berlin: Junker und Dünnhaupt.
Rancière, Jacques. 1995. *La Mésentente. Politique et philosophie*. Paris: Galilée.
Rancière, Jacques. 2009. *Hatred of Democracy*. London: Verso.
Ranieri, John. 2009. *Disturbing Revelation: Leo Strauss, Eric Voegelin, and the Bible*. Columbia: University of Missouri Press.
Raulff, Ulrich, ed. 2006. *Vom Künstlerstaat. Ästhetische und politische Utopien*. Munich: Carl Hanser Verlag.
Rawls, John. 2001. *The Law of Peoples*. Cambridge, MA: Harvard University Press.
Rees, Dafydd Huw. 2017. "Decolonizing Philosophy? Habermas and the Axial Age." *Constellations* 24 (2): pp. 219-31.
Reeves, Marjorie. 1969. *The Influence of Prophecy in the Later Middle Ages. A Study of Joachimism*. Oxford: Clarendon Press.
Rodríguez, Rubén Rosario. 2018. "Political Theology as *Liberative* Theology." *Political Theology* 19 (8): pp. 675-80.
Rorty, Richard. 2001. "Human Rights, Rationality, and Sentimentality." In *The Philosophy of Human Rights*, edited by Patrick Hayden. St. Paul, MN: Paragon Press.
Rosanvallon, Pierre. 1998. *Le peuple introuvable*. Paris: Gallimard.
Rosanvallon, Pierre. 2006. *La contre-démocratie. La politique à l'âge de la défiance*. Paris: Éditions du Seuil.
Rose, Nikolas. 2007. *The Politics of Life Itself. Biomedicine, Power, and Subjectivity in the Twenty-first Century*. Princeton: Princeton University Press.
Rosenstock, Bruce. 2009. *Philosophy and the Jewish Question. Mendelssohn, Rosenzweig, and Beyond*. New York: Fordham University Press.
Rosenstock, Bruce. 2014. "Palintropos Harmonie: Jacob Taubes and Carl Schmitt 'im liebenden Streit.'" *New German Critique* 41 (1): pp. 55-92.
Rosenstock-Huessy, Eugen. 1969. *Out of Revolution. Autobiography of Western Man*. Norwich, VT: Argo Books.
Ross, Alison. 2015. *Walter Benjamin's Concept of the Image*. London: Routledge.
Royal, Robert, ed. 1994. *Jacques Maritain and the Jews*. Notre Dame, IN: University of Notre Dame Press.
Rubinelli, Lucia. 2018. "Taming Sovereignty. Constituent Power in Nineteenth-Century French Political Thought." *History of European Ideas* 44 (1): pp. 60-74.
Runciman, David. 2005. *Pluralism and the Personality of the State*. Cambridge, UK: Cambridge University Press.

Runciman, David. 2007. "The Paradox of Political Representation." *Journal of Political Philosophy 15* (1): pp. 93–114.
Rust, Jennifer. 2012. "Political Theologies of the *Corpus Mysticum*: Schmitt, Kantorowicz, and de Lubac." In *Political Theology and Early Modernity*, edited by Graham Hammill and Julia Reinhard Lupton. Chicago: University of Chicago Press.
Sandoz, Ellis. 1998. "Voegelin's Philosophy of History and Human Affairs, with Particular Attention to 'Israel and Revelation' and Its Systematic Importance." *Canadian Journal of Political Science/Revue canadienne de science politique 31* (1): pp. 61–90.
Sandoz, Ellis. 2009. "The Philosopher's Vocation: The Voegelinian Paradigm." *The Review of Politics 71*: pp. 54–67.
Santner, Eric L. 2015. *The Weight of All Flesh: On the Subject-Matter of Political Economy*. New York: Oxford University Press.
Santner, Eric L. 2011. *The Royal Remains. The People's Two Bodies and the Endgames of Sovereignty*. Chicago: University of Chicago Press.
Saward, Michael. 2010. *The Representative Claim*. New York: Oxford University Press.
Schall, James V. 1975. "Political Theory and Political Theology." *Laval théologique et philosophique 31* (1): pp. 25–48.
Schall, James V. 1981. "Metaphysics, Theology, and Political Theory." *Political Science Reviewer* (11): pp. 1–26.
Schmidt, Christoph. 2009. *Die theopolitische Stunde*. Muenchen: Wilhelm Fink.
Schmitt, Carl. 1982. *Der Leviathan in der Staatslehre des Thomas Hobbes*. Stuttgart: Klett-Cotta.
Schmitt, Carl. 1988. *Political Theology. Four Chapters on the Concept of Sovereignty*. Cambridge, MA: MIT Press.
Schmitt, Carl. 1995. *Les trois types de pensée juridique*. Paris: PUF.
Schmitt, Carl. 1996a. *The Concept of the Political*. Chicago: University of Chicago Press.
Schmitt, Carl. 1996b. *Politische Theologie II. Die Legende von der Erledigung jeder Politischen Theologie*. Berlin: Duncker & Humblot.
Schmitt, Carl. 1996c. *Roman Catholicism and Political Form*. Westport, CT: Greenwood Press.
Schmitt, Carl. 2001. *The Crisis of Parliamentary Democracy*. Cambridge, MA: MIT Press.
Schmitt, Carl. 2003. *The Nomos of the Earth in the International Law of Jus Publicum Europaeum*. New York: Telos Press.
Schmitt, Carl. 2007. *The Concept of the Political*. Expanded ed. Chicago: University of Chicago Press.
Schmitt, Carl. 2008a. *Constitutional Theory*. Durham, NC: Duke University Press.
Schmitt, Carl. 2008b. *The Leviathan in the State Theory of Thomas Hobbes: Meaning and Failure of a Political Symbol*. Chicago: University of Chicago Press.
Schmitt, Carl. 2008c. *Political Theology II. The Myth of the Closure of Any Political Theology*. Cambridge, UK: Polity.
Schmitt, Carl. 2009. *Tiranía de los valores*. Edited by Jorge Dotti. Buenos Aires: Hydra.
Schmitt, Carl. 2013. *Dictatorship*. Cambridge: Polity.
Schmitt, Carl. 2016. *Land und Meer*. Stuttgart: Klett-Cotta.
Schulz, Fritz. 1945. "Bracton on Kingship." *English Historical Review 60* (237): pp. 136–76.
Schürmann, Reiner. 1979. "The Ontological Difference and Political Philosophy." *Philosophy and Phenomenological Research 40* (1): pp. 99–122.
Scott, Peter, and William T. Cavanaugh, eds. 2008. *The Blackwell Companion to Political Theology*. Hoboken, NJ: Wiley-Blackwell.

Segré, Ivan. 2017. *Les Pingouines de l'universalisme. Antijudaisme, antisémitisme, antisionisme*. Paris: Nouvelles Éditions Lignes.
Sen, Amartya. 2007. *Identity and Violence: The Illusion of Destiny*. New York: W. W. Norton.
Senellart, Michel. 1995. *Les arts de gouverner. Du regimen médiéval au concept du gouvernement*. Paris: Éditions du Seuil.
Shepherd, Frederick M., ed. 2009. *Christianity and Human Rights. Christians and the Struggle for Global Justice*. Lanham, MD: Lexington Books.
Shue, Henry. 1980. *Basic Rights. Subsistsence, Affluence, and US Foreign Policy*. Princeton: Princeton University Press.
Silk, Mark. 2004. "Numa Pompilius and the Idea of Civil Religion in the West." *Journal of the American Academy of Religion* 72 (4): pp. 863–96.
Silvestrini, Flavio. 2013. "L'esistenza virtuosa tra *Monarcha* e *Multitudo*: Una (Composita) Lezione Aristotelica nel *Monarchia* Dantesco." *Il Pensiero Politico* 46 (3): pp. 271–97.
Skinner, Quentin. 1978. *The Foundations of Modern Political Thought*. Vol. II. *The Age of Reformation*. Cambridge, UK: Cambridge University Press.
Skinner, Quentin. 2002. "Classical Liberty and the Coming of the English Civil War." In *Republicanism. Volume 2. The Values of Republicanism in Early Modern Europe*, edited by Martin van Gelderen and Quentin Skinner, pp. 9–28. New York: Cambirdge University Press.
Skinner, Quentin. 2005. "Hobbes on Representation." *European Journal of Philosophy* 13 (2): pp. 157–84.
Skinner, Quentin. 2009. "A Genealogy of the Modern State." *Proceedings of the British Academy* 162: pp. 325–70.
Skinner, Quentin. 2018. *From Humanism to Hobbes. Studies in Rhetoric and Politics*. New York: Cambridge University Press.
Slobodian, Quinn. 2018. *Globalists: The End of Empire and the Birth of Neoliberalism*. Cambridge, MA: Harvard University Press.
Springborg, Patricia. 1996. "Hobbes on Religion." In *The Cambridge Companion to Hobbes*, edited by Tom Sorell, pp. 346–80. Cambridge, UK: Cambridge University Press.
Stein, Peter. 2007. *Roman Law in European History*. Cambridge, UK: Cambridge University Press.
Stepan, Alfred C. 2000. "Religion, Democracy, and the 'Twin Tolerations'." *Journal of Democracy* 11 (4): pp. 37–57.
Stewart, Matthew. 2014. *Nature's God. The Heretical Origins of the American Republic*. New York: W. W. Norton.
Stowers, Stanley. 2007. "The Concepts of 'Religion', 'Political Religion' and the Study of Nazism." *Journal of Contemporary History* 41 (1): pp. 9–24.
Strauss, Leo. 2008. *Hobbes' politische Wissenschaft und zugehoerige Schriften—Briefe*. Edited by Heinrich Meier. Vol. 3, *Gesammelte Schriften*. Stuttgart: Verlag J. B. Metzler.
Streeck, Wolfgang. 2016. *How Will Capitalism End? Essays on a Failing System*. London: Verso.
Sullivan, Winnifred Fallers, Elizabeth Shakman Hurd, Saba Mahmood, and Peter Danchin, eds. 2015. *Politics of Religious Freedom*. Chicago: University of Chicago Press.
Tan, Kok-Chor. 2010. "Nationalism and Global Justice: A Survey and Some Challenges." In *Sovereign Justice: Global Justice in a World of Nations*, edited by Regina Queiroz, Gabriele de Angelis, and Diogo P. Aurelio, pp. 9–24. Berlin: De Gruyter.

Tasioulas, John. 2011. "On the Nature of Human Rights." In *The Philosophy of Human Rights: Contemporary Controversies*, edited by Jan-Christoph Heilinger and Gerhard Ernst, pp. 17–59. New York: Walter de Gruyter.

Tasioulas, John. 2013. "Human Dignity and the Foundations of Human Rights." In *Understanding Human Dignity*, edited by Christopher McCrudden, pp. 293–314. New York: Oxford University Press.

Taubes, Jacob, ed. 1983. *Religionstheorie und politische Theologie. Band 1: Der Fürst dieser Welt. Carl Schmitt und die Folgen*. Munich: Wilhelm Fink Verlag.

Taubes, Jacob. 1993. *Die politische Theologie des Paulus*. Munich: Wilhelm Fink Verlag.

Taubes, Jacob. 2003. *The Political Theology of Paul*. Stanford, CA: Stanford University Press.

Taubes, Jacob. 2010. *From Cult to Culture*. Stanford, CA: Stanford University Press.

Taubes, Jacob. 2013. *To Carl Schmitt. Letters and Reflections*. New York: Columbia University Press.

Taylor, Charles. 2004. *Modern Social Imaginaries*. Durham, NC: Duke University Press.

Taylor, Charles. 2007. *A Secular Age*. Cambridge, MA: Harvard University Press.

Taylor, Charles. 2011. "Why We Need a Radical Redefinition of Secularism." In *The Power of Religion in the Public Sphere*, edited by Eduardo Mendieta and Jonathan VanAntwerpen, pp. 34–59. New York: Columbia University Press.

Taylor, Mark C. 2007. *After God*. Chicago: University of Chicago Press.

Thomassen, Bjorn. 2014. "Debating Modernity as Secular Religion. Hans Kelsen's Futile Exchange with Eric Voegelin." *History and Theory 53*: pp. 435–50.

Thompson, Kenneth. 1988. "The Religious Transformation of Politics and the Political Transformation of Religion." *Review of Politics 50* (4): pp. 545–60.

Thornhill, Chris. 2002. *Karl Jaspers. Politics and Metaphysics*. London: Routledge.

Thornhill, Chris. 2013. *A Sociology of Constitutions: Constitutions and State Legitimacy in Historical-Sociological Perspective*. New York: Cambridge University Press.

Thornhill, Chris. 2018. *The Sociology of Law and the Global Transformation of Democracy*. Cambridge, UK: Cambridge University Press.

Tierney, Brian. 1963a. "Bracton on Government." *Speculum 38* (2): pp. 295–317.

Tierney, Brian. 1963b. "'The Prince Is Not Bound by the Laws'. Accursius and the Origins of the Modern State." *Comparative Studies in Society and History 5* (4): pp. 378–400.

Tierney, Brian. 1964. *The Crisis of Church and State 1050–1300*. Englewood Cliffs, NJ: Prentice-Hall.

Tierney, Brian. 1982. *Religion, Law and the Growth of Constitutional Thought 1150–1650*. Cambridge, UK: Cambridge University Press.

Tierney, Brian. 1997. *The Idea of Natural Rights*. Grand Rapids, MI: William B. Eerdmans Publishing Company.

Tooze, Adam. 2018. *Crashed. How a Decade of Financial Crises Changed the World*. New York: Penguin Random House.

Traverso, Enzo. 1994. *The Marxists and the Jewish Question. The History of a Debate 1843–1943*. Amherst, NH: Humanity Books.

Traverso, Enzo. 2017. "Totalitarianism between History and Theory." *History and Theory* (55): pp. 97–118.

Trepanier, Lee. 2018. "Eric Voegelin on Race, Hitler, and National Socialism." *The Political Science Reviewer 42* (1): pp. 167–96.

Trepanier, Lee, and Steven F. McGuire, eds. 2011. *Eric Voegelin and the Continental Tradition. Explorations in Modern Political Thought*. Columbia: University of Missouri Press.

Trom, Danny. 2019. *La France sans les Juifs? Emancipation, extermination, expulsion.* Paris: PUF.

Tuck, Richard. 2016. *The Sleeping Sovereign. The Invention of Modern Democracy.* New York: Cambridge University Press.

Ullmann, Walter. 1980. *Jurisprudence in the Middle Ages. Collected Studies.* London: Variorum Reprints.

Urbinati, Nadia. 2000. "Representation as Advocacy. A Study of Democratic Deliberation." *Political Theory 28* (6): pp. 758–86.

Urbinati, Nadia. 2006. *Representative Democracy. Principles and Genealogy.* Chicago: University of Chicago Press.

Urbinati, Nadia, and Mark E. Warren. 2008. "The Concept of Representation in Contemporary Democratic Theory." *Annual Review of Political Science 11*: pp. 387–412.

Valentini, Laura. 2012. "In What Sense Are Human Rights Political? A Preliminary Exploration." *Political Studies 60* (1): pp. 180–94.

Vardoulakis, Dimitris. 2009. "Stasis: Beyond Political Theology?" *Cultural Critique 73*: pp. 125–47.

Vatter, Miguel. 2004. "Machiavelli after Marx: The Self-Overcoming of Marxism in the Late Althusser." *Theory and Event 7* (4).

Vatter, Miguel. 2008. "The Idea of Public Reason and the Reason of State. Schmitt and Rawls on the Political." *Political Theory 36* (2): pp. 239–71.

Vatter, Miguel. 2011a. "Eternal Life and Biopower." *The New Centennial Review 10* (3): pp. 217–49.

Vatter, Miguel. 2011b. "Habermas between Athens and Jerusalem: Public Reason and Atheistic Theology." *Interpretation. A Journal of Political Philosophy 38* (2): pp. 243–60.

Vatter, Miguel. 2013. "Machiavelli and the Republican Conception of Providence." *Review of Politics* (75): pp. 605–23.

Vatter, Miguel. 2014a. *The Republic of the Living. Biopolitics and the Critique of Civil Society.* New York: Fordham University Press.

Vatter, Miguel. 2014b. "Republics Are a Species of State: Machiavelli and the Genealogy of the Modern State." *Social Research 81* (1): pp. 217–41.

Vatter, Miguel. 2015. "Political Ontology, Constituent Power, and Representation." *Critical Review of International Social and Political Philosophy 18* (6): pp. 679–86.

Vatter, Miguel. 2016. "Law and Life beyond Incorporation. Agamben, Highest Poverty and the Papal Legal Revolution." In *Agamben and Radical Politics*, edited by Daniel McLoughlin, pp. 234–62. Edinburgh: Edinburgh University Press.

Vatter, Miguel. 2017. "Machiavelli, 'Ancient Theology,' and the Problem of Civil Religion." In *Machiavelli on Liberty and Conflict*, edited by Nadia Urbinati, David Johnston, and Camila Vergara, pp. 113–38. Chicago: University of Chicago Press.

Vatter, Miguel. 2018. "Neoliberalism and Republicanism: Economic Rule of Law and Law as Concrete Order (*nomos*)." In *The SAGE Handbook of Neoliberalism*, edited by Melinda Cooper, Damien Cahill, Martijn Konings, and David Primrose, pp. 370–83. London: Sage.

Vatter, Miguel. 2019. "Liberal Governmentality and the Political Theology of Constitutionalism." In *Sovereignty in Motion*, edited by Neil Walker and Bas Leijssenaar, pp. 115–43. New York: Cambridge University Press.

Vatter, Miguel, ed. 2010. *Crediting God: Sovereignty and Religion in the Age of Global Capitalism.* New York: Fordham University Press.

Vattimo, Gianni. 1999. *Belief.* Stanford, CA: Stanford University Press.

Vattimo, Gianni. 2002. *After Christianity*. New York: Columbia University Press.
Vieira, Mónica Brito. 2009. *The Elements of Representation in Hobbes*. Leiden: Brill.
Vieira, Mónica Brito, ed. 2017. *Reclaiming Representation. Contemporary Advances in the Theory of Political Representation*. New York: Routledge.
Voegelin, Eric. 1952. *The New Science of Politics*. Chicago: University of Chicago Press.
Voegelin, Eric. 1953. "The Origins of Totalitarianism." *Review of Politics 15* (1): pp. 68–85.
Voegelin, Eric. 1994. *Les religions politiques*. Paris: Les Éditions du Cerf.
Voegelin, Eric. 1998a. *The History of the Race Idea: From Ray to Carus*. Edited by Ruth Hein and Klaus Vondung. Vol. 3, *The Collected Works of Eric Voegelin*. Baton Rouge: Louisiana State University.
Voegelin, Eric. 1998b. *Race and State*. Edited by Ruth Hein and Klaus Vondung. Vol. 2, *The Collected Works of Eric Voegelin*. Baton Rouge: Louisiana State University Press.
Voegelin, Eric. 1999. *Order and History. Plato and Aristotle*. Vol. 3. Columbia: University of Missouri Press.
Voegelin, Eric. 2001. *Order and History. Volume 1. Israel and Revelation*. Vol. 14, *The Collected Works of Eric Voegelin*. Columbia: University of Missouri Press.
Voegelin, Eric. 2003. *Hitler and the Germans*. Columbia: University of Missouri Press.
Vries, Hent de. 2001. *Religion and Violence: Philosophical Perspectives from Kant to Derrida*. Baltimore: Johns Hopkins University Press.
Vries, Hent de, and Lawrence Sullivan, ed. 2006. *Political Theologies. Public Religions in a Post-Secular World*. New York: Fordham University Press.
Waldron, Jeremy. 2002. *God, Locke, and Equality. Christian Foundations in Locke's Political Thought*. Cambridge, UK: Cambridge University Press.
Waldron, Jeremy. 2015. *Dignity, Rank, and Rights*. Oxford: Oxford University Press.
Walzer, Michael. 1965. *The Revolution of the Saints. A Study of the Origins of Radical Politics*. Cambridge, MA: Harvard University Press.
Watkin, Christopher. 2013. "Thinking Equality Today: Badiou, Rancière, Nancy." *French Studies 67* (4): pp. 522–34.
Weber, Max. 1958. *The Protestant Ethic and the Spirit of Capitalism*. New York: Charles Scribner's Sons.
Weber, Samuel. 2005. *Targets of Opportunity. On the Militarization of Thinking*. New York: Fordham University Press.
Weber, Samuel. 2013. "The Debt of the Living." *Postmodern Culture 23* (3), doi:10.1353/pmc.2013.0039.
Weber, Samuel. 2014. *Inquiétantes singularités*. Paris: Hermann Éditions.
Weidner, Daniel. 2016. "The Political Theology of Critical Philosophy. Reading Kant's Ideas of Religion." *Modern Language Notes 131*: pp. 1325–46.
Whyte, Jessica. 2012. "'Is Revolution Desirable?' Michel Foucault on Revolution, Neoliberalism and Rights." In *Re-reading Foucault: On Law, Power and Rights*, edited by Ben Golder, pp. 207–228. London: Routledge.
Whyte, Jessica. 2013. "'The King Reigns but He Doesn't Govern'. Thinking Sovereignty and Government with Agamben, Foucault and Rousseau." In *Giorgio Agamben. Legal, Political and Philosophical Perspectives*, edited by Tom Forst, pp. 143–61. London: Routledge.
Whyte, Jessica. 2017. "Human Rights and the Collateral Damage of Neoliberalism." *Theory & Event 20* (1): pp. 137–51.

Whyte, Jessica. 2018. "Powerless Companions or Fellow Travellers? Human Rights and the Neoliberal Assault on Postcolonial Economic Justice." *Radical Philosophy* (2.02): pp. 13–29.
Whyte, Jessica. 2019a. "The Invisible Hand of Friedrich Hayek. Submission and Spontaneous Order." *Political Theory 47* (2): pp. 156–84.
Whyte, Jessica. 2019b. *The Morals of the Market. Human Rights and the Rise of Neoliberalism*. London: Verso.
Wilde, Marc de. 2018. "The Dark Side of Institutionalism: Carl Schmitt Reading Santi Romano." *Ethics & Global Politics 11* (2): pp. 12–24.
Witte, John, and M. Christian Green, eds. 2011. *Religion and Human Rights. An Introduction*. Oxford, UK: Oxford University Press.
Wolterstorff, Nicholas. 2013. "An Engagement with Jürgen Habermas on Postmetaphysical Philosophy, Religion, and Political Dialogue." In *Habermas and Religion*, edited by Craig Calhoun, Eduardo Mendieta, and Jonathan VanAntwerpen, pp. 92–111. Cambridge, UK: Polity.
Wood, Gordon S. 1969. *Representation in the American Revolution*. Charlottesville: The University Press of Virginia.
Woodhouse, John, ed. 1997. *Dante and Governance*. New York: Oxford University Press.
Yelle, Robert. 2015. "Imagining the Hebrew Republic. Christian Genealogies of Religious Freedom." In *Politics of Religious Freedom*, edited by Winnifred F. Sullivan, Elizabeth Shakman Hurd, and Saba Mahmood, pp. 17–28. Chicago: University of Chicago Press.
Young-Bruehl, Elisabeth. 1981. *Freedom and Karl Jasper's Philosophy*. New Haven: Yale University Press.
Yovel, Yirmiahu. 1998. *Dark Riddle: Hegel, Nietzsche, and the Jews*. University Park: Pennsylvania State University Press.
Žižek, Slavoj. 2009. *In Defense of Lost Causes*. London: Verso.

Index

For the benefit of digital users, indexed terms that span two pages (e.g., 52–53) may, on occasion, appear on only one of those pages.

Abraham (biblical character), 88
Abravanel, Isaak, 48–49n65
absolute power, 150–51
absolutism, 42
Action Française, 123–24
Adam Kadmon, 214
Adams, John, 63–64
administration, jurisdiction versus, 161–68
Adorno, Theodor, 193, 196–97, 216–17, 219
Aegidius Romanus, 149–51
aequitas (justice as equity), 164–65
against a god, only a god. See *nemo contra deum nisi deus ipse*
Agamben, Giorgio
   on Christian conception of democracy, 6
   on Christian democratic political theology, 64–65
   on Gnostic *stasis*, 244–45
   on government and providence, 171–72
   on modern governmentality, 246
   on political messianism, 74n15
   on providence in Christian theology, 120–21
   on Saint Paul, 127n79
   on self-steering social systems, 117n60
Ailly, Pierre d', 152
Akhenaton (Egyptian ruler), 82, 88
Albericus de Rosata, 159n56
Albertus Magnus, 152–53
Althusius, Johannes, 43–44
Althusser, Louis, 93–94n67
ambivalent philosemitism, 123–24
anamnestic reason, 217–18
anarcho-communism, 242–43
angels, kingship and, 144–45
Antichrist, 62–63, 176–77

antifascism, 173–74
anti-Judaism, 193. *See also* anti-Semitism
antinomy of sovereignty, 161–72
anti-Semitism, 7, 67, 245–46n12
aporia of the Leviathan, 47–48
Aquinas, Thomas, 109, 164
arcana ecclesiae (mysteries of the Church), 147–48
arcana imperii (secrets of state), 147–48
Arendt, Hannah, 68, 193–94, 197
   on crisis of human rights, 127n80
   on decrees, 171–72n81
   Habermas, influence on, 224
   on Hobbes, 87
   on human multiplicity, 227
   on power, 252–53
   on sacredness of life, 101
Aristotle, 176–77
articulation, as condition of representation, 75
artificial persons, 43–45
artificial representation, 44–45, 46–47
Asad, Talal, 190
Assmann, Jan, 82n35
association, theory of, 32
associations, concession theory of, 47–48
atheism
   in Christianity, 211–16, 219
   Judaism's treatment of, 208
   methodological atheism, 8, 195, 212, 218–19, 220–21
auctoritas interpositio, 34
Augustine, Saint
   on Catholic Church versus political state, 72–73
   doctrine of the Two Cities, 54, 55–56, 70–72, 138–39, 141
   Fortescue's critique of, 77–78

Austin, John, 40–41
authority, 222–24, 225–26
autoimmunity and autoimmunitary hypothesis, 232–33, 237–38
Averroes (Ibn Rushd) and Averroism, 85, 153, 175–76, 215
Avicenna, 215
Axial Age hypothesis, 192–93, 196–97

Baader Meinhof, 210–11
Badiou, Alain
 on Christian-Jewish enmity, 131
 on hope, 130
 Maritain and, 70
 radical democratic thought and, 7
 on Saint Paul, 125–29
 on truth, 129
 on universalism, 68, 123, 125–26
Bakunin, Mikhail, 29–30
balance, nature of, 251–52
Baldus (medieval lawyer), 137–38, 148–49
baptism, sacrament of, 55, 177–78
bare faith, 234–35, 236, 238
Bartolus, 137–38, 148
basic rights, human rights as function of, 100–1
Bellarmine, Cardinal, 36
Benjamin, Walter, 162, 219–20
Bergson, Henri-Louis, 83
Berman, Harold, 163n64, 180–85
Beruf (vocation), 10–11
Bible of the poor (*Biblia pauperum*), 213–14
Bismarck, Otto von, 51, 52–53
Bloch, Ernst, 8, 195, 199, 211–16, 220–21, 237, 242–43
Blumenberg, Hans, 8–9
 on Goethe, 244–45, 247, 250, 251–54, 255–56
 on political theology, 9–10
 Schmitt, critique of, 16–19
 on self-assertion, 241–42
Bodin, Jean, 109
body
 corporate body, immortality of, 143–47
 humankind, body of, 174, 176–77
 incorporated bodies, 43–44
 mystical body, 34, 77–81, 133–34, 136, 137–38
 political Body divinization of, 57–58
Böckenförde, Ernst-Wolfgang, 203–4n33
Boniface VIII, Pope, 148–49
Boureau, Alain, 147–48
Bouretz, Pierre, 197–98n22
Bracton, Henri
 Kantorowicz on, 168–69, 170, 170–71n78, 185–86, 187
 on king's will, 166–67
 on *lex digna*, 167
 McIlwain on, 133–34, 163–64, 165–67, 168
 on royal prerogatives, 162–63
 Tierney on, 139–40
Brown, Wendy, 187
Brunkhorst, Hauke, 142, 180–82, 183–84
Buber, Martin, 226
Bultmann, Rudolf, 16–17n42
Burckhardt, Jacob, 1–2n2, 72

Calasso, Roberto, 159
Canon law, 148, 153–54, 181–84, 183n100
Castoriadis, Cornelius, 68
Catholic Church
 anti-Semitism and, 67
 Empire, separation from, 181–83
 as holder of all powers, 151–52
 identity of, 40n50
 political existence of, 37–38
 political role of, 152
 as representative of Jesus Christ, 40
 Two Cities model, rejection of, 56
catholicity, reason versus, 223–24, 225
Catholic Revival, 51
Charles I, King, 148–49
checks and balances, 161–62
Christ. *See also* Christology
 mystical body of, 78, 136
 nature of, 27, 157–58
 as Son of Man, 214
Christianity
 Bloch and atheism of, 211–16
 Christian democracy, 107–13, 122–32
 Christian democratic political theology, 7

Christian eschatology, Voegelin on, 72–73
Christian humanism, 105
Christian messianism, legal form of, 185
Christian theology, original sin of, 217–18
  hegemonic role in legitimacy of power, 3–4
  Judaism, relationship to, 88–89
  Marx on, 12–13
  Schmitt on, 24
Christian political theology
  after Schmitt, 3–4
  and democratic dictatorship, paradox of, 81–86
  democratic turn of, 101–2
  Gnostic obsession with, 241–45
  Peterson on possibility of, 55–56
  totalitarianism and, 67–70
Christology. *See also* Christ
  adoption into theory of state legitimacy, 64
  legal personality and application of law and, 25–35
  Royal Christology, 141–42
  Schmitt's recourse to, 6
  theory of legal personality and, 39–40
christomimesis, 157–58
Church. *See* Catholic Church
Church law, efforts to constitutionalize, 7–8
Church-State relationship, 35–53, 56, 156
Cicero, Marcus Tullius, 164
Civil Code (Napoleon), 248–51
class struggles, 182
Cohen, Hermann, 193–94, 203, 212
common good, right to govern and, 111
communication
  Derrida on, 197–98
  truth and, 206
constituent power, 24, 76–77
constitutionalism
  constitutional dictatorships, 85–86
  constitutional monarchies, 165
  possible religious nature of, 15
  republican conception of, 255
  republican constitutions, 255–56
  sociology of, Papal legal revolution and, 180–84
contradictions in political theology, 28
Cooke, Maeve, 190–91n7
coronation formula (Dante's), 173–74, 177–78
corporate body, immortality of, 143–47
corporations, 46, 47, 48–49, 144, 145
corpus mysticum (mystical body), 34, 78, 137–38
Cortés, Donoso, 21–22
cosmic order, 81–82, 83, 84
cosmopolitanism (universalism), 122–23
Crane, Richard Francis, 124
critical political theology, 216–20
culture wars, 84–85, 94, 229

Dante Alighieri, 154, 157, 158, 172–80
Declaration of Independence, 254–55
de Maistre, Joseph, 51, 52–53
democracy
  charismatic conception of democratic authority, 110–11
  democracy to-come, 239
  democratic communication, theory of, 196–97
  democratic dictatorship, paradox of, 81–86
  democratic legitimacy, 8, 15–16
  democratic political theology, 1–6, 53–65
  democratic public reason, *khora* and, 237
  democratic representation, question of, 35–53
  democratic turn of political theology, 2–3, 25
  divine providence and, 113–22
  illiberal democracies, 161
  modern representative democracy, 89–90
  representation versus, 43
  right to, 100–1
  universality of human rights and, 97–103
democratic, as term, meaning of, 68
Derrida, Jacques, 8, 197–98, 227–39

destiny, politics as, 250–51
dialectic of Enlightenment, 193
Dibelius, Otto, 245–46n12
dictatorships, 56, 81–86, 241–42
dignity
   human dignity, 98, 173, 178, 179–80, 228, 231–33
   of Man, 178
divine kingship, 128–29
divine law, natural law as reflection of, 113–14
divine providence, 115, 116
divine reason (*Logos*), 205–6, 212
doxa (glory), 64–65
droit politique (*nomos*), 186
Duns Scotus, Johannes, 152–53
duty in following rules, 200
Dworkin, Ronald, 101n18

economy of knowledge, 121–22
economy of mystery, 120–21
enemies. *See also* friend/enemy distinction
   politicization of enmity, 105–6
   public versus private, 60–61
England (Britain)
   Catholic Revival, 51
   English pluralists, 32, 35–53
Enlightenment, dialectic of, 229–30, 231–32
erinnern, wiederholen, durcharbeiten (remember, repeat, work through), 216–20
Esposito, Roberto, 78–79n26
eternal life-force, 215
eternity as political matter, 156
ethical communities, 202
ethical states, 205
Eusebius, 54, 55–56, 175
eyeball test, 253

faith
   acts of faith, 189–90
   bare faith, 233, 234–35, 236, 238
   catholicity of, 233–34
   Derrida's idea of, 234–35
   Jaspers on communication of experience of, 223–24

post-metaphysical thinking's dependence on, 222
reason, conflict with (*see* Habermas, Jürgen)
reflective versus religious, 230–31
role of, 29
universality of, 8, 220–27, 230–32
fascism, 79, 162, 173–74
Feuerbach, Ludwig, 11
fiction theory of legal personality, 43–44
Figgis, J. Neville, 32–33n29, 35–36n35, 40–41, 152, 163
Final Solution, 131
Foisneau, Luc, 60n80
forced historicity, 223–24
form, Schmitt on concept of, 33–34
Fortescue, John, 77–78
Foucault, Michel, 117–18, 247–50
Frankfurt School, 219
fraternity, totalitarianism's rejection of, 103–4
Frederick II von Hohenstaufen
   as Antichrist, 151–52
   on Emperors, role of, 78
   Investiture Struggle and, 158–59
   Kantorowicz on, 141, 153
   as *lex animata*, 168–69
   and modernity, beginnings of, 154–60
   Papal supremacy, struggles against, 149
   political theology of, 137, 159–60
free markets, normative order of, 117–18
Freud, Sigmund, 82
Friedrich, Carl, 85–86
friend/enemy distinction
   Maritain on, 106
   in pagan politics, 105–6
   Saint Paul on, 128
   Schmitt on, 38, 52–53, 56–57, 60–61
fullness of powers (*plenitudo potestatis*), 150, 151–52

Garsten, Brian, 59–60
Gauchet, Marcel, 124–25n74
Gelasius I, Pope, 35–36n35, 136
Genossenschaftsrecht (law of association or trust), 163
George Circle, 143, 150–51, 173–74n86
German Idealism, anti-Judaism in, 193–94

German-Jewish symbiosis, 196–97
Gerson, Jean, 152
Gierke, Otto von, 32–33, 40–42, 50–51, 137–38, 163–64
Giesey, Ralph, 166–67n68
gift of rule, 112–13
Gilson, Etienne, 175–76
Glendon, Mary Ann, 99–100, 100–1n17
global panopticon, 118
glory (*doxa*), 64–65
Gnosticism, 241–56
  Blumenberg and Schmitt on, 19
  Christian political theology, Gnostic obsession of, 241–45
  English Puritanism as, 84–85
  Gnostic mis-archy, 8
  Hitler and *parrhesia* and, 245–50
  polytheism, division of powers, and republican civil religion, 250–56
  Voegelin on, 11n25, 72–73
God
  death of, 231
  forms of omnipotence of, 150–51
  God's rule versus human rule, 115–16
  God the Father, sovereignty of, 170–72
  historical representatives of, 44–45, 57, 59
  incarnation of, 28
  Kelsen on belief in, 29
  as King of History, 157
  personation of, 59–61, 90–91
  political presence of, 5–6
  power of, 152–53
  proximate versus distant, 226–27
  self-negation of, 210
  State and, question of parallelism between, 25
Goethe, Johann Wolfgang von
  absolutes, call for renunciation of, 255–56
  Blumenberg on, 244–45, 247, 250, 251–54, 255–56
  Napoleon and, 247–52, 253, 255–56
  nemo contra deum nisi deus ipse, 16–17n42, 61–62, 242–43, 244–45, 247, 250, 251–54
  pantheism of, 252–53

Goodenough, Erwin, 3–4n7, 54
Gordon, Peter, 209–10n43
Gourgouris, Stathis, 61–62n82
government. *See also* Kantorowicz, Ernst, and government; sovereignty; the state
  absolutist nature of, 167
  constitutionalism, uses of, 187
  governmentality, 118–19
  judiciary-government division, 162
  as King's second body, 146n30
  Maritain on legitimacy of, 116
  medieval origins of modern, 159
  question of legitimacy of, 248
  question of rights of, 111
  representative government, 147
  as the Son, 170–72
grace, gift of, 55, 112, 116, 127
Gregory VII, Pope, 35–36, 158–59, 180–82, 184
Gregory Nazianzus (Church Father), 61–62
groups
  designations of, 76–77
  personalities of, 48–53
  political groups, 52
gubernaculum, iurisdictio versus, 162–63, 164–65, 167–68
guilt, as index of moral truth, 208
Gurian, Waldemar, 103–4n22

Habermas, Jürgen, and public reason, 8, 189–239
  Bloch and atheism of Christianity, 211–16
  Christianity, atheistic reading of, 242–43
  critical political theology, 216–20
  Derrida and messianicity of public reason, 227–39
  Gnosticism and, 241
  Hegel and, 203–11
  Jaspers, universality of faith and, 220–27
  Kant's philosophy of religion, critique of, 198–203
  on modern liberal democracies, 9–10
  on modern nation-states, 181–82
  on modern secularism, 17–18
  postsecularism, public reason and debate on, 189–98

Hägglund, Martin, 236, 237–38
Hauriou, Maurice, 80–81
Haverkamp, Anselm, 169–70n75
Hayek, Friedrich, 117, 121–22, 187
Hegel, Georg Wilhelm Friedrich, 110n40, 193, 194–95, 203–11
Heidegger, Martin, 68, 220–21n61, 234–35
Heine, Heinrich, 253
Hellenistic age, on politics and religion, 17–18
Hickman, Jared, 252–53n32
history, world history and divine order, 74
Hitler, Adolf, 245–50
Hitlerism, 245
Hobbes, Thomas. *See also* Leviathan
   question of democratic representation and, 35–53
     Runciman on, 47–48
     Schmitt and, 6, 23, 24, 33, 35–54, 57
     on sovereignty, 86, 109
     Trinitarianism and, 57–58, 59–61
     Voegelin on, 86, 87–89
Hoekstra, Kinch, 146
Hofmann, Hasso, 45–46, 49n67
Holmes, Stephen, 169–70
Holy Spirit, 60, 62
Hooker, Richard, 85–86
hope, 130–31, 220, 237
Horkheimer, Max, 193, 219
Hostiensis (13th-century canonist), 152–53
human dignity, 98, 173, 178, 179–80, 232–33
human freedom. *See* universal human rights
humanism, 104, 105
humankind, double body of, 176–77
human multiplicity, 227
human nature, 119–20
human practical reason, 198–201, 202–3
human rights, 97–103, 131. *See also* Maritain, Jacques, and human rights
human rights violations, 100–1
Hunter, Ian, 201–3
hypostatization of personification, 26–28, 31–32

identity, as formative principle of states, 38–39
Ihering, Rudolf von, 164n66
imperial truth versus theoretical truth, 82–83

Incarnation, dogma of, 185
incorporated bodies, 43–44
Innocent III, Pope, 141–42, 148, 150, 152–53, 158–59
Innocent IV, Pope, 158–59
intelligible world, 236
intersubjectivity, 206
Investiture Struggle, 158–59
invisible Church, 201–5, 212, 214–15
Isidore of Seville, 111
Islamic political theology, 3–4
Israel's occupation of West Bank and Gaza Strip, 123
iurisdictio, 134–36, 149–50, 162–63, 164–65, 167–68

Jacobi, Friedrich Heinrich, 250
James I, King, 148–49
Jaspers, Karl, 8, 192–93, 197, 219, 220–27, 233–34
Jefferson, Thomas, 254–55
Jesus, Bloch on, 214–15. *See also* Christ
Joachim of Fiore, 74, 156–57, 181–82
John of Salisbury, 159
Jonas, Hans, 16–17n42, 193–94
Judaism
   anti-Judaism, 193
   Augustine on, 73
   divinely revealed law, tradition of, 207
   Jewish messianism, 72–74
   Jewish people, exemplarity of, 216–17
   Jewish political theology, 3–4, 239
   Jewish Question, 87–89, 122–32
   Jewish theocracy, 87
   Maritain and, 111–12
   Marx on true realization of, 13
   prophetic, Weber and, 10
   tradition of, 203–11
   universalism and, 130–31
judiciary-government division, 162
Junker-Kenny, Maureen, 192–93n12
juridical persons, 26–27, 30–31
jurisdiction, 34–35, 161–68
justice, administration of, 171–72
Justinian, 166–67

Kabbala, theory of divine contraction, 210
Kahn, Victoria, 57–58n77, 173–74
Kalyvas, Andreas, 24, 76–77

Kant, Immanuel
  Derrida on, 230–31
  Habermas and, 193, 198–203, 229
  on human dignity, 179
  invisible Church, 201–5, 212, 214–15
Kantorowicz, Ernst, and government, 7–8, 133–87
  antinomy of sovereignty, 161–72
  corporation sole and, 47
  Dante and government of humanity, 172–80
  Gnosticism and, 241
  on King's Two Bodies problem, 78
  liberal government, nature of, 133–42
  on modern secularism, 17–18
  modern sovereignty as immortal corporation, 143–47
  Papal legal revolution and sociology of constitutionalism, 180–84
  on sovereignty of artists and the state, 248–50
  sovranist-globalist debate, influence of, 184–87
  theological sphere, overlap with secular sphere, 147–53
  topic of narrative of, 57–58
  Trinitarianism and secularization, 154–60
katechon, 72–73, 243–44
Kelsen, Hans, 6, 25–35, 63–65, 113–14
Kierkegaard, Søren, 193–94, 196, 220–22
the king
  coercion of law and, 168, 169–70
  divinization of, 57–58
  dual nature of, 155–56
  immortality of, 47
  as last judge, 139–40
  law-centered kingship, 158–59
  lex Digna, 162–63, 165–66, 167–68, 170–71
  lex regia, 162–63, 164, 165–69
  McIlwain versus Kantorowicz on, 168
  Norman kings and kingship, 155–56, 157–59, 182–83, 184
  powers of, 151–52
  representative functions of, 45–46
  sacralization of, 78
  second body of, 145, 147
  as spiritual man, 149
  universal monarchs, 176–77
Kingdom, doctrine of, 212
Kingdom of Christ, ground of legitimacy for, 63–64
Kingdom of God, 204–5, 212–13
Klossowski, Pierre, 105–6n28
knowledge, economy of, 121–22
Kojève, Alexandre, 194–95
Kulturkampf, 51

Laborde, Cécile, 15–16
labour unions, 48–49n65
Laclau, Ernesto, 68, 70, 89–95
Laski, Harold, 40–41, 48, 50–53, 110
last judges, 139–40
last judgment, 170–71
law
  application of, legal personality and Christology and, 25–35
  coercive law, 51, 189–90
  as a command, 27
  forms of, 33–34
  law of association or trust (*Genossenschaftsrecht*), 163
  legal fictions, 164–65
  legal ideas, application of, 33–34
  legality, Blumenberg on, 16
  legal order, 27n21, 28, 33
  legal reason, 168–70
  legal systems, question of unity of, 31
  lex digna, 162–63, 165–66, 167–68, 170–71
  lex regia, 162–63, 164, 165–69
  of love, 128–29
  natural (*see* natural law)
  origins of, 80
  Papal legal revolution, sociology of constitutionalism and, 180–84
  positive versus natural, 117–18
  question of interpretation of, 34–35, 35–36n36, 56–57, 135–36, 149–50
  question of source of, 33
  reality, relationship to, 31–32
  reciprocity in, 189–90
  Roman law, 163–65
  sociology of, 181
  spiritualization of, 159
  state, relationship to, 31–32
  written versus living, 248–50

Lawson, George, 161n58
Lee, Daniel, 166–67n68
Lefort, Claude, 1, 1–2n3, 68, 89–90
legal fictions, 164–65
legislatio versus *iurisdictio*, 134–36, 149–50, 164–65
legislators, freedom of application of universal norms by, 149–50
legitimacy, 1–4, 16, 19, 64, 246, 248
Leo I, Pope, 155
Lessing, Gotthold Ephraim, 250
Leviathan (Hobbes's)
  civil kingdom of, versus Kingdom of Jesus Christ, 58–62
  deaths of, 48
  Runciman on, 47–48
  Schmitt on, 40–41, 56, 145
  sovereigns and, 46–47
  theoretical construction of, 45
Lewis, Ewart, 166–67n69
lex digna, 162–63, 165–66, 167–68, 170–71
lex regia, 162–63, 164, 165–69
liberalism
  liberal constitutionalism, 162–63, 171–72
  liberal government, 133–42, 161–72
  as religion, 15
  totalitarianism, relationship to, 241–42, 246
liberation theology, 67, 213–14
Liber Augustalis (Frederick II), 159–60, 182
liberty of movement, 121–22
life
  philosophy as form of, 221–22
  sacredness of, 101
life-force, eternal, 215
Lincoln, Abraham, 76, 111
Lindahl, Hans, 24, 76–77
Lippmann, Walter, 107
Logos (divine reason), 205–6, 212
Lorenzini, Daniele, 107–8
Loughlin, Martin 140–41, 169–70, 186–87
love, 106, 195–96
Löwith, Karl, 16–17n42, 171–72
  Habermas and, 194–95, 204–5
  Hegel and, 205
  on Jewish messianism, 74
  on Joachim of Fiore, 157
  Voegelin and, 72
Luhmann, Niklas, 183–84

Mahmood, Saba, 190
Maimonides, Moses, 82, 112
Maitland, Frederic, 40–41, 48–49, 163
Maritain, Jacques, and human rights, 7, 67–68, 69–70, 97–132
  on Christian political theology, 137
  critique of sovereignty and, 107–13
  democracy and divine providence, 113–22
  Gnosticism and, 241
  human rights, democracy and universality of, 97–103
  Jewish Question and, 122–32
  on political representation, 138–39
  totalitarian ideologies, 103–7
Marquard, Odo, 16–17n42, 252–53n32
marriages, as example of group personality, 49–50
Marsilius of Padua, 154
Martel, James, 59–60
Marx, Karl, and Marxism, 11, 12–14, 213
Masuzawa, Tomoko, 99–100n11
material intellect theory, 215
matter, as Platonic *khora*, 229–30
Maurras, Charles, 123–24
McCormick, John, 101–2n20
McIlwain, Charles, 133–34, 161–68
medieval constitutionalism, 167
medieval political world, 134–36
Mehring, Reinhard, 21–22n2, 21–22n3, 40
Meier, Heinrich, 22–23n9, 55–56n74
Mendieta, Eduardo, 193n13
messianicity and messianism, 202–3, 227–39
metaphysics
  end of, 222
  Kant's destruction of, 198–99
methodological atheism, 8, 195, 212, 218–19, 220–21
Metz, Jean-Baptiste, 67, 196–97, 216–18
Milbank, John, 104
millennialism, 73
mis-archy, 19, 252, 255–56

modernity
    beginnings of, 154–60
    Gnosticism of, 72–73
    modern constitutionalism, McIlwain on, 133–34
    modern public law, Loughlin versus Tierney on, 140–41
    modern representative democracy, nature of, 89–90
    modern sovereignty, as immortal corporation, 143–47
    as secularization, 10
Moltmann, Jürgen, 67
monarchy and monarchism. *See also* the king; sovereigns
    Hellenistic idea of, 248–50
    political theology of, 82–83
    Schmitt on, 57–58
Monod, Paul, 173–74n86
monotheism, 127, 226–27, 237
moral action, 200–1
moral intuitions, 208
morality, Kant's conception of, 199
moral relativism, 202–3
Moses, 63–64, 82
Mouffe, Chantal, 24
movement, liberty of, 121–22
Moyn, Samuel, 97–98n4, 108–9n38, 118
multiculturalism, 122
Munro, Bradley, 114–15n51
mysteries of the Church (*arcana ecclesiae*), 147–48
Mystery of God, 236
Mystery of God as One, 223
Mystery of Israel doctrine, 122, 124–25, 130
mystery of salvation, 171–72
mystery of state, 147–48, 186
mystery of the economy, 121, 122
mystical body, 34, 77–81, 133–34, 136, 137–38

Naas, Michael, 234–36, 237–38
Napoleon Bonaparte, 247–52, 253, 255–56
Näsström, Sofia, 89–90
National Socialism, 79
nation-states, sovereignty of, 144
natural divine right, 126–27

natural eternity, relationship with political form, 143–44
natural law, 103, 112–22
Nature's God, 254–56
Nazism, 103–4, 245–46
Negri, Antonio, 24, 76–77, 93–94
Nelson, Eric, 146n30, 255
nemo contra deum nisi deus ipse, 8–9, 16–17n42, 61–62, 242–43, 244–45, 247, 250, 251–54
neoconservatism, coupling with neoliberalism, 98
neoliberalism, 70, 98, 107, 117
new political theology, 67
new world order, 122–23, 131–32
Nicholas of Cusa, 42n55
Nietzsche, Friedrich, 72, 220–22
Nolte, Ernst, 88n54
nomos (*droit politique*), 186
nomos pneumatikos (spiritual law), 128–29
non-domination, 8–9, 253, 255–56
Norman Anonymous, 155–56, 157–58
Norman kings and kingship, 155–56, 157–59, 182–83, 184
Nussbaum, Martha, 116n57

Oakeshott, Michael, 47n64
Oakley, Francis, 143–44, 151–53, 163n64
Olivi, Peter, 74n15
On the Jewish Question (Marx), 12
optimus homo, 173–74, 176–77
original sin, 91
Orosius (Roman theologian), 175

pagan civil religion, 254
pagan politics, 106
Palestinian Question, 123
pantheism, 250, 252–53
Papal legal revolution, 180–84
Papal Revolution, 158–59
Papinian (Aemilius Papinianus), 164
Parliamentarianism, 40–41
parrhesia (frank speech), 245–50
Party-States, 94
Paul, Saint, 88–89, 125–29, 136, 242–43
peace, 54–55, 56–57, 60–62, 172–73
Peirce, Charles, 206, 209–10

People
  constitution of, 125–26
  immorality of, 144–45
  unity of, 137–38
personhood, artificial, 43–45
personification, 27
Peter, Saint, 155
Peterson, Erik, 3–4n7, 124
  on doctrine of the Trinity, 243–44
  on existential representation, 81
  on Gnosticism, 243
  on Hellenistic political theology, 175
  Kantorowicz's critique of, 154
  Maritain and, 105–6, 124–25
  on polemical context of political theology, 22
  political theology, critique of, 144–45
  on sacral kingship, 133
  Schmitt, critique of, 6, 25
  Schmitt and, 40, 53–65
  on the Trinity, 61–62n82
  Voegelin and, 70–71
Pettit, Philip, 76–77, 253
Peukert, Helmut, 196–97, 219
Philo Judaeus (Philo of Alexandria), 54, 57, 82, 89, 212, 214
philosophers, as advisers to princes, kings, and emperors, 248
philosophy
  as form of life, 221–22
  increased political importance of, 248–50
  philosophical faith, 199, 226–27
  philosophical reason, 223
  philosophic truth, 223
  philosophy of religion, critique of Kant's, 198–203
  post-metaphysical, 206
  religion, relation to, 212
  religion's translation into, 194–96, 197, 202–5, 218
  revelation, relation to, 225
Pitkin, Hannah, 43, 89–90
Plato, 83–84, 86n49
Platonic *khora*, 229–30, 236
plebs versus *populus*, 91–94
plenitudo potestatis (fullness of powers), 150, 151–52

Plessner, Helmuth, 79n28
Plotinus, 82
pluralism, 25, 183
pneumatikos (spiritual man), 136, 138–40, 141, 147–53
Pocock, John, 143–44
Pogge, Thomas, 100–1
Pöggeler, Otto, 194n37
polemical meanings of political theology, 21–25
political theology, 1–19
  Gnosticism and, 241–56 (*see also* Gnosticism)
  Habermas and public reason, 189–239 (*see also* Habermas, Jürgen, and public reason)
  Kantorowicz and government, 133–87 (*see also* Kantorowicz, Ernst, and government)
  Maritain and human rights, 97–132 (*see also* Maritain, Jacques, and human rights)
  Schmitt and sovereignty, 21–65 (*see also* Schmitt, Carl, and sovereignty)
  Voegelin and representation, 67–95 (*see also* Voegelin, Eric, and representation)
politics. *See also* government; representation
  as destiny, 250–51
  great politics as works of art, 248–50
  liberal democratic versus populist democratic, 91–92
  pagan politics, Christian politics versus, 106
  political Body, divinization of, 57–58
  political form, relationship with natural eternity, 143–44
  political monotheism, 70–71n11, 178–79
  political religion, 68, 87–89, 137
  political theology without sovereignty, 2–3, 5–6
  political theory, 3–4n7
  political unity, 23–24, 38n43, 53, 57, 145
polytheism, 250–56
Popes, 35–36, 155
Popper, Karl, 83

INDEX

populism, 89–95
populist social movements, 92–93
populus versus *plebs*, 91–94
Porter, Jean, 116
positive divine right, 126–27
Post, Gaines, 159
post-metaphysical thinking, 222
postsecularism, public reason and debate on, 189–98
power
  absolute power, 150–51, 152–53
  Catholic Church as holder of all powers, 151–52
  constituent power, 24, 76–77
  division of, polytheism and republican civil religion and, 250–56
  in law, 30
  mis-archy, 19, 252, 255–56
  problem of legitimacy of, 1–4
  in republican constitutions, 255–56
  restrictions on, 252–53
  sociology on, 30
practical reason, 198–201, 202–3, 212
Protestantism, 10, 12
public law, 29, 186
public reason, 8, 189–91, 227–39, 246–47. *See also* Habermas, Jürgen, and public reason
Puritanism and Puritan revolution, 56, 57–58n77, 84–85

quod principi placet (q.p.p.), 165–67

radical egalitarianism (universalism), 125–26, 132
Rancière, Jacques, 91
Rawls, John, 189–90, 245–46
reason
  anamnestic reason, 217–18
  catholicity versus, 223–24, 225
  communicative reason, 206
  divine reason (*Logos*), 205–6, 212
  human practical reason, 198–201, 202–3
  practical reason, 198–201, 202–3, 212
  public reason, 8, 189–91, 227–39, 246–47 (*see also* Habermas, Jürgen, and public reason)

Rees, Dafydd Huw, 192–93n12
religion. *See also* Catholic Church; Christ; Christianity; Christology; God; Judaism; Trinitarianism
  atheistic translation of, 206–7 (*see also* atheism)
  death of, 13–14
  individuals' affiliation with, 189–90
  philosophy, relation to, 212
  religious constitutionalism, 202–3
  religious values, realization of, 12
  republican civil religion, 202–3
  science versus, 229–32
  theology versus, 211 (*see also* theology)
  translation into philosophy, 194–96, 197, 202–5, 218
representation
  artificial representation, 44–45, 46–47
  constituent power versus, 24
  description of, 23
  electoral representation, 75–76
  existential representation, 75, 80–81
  as formative principle of states, 38–39
  Gierke on, 41–42
  group personalities and, 50–51
  Hobbes's conception of, 42–48, 49
  Kelsen on, 28
  Lefort's conception of, 89–90
  liberal democratic politics versus populist democratic politics and, 91–92
  Maritain's conception of, 138–39
  need for, 27
  paradox of, 89–90
  in Persons of the Trinity, 59–61
  question of, in Church-state relations, 36–42
  representative government, 147
  Schmitt on, 25, 30, 32, 34, 42
  symbolic representation, 74–77, 91–92
  theocracy, opposition to, 68
  unification of people and, 2–3, 44–46
  vicariate representation, 39, 110–11
  Voegelin's conception of, 6–7, 74–77, 81, 89, 90–91, 138–39 (*see also* Voegelin, Eric, and representation)
  Žižek on, 93–94
republican civil religion, 202–3, 250–56

republican ethical communities, 203
republics, monarchism of, 146
revealability, distinction from revelation, 234–35
revelation, 225, 234–35
revelational faith, philosophical faith versus, 226–27
ritual praxis, 211
Roman legal system, 140–41n19
Rosenstock-Huessy, Eugen, 74n15, 180–81, 182
Rosenzweig, Franz, 193–94, 226
Rossiter, Clinton, 85–86
Rote Armee Fraktion, 210–11
Rousseau, Jean-Jacques, 126–27
Royal Christology, 141–42
rule, gift of, 112–13
rule of law, 3, 182–83, 185, 186
Runciman, Steven, 47–48, 49–50

Sabbatian movement, 210–11
sacral kingship, 133
the sacred, linguistification of, 194–95, 203–11
salvation, 10–11, 171–72
Santner, Eric, 170–71n77, 171–72n81
Schelling, Friedrich Wilhelm Joseph, 195
Schmidt, Christoph, 55–56n74, 71–72, 128
Schmitt, Carl, and sovereignty, 6, 21–65
    Augustinian response to, 70–74
    Blumenberg on self-assertion, critique of, 241–42
    on conflict, 14–15
    critiques of, 16–19, 74–75, 110–11
    Derrida and, 232n74
    English pluralists versus, 35–53
    on Gnosticism, threat of, 243–44
    on Goethe's motto, 245
    on Hobbes, 87
    Kantorowicz and, 135–36, 141–42, 154, 160
    Kelsen versus, 25–35
    Laski, critique of, 110
    on legitimation discourse of political theology, 1–2
    Loughlin and, 140–41
    on peace, 136
    Peterson versus, 53–65

political theology, concept of, 9–10, 21–22
political theology, motivation of, 49
political theology, scientific and polemical meanings of, 21–25
    on political unity, problem of, 23, 53, 145
    on public versus private enemies, 60–62
    on representation, 75–76
    on rule of law, 3
    on secularization, 9–10, 154
    on sovereignty, 181, 186
    on theology and jurisprudence, analogies between, 24
    on universal human rights, 101–2
    Voegelin's borrowings from, 73n14
Scholem, Gershom, 196–97, 207, 208–11
Schramm, Percy, 166–67n70
Schulz, Fritz, 168–69n73
science versus religion, 229–32
Second Vatican Ecumenical Council, 67
secrets of state (*arcana imperii*), 147–48
secularization
    Marx on, 12–14
    modernity as, 10
    political theology and, 9–19, 137
    secularization theorem, 21–22
    Trinitarianism and, 154–60
self-preservation, 232
Senellart, Michel, 135n7
September 11, 2001 terrorist attacks, 210–11
Shoah (Holocaust), 196–97, 216–18, 219
Shue, Henry, 100–1, 121–22
Skinner, Quentin, 43, 143–44, 143–44n25
socialization, importance of, 208
social justice, locus for, 171–72
social media platforms, dangers of, 246–47
society
    Kant on, 214–15
    as legal order, 111
    open versus closed, 13–14, 74, 83, 84–85, 88–89, 104, 105
    postsecular, 190
sociology of constitutionalism, 180–84
socio-political realities, 14–15
solidarity, 219–20
Son of Man, 213–15, 241, 242–43

INDEX   297

sovereigns. *See also* the king; monarchy and monarchism
  as legal miracles, 29
  legal order and, 150
  mystical body of, 133–34
  personal will of, 33
  public religion, control of, 86
  question of legitimacy of, 56–57
sovereignty
  as authority to wage war, 63
  Christian democracy and critique of, 107–13
  consensual basis of, 64
  early modern construction of, 148
  God's rule versus, 115–16
  Hobbes on, 42–43, 45, 86
  Kantorowicz on question of, 149–51
  Kelsen's critiques of, 6
  Laski on, 51–53
  Leviathan and, 46–47
  liberal government and antinomy of, 161–72
  Loughlin on, 186
  McIlwain on, 163–64
  medieval legal formula for, 139–40
  modern form of, 133–34, 143–47
  paradox of, 150–51
  possibility of totalitarianism and, 103
  Schmitt on, 42, 52–53 (*see also* Schmitt, Carl, and sovereignty)
  sovereignism, 1–2
  sovereign prerogatives, 185
  of states, opposition of multitude to, 109
  Voegelin on, 74–75
sovranist-globalist debate, influence of, 184–87
Spinoza, Baruch, 24, 48, 132, 155n51, 201, 229
spiritual corporations, 144
spiritual law (*nomos pneumatikos*), 128–29
spiritual man (*pneumatikos*), 136, 138–40, 141, 147–53
spontaneous normative orders, 117–18, 121
Springborg, Patricia, 40–41n52
Stalinism, 103–4
stasis (conflict), 61–62n82
the state
  Church-state relationship, 35–53
  ethical states, 205
  formative principles of, 38
  individual freedom versus, 48
  Kelsen's theory of, 29, 63–65
  as personification of law, 27–28
  providential states, 171–72
  rule of law and, 110
  society-state relationship, 34
  sovereignty, opposition of multitude to, 109
Stewart, Matthew, 254–55
Strauss, Leo, 74n16, 87
subjection thesis, 47–48
symbols
  interpretation of, 211
  symbolic representation, reunification of faith and knowledge and, 225–26

Taubes, Jacob, 242–44
Taylor, Charles, 9–11, 104, 152–53n48
technology, Habermas's critique of, 228
terrestrial paradise, 174–75, 176–77
terrorism, 210–11
theocracy, opposition to representation, 68
theology. *See also* Christian political theology
  critical political theology, 216–20
  Islamic political theology, 3–4
  law, passage to, 155
  liberation theology, 67, 213–14
  politics, parallelism with, 27
  religion versus, 211
  theological enmity, 72
  theological sphere, overlap with secular sphere, 147–53
Thiers, Adolphe, 133
Third Age of Spirit, 182
Thornhill, Christopher, 142
Tierney, Brian, 135, 139–41, 163n64, 165–66
totalitarianism
  Arendt on, 87
  Christian political theology and, 67–70
  liberalism, relationship to, 246
  mystical body problem and, 79
  nature of, 162
  as term, 68
  totalitarian ideologies, 103–7

tradition, 206, 207–10
transcendence, Voegelin on, 71–72
tree of knowledge, 209–10
tree of life, 209–10
Trepanier, Lee, 79n29
Trinitarianism
    as essence of Christian theology, 54
    of Frederick II's political theology, 160
    on Gnosticism, 244–45
    medieval juridical use of, 7–8
    nature of, 243–44
    political unity and, 57
    secularization and, 154–60
Trinity
    civil war within, motif of, 62–64
    Hobbes on, 59–61
    Schmitt on, 61–62, 63, 64–65
    as stasiology, 62–63
truth
    Badiou on, 125, 129
    imperial versus theoretical, 82–83
    Jaspers on, 222
    of man versus of God, 84
    parrhesia (frank speech), 245–50
    theoretical truth, imperial truth versus, 82–83
Tuck, Richard, 146

Ullmann, Walter, 154–55
unity
    of immortality of corporate body, 143–47
    of legal systems, question of, 31
    of people, 53
    political unity, 23–24, 38n43, 53, 57, 145
universal culture of singularities, 235–36
Universal Declaration of Human Rights (UDHR), 97–98, 99–100, 102, 103, 113–22
universal human rights, 97–103, 112–22
universalism, 122–23, 125–26, 132
utopianism, 215

vicar of God, kings as, 168–69n73
vocation (*Beruf*), 10–11
Voegelin, Eric, and representation, 6–7, 67–95
    on Christian political theology, 137
    Christian political theology and totalitarianism, 67–70
    democratic dictatorship, paradox of, 81–86
    Gnosticism and, 11n25, 241
    on Joachim of Fiore, 157
    Maritain, comparison with, 104
    on Marxism, 11
    mystical body of the people, articulation of, 77–81
    political religion and the Jewish Question, 87–89
    on political representation, 74–77, 138–39
    populism, political theology of, 89–95
    on Protestantism and salvation, 10–11
    Schmitt, Augustinian response to, 70–74

war, impact of legal abolition of, 63
Weber, Max, 9–11, 12, 30
Weber, Samuel, 33–34n31
Weidner, Daniel, 201–2
welfare state, 171–72
Wood, Gordon, 147
world government, 177, 183
world religions, 98, 99–100, 101, 119

Žižek, Slavoj, 91, 93–95

www.ingramcontent.com/pod-product-compliance
Ingram Content Group UK Ltd.
Pitfield, Milton Keynes, MK11 3LW, UK
UKHW022230230426
12048UKWH00016BA/1174